TOXIC DEBTS

AND THE SUPERFUND DILEMMA

© 1994 The University of North Carolina Press

All rights reserved

Manufactured in the United States of America

The paper in this book meets the guidelines for permanence and durability of the Committee on Production Guidelines for Book Longevity of the Council on Library Resources.

Harold C. Barnett is professor of economics at the University of Rhode Island.

Chapter 4 is an expanded version of "The Extent of Social Regulation: Hazardous Waste Cleanup and the Reagan Ideology," *Policy Studies Review* 8, no. 1 (Autumn 1988): 15–35, © 1988 by the Policy Studies Organization. An earlier version of chapter 7 appeared in "Political Environments and Implementation Failures: The Case of Superfund Enforcement," *Law and Policy* 12, no. 3 (July 1990): 225–46, © 1990 by Basil Blackwell Ltd. A version of chapter 3 was published in "Hazardous Waste, Distributional Conflict, and a Trilogy of Failures," *The Journal of Human Justice* 3, no. 2 (Spring 1992): 93–110, © 1992 by *The Journal of Human Justice*. Some material in chapter 9 appeared in "Crimes against the Environment: Superfund Enforcement at Last," *The Annals* 525 (January 1993): 119–33, © 1993 by the American Academy of Political and Social Science.

Library of Congress Cataloging-in-Publication Data
Barnett, Harold C.
    Toxic debts and the superfund dilemma / by Harold C. Barnett.
        p.   cm.
    Includes bibliographical references and index.
    ISBN 0-8078-2124-1 (cloth : alk. paper). —
ISBN 0-8078-4435-7 (pbk.: alk. paper)
    1. Hazardous waste sites—Cleaning—Finance—Government policy—United States.   2. Environmental policy—United States.   3. United States.   Environmental Protection Agency.   I. Title.
HC110.P55B37   1994
363.73'84'0973—dc20   93-32059
                                                          CIP

98 97 96 95 94   5 4 3 2 1

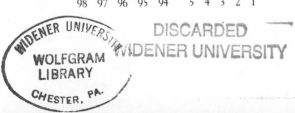

To the memory of my father,

Mark Barnett, who believed in law

TABLES

FIGURES

The passage of Superfund into law on the eve of Ronald Reagan's election as president of the United States set in motion two diametrically opposed forces: a legislative mandate to commit billions of dollars to the cleanup of hazardous waste sites and a White House–interpreted mandate to get government off the backs of the people. Their opposition produced the Sewergate scandal of 1982–83 and kindled my desire to write a political economy of Superfund.

In the early 1980s I was researching government control of illegal corporate behavior. Some of my colleagues perceived a clear tendency for government to take a tougher stand against law violations by large corporations. The progress of the deregulatory movement, gaining strength since the mid-1970s, suggested that their optimism was misplaced. In this context, Superfund appeared a perfect vehicle to gauge the force and direction of government involvement in market relationships and to address a question of increasing relevance as the 1980s progressed: Is it possible to successfully pursue environmental goals in a political economic system that is biased toward the interests of capital and under an administration that unabashedly advocates that bias as in the public interest?

It has taken almost a decade to investigate and write a story of Superfund that spans the Reagan and Bush administrations. As of this writing, there is a new president in the White House and a new EPA administrator. Congress is again addressing Superfund reauthorization issues. The reader might then ask whether this book has relevance to environmental protection under a new administration and a redesigned law. Is it of more interest to academics than to those who must contend with the real world of Superfund cleanup? My best answer to these questions is to state the conclusion of the book: The failure of Superfund to promote an efficient and equitable response to hazardous waste site threats is rooted in an inherent conflict over economic and environmental priorities. This conflict encompasses and goes beyond self-interested political battles. Rather, it emerges, on the one hand, from the fact that a concerted and successful effort to place the burden of cleanup on those corporations responsible for hazardous waste generation and disposal has far-reaching implications for the operation and viability of our capitalist economy. On the other hand, to write off hazardous waste site risks as overstated and shrink the program or to place the burden of cleanup more directly on the public challenges the legitimacy of democratic government. The latter solution must also contend with the government's inability to resolve an apparently intractable budgetary crisis.

Constrained by these structural realities, President Clinton and Congress will be hard-pressed to solve the Superfund dilemma. I complete this book in the hope that it illuminates the hurdles that must be overcome and in so doing contributes to forging a solution.

I accumulated many debts over the course of this project. A list of names and institutions cannot repay the help and support I received from family, friends, and colleagues as well as from diverse participants in the Superfund program.

My research required many visits to Environmental Protection Agency headquarters in Washington, D.C., and to regional offices in New York, Chicago, Atlanta, and San Francisco. I was fortunate to find people willing to take time away from the crisis of the moment to answer my questions and to provide needed materials or direct me to someone who could. They afforded a personal dimension to an often impersonal process.

The University of Rhode Island provided an atmosphere conducive to thinking and writing as well as time and resources. A sabbatical leave in 1986 allowed me to conduct interviews and collect data. A sabbatical leave in 1993 allowed me to complete the book. A grant from the URI Alumni Faculty Development Fund helped to cover the cost of research-related travel.

I received substantial encouragement and support from my editors at the University of North Carolina Press. Paul Betz read each chapter as it was completed (an editorial commitment that few authors seem to experience) and provided invaluable critiques of my prose and the organization of my argument. Lewis Bateman shepherded the project through its final rewrite. Sandra Eisdorfer, aided by an excellent UNC Press staff, carried the book through production.

Friends and colleagues discussed and critiqued this work and helped me in its completion. In particular, James Starkey was a willing and valuable sounding board for theoretical and empirical arguments. Peter Yeager was a valued critic in my search for a political economy of environmental regulation.

My mother, Betty Barnett, an advocate of social justice, provided editorial comment on earlier drafts of the manuscript. My wife, Merle, with love, insight, and good humor, helped me to resolve many of the political and stylistic problems that emerge in writing and to keep the project in perspective. My son, Adam, sustained my belief that a younger generation can succeed in resolving environmental conflicts.

Mountain View, Laurel Park, Lowell, Rose Center, Albion, Sunnyvale. Place names that evoke an image of comfortable communities nestling in natural surroundings. Places where abundant resources were combined with an entrepreneurial spirit to create a historically unprecedented material standard of living. Places named by those with a vision of the future whose progeny now share a crisis of the present—the threat to health and environmental quality from uncontrolled hazardous waste sites.

In 1980, at the close of the environmental decade, Congress passed the Comprehensive Environmental Response, Compensation, and Liability Act.[1] The act created the Superfund as a mechanism to rectify the toxic legacy of the industrial and chemical revolutions. Implementation of the Superfund program became the responsibility of the Environmental Protection Agency (EPA). Over a decade later, there is general consensus that the program has failed. For both supporters and critics of the program, failure is epitomized by the fact that we have spent too much to achieve too little.

The thesis of this study is that Superfund has failed due to conflict over who will pay the toxic debt. The reason for conflict is relatively simple: the bill for cleaning up hazardous waste sites, estimated to exceed $100 billion, must be paid by federal and state governments and by corporations responsible for decades of unsound disposal. Many states, lacking adequate cleanup resources, have sought alternatives to active participation in the federal program. Corporations targeted to bear the financial burden of cleanup have resisted government actions and have attempted to shift the cleanup burden to other private parties and to taxpayers. They also have attempted to reduce the debt by limiting the pace and extent of cleanup. The resulting inaction has left the environmental burden on people living in proximity to Superfund sites: people exposed to contaminated air, soil, surface water, and ground water. With support from advocacy groups, communities that bear the environmental burden of inaction have attempted to counter the forces of opposition. In the process, the cost of cleanup and confrontation has risen while the pace and scope of cleanup has suffered. Superfund has failed to promote efficient or equitable outcomes.

My focus on conflict as the primary source of Superfund failure is not unique. The Office of Technology Assessment attributes failure to the "Superfund syndrome," a condition of confrontation among the broad range of parties and interests affected by cleanup (U.S. Office of Technology Assessment, 1989b: 18). Works reflecting a Law and Economics approach attribute failure to the transaction costs and implementation delays engendered by confrontation and litigation. The current work encompasses and expands on these arguments. The Office of Technology Assessment is particularly concerned with evaluations of hazardous waste site risks and the selection of appropriate remedies. In contrast, I emphasize the political and economic forces that establish the options and constraints faced by legislators and regulatory agencies. Risk evaluations and remedy selection are products of these forces. Those taking a transaction-cost approach emphasize the ability of powerful corporations to oppose regulatory action and to turn Superfund enforcement into an expensive and inefficient funding mechanism. In contrast, I emphasize the manifestations of this power in executive branch and congressional decisions that shape and limit the program's effectiveness. I argue that failure of legislators and regulators to take effective and timely action is related to the economic and political power of major corporate polluters: the power to use government as an instrument of self-interest and the power that derives from a central role in capitalist development.

Agreement that conflict is a root cause of Superfund failure does not produce agreement on how to resolve this Superfund dilemma. Major polluting corporations and their insurers have continuously argued that a socialization of cleanup costs and a related weakening of Superfund liability standards will produce a more equitable and efficient program. Rejecting this position in favor of a make-polluters-pay principle, environmental and labor groups, some congressional advocates of environmental action, and top Environmental Protection Agency administrators have argued that provision of sufficient staff resources can reduce overall costs and enhance efficiency. An adequately funded enforcement program will eliminate some corporate gains from recalcitrance. Expansion in staff resources will allow EPA to carry out many activities currently performed by private contractors and to effectively oversee the behavior of these for-profit companies. Since the vast majority of Superfund expenditures go to contractors, effective oversight will limit their capacity to profit at the expense of program efficiency.

Private parties targeted to bear the toxic debt as well as both the Reagan and Bush administrations have advocated a greater reliance on cost-benefit analysis as a means to control Superfund expenditures and thus to reduce one source of conflict. They contend that a more realistic assessment of hazardous waste site risks and a related selection of cost-effective remedies will enhance equity and efficiency. While acknowledging the potential gains from this approach, critics note that the measurement of risk is highly susceptible to abuse by parties who are primarily concerned with minimizing cost and liability. There is no doubt that industries responsible for creating the problem have consistently understated the risks that flow from their past actions and would clearly prefer cost reduction over risk reduction. It is also clear that at least through 1992 the White House has desired to diminish the burden of cleanup on both the federal budget and the corporate sector.

Advocates of alternative dispute resolution emphasize the gains to be derived through greater reliance on negotiation as opposed to confrontation. However, the effectiveness of negotiation as a means to satisfy Superfund cleanup goals presupposes agreement on a trade-off between risk and cost that satisfies major interests. Further, if agency openness to negotiate is not backed up by strong enforcement when negotiation fails, settlement policy will remain an inefficient procedure for distribution of the toxic debt.

Evaluation of solutions to the Superfund dilemma requires an understanding of the complex, dynamic interactions that have produced failure. The actors, in cooperation or confrontation, both shape and respond to their regulatory environment. Their capacity to influence or to dominate the political decision-making process can enhance or constrain the power of regulators. The interaction of regulator and regulated in turn influences the cost and pace of cleanup and the distribution of the toxic debt.

METHODOLOGY

This is a study in political economy, an approach emphasizing the economic foundations of political decisions. The purpose of the study is to establish the linkage between these foundations and Superfund failure. To trace out this linkage, I examine the responsiveness of legislative and agency decisions to the political and economic power of parties with a stake in regulatory outcomes, the economic consequences of legislative and regulatory action, and the environmental consequences of political inaction. I then demonstrate how the resolution of conflict among competing interests and between contradictory goals is manifest in the Superfund mandate, the strategy adopted by the Environmental Protection Agency to satisfy that mandate, and the resources made available to pursue effective strategy. Finally, I illustrate the relationship between mandate, strategy, and resources, on the one hand, and Superfund failure, on the other.

The story of Superfund failure builds on historical and statistical observation. The chapters on the Superfund Act of 1980 and its reauthorization in 1986 make extensive use of congressional hearings, reports, and legislative histories. These are supplemented with newspaper reportage and the Bureau of National Affairs' *BNA Environment Reporter.*

The analysis of Superfund implementation from 1981 through 1985 draws on a large computerized data base I created in 1986. The data base, containing extensive information on nearly 900 Superfund sites, was compiled from EPA data on site characteristics, cleanup actions, and enforcement actions. These data were supplemented with other measures of program activity contained in reports by the General Accounting Office, the Office of Technology Assessment, and the National Campaign Against Toxic Hazards. A related data base was created to analyze the role of the states in the Superfund program. Measures of state cleanup resources and activities were derived from EPA data as well as from reports published by the Association of State and Territorial Solid Waste Management Officials and the General Accounting Office.

Statistical analysis is used to explain the determinants of state funding and enforcement decisions (chapter 5), the relative accomplishments of EPA's ten regional offices (chapter 6), and the determinants of EPA cleanup and enforcement decisions through 1985 (chapter 7). Statistical methodology and findings are reported in appendices to these chapters and conclusions are integrated into chapter text. It is anticipated that the nontechnical reader can follow the argument without reference to the appendices.

The study also draws on extensive interviews conducted at EPA Washington headquarters, in several EPA regions, and with representatives of environmental and industry groups.

SYNOPSIS

Chapters 2 and 3 provide a factual and theoretical foundation for the study. In chapter 2, I sketch out the relationship between production and use of chemicals and the dangers that flow from the environmentally unsound disposal of hazardous waste products. Studies available prior to the first congressional debate over Superfund are reviewed to establish the link between corporate responsibility for hazardous waste production and disposal and the problems identified at Superfund sites. These studies point to corporations in the petrochemicals, metals, electrical and electronics, and transportation industries as primarily responsible for creating the toxic debt.

Chapter 3 argues that government intervention in environmental affairs is necessitated by the failure of markets to provide incentives for safe disposal and by the failure of private suits to provide appropriate incentives for cleanup. I outline the major issues that must be addressed to establish and implement a cleanup program and emphasize that conflict over the distribution of cleanup costs and benefits pervades all program decisions. Theories of state regulatory activity provide a framework for understanding how these conflicts are resolved in the political arena. Instrumental models point to the relative political and economic power of opposing interests to influence congressional and agency decisions. Structural models, in contrast, highlight the tension between the economic costs of environmental action and the threats to social harmony flowing from environmental inaction. Taken together, these models predict that powerful polluting corporations have great potential to use government as an instrument of self-interest and that this power is enhanced by their central role in the capital accumulation/economic development process. They also predict that organized opposition by environmental interests will blunt corporate power and enhance regulatory conflict. In attempting to resolve conflict and contain its costs, legislative and agency decisions are likely to produce a program that is neither efficient nor equitable. I argue that the resulting inefficiency and inequity define Superfund failure. Building on this perspective, the remaining chapters follow the course of legislative and agency decisions and trace out the relationship between conflict and program failure.

The decade of the 1970s was characterized by a greatly enhanced awareness of environmental degradation and by legislation intended to guarantee that the mistakes of the past would not be reenacted in the future. The Resource Conservation and Recovery Act of 1976 (RCRA) placed controls on operating hazardous waste facilities. The fear and controversy surrounding Love Canal forced acceptance of the fact that efforts to control future disposal must be supplemented by a program to clean up the toxic legacy of the past. Against this background, chapter 4 examines the congressional debate over issues of Superfund cleanup, liability, and victim compensation. The debate highlights areas of conflict between petrochemical and manufacturing interests, on the one hand, and environmental interests, on the other. The imposition of a cleanup tax on the petrochemical industry and the acceptance of a make-polluters-pay principle demonstrate that public pressure can counter corporate power. The defeat of a victim compensation provision and the exclusion of explicit liability standards demonstrate the concessions required to place a major cleanup burden on powerful corporations. Passage of the Superfund Act engendered substantial tension between congressional expectations and the Reagan White House deregulatory agenda. I examine the efforts of the Reagan EPA to eviscerate environmental programs. This episode of regulatory intransigence culminated in the Sewergate scandal of 1983 and led to one of many efforts to revitalize the program.

A full evaluation of Superfund achievements during its first five-year authorization requires an understanding of the role played by the states and EPA regions in the implementation process. Chapter 5 focuses on state/federal government interdependence in hazardous waste regulation. A discussion of efforts to implement the Resource Conservation and Recovery Act emphasizes that inadequate control of operating hazardous waste sites produces new Superfund sites and that an inability to license new facilities compromises both safe disposal goals and the Superfund cleanup effort. The centerpiece of the chapter is an analysis of the environmental conditions and the political and economic forces that explain state hazardous waste program funding and enforcement decisions. Pressures from industry, labor, and environmental groups are shown to impact on state decisions. The inadequacy of state budgetary resources relative to cleanup burden emerges as the most significant limit on state contribution to Superfund achievements. This finding clearly demonstrates that political decisions to impose substantial financial responsibilities on the states limits Superfund potential.

Implementation of Superfund is carried out at the regional level and involves considerable tension between EPA's Washington headquarters and the agency's regional offices. Chapter 6 focuses on the regions and their adaptation to external constraints. The regional office must choose to directly finance cleanup out of the Superfund, to use enforcement powers to induce privately financed cleanup, or to rely on state enforcement efforts. I find that regional capacity to initiate cleanup activity is restricted by insufficient EPA staff resources as well as by the availability of state and private cleanup resources. I then evaluate regional progress in promoting fund-financed and enforcement-induced private cleanup and find progress to be contingent on EPA cleanup guidance and settlement strategy as well as on how each region exercises its discretion to interpret agency intent. I also find that the availability of state cleanup resources constrains regional capacity to promote Superfund-financed cleanups and impacts regional enforcement activity.

Superfund failure through 1985 is examined in chapter 7. I argue that failure is rooted in four intertwined program characteristics: an absence of cleanup standards (the how-clean-is-clean debate), a preference for impermanent versus permanent cleanup technologies, the strategies adopted to promote fund-financed and enforcement-induced cleanup, and the program's budget constraints. These roots emerge from Reagan White House emphasis on minimizing cleanup costs and from executive branch and congressional budgetary decisions. Limited regional and state resources constrain both Superfund-financed and enforcement-induced cleanups. Emphasis on cost minimization diminishes EPA's commitment to address pervasive ground water contamination problems. EPA's post-Sewergate fund-first enforcement strategy is found to be far more effective than the agency's initial nonconfrontational approach. However, the impact of the more recent strategy is diminished by EPA's insufficient reliance on incentives and threats to induce privately financed cleanup.

Superfund reauthorization afforded an opportunity to redesign the program and to wrest success from failure. Chapter 8 examines the issues that dominated the reauthorization debate: cleanup schedules and standards, a preference for permanent remedies, citizen suits, enforcement strategy and liability standards, victim compensation, and the source of funding for an expanded cleanup program. I draw several conclusions from the resolution of these issues as embodied in the Superfund Amendments and Reauthorization Act of 1986 (SARA). First, industrial and White House efforts to limit the scope of the program and to maintain EPA discretion were defeated by recognition of an expanding universe of Superfund sites combined with congressional distrust of Reagan administration commitment to cleanup. Second, industrial efforts to weaken EPA's enforcement program were defeated by the need to finance a more expensive cleanup program and to protect the federal budget from this burden. Third, efforts by a broad-based coalition of environmental and labor groups to include a victim compensation title succumbed again to estimates of the high but uncertain costs associated with this protection. Finally, despite industry claims of being shut out of reauthorization negotiations, a sympathetic hearing of the chemical industry's economic dislocation and fairness arguments allowed it to avoid paying a substantially increased Superfund tax. Over White House protests, Congress imposed higher cleanup taxes on the petroleum industry as well as on corporations in manufacturing and nonmanufacturing industries.

A redesigned Superfund set the stage for a substantial increase in fund-financed and enforcement-induced cleanup activity. Chapter 9 reviews EPA implementation under this new mandate from 1986 to 1988 (the final years of the Reagan EPA) and then through mid-1992 (the Bush EPA). I recount critical evaluations of EPA cleanup and enforcement decisions over the 1986–

88 period and argue that agency preoccupation with mandatory schedules and cleanup costs precluded selection of permanent treatment remedies and initiation of an aggressive enforcement program. I then examine the redirection of Superfund following the election of George Bush and his selection of William Reilly to head EPA. The agency's new aggressiveness under Reilly's enforcement-first strategy enhanced industry's contribution to cleanup. It also produced new industry strategies intended to shift the burden of cleanup onto municipalities and other third parties. These efforts, combined with mounting fear on the part of lending institutions that they would be held liable for the cleanup of foreclosed properties, gave rise to renewed claims that Superfund enforcement was little more than an extremely expensive and inefficient funding mechanism. In evaluating these developments, I argue that maintenance of a strong enforcement program is an essential component of the nation's effort to control future hazardous waste disposal practices. The current conflicts over liability test the nation's willingness to accept the high cost of making polluters pay.

The final chapter highlights the primary cause of Superfund failure. I contend that inability to resolve conflict over cleanup goals and the distribution of the toxic debt has built significant contradictory elements into Superfund. These contradictions have produced a program that is neither efficient nor equitable. The resulting failure is not inevitable. Despite instrumental and structural constraints on Superfund achievements, the substantial costs of failure create strong incentives to solve the Superfund dilemma. In conclusion, I speculate on whether these incentives are strong enough to yield social consensus on a fair and workable hazardous waste site cleanup program.

Hazardous wastes pose a substantial threat to public health and the environment. They are generated as raw materials are extracted, refined, processed, and applied to the production of useful goods. When hazardous wastes are disposed of improperly, they contaminate soil, air, surface water, and ground water and threaten the well-being of humans and other organisms.

Information on generation, disposal, contamination, and risk is integral to the regulatory process. Knowledge of the nature and extent of potential damages creates a demand for legislative action and shapes the regulatory response. At the same time, implementation results in the gathering of additional information that alters perceptions of the problem and evaluations of the regulatory response. Agencies gather information to fulfill legal mandates and to write the rules that give specificity to the law. The regulated and environmental communities gather information to oversee, evaluate, and critique law and its implementation. Despite, or perhaps because of, the centrality of information to the regulatory process, substantial uncertainty surrounds much important data. Uncertainty emerges from the limited ability of scientists and engineers to determine the contents of hazardous waste sites, to identify the pathways of contamination, and to gauge the risks posed to public health and the environment. Uncertainty is enhanced by the political environment within which data are generated and interpreted. With billions of dollars and millions of lives at stake, advocates and opponents of regulation choose and interpret data to give force to their arguments.

While the dangers associated with hazardous waste have been acknowledged for centuries, the threat posed to the United States is of relatively recent origin. It has followed upon the industrial revolution of the nineteenth century and the chemical revolution of the early twentieth century. Despite a century of warnings, systematic efforts to assess this threat have been undertaken only over the past several decades, and these efforts have been limited. Consequently, knowledge of generation, disposal, contamination, and risk is woefully inadequate. For example, a 1984 study by the National Academy of Sciences states that of the almost 710,000 different chemicals in commercial use, only about 20 percent have been subjected to extensive toxicity testing and one-third have never been tested at all for toxicity. A 1984 Senate report lists nearly 100 chemicals with substantial evidence of carcinogenicity that have not been subject to regulation (U.S. Congress, Senate, 1984b: 158). By early 1987 EPA listed only 450 of an estimated 35,000 potentially hazardous chemicals as being hazardous (Miller, 1988: 500–508). After carefully examining the availability of information on management of hazardous waste, the Office of Technology Assessment (OTA) concluded in 1983 that inadequate data conceal the scope and intensity of the national hazardous waste problem and hinder the effective implementation of government programs (U.S. Office of Technology Assessment, 1983: 131–33).

Information acquired over the past several decades does suggest the broad dimensions of the threat posed by hazardous wastes. In this chapter, I use available information to provide the reader with an overview of the problems addressed in the book and to sketch out perceptions of these problems during the 1979–80 debate over hazardous waste site cleanup legislation. The chapter begins with a brief primer on hazardous substances and their contribution to the need for Superfund cleanup. I then review data linking hazardous waste generation and disposal to industries and to private- and public-sector organizations. The next section examines early investigations into the scope of the hazardous waste disposal problem and the threats posed by hazardous waste sites. Finally, I review more recent data on the characteristics of Superfund sites.

HAZARDOUS WASTE AND CHEMICAL FEEDSTOCKS

Hazardous wastes are defined with reference to the dangers they pose to public health and the environment. The Resource Conservation and Recovery Act (RCRA) defines a hazardous waste as "a solid waste or combination of solid waste which because of its quantity, concentration, physical, chemical, or infectious attributes may (a) cause or significantly contribute to an increase in mortality or an increase in serious irreversible or incapacitating reversible illness; or (b) pose a substantial present or potential hazard to human health or the environment when improperly treated, stored, transported, or disposed of, or otherwise managed." The criteria for identifying a hazardous substance under RCRA include toxicity, persistence, and degradability in nature; potential for accumulation in tissue; and other related factors such as flammability and corrosiveness (U.S. Office of Technology Assessment, 1983: 271).

The definition of hazards requiring a response under Superfund is considerably broader, specifying pollutants and contaminants as well as hazardous substances. The latter include substances defined as hazards under other environmental laws (e.g., Clean Air Act, Clean Water Act, RCRA, Toxic Substances Control Act) and under Superfund. The former include "any element, substance, compound, or mixture, including disease-causing agents, which after release into the environment and upon exposure, ingestion, inhalation, or assimilation into any organism, either directly from the environment or indirectly by ingestion through the food chain, will or may reasonably be anticipated to cause death, disease, behavioral abnormalities, cancer, genetic mutation, physiological malfunctions (including malfunctions in reproduction), or physical deformations in such organism or their offspring" (U.S. Office of Technology Assessment, 1983: 300–301).

Superfund addresses the problem of contamination caused by the environmentally unsound disposal of inorganic and organic chemicals. A site is generally considered a Superfund site when the threat posed by contamination exceeds a minimum threshold established under the Environmental Protection Agency's hazard ranking system (HRS). The HRS is a tool for selecting and ranking the nation's worst sites. Sites that qualify for cleanup under the Superfund program are placed on a National Priorities List (NPL). The data base produced through application of the hazard ranking system is the primary source of information on chemicals found at Superfund sites. EPA has traced these chemicals back to the raw materials or feedstocks from which they most likely derive. Data on feedstocks have in turn been used to link industries to hazardous waste disposal. This information has played a central role in determining responsibility for Superfund problems and in crafting a tax system to fund site cleanup.

With minor exceptions (e.g., infectious waste), all hazardous wastes trace back to a set of inorganic and organic feedstocks used in the manufacture of useful goods and services. Inorganic feedstocks include asbestos, radioactive elements, acids and bases, metals and metallic compounds, and nonmetallic chemical elements. Organic feedstocks are predominantly petrochemicals. Some raw materials and feedstocks are inherently hazardous while others only become hazardous as they are processed and/or combined with other materials in manufacture and disposal.[1]

The goal of the inventory contained in the following sections is to highlight the integral role that major organic and inorganic chemical feedstocks play in modern industrial society and to demonstrate that they are the foundation upon which rests our consumption-oriented, high-technology, middle-class culture. Further, the inventory serves to emphasize the threats to human health and the environment consequent upon the unsound disposal of these same feedstocks. Finally, it establishes the link between industries that extract, process, or use these feedstocks and the hazardous wastes found at Superfund sites.

Inorganic Feedstocks

The use of metals such as lead, cadmium, copper, zinc, arsenic, and mercury generated the first hazardous wastes. Lead is a neurotoxin causing learning disabilities and chronic toxic effects in a variety of organs. Mercury, a more powerful neurotoxin, causes kidney damage and birth defects. Arsenic is a cumulative poison at higher levels and is a carcinogen. Cadmium is a carcinogen and a teratogen and is associated with high blood pressure, heart disease, and disease of the liver, kidney, and lungs. Other metallic chemical elements that contribute to Superfund cleanup problems include selenium, beryllium, and chromium. Beryllium is a carcinogen associated with skin lesions, ulcers, and respiratory disease. Chromium is also a carcinogen.

The smelting, refining, and basic processing of lead, copper, and zinc is conducted by firms in the primary metals industry. The remaining metals and nonmetallic inorganic elements are products of firms in industrial inorganic chemicals. Lead is used in the production of lead batteries and lead-based paints and in the smelting of nonferrous metals. Copper serves extensively as electric wiring while zinc is used in the production of batteries and cosmetics. Arsenic is used in the smelting of nonferrous metals, in pesticides, and as an additive to glass; cadmium in zinc mining and processing, in batteries and tires, in fertilizer processing, and in electroplating; mercury in the manufacture of paints, chlorine, and drugs. Beryllium finds application in ceramics and rocket propellants; chromium in electroplating, steel production, and leather tanning.

Elemental metals and their compounds are present in the hazardous waste streams of firms in the nonferrous primary metals and industrial inorganic chemicals industries. They also are present in the waste streams of industries which use metals and their compounds as production inputs: petroleum refining, chemicals, electrical and electronic, ferrous metals, and fabricated metals. EPA's recently compiled Toxics-Release Inventory shows that the primary metals and the chemical industries accounted for 23 percent and 62 percent, respectively, of metal and metal compounds released into the environment in 1987. Petroleum refiners are the next major source, accounting for nearly 5 percent.[2] Hazard ranking system data show that metals and their compounds account for some 20 percent of the contamination problems identified at Superfund sites.[3]

Nonmetallic inorganic chemical industry products, such as chlorine, bromine, and iodine, also contribute substantially to hazardous waste streams. Over 10 million tons of chlorine are produced annually for use in killing bacteria in drinking water, as inputs into the production of bleaching agents and other inorganic compounds, and as a basic element in the production of a broad class of synthetic organic chemicals (halogenated hydrocarbons). Chlorine, bromine, and iodine are highly toxic.

Hazard ranking system data trace 25 percent of contamination problems at Superfund sites to chlorine. The production of chlorinated synthetic organic chemicals is the predominate channel through which this contamination occurs. The use of chlorination to control bacteria in drinking water also is a contributing factor. Chlorine combines naturally with traces of bromine and organic compounds to produce trihalogenated methanes (e.g., chloroform). This occurs as a by-product of chlorination and when drinking water combines with organic matter in untreated water or with synthetic organic chemicals released into the environment. The Toxics-Release Inventory reports that the chemical and primary metals industries account for 56 percent and 20 percent, respectively, of nonmetallic organic materials released into the environment.

Materials that are very acidic or basic are extremely chemically reactive and corrosive; they do considerable damage in large concentrations. Acids may dissolve heavy metals out of soil or sediments, leaving the latter in suspension after the acid is neutralized. Sulfuric acid is an input in production of fertilizers, explosives, lead storage batteries, dyestuffs, other acids, paper, and glue. It is corrosive to skin and causes damage to lungs if inhaled. Hydrochloric acid is used to clean bricks, cement, and metals; nitric acid to produce fertilizers, dyes, plastics, and explosives. The bases that contribute to Superfund cleanup problems include ammonia (ammonium hydroxide), used in production of textiles such as rayon and in plastics and fertilizers, and sodium hydroxide (lye), used in production of soaps and cellophane.

Acids and bases are produced by firms in the industrial inorganic chemicals industry. They have wide application and are present in the hazardous waste streams of many manufacturing industries—including petroleum refining; chemicals; stone, clay, and glass; primary metals; fabricated metals; electric and electronic; transportation equipment; instruments and related products— as well as those of nonmanufacturing industries and households. According to the Toxics-Release Inventory, the chemical industry accounts for 69 percent of acids and bases released into the environment in 1987. Hazard ranking system data suggest that some 5 percent of contamination problems at Superfund sites are traced to acids and bases.

Organic Feedstocks (Petrochemicals)

Petroleum is the foundation of the modern organic chemical or petrochemical industry. Over the past half century, products derived from petrochemicals have replaced natural materials such as cotton, wood, rubber, metals, soap, manure, and natural solvents. Growth in synthetic organic chemical production has accelerated in the past several decades: in 1940 some 1 billion pounds were produced, increasing to 30 billion pounds by 1950, and to 300 billion pounds in 1976.

Petrochemicals are derived from petroleum and from natural gas. Primary petrochemicals, the initial direct chemical derivatives of these hydrocarbons, include benzene, butadiene, ethylene, propylene, styrene, toluene, and xylene. They are used as end products or are further processed into intermediates for production of petrochemical products which are sold to a wide range of industries to be further processed and incorporated into goods for industrial, commercial, and household use.

All primary petrochemicals are highly toxic. Benzene causes aplastic anemia and leukemia; toluene causes central nervous system depression with acute exposure. Benzene, toluene, and xylene are associated with adverse reproductive effects. In many applications, petrochemicals are used to create nonhazardous products; in others, the product is far more hazardous than the primary petrochemical from which it is derived.

As end products, the primary petrochemicals benzene and toluene are used as industrial solvents. As intermediates, ethylene and styrene are polymerized to form long chain plastics such as polyethylene and polystyrene. These are used to produce plastic bags, toys, auto parts, wire insulation, packaging, and furniture. Benzene is the starting material for synthetic fibers (e.g., nylon), pharmaceuticals, perfumes, and synthetic drugs. Toluene is used to produce explosives and dyes while butadiene is applied extensively in the manufacture of tires. Polypropylene, a plastic, is the major derivative of propylene. A minor derivative, cumene, is an input in the production of phenol. Phenol is used principally in construction materials (e.g., as a "glue" for plywood). Like other plastics, polypropylene is nonhazardous; in contrast, phenol is a carcinogen and extremely hazardous.

Halogenated hydrocarbons, created by adding chlorine, bromine, and iodine to hydrocarbon chains, are the basis for the production of modern synthetic organic chemicals. Trichloroethylene (TCE) is used extensively as an industrial solvent or degreasing agent. Polybrominated biphenyls (PBBs) are an effective fire retardant. Polychlorinated biphenyls (PCBs) resist breakdown from heat and electric charge. They were used widely as insulating material in transformers and electric machinery during the period from 1930 to 1980 and were once used to add pliability to plastics. Vinyl chloride is polymerized to form polyvinyl chloride, a tough synthetic material used for such products as floor coverings, unbreakable bottles, clear plastic wrap, and plastic pipes. Among synthetic agricultural chemicals, DDT, mirex, and chlordane are important pesticides and insecticides; 2,4,5-T was used extensively as a herbicide; and agent orange was used as a defoliant.

The characteristics of synthetic organic chemicals that make them extremely useful often make them extremely hazardous as well. They are variously able to suppress or alter chemical reactions involving naturally occurring organic processes and are resistant to degradation by natural biological reactions. Chlorine, bromine, and iodine, when attached to hydrocarbons, can remain toxic. When used as agricultural chemicals, they enter the metabolic systems of both targeted and nontargeted organisms. Once in the ecosystem, many halogenated hydrocarbons are almost insoluble in water but are more soluble in fats. They accumulate in living organisms and are passed up the food chain to humans.

Synthetic organic chemicals are not indestructible. They can be incinerated and eventually lose their toxicity through biodegradation. In some cases, however, biodegradation produces substances that are more toxic. For example, PCBs can break down into highly toxic dibenzofurans; as a result, they are no longer used in the production of plastics.

Synthetic organic chemicals have both known and suspected health effects. Trichloroethylene is a suspected mutagen, carcinogen, and neurotoxin; vinyl chloride is a known carcinogen. Many chlorinated hydrocarbon pesticides have adverse reproductive effects in animals and are carcinogenic. PCBs are carcinogenic and impair fertility. Dioxin (TCDD), a contaminant of herbicides such as 2,4,5-T and agent orange, is widely considered the most toxic known chemical.[4]

With their wide application in modern production, organic chemicals are present in waste streams of many manufacturing industries and also in those of nonmanufacturing industries and households. The Toxics-Release Inventory reports that 49 percent of nonhalogenated organic material released into the environment (mainly methanol, toluene, acetone, xylene, and methyl ethyl ketone) are attributable to the chemical industry. The paper, plastics, and transportation industries each account for 8 to 10 percent. In contrast, only 27 percent of halogenated organic releases are attributable to the chemical industry. The transportation and electrical industries each account for about 13 percent while plastics, primary metals, fabricated metals, and instruments each account for 6 to 9 percent. EPA notes that this broad distribution across industries may reflect the widespread use of synthetic solvents and degreasers. Hazard ranking system data show that 38 percent of the cleanup problems at Superfund sites are traced to organic chemicals.

HAZARDOUS WASTE AND INDUSTRY

The hazardous wastes deposited at Superfund sites reflect decades of production and consumption. If the contents of a "composite" site were stratified by decade, the thickness of each strata would indicate production quantities and disposal practices while characteristics of these wastes would indicate contemporary technologies and production processes. Growth in industrial production over the past century suggests that thickness would increase as more recent strata were observed. The top strata would contain more petrochemicals and would be considerably thicker than the lower strata.

Who bears responsibility for disposal of these wastes and for creation of the toxic debt remains a central Superfund policy issue. If responsibility can be traced to specific corporations, they can be held liable for the cost of cleanup. If specific responsible corporations cannot be identified, cleanup can be financed by taxing those industries that disposed of their hazardous wastes at Superfund sites. As more fully explained in chapter 4, the Superfund program incorporates both approaches. In what follows, I draw on government and private studies to suggest the distribution of responsibility for hazardous waste disposal and for Superfund cleanup problems across United States industry. These studies highlight the fact that the petrochemical industry is a most important source of hazardous waste generation and disposal. Not surprisingly, that industry has been a major target of Superfund taxation and enforcement.

In the early 1970s the newly established Environmental Protection Agency contracted for studies of waste generation by major industries (mostly manufacturing). Applying various methodologies and definitions, contractors produced fifteen industry studies which served as a data base for subsequent national estimates. A Booz Allen Hamilton (Booz Allen) study estimated that 41 million tons of waste regulated under the Resource Conservation and Recovery Act were generated in the United States in 1980 (U.S. Environmental Protection Agency, 1980). A survey of state data for the same year conducted by the Association of State and Territorial Solid Waste Management Officials estimated that some 265 million tons of hazardous waste were generated. The wide disparity between this estimate and that of Booz Allen is due primarily to the fact that many states included hazardous wastes that EPA had exempted from regulation (U.S. Office of Technology Assessment, 1983: 117–23).

Subsequent studies by Westat (U.S. Environmental Protection Agency, 1983a), the Congressional Budget Office (U.S. Congressional Budget Office, 1985), and the Chemical Manufacturers Association (U.S. General Accounting Office, 1987a) estimated national hazardous waste generation in the early 1980s to be in the range of 247 to 266 million tons. The similarity among these estimates is misleading. In a 1987 review, the General Accounting Office stated that it is virtually impossible to use these studies collectively to derive an accurate national estimate in that there are too many missing classes of waste and too much double counting. Further, there is wide variation in definition across studies, ambiguity with respect to the unit of measure, and errors in sampling and response (U.S. General Accounting Office, 1987a). Nonetheless, these various estimates support the oft-repeated observation that at least one ton of hazardous waste is generated annually for each man, woman, and child in the United States. At this rate, average daily production would fill the New Orleans Superdome from floor to ceiling four times.[5]

The Booz Allen, Westat, and Congressional Budget Office studies estimated hazardous waste generation by industry as a basis for national estimates (see table 2.1). Taken together, they show that chemicals and allied products account for between 48 and 71 percent of hazardous waste generation in 1980. Within this industry, one-third of total generation is attributed to industrial organic chemicals, pesticides, and related agricultural chemicals and 20 percent is attributed to industrial inorganic chemicals. An additional 8 to 40 percent of generation is attributed to petroleum refining, primary metals, and fabricated metals. The higher percentages recorded for these industries in the Congressional Budget Office study reflect in part its inclusion of RCRA exempted wastes. The findings of these studies is generally confirmed by the more recent EPA Toxics-Release Inventory data compilations reported in the last column of table 2.1. The chemical industry accounts for 55 percent of releases into the environment, and an additional 19 percent is attributed to petroleum refining and primary metals. The share of fabricated metals is less than suggested by earlier estimates.

A basic limitation of estimating hazardous waste generation by industry is that it does not focus our attention on the corporations that own and control these industrial establishments, that have earned the profits associated with the

Table 2.1. Generation of Hazardous Waste by Industry

Industry	Booz Allen (1980)	Westat (1981)	CBO (1982)	EPA (1987)
Textile Mill Products	<1			2
Lumber and Wood Products	<1		1	<1
Furniture and Fixtures	<1			<1
Printing and Publishing	<1			<1
Chemicals and Allied Products	62	71	48	55
Industrial Inorganic Chemicals	(20)			
Industrial Organic Chemicals	(32)			
Petroleum Refining and Related Industries	5	3	12	4
Rubber and Plastic Products	<1			2
Leather Tanning and Finishing	1			<1
Stone, Clay, and Glass	<1			<1
Primary Metals	10	3	28	15
Fabricated Metal Products	5	2	10	1
Machinery (except Electric)	<1	6	2	<1
Electric and Electronic	3	1	1	2
Transportation Equipment	3	6	1	2
Instruments and Related Products	<1		2	<1
Nonmanufacturing	5	8	1	

Sources: U.S. Environmental Protection Agency, 1980, 1983a, 1989; U.S. Congressional Budget Office, 1985.
Note: Not all industries are shown. Figures are in percent and may not add to 100 percent due to rounding.

environmentally unsound disposal of waste products, and that are parties to the political and legal debate over liability for Superfund cleanup. The major contribution of the chemical and petroleum refining industries to hazardous waste generation suggests that substantial responsibility can be traced to those corporations that make up the petrochemical industry.

The petrochemical industry is comprised of corporations nominally defined as in petroleum refining or chemicals. The distinction is based on the primary source of the firms' revenues. The major petroleum and chemical corporations are highly integrated with units or subsidiaries variously involved in the exploration, extraction, and refining of petroleum; the production and processing of primary petrochemicals; and the production of industrial, commercial, and household chemicals along with other petrochemical-based final products.

The twenty largest petroleum refiners earn, on average, some 20 percent of their revenues from petrochemical industry activities.[6] Exxon, with 1988 sales of nearly $80 billion, is the third largest U.S. corporation, the largest petroleum refiner, and the tenth largest petrochemical corporation. Mobil, the second largest petroleum refiner, had 1988 sales of $48 billion. Other major petroleum refiners prominent in the petrochemical industry include Texaco, Chevron, Occidental Petroleum, Amoco, Atlantic Richfield, Phillips, and Unocal.

The fifty-one largest U.S. (domestic) chemical corporations (not including petroleum refiners) are Fortune 500 companies with total 1988 sales of $163 billion and after-tax profits of $124 billion. The top eight companies (DuPont, Dow, Union Carbide, Monsanto, Hanson Industries, W. R. Grace, Hoechst Celanese, and PPG Industries) account for over half the sales and profits of these firms, while the two largest (DuPont and Dow) account for 30 percent of sales. Like the petroleum refiners, the major chemical companies are highly integrated and diversified across chemical product markets.

The contribution of very large petrochemical corporations to hazardous waste generation and disposal and to Superfund cleanup problems cannot be easily demonstrated. However, it is suggested by a number of statistics. First, if the magnitude of environmentally unsound hazardous waste disposal is roughly proportionate to chemical industry production, it follows that the major petrochemical corporations bear a substantial share of the responsibility for Superfund site problems. The petrochemical industry is comprised of approximately 1,200 companies that operate some 11,500 chemical production facilities. The industry was highly concentrated in the 1950s and remains so today. For industrial organic chemicals the fifty largest companies accounted for 91 percent of shipments by value in 1958 and 88 percent in 1987. For agricultural chemicals the fifty largest companies accounted for 85 percent of shipments by value in 1963 and 91 percent in 1982. For industrial inorganic chemicals the fifty largest companies accounted for 86 percent of shipments by value in 1972 and 79 percent in 1982.[7] The Booz Allen study reports that these three industry segments are the major source of petrochemical industry hazardous waste.

Concentration data can overstate the responsibility of the major companies for Superfund problems in that many large generators dispose of their hazardous waste on-site. A 1979 congressional survey found that the fifty-three largest domestic petrochemical companies (chemical companies and chemical divisions or subsidiaries of petroleum companies) owned or operated 14 percent of domestic chemical production facilities, about thirty facilities per company (U.S. Congress, House, 1979b). These 1,605 facilities generated an estimated 762 million tons of chemical-process waste between 1950 and 1978 and disposed of it at 3,383 on-site and off-site locations known to the companies. The companies disposed of 94 percent of this waste at sites located on their immediate property. The remainder was sent to the 2,334 off-site locations. One-third of these latter sites were closed at the time of the survey, and another 9 percent may have been closed. Nearly 5 million tons were transported off-site for disposal by some 960 haulers to locations unknown to the facility operator.

A second index of the contribution of major petrochemical companies to Superfund cleanup problems is the extent to which sites listed in the 1979 survey appear on EPA's list of Superfund sites. Since EPA lists nearly 900 Superfund sites as of 1986 and the 1979 survey lists over 3,000 sites, a match was conducted for only three states: New Jersey, Ohio, and Texas. These states account for roughly one-quarter of the facilities and sites reported in the survey as well as one-quarter of reported nonmining wastes. This name-matching exercise establishes that at least 18 percent of the New Jersey Superfund sites received wastes from the major petrochemical companies and at least 31 percent and 21 percent, respectively, of the Ohio and Texas sites received their wastes. In the absence of volume and toxicity data, it is not possible to fully assess the contribution of the major companies to cleanup problems at these sites. Further, it is not possible to determine how many Superfund sites in these states received waste from haulers, under contract to major companies, who did not report where wastes were disposed.

A third index of the contribution of the major petrochemical companies to Superfund cleanup problems is the frequency with which their names appear as potentially responsible parties (PRPs) targeted by EPA to cover cleanup costs.[8] In 1984 the Clean Water Project obtained an EPA list of PRPs at 195 Superfund sites; thirty-six companies were identified which appear as potentially responsible parties at seven or more of these sites. Twenty-five are petrochemical companies; of these, fourteen are among the twenty-five largest companies in that industry. On average, each is identified as a potentially responsible party at 11 of the 195 Superfund sites (Cole and Roberts, 1984). This study also shows that some small chemical companies made disproportionately large contributions to cleanup problems. Velsicol, a producer of pesticides and industrial chemicals, was named as a potentially responsible party at seven sites. It had 1,587 employees in 1987.

The findings of the Clean Water Project study are supported by a listing of potentially responsible parties released by EPA in 1987. Of the twelve companies associated with the largest number of sites, eight are major petrochemical producers (DuPont, Monsanto, Union Carbide, Rohm and Haas, Mobil Chemical, Allied, Ashland Chemical, and Exxon). On average, each is named as a PRP at twenty-five sites.[9]

The contribution of major corporations to Superfund cleanup problems is not unique to the petrochemical industry. Three of the thirty-six companies identified in the Clean Water Project study are in electronics. Of these, General Electric was named at twenty-two sites and Westinghouse at nine. The 1987 EPA list includes General Electric among the twelve companies associated with the largest number of sites. With thirty-five sites, it is second only to DuPont. Westinghouse identified itself as a potentially responsible party at ninety hazardous waste sites. GE and Westinghouse are the two largest companies in electronics, together accounting for 37 percent of sales of the largest forty-five companies in that industry. Their contribution to Superfund problems derives substantially from the use of PCBs in transformers and other electric equipment. Another three of the thirty-six companies identified in the Clean Water Project study and two of the companies identified by EPA are in motor vehicles production. Ford and General Motors both had eleven sites in the former study and nineteen and twenty-one, respectively, in the more recent EPA listing.

The contribution of large entities to Superfund cleanup problems is not unique to the private sector. The Clean Water Project study identified fifteen sites (8 percent of the total) where the U.S. government is among the potentially responsible parties. The vast majority of these are the responsibility of the Department of Defense (DOD). At many of these sites production or storage was conducted by a private company under contract to DOD or by a private company on land leased from DOD. The Rocky Mountain Arsenal site near Denver provides an example of the latter situation. From 1959 to 1982 the Shell Oil Company leased U.S. Army land at the arsenal for a pesticide production plant. Soil and ground water was polluted by Shell and army operations; the pollution seeped into nearby drinking water wells. A projected $2 billion cleanup at this site is to be shared by Shell and the army (New York Times, 1988). Recent investigations of Department of Energy operations at nuclear weapons plants reveal disposal practices through the mid-1980s that were prohibited for private concerns in the mid-1970s. The Department of Energy disposed of trichloroethylene and other solvents, asbestos, PCBs, insecticides, herbicides, dioxins, and heavy metals in unlined pits, lagoons, and ditches, causing contamination of soil and ground water (see Wald, 1988).

HAZARDOUS WASTE AND CONTAMINATION

The "discovery" of Love Canal in 1978 and Michael Brown's reporting of the threats faced by the residents of this Niagara Falls community sensitized

Congress, EPA, and the public to the potentially immense problems posed by uncontrolled, closed, and abandoned hazardous waste sites.[10] At that time, it was known that industry utilized various land-based facilities for hazardous waste disposal: landfills, surface impoundments, deep well injection, above-ground tank and drum storage, piles, and land farms. It was also known that industrial sites were contaminated both through production and in efforts to manage waste by recycling, chemical treatment, and solvent recovery. It was recognized that regulatory efforts to clean up surface water through restrictions on release of liquid waste into rivers and lakes and to clean up the air through restrictions on particulate emissions had led to an increased reliance on unregulated land-based disposal. Further, it was understood that any land-based hazardous waste disposal method could contaminate soil, air, surface water, and ground water. These methods could also cause damage to sensitive ecosystems such as wetlands, aquifers, and streams, as well as to humans and other living organisms. What was not known was the true extent of the problem. Representative Robert Eckhart (D-Tex.) offered a characteristic statement on the degree of public ignorance: "Neither EPA nor any other agency has any reliable figures even approximating the number of these potentially dangerous sites that exist. In short, how many past dump sites are time bombs of hazardous materials ticking toward catastrophic health and property damage?" (U.S. Congress, House, 1979a: 1–2).

In this section I review major studies of hazardous waste site threats that informed the congressional debate over Superfund. On the one hand, these studies make abundantly clear that U.S. industry had for decades been disposing of highly toxic wastes in a manner that afforded scant protection to human health and the environment. They point to the significant and pervasive problem of ground water contamination by toxic chemicals and establish the need for a cleanup program. On the other hand, wide disparity in estimates of the number of problem sites provided support in congressional debate for proponents of both more and less ambitious programs. As becomes evident in chapter 4, disagreement among scientific studies allowed political pressure from generator industries to play a substantial role in legislative debate. This was due, first, to uncertainty with regard to the industrial sources of hazardous waste disposal; second, to the obvious fact that hazardous waste disposal was a clear by-product of a contemporary industrial-based culture; and third, to often sketchy data on how many sites required cleanup to protect public health and the environment.

By 1980 the extent and nature of the hazardous waste disposal problem began to emerge as the Environmental Protection Agency and others released studies initiated in the last years of the 1970s. The 1979 congressional study of major chemical manufacturers found that surface impoundments and landfills were the most commonly used land-based disposal methods for nonmining wastes. In 1978, 17 percent of this waste was placed in pits, ponds, and lagoons while 12 percent was placed in landfills. An additional 10 percent was injected into deep wells. Chemical industry liquid waste and sludge was sent to industrial landfills and often mixed with waste streams from other industries. Chemical waste was also sent to municipal landfills. While the study noted that 33 to 42 percent of the sites receiving waste were closed by 1978, no information was collected on the risks these sites posed to public health and the environment (U.S. Congress, House, 1979b: xviii–xix).

Under prodding from Congress, EPA contracted with Fred C. Hart Associates to estimate the extent of the hazardous waste site problem (U.S. Environmental Protection Agency, 1979). The consultant estimated that there were approximately 30,000 to 50,000 active and inactive hazardous waste sites nationwide and that 1,200 to 34,000 posed significant problems. Following upon the Fred C. Hart study and drawing on some of the same regional data, EPA released a study in 1980 documenting the extent and variety of risks associated with 350 hazardous waste disposal sites.[11] Half of these sites had contaminated surface water supplies or ground water while 13 percent had resulted in the closure of over 468 drinking water wells.

In the same year, the Chemical Manufacturers Association (CMA) released its own estimate that 4,800 sites nationwide contained hazardous waste and that 400 of these posed significant problems. The CMA estimate was based on a telephone survey of the states. The association did not say how many states provided data or how they derived their figures (U.S. Office of Technology Assessment, 1983: 131). The CMA study did cast doubts on "official" estimates and highlighted the fuzziness of the numbers upon which legislation would be based.[12]

Evidence also was accumulating that toxic chemicals released from hazardous waste sites posed a substantial threat to a resource once thought pure— ground water. The Council on Environmental Quality (CEQ) conducted a study of contamination of ground water by toxic organic chemicals and reported that "[i]n both relative and absolute terms, the contamination of drinking water supplies by toxic organic chemicals is worse for ground water supplies than for surface water supplies. This conclusion runs counter to the previously unquestioned assumption that drinking water from ground water supplies can be used as a standard of purity in epidemiological and medical studies of human health" (U.S. Council on Environmental Quality, 1981: 579).

In mid-1980 the House Committee on Government Operations conducted hearings on toxic chemical contamination of ground water. In opening comments, Representative Toby Moffett (D-Conn.) called this a problem of frightening dimensions and one of the most tragic and least understood environmental facts confronting the nation. He went on the say that "the fact is that we have already carelessly, and perhaps irreversibly, contaminated one of the nation's most precious resources—the ground water that we drink, that we use to irrigate our crops, and the water we use for a host of vital industrial activities" (U.S. Congress, House, 1980b: 1).

Moffett's characterization was based on EPA's Surface Impoundment Assessment, a systematic study of the extent to which the storage, treatment, and disposal of liquid wastes in surface impoundments such as pits, ponds, and lagoons threatened ground water quality.[13] The study located 25,749 impoundments at 10,819 industrial sites and assessed over 8,000 of these sites. Impoundments at over 70 percent of the assessed industrial sites were found to be unlined, potentially allowing contaminants to infiltrate unimpeded into the subsurface. Further, nearly 95 percent of the impoundments were found to be virtually unmonitored as to possible ground water contamination. Approximately 50 percent were found to contain liquid waste with potentially hazardous constituents while the remaining 50 percent were found to contain constituents that could cause degradation of ground water. Finally, 30 percent of the industrial impoundments were unlined and located above unsaturated zones which freely allowed downward movement of any liquid wastes escaping from the impoundment into a usable aquifer. About one-third of the industrial sites were within one mile of a water supply well which would be in the path of any contaminated ground water flowing from these sites.

Complementing the findings of the Surface Impoundment Assessment, Robert Harris of the Council on Environmental Quality presented Congress with evidence on the contamination of ground water by synthetic organic chemicals from a wide variety of industrial, commercial, municipal, and agricultural sources.[14] To place the evidence in context, Harris reiterated the following basic facts: The volume of ground water under the United States is estimated to be about fifty times the volume of annual surface water flow. Ground water supplies 25 percent of the fresh water used for all domestic purposes. The overall use of ground water has increased at a rate of approximately 25 percent per decade. Nearly 70 percent is used for irrigation, while industry utilizes 14 percent, urban drinking water 13 percent, and rural drinking water 5 percent. Approximately 50 percent of all U.S. residents rely on ground water as their primary domestic drinking water supply. An estimated 96 percent of all rural drinking water comes from ground water sources, in contrast to 20 percent of urban needs.

Harris also emphasized that the importance of ground water as a natural resource is matched by its vulnerability to contamination. Ground water is the subsurface water that occurs beneath the water table in soils and geologic formations that are fully saturated. Aquifers, the subsurface permeable formations that can yield significant amounts of water to wells and springs, underlie most of the nation. Once contaminated by toxic organic chemicals, ground water remains so for hundreds or thousands of years, if not for geologic time—the contamination is irreversible by natural forces. Ground water moves very slowly. Contamination moving with the ground water will spread by flow and dispersion into a "plume," the dimensions of which are controlled by the structure of the aquifer. It may take decades for ground water pollution which occurs in one location to appear in a water well only a few miles away. By its very nature and location, ground water is expensive to test and monitor. The qualities and quantities of ground water and surface water are interdependent because they are part of the hydrologic cycle. Fresh water wetlands are commonly in close hydrologic connection with both surface and ground water. Consequently, contamination of the wetland or surface water may pollute ground water in an aquifer.

The CEQ had compiled available information on incidents of ground water contamination and determined that hundreds of drinking water wells affecting the domestic water of millions of people had recently been closed. For example, contamination by trichloroethylene (TCE) resulted in the closure of public wells serving more than 400,000 people in California's San Gabriel Valley. Contamination by TCE and dioxane resulted in closure of wells providing 80 percent of the drinking water in Bedford, Massachusetts. At least one-third of the state's 351 communities were affected by organic or inorganic chemical contamination of drinking water supplies. Massive ground water contamination also confronted the millions of Long Island residents who relied on ground water for all domestic and industrial purposes.[15]

Testimony on behalf of the council argued that these specific incidents only hinted at the nationwide magnitude of ground water contamination. A contemporary EPA survey of selected volatile organic chemicals in drinking water supplies provided a broader perspective. Samples were taken from thirty-nine cities with populations of 10,000 to 1,000,000 without regard to potential contamination. Eleven volatile organic chemicals were found frequently, sometimes in high concentrations. The solvent and degreaser TCE was found most frequently. EPA regional offices also had detailed information on contamination of drinking water wells in thirty-four states indicating that almost all states east of the Mississippi had major problems, and that even the relatively nonindustrial, lightly populated western states had major problems.

At least thirty-three toxic organic chemicals were found in concentrations exceeding any previously measured in surface water or ground water supplies.

The council acknowledged that there was uncertainty regarding the health risks posed by high concentrations of these toxic organic chemicals found in drinking water wells. Qualitative data from occupational studies identified adverse effects, including reproductive problems, from two-thirds of these thirty-three most commonly found chemicals. Epidemiological studies of populations consuming chlorinated water provided insights into the cancer risks associated with some of these. Epidemiological studies also provided evidence that benzene and vinyl chloride were human carcinogens. Studies of laboratory animals provided evidence that an additional thirteen of the thirty-three organic chemical compounds were carcinogenic. The CEQ offered crude estimates of the carcinogenic risks from drinking water that contained fifteen of the thirty-three synthetic organic chemicals at various concentrations assuming lifetime consumption of water containing one part per billion of the chemical. Two of the chemicals would be expected to result in one cancer per million population, twelve would be expected to result in two to four cancers per million population, and one chemical (tetrachloroethylene) would be expected to result in nine cancers per million population. These incidence levels were compared to the state and federal risk assessment rule of thumb that a lifetime cancer risk of one per million is acceptable.

In the absence of nationwide data on the extent and severity of ground water contamination, nationwide risks could not be calculated. Two "worst case" scenarios were analyzed based on chemicals present in a New Jersey well and in 372 Nassau County, New York, wells. For the former, the lifetime cancer risk was estimated at 1 in 400 and for the latter at 1 in 1,300.

THE NATION'S WORST SITES?

As suggested at the beginning of the chapter, information shapes legislation and implementation of legislation generates new information. The pre-Superfund studies discussed above provided sufficient evidence to establish that the nation faced an extremely serious hazardous waste disposal problem. Information was not available to narrowly define its extent and severity. Further, neither time nor resources were available for on-site investigations to establish the percentage of known sites that posed significant threats to public health and the environment. In the absence of such systematic investigation, it could not be determined whether the hundreds of sites with problems known to EPA regional offices and state officials were the "tip of the iceberg" or the majority of problem sites. As discussed in chapter 4, the determination of the true extent of the threat posed was a major issue in the debate over Superfund legislation.

By 1984 a clearer picture of the hazardous waste disposal problem began to emerge as EPA compiled a list of known sites and sifted through these to identify sites that posed significant threats to public health and the environment. In December of that year, EPA submitted a progress report to Congress. EPA's inventory of potential Superfund sites now contained 19,000 sites with a wide range of potential hazardous waste problems. The National Priorities List of the nation's worst sites included 538 sites with an additional 248 proposed, for a total of 786 proposed and final sites requiring cleanup. On the basis of its experience to date, EPA projected that 1,500 to 2,200 sites would eventually require cleanup. However, it noted that this projection was for "traditional sites" with "obvious hazardous release problems." The number of needed cleanups would greatly expand were Superfund reoriented to encompass a range of emerging problem areas.[16] By EPA estimates, these problem areas encompassed an additional 131,000 to 379,000 sites of potential concern (U.S. Environmental Protection Agency, 1984b: 5-2–5-14).

Early 1980s estimates by the Commerce Department and the Chemical Manufacturers Association suggested that EPA's projections were excessive. (The CMA identified 1,000 likely NPL sites and 3,681 potential sites through a state survey.) An estimate by the General Accounting Office of 1,270 to 2,546 NPL sites was in accord with EPA's projection. At the same time, the National Audubon Society projected 2,200 to 7,000 NPL sites, The Association of State and Territorial Solid Waste Management Officials projected over 7,000 sites based on a state survey (1,500 of these were most serious), and the Office of Technology Assessment projected a National Priorities List of 10,000 sites (U.S. Office of Technology Assessment, 1985: 14, 167). In its critique of EPA projections, OTA argued that the agency had not even considered some 340,000 surface impoundments, regardless of their prominence on the National Priorities List, and that EPA did not acknowledge as many as 150,000 closed industrial landfills (U.S. Office of Technology Assessment, 1985: 168).

In light of the narrowness of Superfund's focus through 1984, the characteristics of priority list sites cannot be assumed identical to those of a representative sample of the nation's hazardous waste problem sites broadly defined. At the same time, the characteristics of the NPL sites are generally consistent with the findings of pre-Superfund studies discussed above. In its 1984 report to Congress, EPA identified nonexclusive types of activities demanding cleanup at 786 proposed and final National Priorities List sites: Surface impoundments posed problems at 34 percent of these sites, while buried or surface drums were present at 24 percent. Over 20 percent of the sites were unclassified landfills, 17 percent were commercial/industrial landfills, 17 percent were open dumps, 13 percent were municipal landfills, 12 percent contained above ground tanks, and 11 percent contained piles (U.S. Environmental Protection Agency, 1984b: 3–6).

The twenty-five hazardous substances found most frequently at these sites were seen to present serious hazards to humans and animal life. Seven were toxic to aquatic life, nearly half were known or probable human carcinogens, nine were mutagens, seven were teratogens, seven would ignite at room temperature, seven could bioaccumulate in the environment, and nearly nineteen resisted biodegradation and were persistent especially in ground water. Release of hazardous substances into ground water had occurred at three-quarters of the sites and was highly likely at another 18 percent. Releases into surface water had occurred at over half the sites and was highly likely at another 17 percent. Releases into the air had occurred at one-fifth of the sites (U.S. Environmental Protection Agency, 1984b: 2-7, 2-11).

To estimate population at risk from surface water–borne contaminants, EPA counted persons who used water drawn from an intake within three miles downstream of the facility or waste site. To estimate population at risk from ground water–borne contaminants, EPA counted persons who actually used ground water from wells, but only those wells within three miles of where hazardous substances were deposited or were known to have migrated. For 546 National Priorities List sites, EPA estimated the population at risk from each of these media at approximately six million persons (U.S. Environmental Protection Agency, 1984b: 2-12). The author's calculations using EPA data on exposed population at 858 proposed and final National Priorities List sites as of early 1986 suggests that nearly 4 percent of the nation's population is at risk from surface water–borne contamination (9.24 million persons) and 10 percent is at risk from ground water–borne contamination (24.2 million persons).[17] Given EPA's prediction of a fourfold increase in the size of the National Priorities List, these may be low estimates of the population at risk from hazardous waste site contamination.

A FINAL COMMENT

Over a decade has passed since Congress debated and passed Superfund. In that time, EPA has identified over 34,000 potential Superfund sites and has placed 1,236 on the National Priorities List (see table 2.2). The states also have identified tens of thousands of sites needing attention, many of which will not

Table 2.2. Superfund Sites by State and EPA Region, 1989

REGION 1	84		REGION 6	.73
Connecticut	15		Arkansas	11
Maine	9		Louisiana	11
Massachusetts	25		New Mexico	10
New Hampshire	16		Oklahoma	12
Rhode Island	11		Texas	29
Vermont	8			
			REGION 7	62
REGION 2	192		Iowa	21
New Jersey	109		Kansas	11
New York	83		Missouri	24
			Nebraska	6
REGION 3	152			
Delaware	20		REGION 8	46
Maryland	10		Colorado	16
Pennsylvania	97		Montana	10
Virginia	20		North Dakota	2
West Virginia	5		South Dakota	3
			Utah	12
REGION 4	155		Wyoming	3
Alabama	12			
Florida	51		REGION 9	109
Georgia	13		Arizona	11
Kentucky	17		California	91
Mississippi	3		Hawaii	7
North Carolina	22			
South Carolina	23		REGION 10	62
Tennessee	14		Idaho	9
			Oregon	8
REGION 5	267		Washington	45
Illinois	38			
Indiana	35			
Michigan	79			
Minnesota	42			
Ohio	33			
Wisconsin	40			

Source: U.S. Environmental Protection Agency, press release, October 1989.
Note: Includes final and proposed National Priorities List sites.

be addressed under Superfund. Although EPA has only certified thirty-three sites as "clean," it has made progress toward permanent cleanup at over 300 sites. The program remains under attack for the slow pace and high cost of cleanup. Critics of the program as well as some in EPA have begun to question whether hazardous waste sites in fact pose risks to public health of sufficient magnitude to justify the billions of dollars spent to date and the billions more to be spent over coming years. The following chapters are intended to provide insight into how we have arrived at this current impasse.

Social regulation emerges out of conflict between an industrial drive for profit
and public demands for protection from production-related harms to health,
safety, and the environment.[1] Regulation orders this conflict and channels it
through a set of interacting decision-making bodies: legislatures, administrative agencies, and courts. The success or failure of regulation reflects the terms
on which conflict is resolved by successive decision makers.

Analyses of Superfund reveal a broad consensus that the program has failed
to provide effective and fair social regulation. There is far less consensus on
what the program has achieved and should achieve, the cause of its failure, and
the relationship between failure and program-engendered conflict. The thesis
of this study is that inability to resolve these conflicts in a consistent manner
has contributed substantially to Superfund failure. The purpose of this chapter
is to identify the conflicts that surround Superfund and set them within a
framework that links conflict, conflict resolution, and program failure.

The starting point is an examination of environmentally unsound hazardous
waste disposal as an instance of market failure. Contrary to a popular position,
I argue that tort law faces severe limits as a mechanism to correct market failure
and to promote efficient and equitable cleanup and compensation. The case
for centralized, direct government regulation is then based on the failure of
private torts. Direct regulation by the state requires explicit decisions on issues
of hazardous waste cleanup program design and implementation. I outline the
major issues confronting decision makers and emphasize that conflict over the
distribution of program costs and benefits pervades all design and implementation decisions. Parties are identified that have a direct interest in program
outcomes. Next, political economic perspectives on government decision
making are discussed and used to summarize expectations regarding barriers to

the resolution of program-engendered distributional conflict. Finally, program failure is related to distributional conflict.

MARKET FAILURE AND STATE INTERVENTION

The improper disposal of hazardous waste enhances generator and site owner profits at the expense of damage to public health and the environment. For example, dumping toxic waste in an abandoned gravel pit is less costly than sending waste to a state of the art landfill with double liners and continuous monitoring of site integrity. The former is more likely to result in waste migration, contamination of surface or ground water, exposure of population to contaminated drinking water supplies, and increased incidence of injury. If a generator chooses the first option, production costs are reduced and output and profits are increased. As a consequence of this decision, either the exposed population suffers injuries and society loses resources or population and society bear the cost of cleanup to gain protection from injury and natural resource damage. This is a classic instance of market failure. The firm is able to shift a production-related cost onto a third party, thereby externalizing the cost. Since the firm avoids absorbing the cost, it expands production beyond the level that would be profitable were all costs of production internalized.

Market failure results in a loss in economic efficiency and a reduction in social welfare. Economic efficiency measures the benefits society derives from use of its productive resources while social welfare measures the costs imposed and benefits received by members of a society in the aggregate. Social resources are used inefficiently and society as a whole is made worse off when the cost of redressing production-related damages exceeds the benefit associated with the enhanced production and profits allowed by externalization of cost. Market failure also results in inequities and a related loss in social welfare when there is consensus that those who profit should absorb all associated costs. Market failure justifies government intervention as a means to achieve efficiency and equity and to promote social welfare.

Intervention by the political state to correct market failure can work through two interrelated mechanisms: tort law and direct regulation. Tort law protects interests in property and persons from damage by others. Legislation and the evolution of common law has established personal and property rights as well as procedures for asserting rights. The correction of hazardous waste disposal problems through private civil action requires courts to enforce the principle that hazardous waste generators and disposers are responsible for the damages they cause. Responsible parties are forced to arrange for site cleanup and/or to compensate those who suffer waste disposal damages. In contrast to the de-centralized decision making inherent in private tort law, direct regulation involves centralized decisions on standards for corporate behavior and pro-cedures for achieving compliance with these standards. Direct regulation often relies on tort law as a means of asserting society's interests. The correction of disposal problems through direct regulation requires that government assert the liability of hazardous waste generators and disposers, enforce these liability standards, and act to clean up hazardous waste sites when correction is not forthcoming from a private responsible party.

The need for direct government intervention to promote cleanup and compensation is a subject of heated political and academic debate. The environmental legislation of the 1970s (discussed in the next chapter) clearly built on the expectation that direct regulation is in the social interest. Critics of direct regulation, in particular many associated with the Law and Economics movement, argue that reliance on markets and marketlike devices such as bargaining will often produce outcomes more efficient than those resulting from direct government regulation.[2] The cost of market transactions is a pivotal factor in the case for reliance on the market. In the instance of waste site cleanup, transaction costs include identification of those responsible for site conditions, determination of the damages resulting from these conditions, establishment of relevant property and personal rights, conduct of negotiations leading up to a bargain, drafting and execution of a cleanup or compensation plan, and inspection to make sure that the terms of the agreement are being observed (Coase, 1960: 15). If transaction costs are minimal, those responsible for waste site conditions and those who suffer the associated damages will bargain and reach an agreement that is efficient and that benefits both parties. The agreement may require the responsible party to clean up the site and to compensate people for damages already suffered or may require that local population sell their homes and move away, leaving disposal site conditions unchanged. These outcomes suggest alternative distributions of the costs of public health and property protection. Their equity or inequity is not an issue for many advocates of the Law and Economics approach since efficiency is taken to be the sole criteria for evaluation. If negotiation promotes efficiency through minimizing collective cost, regardless of who bears the cost, the social interest is served.

From this perspective, the appropriate role for government is to see that the law minimizes transaction costs and thus promotes efficiency. Direct govern-ment regulation is costly, for example, due to public expenditures on admin-istration, staff, and overhead, and due to private expenditures on record keeping. Were direct regulation to specify the same solutions reached through private bargaining, transaction costs would be higher and therefore outcomes would be less efficient than if these solutions were derived in the absence of government intervention. Were direct regulation to specify a solution that did not minimize collective costs, efficiency would suffer more substantially. Government involvement therefore should be limited to writing the rules and procedures for private bargaining.

When transaction costs are substantial, a negotiated agreement between parties becomes less likely. If the cost of asserting rights exceeds the expected gains to be achieved, waste disposal victims withdraw and waste site conditions remain unaltered even though agreement in the absence of transaction costs would promote the social interest. In such situations, proponents of the Law and Economics approach acknowledge that direct regulation to command change in responsible party behavior may be justified (Coase, 1960: 18).

The case for direct regulation is integrally related to the failure of tort law to achieve cleanup and compensation.[3] A successful tort action requires that there is a breach of duty owed to the plaintiff by the defendant, that there is a harm suffered by the plaintiff, and that the breach is the immediate or proximate cause of the harm (Cooter and Ulen, 1988: 327). One source of failure is the substantial transaction costs associated with promoting waste site cleanup and compensation through private torts. A victim must be able to locate a defendant who is liable under common law and who is worth suing. When many defendants are responsible for conditions at the site and all must be brought into the case, transaction costs increase exponentially. The victim must bear the considerable cost of testing and expert testimony to establish injury and causation. While per capita transaction costs can be reduced through class action suits, courts may not allow a class action where injuries arising from a single waste disposal site are of disparate types and appear at different times.

The practical and legal barriers faced by the plaintiff in meeting tort law requirements are an additional source of failure. First, some state statutes of limitations for tort actions begin to run at the time of the defendant's tortious act. These traditional limitation periods are often violated by the time required for toxic waste leakage and migration, for exposure to contaminated surface or ground water supplies, for the onset of an injury such as cancer with long latency periods, and for awareness of the relationship between exposure and injury.[4] Second, while several tort law principles such as strict liability, negligence, trespass, and nuisance are available in theory, the fact that the plaintiff may be indeterminate renders them inapplicable. We may know that a group of people has a specific type of cancer and that some of them contracted that cancer from exposure to the defendant's waste; however, we will not necessarily know which individuals in that group were affected by the waste. Third, a defendant will be held liable if it is proven to be more likely than not that the defendant's action caused the plaintiff's injury. A plaintiff, however, typically can show only a causal link between exposure to a toxic substance and an injury. Further, medical and epidemiological evidence linking contamination to injury in a statistical sense may be excluded by evidentiary rules. Causal indeterminacy imposes great difficulties on the party with the burden of proof. High transaction costs combine with the uncertainty of eventual recovery to discourage many victims from suing and to encourage many who do sue to accept settlements which do not reflect the merits of their claim.

Even in the absence of high transaction costs, legal barriers, and practical barriers, the private tort law mechanism will fail to promote a socially efficient response if three other conditions are not met. First, responsible parties must have perfect foresight: they must accurately project and fully internalize the future costs of their actions. It is highly unlikely that this condition will be met. Since the relationship between disposal, migration, contamination, and injury is very uncertain, the cost of future compensation is also uncertain. Faced with uncertainty, the responsible party may underestimate future costs and fail to take appropriate action. Further, when many responsible parties are involved, each may underestimate their share of future costs. Second, property rights must be attached to all resources that suffer hazardous waste site damages. If contaminated surface or ground water does not have an owner to bring suit, tort law cannot achieve internalization and responsible parties do not select a socially efficient action.[5] Third, responsible parties must exist with sufficient resources for cleanup and compensation. If all responsible parties are bankrupt, this condition cannot be met. Further, when cleanup costs are likely to bankrupt an otherwise profitable firm, shareholders may deem it in their interest to put off the day of reckoning.

The limitations of tort law make it most unlikely that compensation will occur when justified by damages or that cleanup will occur when justified by social efficiency. The failure of tort law therefore necessitates direct regulation as the next best viable option to protect public health and the environment.

SUPERFUND ISSUES

Hazardous waste site cleanup poses a set of interrelated issues that must be addressed to design and implement a program of direct regulation. The following brief overview of Superfund issues highlights a root cause of the Superfund dilemma: the fact that all program decisions impact on the distribution of cleanup costs and benefits either by specifying who will pay and who will gain or by determining the amount of these expenditures and benefits. As developed at greater length in subsequent chapters, the history of Superfund reveals substantial conflict over decisions on such major issues as the appropriate scope of the program, the selection of cleanup remedies, and the mechanisms to distribute the costs and benefits of cleanup and compensation. The purpose of this section is simply to give the reader a sense of the issues and the conflicts that surround them.

The range of problems to be addressed by the program and the selection of cleanup remedies to correct these problems are primary determinants of cost and potential benefits. The policy debate has focused on whether Superfund should be limited to cleanup of abandoned hazardous waste sites or should be expanded to include unsound operating hazardous waste facilities, leaking underground storage tanks, radon in homes, and contaminated federal government facilities. It also has focused on whether cleanup actions should be limited to protection of public health and currently utilized ground water supplies or should be expanded to protect unused aquifers and other sensitive environments.

The debate over how clean is clean has focused attention on social goals for minimization of threats to public health and the environment. At issue are the cleanup standards that define cleanup objectives. At one extreme, standards are specified in terms of maximum acceptable contamination levels for each toxic substance present at a site and cleanup objectives are chosen that satisfy these standards. At the other extreme, the risk posed by toxic substances at a site is evaluated on a case-by-case basis in the absence of specific standards. The role of cost in defining cleanup objectives is an integral part of the debate. At issue here is whether cost should enter as a secondary factor once standards and objectives are defined or as a primary factor in choosing among alternative objectives. The former approach emphasizes cost-effectiveness; the goal is to select the least costly remedy that meets predetermined cleanup objectives. The latter approach is that of cost-benefit analysis; the goal is to select a remedy with greatest risk reduction per dollar of cleanup expenditures. When cleanup costs are high and risk reduction is uncertain, a cost-benefit approach will often result in selection of a less ambitious and less costly remedy.

A related debate over selection of cleanup remedies has focused attention on whether less expensive, less effective remedies should be applied that simply contain the threat posed by hazardous waste sites or whether more expensive and permanent cleanup technologies should be chosen to minimize risk over the long term. A broader program that aims to achieve greater risk reduction through more complete and permanent cleanups will be substantially more expensive than one that applies temporary fixes to a narrow range of problems. Whether the benefits of the broader program justify its cost remains a major Superfund issue. Debate divides the scientific community as well as those who have a clear stake in program outcomes as beneficiaries of cleanup or as targets of taxation and enforcement.

The design of tax and liability/enforcement schemes are major determinants of who bears the toxic debt. The policy debate has focused on the efficiency and equity implications of alternative taxing mechanisms: a feedstock tax to place the cleanup burden on industries that produce the organic and inorganic chemicals that ultimately give rise to hazardous wastes, a waste-end tax to place the burden on industries that generate or dispose of hazardous wastes, a broad-based tax on all manufacturing and nonmanufacturing industries regardless of direct contribution to Superfund problems, and a claim on general revenues to place the burden on taxpayers as the beneficiaries of industrial production. At one extreme, the major hazardous waste–generating industries argue that society as a whole has benefited from chemical-based production and the high standard of living associated with the chemical revolution and therefore should bear the toxic debt. A broad-based tax or funding through general revenues is most equitable. At the other extreme, environmentalists argue that generator industries are ultimately responsible for Superfund problems. These industries have promoted the chemical revolution in their own interest and have profited from unsound hazardous waste disposal. Taxes should be imposed on their feedstocks or on their waste-end products.

The extent to which the cleanup burden should be borne by the states or the federal government is a related funding issue. Advocates of placing a substantial burden on the states argue that this will promote efficiency: the states will more seriously evaluate whether cleanup benefits are justified by their cost if they more fully participate in financing cleanup. Advocates of a minimum state burden argue that cleanup is a national problem and that the individual states face more severe budgetary problems than does the federal government. Placing a large burden on the states guarantees inadequate funding and promotes inefficiency.

Cleanup that is not financed through taxation must be financed through enforcement. The policy debate has focused on the severity of liability standards and their implications for Superfund enforcement. Liability can be retroactive, thereby holding industry responsible for actions taken prior to the more demanding environmental legislation of the 1970s, or liability can be prospective, thereby holding industry responsible only for actions taken in recent decades. Corporations can be held liable regardless of negligence in production and disposal practices (strict liability), or they can be held liable only when they were negligent within the weak requirements of pre-1970s environmental law. Corporations can be held liable only for their specific contributions to site cleanup problems, or they can be held liable for cleanup costs regardless of their proportionate contribution (joint and several liability). Proportionate responsibility requires that contribution to Superfund problems be clearly apportioned among all responsible parties before they can be asked to pay for their share of the cleanup burden. The more radical doctrine of joint and several liability removes this potentially insurmountable barrier. A retro-active, strict, joint and several liability standard is advocated by those who wish government to cast the broadest liability net and to have the greatest power to induce industry to pay for hazardous waste site cleanup. It is strenuously opposed by corporations and industries most likely to be ensnared in that net, in particular deep-pocket corporations in major hazardous waste–generating industries.

The extent to which cleanup should be financed by taxes versus enforce-ment of a liability standard has been hotly debated. Major generator industry corporations and their insurers have argued that the transaction costs associ-ated with an aggressive enforcement program are excessive. Superfund would be far more efficient were enforcement minimized at the expense of taxation. Advocates of aggressive enforcement argue that this is the only mechanism to impose cleanup costs directly on those responsible for Superfund problems. Controversy has surrounded the enforcement strategies EPA has adopted to assign liability to potentially responsible parties; they have been variously criticized as too aggressive and as too accommodative of industrial interests. Equally controversial have been proposals to ease the legal requirements for compensation of personal injuries that are caused by exposure to hazardous waste sites and to compensate victims out of the Superfund.

How these issues are resolved determines the total cost of the program, the extent of risk reduction, and the distribution of cost and benefits. The burden imposed and benefits received by any party depend on both the size of the program and the way in which costs and benefits are distributed. Conflict over distribution therefore pervades debate over all Superfund issues.

WHO BENEFITS? WHO PAYS?

An individual's or corporation's perception that it will bear the cost or receive the benefits of a policy decision motivates self-interested participation in the Superfund debate. Political theorists argue that participation also depends on whether costs and benefits are concentrated or diffuse. Members of a narrowly defined group who anticipate absorbing a substantial share of costs or benefits are more likely to be active participants than are members of a large group each of whom anticipates absorbing only a minimal share (Wilson, 1980).

The primary direct beneficiaries of Superfund are people and communities exposed to health risks and to loss in natural resources and private property as a result of proximity to hazardous waste sites. Prior to Superfund passage in 1980, perceptions of risk were fueled by discussion of environmental problems, by the discovery of major hazardous waste sites and identification of adverse health effects, and by published accounts of often unsuccessful local efforts to close down or clean up hazardous waste sites.[6] Debate over Superfund legislation, the subsequent site discovery process, and extensive public controversy over initial Reagan administration implementation substantially increased perceived risk.

An enhanced perception of risk motivated many communities to coalesce around the need to remove the threats posed by hazardous waste sites. However, large numbers and anticipation of concentrated benefits did not always result in collective action. In some communities, people did not perceive themselves as equally at risk. In others, some members of the community desired to minimize knowledge of waste site conditions out of concern for property values, to protect local employers from being driven out of business if burdened with cleanup costs, or to attract business to the area. For small, poor, and rural communities, effective action was less likely even with concentrated benefits. The income, ethnic, and educational characteristics that made these communities attractive sites for hazardous waste facilities also made them less successful advocates for cleanup.[7]

In some threatened communities, the barriers to political action associated with diffusion and small numbers were offset by the presence of effective local organizers. Lois Gibbs, a housewife turned activist, was most influential in directing national attention to the dilemma faced by the people of Love Canal.[8] Access to technical knowledge also increases community leverage when confronting EPA and industry representatives over cleanup plans. The Superfund Amendments and Reauthorization Act of 1986 enhanced the potential for local involvement through a technical grants program. In some instances this potential was an illusion. One of the first grants was awarded to a community group in Jacksonville, Arkansas, the site of three dumps contaminated with dioxin. The group receiving the grant included Hercules, Inc., identified by EPA as a principal party responsible for the town's toxic waste sites, and the town's business interests, who desired to play down the problem so that business would not be frightened from the area (see Shabecoff, 1989; Russell, 1989).

Community perception of gain from political action becomes more tenuous when the locus of conflict shifts from the local to the state and national levels. Benefits become more diffuse and local community gain becomes less certain. At these levels of decision making, the negative consequences of diffusion and small numbers has been offset to some degree by the formation of environmental advocacy groups. Environmental organizations such as the Environmental Defense Fund, the Natural Resources Defense Council, the Sierra Club, the National Wildlife Fund, the National Audubon Society, Greenpeace, the National Campaign Against Toxic Hazards/Clean Water Project, and the Conservation Foundation have been variously active in the debate over Superfund legislation, in overseeing implementation, in adjudication, and in promoting public awareness. Unions representing workers at risk from chemical hazards in occupational settings also have promoted the interests of waste site host communities. The involvement of the Chemical Workers Union and the Union of Oil, Chemical, and Atomic Workers have stemmed in part from their promotion of right-to-know legislation. Their involvement also reflects the fact that the proximity of disposal sites to generator industries and to the households of industry labor places their members within threatened communities. In some instances, however, the involvement of unions and their membership has been constrained by fear of employer flight and employment loss.

Communities at risk are not the sole beneficiaries of a cleanup program. An expanded program also serves the interests of the hazardous waste management industry. While ninety-three firms managed 125 facilities in 1980, 40 to 60 percent of revenues were received by seven industry leaders: Waste Management, Browning Ferris Industries, Rollins Environmental Services, SCA Services, Cecos International, IT Corporation, and Chem-Nuclear Systems (see U.S. Office of Technology Assessment, 1983: 30; Mahoney and Bowman, 1985: 30). Industry revenues and profits have increased substantially with the implementation of Superfund and the removal of Superfund wastes for off-site treatment, incineration, and disposal. For example, the annual profits of Waste Management, the leader in solid and hazardous waste disposal, grew more than tenfold to $464.2 million from 1978 to 1988 and reached nearly $700 million in 1990.[9] The National Solid Waste Management Association represents this industry and has been very vocal in Superfund debates.

Waste site cleanup also yields revenue and profits to the private contractors that conduct hazardous waste site studies, propose feasible remedies, and design and implement cleanup. Contractors that produce Superfund-related reports and studies for EPA earn substantial profits. Over the first eight years of the Superfund program, contractors have received some $4 billion for their services.[10]

The extensive litigation surrounding Superfund has led an editorial writer to call Superfund a welfare program for lawyers. One estimate suggests that the cost of litigation equals 40 percent of the private cost of waste site cleanup (Butler, 1985). For some critics of the program, these high transaction costs define a basic element of Superfund failure.

Conflict over funding options, cleanup and liability standards, and enforcement strategy brings industrial interests into the program design and implementation debate. The profits of major industrial generators have been threatened by decisions to finance cleanup via taxes on chemical feedstocks, to apply cleanup standards and more expensive permanent cleanup remedies, and to apply a retroactive, strict, joint and several liability standard. In contrast to communities at risk, major generators can expect concentrated benefits from political action and have substantial resources to promote their interests. Data presented in chapter 2 make clear that the petrochemical industry is the most exposed among manufacturers. The largest petrochemical firms and their trade group, the Chemical Manufacturers Association, have a continuous presence in the Superfund policy debate and in litigation stemming from implementation. Leading firms in other major generator industries and their trade associations are also substantially involved. The interests of manufacturers in general have been represented by the National Association of Manufacturers. Nonmanufacturing industries such as dry cleaners and service stations also are represented by trade associations.

Manufacturing and most nonmanufacturing industries have a shared interest in minimizing the size of the cleanup program. At the same time, they have substantial conflict of interest regarding a number of specific issues. Nongenerator firms support feedstock taxation but strongly oppose proposals for a broad-based tax on corporate revenues or profits that shifts the cleanup burden onto a wider set of industries. There is conflict of interest between large and small manufacturing firms as well. Joint and several liability magnifies the exposure of Fortune 500 companies as deep pockets and makes smaller companies less attractive targets for enforcement actions. Smaller firms also are more likely to oppose strict disposal standards that limit future Superfund problems and that can be more easily met by their larger competitors. Conflict of interest also exists between generators and their insurers. Generators carry comprehensive insurance that has been interpreted to cover pollution damages. On the one hand, this motivates coordinated action by generators and their insurers to promote narrowly defined liability standards. On the other, it leads to substantial conflict over who will pay the cleanup costs imposed on generators through enforcement actions.

Liability issues bring other parties into the Superfund debate: for example, the owners and operators of off-site treatment, disposal, and storage facilities; waste haulers; and cleanup contractors. While the hazardous waste management industry benefits in the receipt of Superfund site wastes, these firms appear also as responsible parties at Superfund sites.

The states receive benefits and bear costs resulting from a hazardous waste cleanup program. They have an interest in a program that is more inclusive with respect to contamination problems and is financed primarily at the federal level. They have strongly opposed efforts to make them absorb an unrealistically high share of cleanup costs. At the same time, states desire to maintain discretion in selection of cleanup standards and remedies and in the prioritization of sites for cleanup. Representatives of state government are confronted with the contradictory needs to impose a cleanup burden on firms responsible for site conditions and to promote the interests of polluting industries important to the local economy. Recently the states have had to deal with industry-initiated suits that would hold municipalities liable for Superfund cleanup costs. The National Governors Association, the Association of State and Territorial Solid Waste Management Officials, the National Association of Attorneys General, and representatives of individual states are all involved in the Superfund policy debate.

POLITICAL ECONOMY OF REGULATION

Direct regulation shifts the locus of conflict over distributional issues to the state. How these conflicts are resolved determines whether regulation succeeds or fails. Political economies of regulation conceptualize the state as a decision-making apparatus that includes the branches of government and the bureaucracy that administers government programs. Instrumental and structural analyses of regulation provide alternative perspectives on this public decision-making process and on the ability of economic and environmental groups to promote their goals through state action. These analyses help to explain congressional and agency policy decisions in the presence of distributional conflict and the link between this conflict and program failure.

The Instrumental Perspective

The instrumental perspective[11] casts the state as a passive mechanism to process political demands. Public sector decision makers are seen to be motivated primarily by self-interest. Members of Congress, for example, are assumed to be influenced substantially by prospects for reelection and pecuniary gain. They are expected to make decisions that will maximize the political support required to achieve these ends. This leads them to make decisions that satisfy the desires of supporters while placating the concerns of opponents.[12]

Self-interested legislators respond to political leverage exerted by groups that are affected by their decisions and are inclined to promote programs that are most acceptable to those with the greatest political leverage. In advocating private interests, the legislator is rewarded through campaign contributions and other financial support and through positive publicity. For major economic interests, political leverage builds on corporate assets, sales, employment, and profits. For environmental interests, political leverage builds on contributions, membership, and, of greatest importance, popular support. Competing interests use the resources at their command to define the nature and extent of an environmental problem and to shape congressional perceptions of the feasibility and equity of alternative solutions. Those with extensive resources can achieve a continuous presence at congressional hearings and secure access to key congressional committee members and other key legislators. They can promote reelection of sympathetic legislators through political action committee contributions and other campaign support as well as through the media.

Regulatory ideologies play an important role in the merging of legislator and private interests. Ideological positions on regulation and deregulation encompass philosophical convictions regarding the appropriate role of government in legal and market relationships as well as beliefs regarding whether government intervention will bring about better or worse economic and environmental outcomes. Short of total opportunism, a legislator is more inclined to advocate the position taken by a private interest when the two have a shared perception of current economic and environmental conditions and a shared expectation of the efficacy of government action. Regulatory ideologies shape these latter expectations. The more opportunistic legislator may simply justify support for private interests in terms of regulatory ideology.

Conservatives and radicals both predict that the desire to maximize political support will result in powerful private interests dominating the legislative process. Conservatives emphasize the ability of environmental interest groups to rouse latent public fears by exaggerating the consequences of regulatory inaction. According to this view, the environmental groups' leverage on Congress is enhanced by the presence of pro-environment legislators and by sympathetic reporting of their predictions in the media. Their promotion of a zero-risk ideology provides a rationale for legislator imposition of costly regulation.

In contrast, radicals emphasize the class backgrounds of legislators and their inclination to support the interests of capital. Promotion of class interests merges with promotion of self-interest. The vast financial and economic resources of industrial polluters makes opposition to their interests more likely to reduce the chance of reelection than opposition to the environmental movement. While journalists may be sympathetic to an environmental cause, the media is tied to polluting industries through ownership and advertising revenues. Industry also provides ample opportunity for pecuniary gain in office or upon return to the private sector. Further, legislators are seen to respond to industry claims that loss in employment and tax revenues will result from strong environmental policies and to industry predictions that legislators will be held accountable for these consequences by their constituencies. Finally, legislators are likely to respond to industry assertions of the need to fully recognize the costs of regulatory action and balance these against minimal expected benefits. Having a near monopoly over the information necessary to predict the cost of regulatory action, industry is in a position to overstate these costs.

While conservatives expect that environmentalists will dominate the legislative process and radicals assign the dominant role to capital, liberals anticipate a counterbalancing of these efforts to exert political leverage. Decisions which appear to strongly favor one of these interests will result in a redoubling of effort on the part of the interest which suffers. Further, they note, the interests of industry are not singular. Individual firms or industries will form coalitions with environmentalists in support of strong legislation that serves mutual interests. Since competition for influence generates information and predictions from all parties, Congress is in a position to more accurately assess the consequences of its actions. In general, while environmental or industrial interests can win on specific legislative points, they need to accept compromise or defeat on others.

From an instrumental perspective, agency implementation decisions also are guided by self-interest. Like legislators, the agency administrator and staff have diverse goals and motives. In general, the capacity to pursue and achieve these goals, even when contradictory, is enhanced if the agency can maintain or increase its discretionary power.

Agencies have multiple masters that can rein in discretionary power. Congress endows an agency with powers and appropriates the funds to implement the agency's agenda. Positive congressional oversight is necessary to maintain the agency's exercise of discretion. At the same time, federal agencies are within the executive branch of government and therefore subject to some White House direction and control. An agency administrator is nominated by the president based on White House goals and regulatory expectations. Agency rule making and budget requests are subject to review by the Office of Management and Budget. The agency can negotiate with the executive branch on issues of program policy and funding but must commit itself to follow White House direction once set. Within the limits of prior White House constraint, the agency will attempt to maintain its discretionary power by producing implementation outcomes that pass congressional oversight. During the Reagan and Bush administrations, the president and Congress had conflicting interpretations of environmental mandates and conflicting views on the effectiveness of alternative regulatory strategies. In the 1980s the EPA followed White House guidance on deregulation and suffered a loss in discretionary powers at the hands of the Congress.

The exercise of political and economic power by interested parties affects regulatory outcomes and, consequently, forces a regulatory agency to refine or alter its strategy in light of the expected behavior of these parties. In the case of Superfund, for example, the outcome of actions to induce compliance with demands for private cleanup depends on industrial cooperation/recalcitrance and resource endowments as well as on agency implementation strategy. Significant economic resources allow industry to delay implementation by challenging agency actions in court while significant political power allows industry to seek redress from the White House and to influence congressional oversight. Aggressive agency implementation promotes conflict with industry and results in proposals to limit agency power or to reduce agency funding. Accommodative implementation diminishes conflict with industrial interests. However, when less satisfactory cleanup or cost recovery settlements emerge, local communities, states, or environmental groups challenge agency actions in court and demand that Congress exercise tighter control over the agency. The agency's selection of cleanup technologies and cleanup standards engenders similar tensions: industry protests the greater cost of more permanent and more extensive cleanup while local communities, states, and environmental groups protest the greater risks resulting from less costly and effective remedies. Placed in a potential no-win situation, the self-interested environmental agency will choose an implementation strategy that maximizes its achievements while minimizing conflict with those most likely to successfully convert dissatisfaction into negative congressional oversight.

Conservatives and radicals expect the pursuit of self-interest to expose an environmental regulatory agency to capture by powerful private interests. Capture means that the agency identifies the promotion of its interests with promotion of the interests of a private participant in the regulatory process.[13] Conservatives argue that the capture of economic regulatory agencies such as the Interstate Commerce Commission and the Civil Aeronautics Board led

Congress to insulate social regulatory agencies from industry influence, for example, by allowing agency authority to cut across industry lines. However, insulation from industry influence then combined with easier access to the courts to open an environmental protection agency to capture by environmental groups. Since Congress is characterized as highly responsive to environmental interest group pressure, environmental groups became the natural ally of an environmental protection agency. To satisfy this ally and promote its own interests, the agency would adopt more confrontational strategies vis-à-vis the regulated. The agency achieves a positive evaluation from Congress even though its outcomes are inferior to those associated with a more cooperative strategy.

Radicals argue that social regulatory agencies are dependent on the cooperation of the regulated to achieve positive outcomes and evaluations. The legal budgets of major firms in regulated industries far exceed those of social regulatory agencies, allowing the regulated to delay, if not deny, the success of agency actions. The agency is also dependent on industry for much of the data that feeds into the regulatory process. A lack of cooperation delays satisfaction of agency mandates. The economic power of industry combined with its political leverage in Congress leads the agency to eschew confrontational strategies that result in industry opposition. The agency achieves a positive evaluation from Congress through accommodation even though outcomes are inferior to those associated with a more confrontational strategy.

In contrast to these extreme expectations, liberals argue that countervailing political leverage works against capture by industry or environmental groups. Undue concern for the interests of either results in challenges that delay implementation and in negative congressional evaluation. The agency identifies promotion of its interests with promotion of the legislative mandate.

The Structural Perspective

The structural perspective[14] on regulation highlights contradictory economic and political constraints that surround the decision-making process. Social legislation that holds corporations liable for their harms to public health and the environment must impose substantial costs on industry. Absorption of these costs impairs capital accumulation, the engine of growth in a capitalist system. At the same time, an absence of legislation in the face of certain harm to public health and the environment threatens the legitimacy of the state. A capitalist state that openly uses its coercive powers to help one class accumulate capital at the expense of other classes loses its legitimacy and undermines the basis of its loyalty and support (O'Conner, 1973: 6).

To stabilize the capitalist system, the state must resolve conflict between promotion of capital accumulation and maintenance of social harmony. Resolution of conflict can take several forms. First, the state can engage in regulatory actions that are essentially symbolic. When the cost of correcting social problems exceeds the ability of the private or public sectors to pay, Congress may pass strong legislation but provide inadequate funding for effective implementation. The legislative mandate satisfies public demands for action while constrained funding limits the costs to be borne. Alternatively, the state can resolve conflict through socializing the cost of correction: the public sector pays for correcting social harms imposed by industry. Public demands for action are satisfied while the impact on capital accumulation is minimized. However, while socialization of cost avoids imposing a direct burden on industry, increased public expenditures can impose indirect burdens on capital accumulation. Public funding must come from higher taxes, reductions in other public programs, or increased debt. When higher taxes reduce consumption or public debt raises the cost of private finance, corporate profits suffer. When reduced public expenditures are at the expense of programs which underwrite private production costs such as agricultural or dairy subsidies, corporate profits also suffer. When reduced public expenditures come from other socialized programs, pressure can mount for compensatory corporate expenditures. In times of budgetary strain and rising public debt, the need to promote capital accumulation therefore can effectively constrain socialized as well as privately funded correction.[15]

With a social consensus that capital must pay for the harms it imposes, symbolic action and socialization of cost can promote social harmony only when their distributional outcomes are not transparent. Public perceptions must be manipulated through the mystification of policy. For example, Congress can impose a tax on industry with every expectation that it is passed on to consumers. The financing of Superfund through a feedstock tax fits this case. The recent challenge to the belief that Superfund sites pose significant threats to public health provides another example. If policy makers accept the argument that Superfund site threats are overstated despite an absence of firm scientific evidence in support of this position, the public can be exposed to greater risk though policies billed as enhancing the efficiency of environmental protection. Public perceptions can also be manipulated through use of regulatory ideology. For example, inferior program outcomes due primarily to a lack of agency funding can be attributed to bureaucratic inefficiency or the application of an overly aggressive or accommodative implementation strategy.

The structural perspective predicts that contradictory pressures to promote capital accumulation and social harmony will constrain the exercise of economic and political pressure. It therefore challenges many predictions offered by instrumentalists. The conservative instrumental perspective predicts that environmental groups will achieve their ends at considerable cost to capital. The structural perspective suggests that this outcome is highly unlikely. The need to promote capital accumulation makes the interests of capital coincident with the needs of the system, thereby enhancing industry's political leverage. The radical instrumental perspective predicts that the power of capital will rule out any effective social regulation. In contrast, the structural perspective suggests that in the presence of a strong environmental movement, regulatory agencies must be given limited autonomy to punish some powerful corporations as a means to maintain social harmony. In the case of Superfund, this means that the agency must have sufficient latitude to impose cleanup liability on responsible corporations via an enforcement program. When progress toward this goal is clearly inadequate, enforcement loses its legitimating force.

The structural perspective also challenges the liberal belief in a counterbalancing of political power to produce workable compromise. The structural argument suggests that the existence of potentially irreconcilable economic and environmental goals leads to a regulatory system with some elements that reinforce the interests of industry and some that reinforce the interests of environmentalism. When a program such as Superfund contains a multiplicity of decision points and of decision makers, there is ample opportunity for design elements that benefit one party to be offset by elements that benefit another. Each party has some limited victories that partially negate those achieved by the opposition. In this context, congressional and environmental agency decisions do not, perhaps cannot, coalesce into a program that is free of contradictions and unencumbered by conflict. Regulation therefore allows a perpetuation of conflict. The resulting system embodies contradictions and promotes neither efficiency nor equity.

The analysis presented in this book draws on both instrumental and structural perspectives to explain the failure of Superfund. The instrumental perspective is most useful in its emphasis on the link between private interests and public decisions. The structural perspective is essential for its emphasis on the link between failure to resolve basic system conflicts and failure to construct an efficient and equitable regulatory program.

SUPERFUND FAILURE

Regulation is forged in a political arena. Its design and implementation are influenced by private conflict over distribution and public conflict over the need to promote capital accumulation and social harmony. In the presence of these conflicts, there is ample reason to expect that the multiplicity of executive, legislative, and agency decisions that define a regulatory program will yield inefficient and inequitable regulatory outcomes. If efficiency and equity are basic measures of program success, inefficiency and inequity are the corresponding measures of program failure. The failure of Superfund thus resides in the inability of society to resolve underlying conflicts over cleanup and compensation. The purpose of this book is to trace out the relationship between this conflict over the toxic debt and program failure.

The centrality of conflict to Superfund failure has been highlighted in other major analyses. The Office of Technology Assessment attributes failure to what it calls the "Superfund syndrome": a condition of constant confrontation among nearly everyone affected by and working in the program. A diverse set of interests have opposing views on risk and on necessary cleanup costs. These combine with excessive policy flexibility to provide ample opportunity for competing interests to achieve their objectives at too great an expense to their adversaries (U.S. Office of Technology Assessment, 1989b: 18). Another critique, echoing the Law and Economics approach, expresses the link between conflict and failure in terms of the transaction costs that result from excessive confrontation and litigation. Guided by the social judgment to make polluters pay, regulators attempt to impose costs on responsible parties, who in turn resist these efforts. The resulting conflict generates substantial enforcement and litigation expenses and delays cleanup. Cleanup delays result in deterioration of site conditions and increased risk of exposure. Increased costs combined with reduced benefits compromise program efficiency. Distributional outcomes either do not satisfy demands for equity or satisfy them only at great loss in efficiency.[16]

The analysis presented in this book encompasses and expands on these arguments. The Office of Technology Assessment analysis hones in on the identification of hazardous waste site risks and the selection of cleanup remedies. In contrast, I focus on the political and economic environment that establishes the options and constraints faced by decision makers. The transaction cost analysis emphasizes the power of polluting industries to effectively oppose regulators and to avoid acceptance of financial responsibility. In contrast, I focus on the manifestations of this power in the design and implementation of the Superfund program. I argue that the failure of legislators and regulators to render this opposition less attractive or less effective is related to the political and economic power of polluting industries: the power to use government as an instrument of self-interest and the power that derives from the role of major corporations in the capital accumulation process.

Superfund was to complete the environmental agenda of the 1970s, the environmental decade. A unique convergence of economic and political forces produced an unprecedented surge in environmental legislation to limit and control disposal of pollutants and hazardous substances in the air, in the water, and on the land. The decade was also a period of transitions from an era of regulation to one of deregulation. The election of Ronald Reagan in 1980 ushered in a concerted attack on social regulation, in particular that relating to the environment. Superfund was a first target for social deregulation in the Reagan decade. This chapter begins with an overview of the environmental movement and the environmental legislation of the 1970s. Next, congressional debate and conflict over Superfund cleanup and liability issues are examined. The factors accounting for the compromise legislation eventually signed into law are analyzed. A discussion of the conflict between congressional expectations for Superfund and the incoming Reagan administration's deregulatory ideology serves as introduction to examination of the program's tumultuous initial implementation. The Reagan EPA Superfund strategy is assessed as a primary cause of the agency's 1983 Sewergate scandal. The chapter ends with an evaluation of the efficiency and equity consequences of Superfund implementation over its first two and one-half years.

THE ENVIRONMENTAL DECADE

The massive industrialization accompanying and following World War II raised living standards as goods production outpaced population growth and lowered environmental quality as waste generation outpaced the absorptive capacity of the environment. Production increasingly relied on the technological advances of the chemical revolution. Between 1945 and 1970, production in manufacturing more than doubled while production in the chemicals and allied products industry increased nearly sevenfold. Energy production and the related consumption of fossil fuels kept pace with growth in manufacturing output. Driven by a desire to minimize costs and effectively unconstrained by law, industry used the air and the water as dumping grounds for its waste byproducts. The notion of free disposal in the environment informed the design and packaging of consumer products in general as well as the design and use of the automobile. In the three decades preceding 1970, sulfur dioxide air pollution emissions increased by 54 percent, carbon monoxide by 26 percent, hydrocarbons by 68 percent, and nitrogen oxides by 191 percent. Severe deterioration in water quality occurred in many rivers and lakes as industrial and municipal pollutants were dumped into the nation's waterways. In the Great Lakes (Erie and Ontario in particular), concentrations of dissolved solids, sulfates, calcium, chloride, sodium, and potassium doubled between 1940 and 1970 (Baumol and Oates, 1979: 17, 25).

Popular pressure for a federal response to environmental degradation was fed by aspirations for an improved quality of life as material needs were increasingly satisfied by economic expansion. Changing public attitudes toward the environment reflected the idealism and activism of the 1960s and an enhanced awareness resulting from media dissemination of ideas, images, and reports emerging from environmental advocacy groups—the latter in turn growing with support from a concerned public. By 1970 environmental protection was cast in terms of a moral right or entitlement, linking the fundamental principle of equality of opportunity (a cornerstone of the Kennedy/Johnson Great Society program) to the right to a decent environment (Yeager, 1991: 130; Mitchell, 1984). The "ecological paradigm" of the 1969 Earth Day organizers asserted that "environmental limits are real, and natural ecosystems are subject to serious, sometimes irreversible, harm by human activity. Economic growth should be pursued in a way consistent with the need to maintain the quality of life" (quoted in Mitchell, 1984: 58).

National political leaders were captured by the momentum of the environmental movement. President Nixon advocated a strong and comprehensive federal role in environmental policy to generate needed public support after his unsuccessful and increasingly unpopular continuation of the war in Vietnam and to counter the expected presidential challenge of Democrat Edmund Muskie. Muskie, whose Senate subcommittee had drafted air quality legislation in the late 1960s, was expected to base his campaign on environmental issues. He was in turn being accused of not taking a tough enough stand against industrial polluters (Marcus, 1980: 171–72).

Many members of Congress supported federal action, some out of conviction and others out of political expediency. Industry worked to minimize the impact of pending legislation on profits and to convince Congress and the public that it was capable of correcting past practices without increased regulation. But polluting industries could not directly and publicly oppose legislation to promote a clean environment. Their opposition could only be interpreted as advocacy of further environmental deterioration.

Popular pressure for federal action was buttressed by the fact that pollution was an interstate problem: both air and water carried industrial and municipal emissions across state borders. Evidence of severe environmental deterioration demonstrated that state-level regulation was unsuccessful in solving intrastate problems and offered little hope as a regulatory solution to interstate problems. Further, common law remedies based on the principles of trespass, nuisance, and negligence were perceived as inadequate to the task of limiting industrial waste disposal methods and their environmental consequences. The common law was inconsistently applied by the courts as a remedy for past damages and, given its emphasis on past damages, was not a suitable means for halting activity likely to result in future damages (Harris, Want, and Ward, 1987: 49–60; Harvard Law Review, 1986: 1602–30). The need for collective action by pollution victims was another major obstacle to redress through common law. The diffusion of harms and the high cost of litigation would deter most suits by individual plaintiffs. At the same time, the use of class action suits was limited by the reluctance of the courts to certify class actions by plaintiff classes whose members varied significantly with respect to the types and magnitudes of the harms they suffered (Harvard Law Review, 1986: 1468–69).

In 1970, against this background of mounting problems and inadequate solutions, President Nixon established the Environmental Protection Agency. During the following decade, it would be given responsibility for implementing a complex web of environmental regulations. In his "Message Relative to the Reorganization," Nixon offered a vision of comprehensive waste management:

Despite its complexity, for pollution control purposes the environment must be perceived as a single interrelated system . . . a single source may pollute the air with smoke and chemicals, the land with solid wastes, and a river or lake with chemicals and other wastes. Control of the air pollution may produce more solid wastes which then pollutes the land or water. Control of the water may convert it into solid wastes which must be disposed on land. . . . A far more effective approach to pollution control would: Identify pollutants—trace them through the entire ecological chain, observing and recording changes in form as they occur—determine the total exposure of man and his environment—examine interactions among forms of pollution and—identify where in the ecological chain interdiction would be more appropriate. (Quoted in Marcus, 1980: 275–76)

Although this perspective did not come to guide the structure of EPA's interacting and overlapping programs, it does describe the industrial/ecological dynamic which drove environmental legislation in the 1970s: each new environmental initiative was followed by another to deal with unanticipated regulatory consequences or to address problems recognized in debate over previous legislation but not yet subject to regulation. Since a depiction of the total regulatory mosaic goes well beyond the scope of this work, the following discussion of legislation focuses primarily on regulation relevant to the generation and disposal of hazardous waste. It must be noted that legislation does not in itself result in implementation. As discussed below, the record of implementation is far less impressive than the legislative effort to address environmental deterioration.

The Clean Air Act of 1970 was intended to sharply reduce the quantity of conventional chemical pollutants dispersed in the air. The act mandated that EPA identify air pollutants having an adverse effect on public health and welfare and establish threshold values. EPA was also to develop a list of hazardous pollutants which may cause severe health damage and to establish control regulations for all emission sources. The Clean Water Act of 1972 (formerly the Federal Water Pollution Control Act) was intended to completely eliminate discharge of pollutants into navigable waters. The act required all industrial plants to achieve by 1977 that level of discharge which indicates the application of the best practicable control technology economically available and to achieve by 1983 that level which indicates the use of the best available technology economically achievable. It mandated that EPA establish waste performance standards for all new sources of emissions within comprehensive industrial classifications and develop specific effluent standards for existing sources.[1] The Clean Air and Clean Water Acts focused on the emission of chemical pollutants from point sources. Permits would be required to limit the allowable amount of pollution (pollutant by pollutant) from factory smokestacks, auto tailpipes, city sewers, and factory sewers. These acts gave EPA no guidance as to what was to happen to toxic substances once industry was prevented from disposing of them into the air or the water. The Solid Waste Act of 1970 did call, however, for study of hazardous waste practices. Several years later, EPA would estimate that about two-thirds of the increase in industrial waste generation resulted from air and water pollution control regulations (Epstein, Brown, and Pope, 1982: 191).

As the decade progressed, legislation was passed to further control and restrict disposal practices as well as to protect the water supply from contamination. The Marine Protection, Resources, and Sanctuaries Act of 1972 curtailed ocean disposal of solid and hazardous wastes. The Safe Drinking Water Act of 1974 authorized EPA to develop drinking water standards to guard against consumption of contaminated ground water. The act established a regulatory system for compliance with EPA standards and for promoting safer siting and construction of water storage and delivery systems. EPA was instructed to regulate the underground injection of hazardous waste and to determine acceptable levels of chemical contamination of public drinking water supplies. This first congressional effort to address hazardous waste disposal as a ground water problem did little to protect the public against harm from contaminated ground water caused by means other than ingestion. It also failed to address unsafe means of hazardous waste disposal other than underground injection (Harvard Law Review, 1986: 1470).

In 1974 Congress began to more fully address hazardous waste issues within the context of the general problem of solid waste disposal. The Nixon administration, wanting to keep municipal trash and garbage a state and local responsibility, proposed that the federal role in solid waste be limited to dealing with the disposal of toxic waste. Opponents of expanded solid waste regulation expected that a focus on hazardous waste would keep EPA busy and deflect its efforts from pursuing industrial source reductions. This tended to make hazardous waste regulation a noncontroversial issue (Epstein, Brown, and Pope, 1982: 187–88). At the same time, the chemical industry was more concerned with the impact of the proposed Toxic Substances Control Act on profits and standard industry practices than with the issue of hazardous waste disposal. Industry efforts were directed at opposing and shaping this act, which became law in 1976. The accompanying Resource Conservation and Recovery Act of 1976 did not establish a major role for the federal government in solid waste disposal, but it did contain strong provisions for hazardous waste disposal. Chemical industry representatives found it almost impossible to argue against safe disposal of toxic waste (Epstein, Brown, and Pope, 1982: 190–93).

The goal of the Toxic Substances Control Act (TSCA) was to protect public health and the environment from excessive risk due to the production, use, and improper disposal of toxic chemical substances. TSCA was spurred by public concern over the discovery of suites of chemicals that were present— often in unknown levels—in soil, air, and water and were associated with cancers and other long-term chronic health effects (Dowd, 1988: 16). It focused on substances different in nature, concentration, and behavior from the conventional bulk pollutants brought under regulation in the early 1970s. This change in focus was driven, in part, by advances in analytical chemistry and improvement in the sensitivity of detection methods as well as by biological experimentation on the carcinogenic characteristics of chemical substances (Dowd, 1988: 15–16). Under TSCA, manufacturers and processors of chemical substances and mixtures were to develop adequate data to determine the effect of these substances and mixtures on health and the environment. To fulfill TSCA objectives, EPA was to require testing of chemicals identified as possible risks, scrutinize new chemicals prior to manufacture, regulate chemicals known to present a health risk, and report and maintain data on all chemical substances (Riley, 1983: 25–26). TSCA also required EPA to regulate the use and disposal of polychlorinated biphenyls (PCBs).

The goal of the Resource Conservation and Recovery Act (RCRA) was to control toxic substances at the waste end of the production/consumption process. RCRA mandated a cradle-to-grave system for hazardous waste control.[2] EPA was to publish criteria for the identification of hazardous waste materials and to establish standards for hazardous waste disposal facilities. It required that all operators of these facilities receive a permit from EPA. Under pressure from the Office of Management and Budget (OMB), Congress allowed applicants to receive an interim permit to operate while EPA processed the application and wrote guidelines for final permits.[3] It directed EPA to establish a manifest system to assure that all hazardous waste generated is designated for treatment, storage, or disposal in treatment, storage, or disposal facilities for which EPA has issued a permit. RCRA provided civil and criminal penalties for violation of its hazardous waste provisions and also gave EPA a broad mandate to act when waste-handling practices presented an imminent and substantial endangerment to health or the environment.

Epstein, Brown, and Pope argue that few in Congress or among the public had any notion of what would be required to carry out the mandate for safe disposal of hazardous waste. This absence of foresight helps explain the minimal opposition to RCRA on the part of generator industries. Further, it was not yet recognized that past disposal practices had created a legacy of environmentally unsound hazardous waste sites that required a collective federal response. The House Commerce Committee report on RCRA states that

> the Committee believes that the approach taken by this legislation eliminates the last remaining loophole in environmental law, that of unregulated land disposal of discarded materials and hazardous waste. Further the Committee believes that this legislation is necessary if other environmental laws are to be both cost and environmentally effective. At present, the federal government is spending billions of dollars to remove pollutants from the air and water, only to dispose of them on the land in an environmentally unsound manner. The existing methods of land disposal

often result in air pollution, subsurface leachates, and surface run-off, which affect air and water quality. This legislation will eliminate the problem [of disposal associated with previous laws] and permit environmental laws to function in a coordinated and effective way. (Quoted in Epstein, Brown, and Pope, 1982: 193)

President Ford signed the Resource Conservation and Recovery Act into law on October 22, 1976. Although technically violating his administration's stance against new programs, it was seen as a small and, in budgetary terms, insignificant violation (Epstein, Brown, and Pope, 1982: 194).

LEGISLATING SUPERFUND

By the end of the decade, it was clear that control over current disposal practices did not close the last remaining loophole in the nation's regulation of hazardous waste. In 1978 Michael Brown horrified the nation with his exposé of the Love Canal toxic waste scandal in Niagara Falls, New York. In a series of *Niagara Gazette* articles and his book *Laying Waste*, Brown described John Love's failed vision of an industrial city served by a navigable power canal and the eventual use of the abandoned canal by Hooker Chemical Company to dispose of "a veritable witch's brew of chemistry, compounds of truly remarkable toxicity. There were solvents that attacked the heart and liver, and residues from pesticides so dangerous that their commercial sale had subsequently been restricted or banned outright by the government" (Brown, 1981: 9). By the 1960s a school, playground, and homes sat atop the closed dump site. Brown's reporting of the chemicals dumped by Hooker (e.g., mercury, benzene, chlorinated compounds, dioxins), the contamination of aquifers and drinking water supplies, and the likely injuries from exposure provided an objective picture of environmental disaster. His images of life in Love Canal made an abstract threat palpable: children coming home from the playground with hard pimples on their bodies, women giving birth to deformed and mentally retarded children, a strange black sludge seeping through basement walls, chemical water flooding yards, and families torn between abandoning homes and protecting their children's health. His description of avoidance, cover-up, and inaction by the city, the board of education, the state, and Hooker made it clear that homeowner pressures were not enough to force containment, let alone clean-up. Three years of congressional hearings would subsequently document in detail the story of Love Canal: the irresponsible behavior of the Hooker Chemical Company in its disposal of tens of thousands of tons of waste residues in an unlined canal, the faltering efforts of local and state officials to respond, and the absence of EPA legal authority to provide more than technical assistance.[4] Congressional hearings would also provide testimony and documentary evidence on the conditions of waste disposal facilities nationwide, the contamination of ground water, and the risk posed to public health and the environment (see chapter 2). Opinions on the real and perceived threats posed by hazardous waste sites would be widely disseminated by the national media.

At the same time that awareness of this new environmental threat was growing, federal government capacity to finance and implement additional environmental action was declining and resistance on the part of industry to bear additional costs was mounting. During the 1970s federal expenditures on natural resources and the environment grew from 1.5 percent of federal budget outlays to over 2 percent. From 1971 to 1979 federal government expenditures for environmental quality control increased from nearly $900 million to $5.7 billion, a real increase of 454 percent. Water quality control accounted for 84 percent of these expenditures and land-based environmental quality control accounted for only 3 percent. The double-digit inflation of the late 1970s and the related expansion in the federal budget deficit placed great pressure on government to reduce its spending.

Growth in EPA's budget mirrored growth in federal expenditures on the environment and comprised some 85 percent of these expenditures. Nevertheless, the agency was having serious difficulty in meeting deadlines for writing the regulations mandated by a decade of legislation.[5] By 1978 EPA had issued standards for only four pollutants under the Clean Air Act (asbestos, beryllium, mercury, and vinyl chloride) and had issued no final effluent standards for hazardous pollutants under the Clean Water Act. Under the Safe Drinking Water Act, the agency promulgated interim maximum contaminant-level standards for arsenic, other inorganic substances, and some pesticides but promulgated no standards for the other organic compounds found in drinking water (primarily chlorinated hydrocarbons) even though the carcinogenicity of some of these compounds had been known for twenty years. EPA argued that delay in regulating organic compounds was due to a lack of information on their health effects. The agency acted to limit the production, distribution, and disposal of PCBs and had proposed regulations for chlorofluorocarbons under the Toxic Substances Control Act. Also under this act's authority, it ordered the chemical and petroleum industries to begin to supply information on the production and composition of their new chemicals. EPA missed the 1978 deadline for establishing treatment, storage, and disposal regulations under the Resource Conservation and Recovery Act and was, in 1979, placing primary emphasis on this mandate. The agency was aware of disposal sites which could be regulated or closed under RCRA's imminent hazard provisions. The power to act was expanded in 1979 amendments with the significant substitution of "may present" for "is presenting" an imminent and substantial endangerment. Nevertheless, EPA was hesitant to direct its resources and efforts to the problem posed by these uncontrolled sites.[6]

By 1978 polluting industries were spending $3.3 billion on pollution abatement equipment to meet air and water pollution control standards, an amount equal to 6 percent of total new capital expenditures. Their operating costs related to pollution abatement activities exceeded $6 billion. They were aware of the additional costs associated with EPA's proposed regulations for hazardous waste disposal under RCRA. Many lobbied Congress, some successfully, to exempt their waste streams from regulatory control (Epstein, Brown, and Pope, 1982: 197–98).

THE CLEANUP AND LIABILITY DEBATE

Congressional design of a program to address uncontrolled hazardous waste sites required decisions on the set of interrelated issues outlined in the previous chapter: the scope and nature of spills or releases needing a federal response, the extent and funding of the response, the liability of responsible parties, and the compensation of third party damages. A brief overview of Carter administration and House and Senate bills provides a contextual background to the debate and conflict over Superfund legislation.[7]

Hazardous waste site cleanup was initially linked to previously debated issues of oil and hazardous substance spills. However, the prospect of a nation dotted with Love Canals focused primary attention in 1979 on uncontrolled toxic waste dumps and provided the driving force that ultimately brought forth Superfund as law. In mid-1979 the Carter administration proposed creation of a $1.6 billion fund to allow for a federal emergency response in the event of an oil spill, hazardous substance spill, or leakage from an old dump site. Industry would finance 80 percent of the fund via a fee on chemical feedstocks with the remaining 20 percent coming from general governmental revenues.[8] To give producers a strong incentive to improve standards of care throughout the chain of commerce, the bill would impose strict, joint and several liability for all costs and damages covered by the fund. Strict liability held a responsible party liable for damages whether or not their actions were negligent. Joint and several liability held each responsible party liable for total damages when the harm was indivisible, that is, when the relationship between each responsible party's actions and the resulting share of total damage could not be established.

No provision was made for the compensation of third party personal injury or for medical costs.

The House and Senate considered the administration bill and then proceeded to design their own versions of cleanup legislation. Two bills were passed in the House and sent to the Senate. The first, H.R. 7020, provided "authority to respond to releases of hazardous waste from inactive, hazardous waste sites which endanger public health and the environment." The definition of inactive hazardous waste site excluded facilities with Resource Conservation and Recovery Act permits, but an emergency response was authorized when interim RCRA sites posed an imminent and substantial endangerment. Oil spills were not covered. A proposed tax on chemical feedstocks provided 75 percent of a $1.2 billion emergency response fund with the remaining 25 percent coming from general government revenues. The federal government would act only if it determined that a responsible party or a state or local government would not take proper action. The states were required to cover at least 10 percent of total federal response costs, to provide assurance that nonfederal funding was available for long-term site maintenance, and to provide disposal capacity for any wastes removed. Liability was strict, joint and several, and significant defenses to liability were provided (U.S. Congress, House, 1980a: 34). The second House bill, H.R. 85, provided over $700 million to cover oil and chemical spills. The latter bill died in the Senate.

The leading Senate bill (S. 1480), as reported after the November 1980 presidential election, proposed creation of a $4.1 billion fund to respond to any release to the environment of any hazardous substance when action by a responsible party was not forthcoming. Oil spills were excluded. To finance the fund, industry would pay 87.5 percent via a chemical feedstock tax with the remainder coming from general government revenues. In contrast to the House bill, this fund could be used for costly, long-lasting remedial response as well as for emergency removal. The former included construction of major facilities proceeded by considerable study, investigation, and planning. Damage to natural resources was also covered. State responsibilities were similar to those stipulated in H.R. 7020. The Senate bill established a no-fault victim compensation scheme (with claims paid out of the fund) and a federal cause of action for those injured by poisonous chemicals. Parties responsible for releasing hazardous substances were held to a standard of strict, joint and several liability. As in the House bill, there were provisions for limiting liability. The magnitude of the cleanup funds contained in the House and Senate bills resulted in their being referred to collectively as the Superfund. Industry, in an expression of opposition, chose to refer to them as the Ultrafund.

The most general issue to be resolved was whether the Superfund should be limited to the problem of abandoned hazardous waste sites or expanded to include oil and hazardous substance spills. The Chemical Manufacturers Association (CMA), whose 200 members produced more than 90 percent of industrial chemicals, opposed addressing all three problems in one legislative package. CMA argued that these were three completely different problems requiring different approaches and remedies. A broad response authority would duplicate existing law, in particular section 311 of the Clean Water Act pertaining to oil and chemical spills. The chemical industry did accept the need to create a federal/state fund to solve problems stemming from orphaned dump sites, defined as "a site that does not achieve interim Resource Conservation and Recovery Act standards; whose failure is causing a health danger; and where no action is being taken to arrest the danger because of the inability of the responsible party, if they can be found, to pay, the inability to locate a liable party or where a legal dispute would lead to an inordinate delay" (U.S. Congress, House, 1979c: 347). The National Association of Manufacturers (NAM), representing 12,000 corporations accounting for 75 percent of national goods production, agreed with CMA that legislation should be limited to the problem of abandoned sites. Given the likelihood that RCRA would restrict the availability of adequate waste disposal sites, generators recognized that control of the most egregious facilities was necessary for the acceptance of additional waste disposal capacity in local communities.

In contrast to industry's position, EPA Administrator Douglas Costle argued that existing law recognized the relationship of oil and chemical spills, that spill incidents often involved both oil and chemical substances, and that from a programmatic point of view, government emergency response to spills and abandoned sites cannot be readily separated. In terms of bureaucratic and regulatory reform, different programs would be extremely inefficient. Further, gaps in the existing law necessitated a broad approach. The authority to respond under section 311 of the Clean Water Act, the only such fund to have received appropriations, "does not authorize government action for spills onto the ground only, or spills that result only in the release of gases into the air. It does not adequately cover spills that contaminate only ground water" (U.S. Congress, Senate, 1983, 1:407). In support of Costle's argument, Congress was presented with the fact that chemical spills capable of inflicting environmental harm occurred about 3,500 times each year, with some 50 percent reaching navigable waters and the remainder reaching ground water, air, or land. At least $65 to $260 million was needed for their cleanup. Serious incidents were recounted which neither fit the definition of abandoned waste sites nor could be addressed under the Clean Water Act: PCBs had been dumped into the Hudson River by General Electric, and trichloroethylene (TCE) was found in drinking water in California's San Gabriel Valley (U.S. Congress, Senate, 1983, 1:683–84). The April 1980 explosion of the Chemical Control warehouse in Elizabeth, New Jersey, in the midst of the House debate on H.R. 7020, also provided graphic evidence of the need for immediate response without elaborate bureaucracy. In the absence of a favorable wind, clouds of toxic smoke billowing from the warehouse fire would have blanketed heavily populated areas including Manhattan. New Jersey Senator Bradley argued that such incidents established the need for the comprehensive approach contained in the Senate bill 1480: "In the face of imminent peril to the public, Government should not have to determine first whether the cause of the problem is a spill, a leaking pipe, or buried toxic substances leaking into a water supply. It should be able to respond. The comprehensive scope of the Senate bill makes it far superior to the more narrow House approach" (U.S. Congress, Senate, 1983, 1:707). Environmentalists and representatives of state government generally supported the need for a comprehensive approach.

The case for a comprehensive approach did not prevail against industry opposition. Coverage of oil spills was excluded from both House and Senate bills. Debate over the scope of the proposed Superfund program now focused on two crucial issues: the extent of the abandoned waste site problem and the cost of cleanup. The environmental and health hazards associated with Love Canal, the Valley of the Drums in Kentucky, and the LaBounty site in Iowa were generally accepted as serious, but little evidence existed to determine whether these sites were just the tip of the iceberg or extreme and noncharacteristic waste site problems. A Fred C. Hart Associates study commissioned by EPA was generally cited by supporters of a multibillion-dollar fund as the best current estimate of the extent of the problem and the cost of correction. Hart estimated that there were 1,200 to 2,000 potentially significant problem sites. It would cost $3.6 to $6.1 billion to finance emergency measures nationwide. For ultimate remedies, including off-site treatment and disposal, the nationwide range was estimated as $26.2 to $44.1 billion (U.S. Congress, Senate, 1983, 1:61). To challenge the conclusions of the Hart study, the Chemical Manufacturers Association conducted a telephone survey of state environmental agencies and concluded that there were some 400 potentially hazardous sites requiring action. At $1 million per site, cleanup would cost $400 million (U.S. Congress, House, 1979c, 346–50). Proponents of a multimillion-dollar fund asserted that the Hart study was guesswork, a position that EPA could not fully deny. The CMA estimate, however, carried even less weight given the unwillingness of the association to release the full study to EPA, members of Congress, or congressional committees (Mahon and Post, 1987: 67). In light of uncertainty regarding the scope of the problem, Superfund opponents such as the National Association of Manufacturers argued that appropriations be limited to the $20 to $50 million needed to conduct site inventories authorized in House and Senate bills. Further legislative action was imprudent in the absence of solid evidence.

The Superfund envisioned in both the House and Senate bills would be financed primarily through taxes imposed on chemical feedstocks: crude oil, inorganic chemicals, and organic chemicals.[9] Supporters of the feedstock tax—the Carter administration, EPA, environmental groups, representatives of state government, and many influential members of Congress—argued that it was desirable on grounds of equity, administrative complexity, and economic impact. The chemical industry and other industrial hazardous waste generators were viewed as major beneficiaries of the profits associated with historic hazardous waste production and environmentally unsound disposal. As a matter of equity, it was appropriate that taxes be imposed on these industries rather than directly on the taxpayer. A case could be made that a tax on hazardous waste generators (i.e., a waste-end tax) would promote waste reduction and directly penalize waste disposal. However, it was deemed to be far easier to impose and collect a tax on perhaps 1,000 chemical producers than on at least 260,000 generators. Further, it was widely believed that the chemical industry would be able to pass a feedstock tax through the chain of commerce to other generators and that industry would not therefore bear a disproportionate burden of the cleanup fund. EPA Administrator Costle cited recent articles in *Chemical and Engineering News* and the *Wall Street Journal* that discussed the ability of the chemical industry to pass along feedstock price increases (in excess of Superfund fees) by raising product prices. EPA projected that a $400 million per year feedstock tax would have a negligible impact on the economy: petrochemical feedstock prices would rise by less than 2 percent, final organic chemical product prices would increase by 0.6 percent, and the rate of growth in chemical industry sales would be only slightly damped.[10] Finally, a feedstock tax was seen as the best approach to assure the availability of cleanup resources. The Treasury Department was not able to pay for the fund given a mounting federal deficit and a resolve to fight inflation. State representatives and environmentalists feared, with good cause, that if the fund was not guaranteed through feedstock tax revenues, it would not be funded through congressional appropriations. The states were less concerned with the percentage share coming from the Treasury and industry than with there being a fund available to finance an immediate response. The states would be left to deal with the consequences of abandoned sites if no one else would or could act. Their resources were inadequate to finance cleanup costs, and some questioned whether they would be able to meet cost-sharing requirements. The states were prepared to take the lead on cleanup if the federal government provided the financial resources (U.S. Congress, House, 1979c: 535–48).

The chemical industry took strong exception to the feedstock tax, arguing that the fund should come from the federal Treasury, cost recovery from responsible parties, and a state matching contribution. Chemical Manufacturers Association President Robert Roland, voicing a common industry position, asserted that a feedstock tax was inequitable and punitive and "unfairly singles out the chemical and related industries to bear a disproportionate burden of cleanup costs. In doing so, it fails to adequately reflect the society's responsibility for resolving problems which everyone has helped create and for whose solution everyone should help pay" (quoted in Mahon and Post, 1987: 67). The CMA also argued that the feedstock tax would have a serious economic impact on an industry already burdened by regulation and facing severe foreign competition, often from producers with government subsidy. When asked for an economic impact analysis, the CMA informed the Senate that no analysis had been conducted in that the "boundless nature of the fee collection proposed . . . renders an analysis difficult without making wide-ranging assumptions" (U.S. Congress, Senate, 1979: 463–66, 474). Neither supporters nor opponents noted that the feedstock tax would be treated as a business expense and thus shifted in part back onto the taxpayer.

The Superfund would finance the cost of cleanup in those situations where a responsible party could not be identified or where a responsible party was unwilling to take prompt and appropriate action. Cleanup at sites where a responsible party could be identified required enforcement authority. Hart Associates warned EPA that at most half of the cost of cleanup could be recovered through enforcement. Strong liability provisions were essential for EPA to pursue rapid cost recovery when responsible parties could be found and their recalcitrance necessitated fund-financed cleanup. They were also essential to induce responsible parties to pursue appropriate environmental response actions to save fund resources for orphaned sites. The House and Senate committees writing Superfund legislation, the Carter administration, state representatives, and environmentalists all believed that liability must be strict, joint and several. Given the extreme problems of proof associated with conventional tort law standards, strict liability was necessary in order to fully compensate victims, to repair natural resource damages, and to serve as an adequate deterrent to those who would engage in highly risky activities without adequate safeguards. Joint and several liability held any responsible party potentially liable for the whole cost of cleanup even if others were also responsible. Fairness dictated that all significant contributors to hazardous substance damages should bear responsibility and liability at least in rough proportion to their contribution to the problem. It also dictated that it should not be up to the state or a hapless victim to attempt to allocate liability among a potentially large number of contributing individuals and companies. Supporters of these liability standards argued that "many American courts hold joint tortfeasors jointly and severally liable for the whole damage, where the negligence of each of them concur in producing a single indivisible injury—even though those responsible acted without concert or common design" (Kamlet testimony on behalf of National Wildlife Federation, U.S. Congress, House, 1979c: 619). Further, these liability provisions "merely codify long standing common law rules relating to liability for hazardous products and undertakings. Existing common law principles hold that in areas of ultra-hazardous activity, liability is attached to any injury resulting directly or indirectly from the activity. This is true regardless of whether the injury was foreseeable or whether negligence or contributory negligence was involved. There is a great deal of precedent in case law. . . . As the common law has recognized, knowing failure to take action now to protect society from a hazard created previously, is in practical effect, the same as originally creating the hazard" (Costle testimony, U.S. Congress, Senate, 1983, 1:405–6).

Joint and several liability held out the potential for highly inequitable outcomes such as a minor contributor to a site bearing the full cost of cleanup. The proposed legislation therefore modified the rule when (1) a liable party could demonstrate by a preponderance of the evidence that its contribution to the discharge, release, or disposal could be distinguished or apportioned and (2) its contribution was not a significant factor or cause. The court could then limit liability or the liable party could seek contribution from other involved parties.

Strict, joint and several liability could reduce the government's transaction costs since neither proof of negligence nor proof of proportionate responsibility was required. At the same time, responsible party transaction costs increased if the parties acted to limit their exposure to liability and to apportion liability among themselves.

The Chemical Manufacturers Association considered the proposed liability standards to be most dangerous and precedent setting. They amounted to a denial of due process and potentially violated the principle of constitutional rules against ex post facto laws. Testimony on behalf of the CMA developed the following scenario: "I'd like to give you an example of our concern. Let's envision, for a moment, that an orphan dump site has been discovered. It is known that at least 50 disposers have used the site. But the Justice Department decides that just one of those companies—likely to be one with sales exceeding several billion dollars per year—should be singled out for attack. . . . [It] would be entirely possible that one company might have to bear the entire cost of the cleanup, while at the same time it has been making fee payments into the cleanup fund. This is what is meant by joint and several liability."[11]

Manufacturers and the waste management industry were also strongly opposed to the "argument assigning liability to any and all involved in generating and handling waste which subsequently became a problem" (U.S. Congress, House, 1979c: 482). Like CMA, they saw existing tort law as adequate to induce responsible party action and to achieve cost recovery.

Industry's opposition to the codification of liability standards was greatly magnified by the possibility that the standards would be applied to compensate personal injuries as well as to promote waste site cleanup. The Senate bill proposed a substantial change in the treatment of compensation claims by hazardous substance release victims. The standard of strict, joint and several liability applied to all damages for economic loss, loss due to personal injury (including medical expenses), or loss of natural resources resulting from a hazardous substance release. The bill authorized the admission of medical and scientific studies in a court of law and provided that when a plaintiff has shown a reasonable likelihood that his disease resulted from the release of the toxic substance, a presumption was created in his favor. Although the latter provided a significant procedural advantage, the burden of proof was still on the plaintiff. Finally, where the claimant was unable to obtain satisfaction from a liable party, he could elect to pursue his claim against the fund rather than in a court against the liable party. If the claim was honored, the government could seek recovery of costs from the liable party.

The authors of the Senate bill noted that Congress was generally reluctant to create a federal cause of action which might duplicate state law. In the case of injury from a hazardous substance release, however, the barriers to obtaining redress via the common law justified federal action: Common law traditionally required proof of actual harm as a basic condition for recovery under tort law. Further, to prove causation, the plaintiff needed to (1) isolate the harm-causing substance, (2) trace its pathway of dispersal from the polluter to the victim, and (3) show the etiology of the harm-causing substance. Without extensive scientific data, these elements of causation cannot be firmly established (U.S. Congress, Senate, 1983, 1:348). The conclusions of an in-depth Library of Congress study of victim compensation in six states supported the need for change: "(1) [T]he legal mechanisms in the states studied are generally inadequate for redressing toxic substances–related harms, and traditional tort law presents substantial barriers to recovery. (2) [S]eeking compensation for pollution-related injuries is usually cumbersome, time-consuming and expensive. In the releases studied, few cases were filed and final judgments were rarely obtained. (3) [A]s a consequence of these difficulties, the compensation ultimately provided to injured parties is generally inadequate" (U.S. Congress, Senate, 1983, 1:320–21). If the victim's burden of proving causation was reduced and if the fund could stand in the shoes of the victim, this situation would be changed (U.S. Congress, House, 1979c: 424–29).

All parties to the debate expected the cost of compensation to be many times greater than the cost of cleanup. Neither the House nor the Carter administration strongly supported the inclusion of victim compensation in Superfund legislation. It was frequently noted that personal damage claims of $2 billion were filed by residents of Love Canal. EPA, speaking for the Carter administration, opposed this potential application of fund resources, noting that "if we take Love Canal's $2 billion in claims as at least indicative of [the] situation, we could clean up an additional 555 sites for that money" (U.S. Congress, Senate, 1983, 1:65). The administration argued that this scheme was inequitable in that it tended to subsidize those who did not undertake high standards of care at the expense of others. Further, the federal court system and the case load handled by the Department of Justice was already overwhelming the federal judicial system. The administration took the position that decisions regarding compensation for personal injury should be made in the context of governmentwide policy on health care (U.S. Congress, Senate, 1983, 1:117–22).

The Chemical Manufacturers Association opposed legislative changes in the law governing victim compensation. The chemical industry was a prime deep pocket. It was willing to pay its fair share but needed assurance that its liability would not be indefinitely expanded. The National Association of Manufacturers also strongly opposed these changes in legal relationships among parties, arguing that they would be "extremely litigious and would encourage speculation in groundless litigation" (U.S. Congress, House, 1979c: 581). Some members of Congress predicted that provision for third party damages on top of strict, joint and several liability would have adverse consequences for the national economy, in particular causing business failures, reduced investment, and capital flight abroad (U.S. Congress, Senate, 1980: 119–22).

THE SUPERFUND ACT

The Comprehensive Environmental Response, Compensation, and Liability Act of 1980 (CERCLA or Superfund) was a compromise reached in the closing days of a lame-duck session by an outgoing Congress. With the election of

Ronald Reagan and of a Republican majority in the Senate, substantial compromise was required for S. 1480 to pass the Senate. The legislation, designed by an informal committee of senators, contained many ambiguities and did not address other issues contained in earlier House and Senate versions. The size of the fund was cut and the provisions for compensating victims of environmental disasters were deleted, as were references to joint and several liability.[12] This version passed by a 78 to 9 vote; its provisions were substituted for the language of H.R. 7020, and the resulting bill was returned to the House. Senators Stafford (R-Vt.) and Randolph (D-Va.), the authors of the Senate bill and compromise, writing to Representative Florio (D-N.J.), the author of the House bill, noted "that the bill passed [the Senate] at all is a minor wonder. . . . [It] represents an extremely delicate balancing of interests. . . . [It] was the only bill we could pass at the time and we do not believe it can be passed again" (U.S. Congress, Senate, 1983, 1:774–75). The House was presented with a take it or leave it choice on a complicated bill. In light of the anticipated hostility of the incoming Reagan administration to strong environmental regulation and the likelihood of extensive delay and revision by a new Congress, the House grudgingly accepted the compromise by a 274 to 94 vote. President Carter signed Public Law 96-510 on December 11, 1980.

CERCLA created a five-year, $1.6 billion fund for remedial, permanent cleanup at inactive or abandoned hazardous waste disposal sites and for removal action in emergencies when (1) an imminent threat of damage was posed to public health and the environment and (2) it was determined that a responsible party would not take this action. The chemical and petroleum industries were required to pay $1.38 billion into the fund, with some 85 percent of these payments to come from the chemical industry.[13] The states were required to contribute 10 percent of the cost of cleanup (50 percent if the state or a municipality owned the site) and to provide long-term maintenance of the site as well as disposal capacity for the waste removed.

EPA was required to revise the National Contingency Plan (NCP), originally prepared under the Clean Water Act, to provide a comprehensive document detailing emergency response and remedial action procedures and to provide guidance on cost-effectiveness. EPA was also required to inventory the nation's hazardous waste sites and to place at least 400 of the worst sites on a National Priorities List (NPL) for remedial action. Each state could designate a top priority site to be included in the NPL. The fund was expected to be sufficient to clean up at most 60 percent of this minimum number of priority sites. Strong enforcement powers were considered necessary to induce private parties to cover, at a minimum, the remaining 40 percent of site cleanups.

The EPA and the Justice Department were given legal authority to induce responsible private parties to undertake cleanup or to recover from them the cost of cleanup paid out of the fund. Section 106 authorized EPA to issue administrative orders or to pursue civil actions in the courts compelling responsible parties to take appropriate cleanup action in response to a release that might present an imminent and substantial endangerment to public health or welfare or the environment. Section 107 held responsible parties liable for the costs incurred by federal or state government or private parties taking appropriate response to a release. This section also held responsible parties liable for up to three times the cost of any response made necessary by their failure to comply with an administrative order issued pursuant to section 106. In addition, responsible parties were liable for the costs of natural resource damages. CERCLA required EPA to develop guidelines for use of the imminent hazard and enforcement authority of other major environmental laws given the additional authority provided by Superfund.

That the bill passed at all was a reflection of political and economic forces and of regulatory ideology at the close of the environmental decade. A large segment of the public and many members of Congress perceived the magnitude of the hazardous waste threat to be extremely large. This is clearly indicated in congressional hearings (for example, U.S. Congress, House, 1979c, and U.S. Congress, Senate, 1979) and in public opinion polls. A mid-1980 Harris survey reported that 76 percent of Americans felt that the dumping of toxic chemicals was a very serious problem. A 93 to 6 percent majority wanted strict federal standards. An 83 to 12 percent majority favored federal investigation of hazardous waste sites even though this could lead to well over $10 billion in suits against the federal government and the chemical industry (Harris, 1980). Surveys commissioned by the chemical industry also revealed strong public support. A Cambridge Reports, Inc., survey for the Chemical Manufacturers Association found that the issue most on the minds of politically active people as far as the chemical industry was concerned was chemical waste disposal. Most of those polled did not believe that the industry was properly concerned. A Union Carbide poll found that the public favored stronger laws protecting workers and consumers and more rigorous control over water and air pollution (U.S. Congress, Senate, 1983, 1:709).

Evidence of public support provided environmental interests the leverage to counter the political power of the chemical industry, but not enough leverage to block exclusion from CERCLA of a victim compensation title (also opposed by the Carter EPA) and of clear language on provision of a strong liability standard. At the same time, the ability of the chemical industry to fully exercise its substantial political power was limited by internal divisions and strategic blunders. The chemical industry's initial unified opposition began to erode after H.R. 7020 was reported out of committee.[14] Union Carbide, DuPont, Rohm and Haas, Olin, and Monsanto moved to accept a compromise involving the use of public funds for cleanup of orphan sites and an elimination of third party liability. The more threatening Senate proposals in S. 1480 amplified disagreement on compromise versus increased opposition. Intense grass-roots pressure by Monsanto helped to tie up competing Senate bills in the Senate Finance Committee as some senators voiced their concern about the shape of the proposed legislation.

Positive that Superfund could be stopped after the November election, CMA now voiced opposition to the House bill. Given previous public comments, it appeared to reverse its position. The statement put the Republicans in an untenable public position: if they did not act in support of Superfund, it would appear that they were merely servants of the chemical industry. Reports in the media of chemical industry political action committee contributions to Senate Finance Committee members cast senators in an even more unfavorable light. The Senate reported S. 1480 out of committee. Irving Shapiro, chairman of DuPont, told the *New York Times* that rational legislation dictated by the facts should be passed in the current congressional session, a position immediately supported by Rohm and Haas and Union Carbide. With the industry divided and its credibility damaged, the Senate compromise was fashioned in expectation of Superfund passage into law.

Beyond these political considerations, the state of the national economy was conducive to shifting the burden of cleanup onto the chemical industry. The economy went into a steep recession in 1980, contributing to a near doubling of the federal deficit. In contrast, chemical and petroleum industry profits remained high after increasing in the mid-1970s. The cost to these industries of the Superfund tax burden was characterized as small though not insignificant. At the same time, predictions of the adverse economic consequences of promoting victim compensation appeared credible.

In addition to favorable political and economic conditions, CERCLA gained support from the view still dominant in the lame-duck Congress that strong federal regulatory authority was necessary to solve environmental problems such as hazardous waste cleanup. Left to themselves, states, localities, and industry would not or could not be expected to provide adequate solutions. A vocal minority, however, were far more sympathetic to the *Wall Street Journal* editorial view that "[i]n the wake of a resounding national mandate against intrusive government . . . the outgoing Congress has decided to have a few for the road" (quoted in U.S. Congress, Senate, 1983, 1:725). Although not necessarily typical of opposition viewpoints or language, the critique of the House bill and the Superfund concept offered by Representatives Stockman

(R-Mich.) and Loeffler (R-Tex.) expresses an ideological position that would come to dominate Reagan administration environmental policy in the early 1980s:

> H.R. 7020 . . . is a replay of the patented formula for environmental legislation developed over the past decade. . . . Having established this pattern of regulatory overkill in the 1970s, the nation is now paying the price in the form of worsening economic conditions, stagflation, collapsing productivity and international competitiveness, declining living standards, and rising welfare costs. . . . The bill as reported inadvertently embodies an anti-industrial zero-discharge mentality. . . . [T]here never existed, especially in recent times, a regulatory or legal vacuum that permitted widespread gross irresponsibility and negligence in disposal and storage, nor are we consequently faced today with a national landscape thickly littered with industrial time bombs. The underlying notion of the bill—presence of a latent public health and environmental catastrophe— is wrong and the vast machinery it erects to combat this imagined hazard is wasteful and unnecessary. (U.S. Congress, House, 1980a: 70–71)[15]

SUPERFUND AND THE REAGAN ERA

The conflict over Superfund legislation mirrored essential disagreements between advocates and opponents of government regulation and reflected the evolution and victories of the deregulatory movement. Conflict would intensify greatly as the Reagan administration began to implement Superfund.

The deregulation movement emerged with the perception that economic regulation often protected entrenched business interests at the expense of competitors and customers and the related belief that economic regulatory agencies were captured by the regulated. This critique, shared by liberals and conservatives, gained prominence in the 1970s as the nation was confronted with new economic problems: stagflation, increased international competition, declining productivity, and structural maladjustment in U.S. industry. With the apparent failure of old solutions to effectively address these problems, Washington, the business community, and the general public accepted the dismantling of economic regulations as a viable, alternative solution. The late 1970s witnessed major deregulation of banking, airlines, trucking, and railroads.

The structure of the social regulatory agencies created in the 1970s was also affected by the critique of economic regulation. As an agency of social regulation, EPA was designed to avoid capture by the industries it was to regulate: its authority cut across industries to negate development of a symbiotic relationship with a single industrial constituency. Its legislative mandates stipulated specific goals in contrast to the vague objectives thought to allow industry welfare to substitute for social welfare in regulatory decision making (Marcus, 1980). Its implementation style reflected the regulator's need to impose an economic burden upon the regulated. The interdependence of regulator and regulated in areas of economic regulation supported a negotiated compliance style of regulatory implementation, a style emphasizing bargaining, discretion, flexible guidelines, and an accommodative stance toward the regulated. In areas of social regulation, the inherent conflict between the goals of regulator and regulated, and the historic occurrence of capture in the economic regulatory agencies, suggested the need for a relatively greater reliance on an enforced compliance style of implementation. The enforced compliance style emphasized rules, legal procedures, and a more adversarial orientation toward the regulated.

Many industries perceived the burden of new environmental and workplace safety regulations as posing a potentially immense threat to their profitability. Spurred on by the momentum of economic deregulation, business supported an aggressive lobbying and media campaign to emphasize the costs and downplay the benefits of social regulation. The campaign emphasized that negotiated compliance strategies were more productive of regulatory ends than enforced compliance strategies: the former promoted cooperation while the latter promoted confrontation. The conservative variant of the instrumental model of regulation (see chapter 3) provided scientific legitimacy to business advocacy of deregulation.

The debate over legislation to clean up hazardous waste sites proceeded within these crosscurrents of regulation and deregulation. The election of Ronald Reagan in 1980 marked a watershed in the deregulatory movement and made implementation of the Superfund mandate the responsibility of those who questioned the very need for its existence. The Reagan administration attacked regulation as one piece of a broader program to reorder the nation's priorities and reallocate income, wealth, and power among individuals, groups, and regions. Acceptance of the administration's total program was stated as necessary and sufficient to achieve the primary national goal of economic growth with low unemployment and low inflation (Tobin, 1982: 207).

The stated objective of the Reagan program was to promote substantial and sustained economic growth through a reduction in the size and number of federal spending programs, through tax cuts, and through reform of regulatory agencies.[16] When government intervention was justified by the presence of externalities, as in the case of hazardous waste, several principles were to guide its course. The regulatory agency should make fullest appropriate use of marketlike incentives and rewards to elicit self-interested cooperation. An adversary stance would elicit conflict and be less effective in achieving agency goals. Further, appropriate responsibility should be placed on state and local government. Finally, the agency should avoid government failure resulting from the actions of special interests or an administrator's desire to acquire status through his or her agency's growth.

There was a clear and inherent conflict between the CERCLA mandate to EPA and the ideology underlying the Reagan administration program for economic recovery. First, in contrast to administration emphasis on less government, CERCLA authorized EPA to spend $1.6 billion over five years. These expenditures were just part of the expected growth in EPA's overall authority, which would soon double the agency's work load. David Stockman, director of the Office of Management and Budget, noted in 1980 that "unless swift, comprehensive, and far reaching regulatory policy corrections are undertaken immediately, an unprecedented scale-up of the much discussed 'regulatory burden' will occur during the next eighteen to forty months" (quoted in Claybrook et al., 1984: 122–23).

Second, in contrast to Reagan administration belief in nonconfrontational voluntary compliance, Congress expected EPA to use its enforcement powers aggressively to satisfy site cleanup objectives and to replenish the fund (U.S. Congress, House, 1983c: 21).

Third, in contrast to the Reagan administration belief in local responsibility for local problems, CERCLA required the states to contribute only 10 percent of the cost of fund-financed cleanup at sites owned by neither a state nor a municipality.

Fourth, the EPA personified government failure. It was perceived by David Stockman and others as having accepted a no-growth, zero-discharge ideology; as being willing to spend when the value of the benefits fell far short of the costs; and as being willing to unfairly burden a deep pocket corporation for the total cost of cleanup (U.S. Congress, House, 1980a: 71–75).

Implementation: 1981 to Mid-1983

The Reagan administration acted to resolve this conflict on terms it deemed most consistent with its deregulatory ideology. Office of Management and Budget Director Stockman had advocated "an orchestrated series of unilateral administrative actions to deter, revise, or rescind existing and pending regulations where clear legal authority exists" (quoted in Andrews, 1984: 163). The Paperwork Reduction Act of 1980, signed in the last hours of the Carter administration, gave OMB power to kill unnecessary government forms and eliminate burdensome items. Three weeks after taking office, President Reagan issued Executive Order 12291 making the Office of Management and Budget the clearance center for all regulatory decisions. The order set up new procedures shifting authority over major regulations to that office. It authorized OMB to require sweeping regulatory impact analyses of proposed regulations, to review existing programs, and to postpone and eliminate regulations (Claybrook et al., 1984: xix). Stockman would use this power over agency budgets to shrink the size and influence of regulatory agencies. Prominent on Stockman's hit list of regulations were EPA rules affecting the automobile, steel, and chemical industries. President Reagan created a Task Force on Regulatory Relief, headed by Vice-President Bush, to work with OMB toward the goal of deregulation. The task force compiled its list of burdensome regulations based in part on the OMB list and on industry wish lists. The largest number concerned EPA regulations.

Top positions at EPA remained unfilled during the first three months of the Reagan term. Those eventually selected to administer EPA and to implement the Superfund program were chosen for their ideological conformity with Reagan administration views on regulation.[17] Anne Burford (née Anne McGill Gorsuch), chosen as EPA administrator, was a lawyer from Colorado with no Washington experience and little substantive experience with environmental issues. As a former Colorado state legislator, she fiercely opposed regulating hazardous waste disposal. Rita Lavelle, chosen to head the Superfund program in her capacity as assistant administrator for solid waste and emergency response, was director of communications for a subsidiary of the Aerojet-General Corporation. EPA records showed that Aerojet-General had the third worst pollution record in California. Robert Perry, a former Exxon trial lawyer, was chosen as the EPA general counsel. The administration's appointments to other top positions were drawn primarily from large corporations, the lawyers representing these firms, and Washington lobbyists (Claybrook et al., 1984: 120–21). The decline in staff morale following these appointments would accelerate as many senior employees left the agency.

With the support of a newly elected and more conservative Congress, the administration limited the resources available to EPA and its Superfund program. Between fiscal years 1981 and 1983, EPA's total real outlays were cut by one-third while real outlays in hazardous waste programs declined by 39 percent (Shabecoff, 1983b). Over the same period, EPA abatement and control staff declined by 21 percent, enforcement staff declined by 33 percent, and research and development staff declined by 16 percent (Crandall and Portney, 1984: 68). Appropriations to the Superfund response fund fell far below those initially authorized by Congress. Of the $960 million authorized in the first three years of the program, $74.4 million was appropriated in 1981, $26.6 million in 1982, and $210 million in 1983 (Acton, 1989: 31).

During the first two years of the Reagan administration, EPA Administrator Burford and Assistant Administrator Lavelle made substantial changes in the strategy that had been developed by the Carter EPA in anticipation of Superfund legislation.[18] A Carter EPA draft of the National Contingency Plan, the framework for government action in cleaning up hazardous waste sites, was ready for review in May 1981. The draft plan set the level of waste site cleanup at existing standards for drinking water quality, ambient water quality, and air quality. Rejecting this approach, Burford had the NCP rewritten several times. New draft versions would leave the level of cleanup to be decided on a case-by-case basis. In mid-1982, the Environmental Defense Fund and the state of New Jersey brought suits to force EPA to promulgate the NCP (Hall testimony, U.S. Congress, House, 1982b: 36). The plan was finally published in the *Federal Register* in July 1982. The Office of Technology Assessment, in a 1983 evaluation of the Superfund program, noted that

> [t]he NCP . . . does not establish any specific required environmental standards for the level of cleanup to be achieved, such as the maximum acceptable level of ground water contamination. EPA characterized the development of such standards for the hundreds (if not thousands) of substances that could be found at uncontrolled sites as a potentially time-consuming and costly task that might distract from cleanup efforts. Nonetheless, EPA declined to specify cleanup standards even where they have already been set for other purposes. . . . The NCP would allow contamination levels (that would trigger corrective action at permitted RCRA facilities) to continue to exist after remedial actions have been taken or without requiring any response action at all. (U.S. Office of Technology Assessment, 1983: 267)

The National Contingency Plan contained a hazard ranking system (HRS) for selecting sites for placement on the National Priorities List. These sites were eligible for fund-financed remedial action. CERCLA required that EPA include at least 400 sites on the list based on their hazard ranking system scores. The score would approximate the relative risk posed by a site in terms of air, surface water, and ground water contamination. The maximum possible score was 100. The agency selected 115 interim priorities list sites in October 1981, added 45 expanded eligibility list sites in July 1982, and published a 418-

site list in December 1982.[19] To avoid selecting more than 400 sites as cleanup priorities, the agency set the hazard ranking system cut-off at 28.5. Only sites with scores in excess of the cut-off would be deemed to constitute a risk sufficient to qualify for placement on the National Priorities List. Little scientific basis existed for choosing any score as a cut-off below which a site could be deemed to pose no significant risk. Ironically, this politically motivated cut-off would eventually result in a larger number of priority sites, increased community pressure for cleanup, and greater financial claims on the Superfund.

The National Contingency Plan also included guidance for an emergency removal program and a remedial action program. The Superfund Act defined a removal as a short-term containment or cleanup in response to emergency conditions requiring less than $1 million and six months to complete. In contrast, the plan drafted by the Reagan EPA divided removals into immediate and planned removals. The former were appropriate to prevent or mitigate immediate and significant risk of harm to human life, health, or the environment. The latter were appropriate in situations calling for a short-term, but not an emergency, response. Unlike immediate removals, the states would be subject to contribution requirements nearly identical to those for remedial actions. Remedial actions were more long-term in nature and were to be consistent with a permanent remedy for a release.

Consistent with the guidance now written into the plan, Administrator Burford reorganized the Superfund program to support a cleanup strategy which emphasized conservation of the fund and nonconfrontational voluntary compliance by responsible parties.[20] This is in contrast to the shovels-first-and-lawyers-later approach advocated by the Carter EPA. Burford initiated five reorganizations of the agency's Office of Enforcement, finally dividing Superfund enforcement between the Office of Waste Programs Enforcement under Lavelle and the Office of Legal Enforcement Counsel under an associate administrator. Legal and technical enforcement support personnel were organizationally separated. Enforcement decisions were centralized in Washington.

The decision-making authority to use the Superfund for emergency removals was also centralized in EPA headquarters rather than delegated to the regional administrators who were closer to the problem. If a hazardous substance release was reported, it had to present a current threat before the Superfund would be committed. If the release was at one of the 400 hazardous waste sites on the priority list, the emergency removal was limited to a small-scale stabilization to reduce only the most immediate hazard. To go further than this was considered an infringement on the remedial action program for cleanup of NPL sites. Administrator Burford argued that this frugal use of the

Superfund in emergency situations would conserve its resources to finance remedial cleanup.

The remedial cleanup program, however, also had restrictions on its implementation. Before Superfund resources were used, EPA had to determine that a responsible party would not act. The guideline used for making this determination was whether or not there were financially capable and potentially responsible parties to perform the cleanup. Since there was almost always at least one such party, few NPL sites qualified for a fund-financed cleanup. For those that did, EPA required the states to pay 10 percent of the cost of the remedial planning studies which preceded cleanup. Further, the states needed to provide up-front assurance that they would pay their share of the as yet unknown cost of cleanup.

In limiting fund-financed removals and in forcing the states to bear an unnecessarily large share of the cost of remedial action, progress on cleanup became highly dependent on the willingness of responsible parties to deal with hazardous waste emergencies and to finance cleanup at priority sites. Consistent with its nonconfrontational approach, EPA provided the maximum opportunity for these parties to agree to cover the cost of cleanup. Notably, rather than using Superfund to finance remedial planning studies as a basis for negotiation, EPA conducted rather open-ended negotiations with potentially responsible parties to establish who would perform the planning studies. EPA then negotiated the action to be taken at each subsequent phase of implementation. Congress had provided EPA with strong civil and administrative enforcement authority under CERCLA sections 106 and 107 for the purpose of encouraging private party settlements. Under Administrator Burford, EPA placed little emphasis on the use of this authority, thereby providing little incentive for successfully negotiated settlements.

Oversight and Investigation

The likely consequences of EPA strategy for fund-financed and privately financed emergency response and remedial site cleanup became evident soon after its adoption. In congressional hearings held in late 1981 and early 1982, legislators protested that EPA had done virtually nothing toward the cleanup of high priority sites in their districts.[21] Supporters of Superfund claimed that the Reagan administration intended to build up a fund surplus to help balance the federal budget. This contention was supported by the fact that while the Treasury was collecting some $298 million per year, the administration asked for only $200 million in 1982 and would have preferred less (U.S. Congress, House, 1982b: 26–40). Congressional hearings also documented the near shutdown in EPA's enforcement program during the first year of the Burford tenure (U.S. Congress, House, 1982a). Few consent agreements were initiated, no section 106 unilateral administrative orders (with their treble damage provisions) were issued, and only two cases were referred to the Justice Department for civil prosecution of responsible parties. Consequent on elimination of enforcement as an incentive to settle, few responsible parties showed any inclination to negotiate.

Concern over the implementation of hazardous substance policy was not limited to the Superfund program. [22] In response to requests by the Task Force on Regulatory Relief, EPA adopted unenforceable voluntary testing and self-certification of hazardous substances by chemical manufacturers as a substitute for rule making under the Toxic Substances Control Act. Responding to Office of Management and Budget pressure, EPA sought to delay indefinitely its regulation of toxic water pollutants discharged to public treatment plants, an action reversed by court order as an illegal form of deregulation. The interim final regulations for landfills and surface impoundments under the Resource Conservation and Recovery Act issued in July 1982 represented a significant relaxation of similar rules proposed by the Carter EPA. At Office of Management and Budget behest, reporting and insurance requirements for hazardous waste facilities were eliminated. The agency agreed with industry requests to loosen rules governing the permitting of hazardous waste facilities: permits would be issued for the lifetime of the facility rather than a set term of five or ten years. Further, EPA required no preconstruction review for anything but landfills and other land disposal methods. The agency had not obtained OMB permission to produce RCRA permits for existing facilities, negating the applicability of regulations that were already in place.

The most graphic example of EPA orientation to industry versus public health and environmental needs was the 1982 suspension of a ban on storing drums of hazardous liquid waste in landfills without first giving notice or allowing opportunity for public comment. At the time, James Sanderson, Burford's apparent choice for associate administrator for Policy and Resource Management, was serving simultaneously as a consultant to the EPA as well as to a solid waste firm in Colorado. His client in Colorado apparently dumped thousands of barrels of liquids into landfills during the eighteen days after Burford lifted the ban and before congressional protest forced her to reimpose it. Crandall and Portney note that this simply served to confirm the distrust of EPA developed over the previous eighteen months (Crandall and Portney, 1984: 75).

Industry in general secured benefits from EPA decisions under the Resource Conservation and Recovery and Toxic Substances Control Acts, and those liable for private cleanup costs at hazardous waste sites benefited from EPA's inaction under Superfund. However, industries that had invested in treating waste objected to lifting the ban on liquid waste disposal in landfills. Major industry groups also feared that Administrator Burford's ineptness was working against them and that the inevitable backlash to her style and policies would result in stronger regulation (Davies, 1984: 155–57). An editorial in *Chemical Week*, an industry publication, stated displeasure at seeing a "regulatory agency in turmoil." It noted that "in a highly competitive industry, companies cannot afford to spend their resources on environmental protection, however well conceived the rules, unless they perceive that those rules are backed up by credible enforcement policy." "Without an effective EPA," it concluded, "industry's contribution to pollution, which has been diminishing, is bound to grow again. In the long run, the American people will not stand for that" (quoted in U.S. Congress, House, 1982a: 34). In support of these observations, polls showed broad public opposition to a relaxation of environmental health standards no matter what the resulting cost might be and equally strong public support for strict enforcement of already mandated controls (Harris, 1981 and 1982a). Environmental issues were expected to be important in the November 1982 congressional election.

Sewergate

After the election, a House investigation and oversight subcommittee chaired by Representative Elliot Levitas, a Georgia Democrat, subpoenaed 700,000 EPA documents related to Superfund enforcement and cleanup. The subcommittee members made it clear that they suspected political meddling in lawsuits against waste dumping and were looking for sweetheart deals in which industry was excused from further liability in exchange for cosmetic cleanup (Epstein, Brown, and Pope, 1982: 252). On advice from the Justice Department, Administrator Burford refused to hand over sensitive enforcement documents, based on the doctrine of executive privilege. Her December 1982 decision led to a major confrontation between Congress and the executive branch.[23] Soon six committees were investigating EPA and the Superfund program. These investigations highlighted systematic constraints built into the program and also indicated that EPA administrators were willing to violate the law in support of their preferred implementation.

Cleanup activity financed out of the Superfund (referred to as fund-financed) was clearly limited by EPA's policy that the states should pay as much of the total cost of response as the agency's interpretation of CERCLA would allow. By the agency's own estimates, forty-two out of fifty states did not have adequate resources for a 10 percent matching share (U.S. Office of Technology Assessment, 1983: 314). At the same time, senior administrators discouraged EPA staff from developing creative methods for the states to meet this financial obligation (Shabecoff, 1983c). On the enforcement side, funding was reported to have fallen far short of levels consistent with EPA's Strategic Management Plan enforcement goals. Funding was just sufficient to support on-going litigation. It was not possible, however, to support cost recovery, issue new administrative orders, or enforce orders that were in violation (U.S. Congress, House, 1983b: 416–17).

In addition to these overt limits on cleanup activity, EPA administrators were charged with unlawful acts in relation to their implementation of Superfund. Administrator Burford was charged with manipulating the fund for political ends prior to the November 1982 election. She resigned in March 1983. John Hernandez, a deputy administrator and temporary chief after Burford's resignation, resigned under fire from Congress for his role in altering a draft report to exclude reference to Dow Chemical as a major source of dioxin contamination in Michigan. Rita Lavelle was charged and eventually convicted of perjury in congressional testimony regarding communications with Aerojet-General on impending agency enforcement actions. Other top EPA administrators were accused of perjury in congressional testimony, destruction of records required by Congress, and misuse of authority to the benefit of those regulated (Shabecoff, 1983a, 1983e; Pasztor, 1983; Maitland, 1983). At the same time that Congress was documenting the extremes to which EPA administrators would go to not implement Superfund, the discovery of dioxin contamination at Times Beach, Missouri, magnified public awareness of the problem that EPA was to be addressing.

By early 1983 EPA had lost considerable legitimacy as a regulatory agency. Sewergate dominated the front page of major newspapers during the first three months of that year and continued as major news for several months after Burford's resignation (Szasz, 1986). Polls showed that a slight majority of the public thought the president cared more about firms violating antipollution laws than about enforcing those laws[24] and that many agreed with the charges voiced in Congress (Harris, 1983).

In May 1983 William Ruckelshaus was named the new EPA administrator and Lee Thomas was named assistant administrator in charge of the Superfund program. As EPA's first administrator, Ruckelshaus had already proven his commitment to the agency, his ability to work with its professional staff and political constituencies, and his substantive appreciation of the technical and political issues involved in its decisions. He entered office with a presidential mandate to restore public trust in EPA. Ruckelshaus asserted that the Reagan administration had initially misread its mandate by attempting to deregulate environmental and health regulations along with economic controls; while the procedures of social regulation needed reform, their basic goal did not. He argued that an effective national regulatory program was a necessity for free enterprise and was far preferable to relying on voluntary compliance at the mercy of scofflaw competitors: "[T]he only voluntarism at EPA is if the EPA voluntarily decides not to enforce the law."[25]

Implementation: Mid-1983 through 1985

Ruckelshaus demanded greater influence over the agency's budget as a condition for accepting the position of administrator. Freed from Office of Management and Budget constraint, Superfund received appropriations of $1.07 billion in fiscal years 1984 and 1985 combined, a 343 percent increase over the $311 million appropriated in fiscal years 1981 through 1983. Combined outlays in fiscal years 1984 and 1985 totaled over $600 million, a 261 percent increase over the $233 million spent in fiscal years 1981 through 1983 (see table 4.1 for comparison of Superfund activity in 1981–83 and 1984–85).

Under Ruckelshaus's leadership, EPA adopted a Superfund strategy for removal actions, remedial actions, and enforcement more in keeping with the intent of Congress in passing CERCLA.[26] EPA regional administrators were given substantial authority to conduct fund-financed emergency removals when a significant potential hazard was present. The situation no longer needed to be urgent. The bureaucratically cumbersome and time-consuming distinction between immediate and planned removals was dropped. Further, heavy reliance was placed on executing removal actions at priority sites and using these removals to perform more extensive surface cleanups. With these changes, the Superfund financed 102 removals in the first six months after the resignation of Administrator Burford and removals at an additional 597 sites in 1984–85. In contrast, only 119 removals were conducted between 1981 and mid-1983. Site-specific expenditures for removals in 1984–85 were 254 percent greater than those in 1981–83.

EPA established a site classification system to better determine which National Priorities List sites should be cleaned up with Superfund resources and which should come under the enforcement program, that is, should be cleaned up by responsible parties through application of Superfund enforcement provisions. It waived the excessive burden placed on the states relative to fund-financed remedial cleanups. Most significantly, it ended its negotiation-first posture and returned to the fund-first approach proposed by the Carter EPA. For those remedial cleanups still in the enforcement program, EPA used

Table 4.1. Superfund Activities, 1981–1983 and 1984–1985

	1981–1983	1984–1985
Budget		
Appropriations (in millions)	$311	$1,066.1
Outlays (in millions)	$233.1	$609.3
National Priorities List (additions)	406	135
Cleanup Activities (number of sites)		
Removals	171	597
Preliminary Assessments	5,041	8,813
Site Inspections	3,050	2,831
Remedial Investigation/Feasibility Studies	169	331
Remedial Design	30	31
Remedial Action	21	67
Enforcement		
Enforcement Referrals (Section 106)	13	53
Cost Recovery (Section 107)	35	80

Source: Author's computations based on Acton, 1989, various tables.

the fund to finance remedial investigation/feasibility studies and used these studies as a basis for negotiations with responsible parties. With a greater emphasis on cleanup expenditures out of Superfund, 331 fund-financed studies were completed in 1984–85, in contrast to 169 completed in 1981–83. Of the latter, 115 were completed in 1983. Given the delays involved in moving from study to action, the increase in design of cleanup remedies was less dramatic; the fund financed thirty remedial designs in 1981–83 and thirty-one in 1984–85. Priority sites did begin to reach the final cleanup stage, remedial action, at an increased rate. In contrast to twenty-one remedial actions conducted in 1981–83, sixty-seven were conducted in 1984–85, with fifty-four of the latter conducted in 1985. Remedial program expenditures increased by 578 percent, from $25.8 million in 1981–83 to $149 million in 1984–85.

In the enforcement program, EPA replaced its highly accommodative negotiated compliance strategy with a more aggressive enforced compliance strategy and also delegated increased enforcement discretion to its regional offices. EPA's potential enforcement leverage was greatly enhanced by court rulings during Administrator Burford's tenure: The courts determined that strict liability applied under CERCLA and that joint and several liability was appropriate when the harm is indivisible. The courts determined also that parties liable under CERCLA include past and present facility owners and operators, transporters, and off-site generators of hazardous substances.[27] The new enforcement strategy emphasized these judicial rulings in support of joint and several liability. It also emphasized fund-financed expenditures as an alternative and inducement to negotiation and settlement by responsible parties, and more stringent conditions for negotiation and settlement. The agency began to use its civil and administrative enforcement authority to encourage responsible party settlements when negotiations were stalled. In particular, greater reliance was placed on section 106 treble damage, unilateral administrative orders. The regions were directed to use these orders in every case where compelling enforcement authority was necessary. From mid-1983 to the end of 1984, 107 unilateral administrative orders were issued, in contrast to five issued during the Burford administration. As a consequence of changes in negotiation strategy, the number of settlements and the value of private party–financed cleanups nearly tripled over the mid-1983 through 1984 period compared to outcomes in the 1981 through mid-1983 period. The agency also increased its section 106 referrals to the Department of Justice for civil court actions against responsible parties, from thirteen in 1981–83 to fifty-three in 1984–85. It more than doubled its section 107 cost recovery actions, from thirty-five in 1981–83 to eighty in 1984–85.

ADMINISTRATION OF SUPERFUND FAILURE

It is clear that both advocates and opponents of Superfund expected the incoming Reagan administration to minimize the importance of environmental issues in defining national priorities. It is unlikely that either side anticipated the debacle of initial Superfund implementation, an implementation dominated by the fact that failure of Superfund was a basic goal of the Reagan program. The Reagan administration did not desire failure in the sense that the federal government would not respond to any immediate threat posed by uncontrolled hazardous waste sites or in the sense that all parties responsible for these threats would be fully able to avoid financial responsibility. But the intent was certainly failure relative to public and congressional expectations of a major waste site cleanup program financed in large part by generator industries and other responsible private parties. Industry eventually did come to question whether the evisceration of EPA was in its long-term interest. It is, nevertheless, clear that the promotion of industry interests was at the heart of the Reagan administration policy in general and that the minimization of costs imposed on industry to achieve waste site cleanup was at the heart of EPA hazardous waste policy. In this respect, the failure of Superfund under Administrator Burford was due to the acceptance of industry views on efficiency and equity and the related domination of decision making by polluting industry interests.

As a consequence, Superfund implementation to mid-1983 was both inefficient and inequitable. Critics of the agency argued that EPA efforts to minimize Superfund expenditure were based on a desire to reduce the federal deficit and to weaken the case for reauthorization after 1985. Minimizing cleanup expenditures to preclude a Son of Superfund meant that the agency would forgo the opportunity to proceed with cleanup at the nation's worst hazardous waste sites. In light of strong evidence on the threat posed at many of these sites, the benefits of cleanup would certainly exceed the cost; the decision not to act thus promoted inefficiency and diminished social welfare. Built-in delays in the Superfund remedial cleanup program further reduced Superfund efficiency by allowing site conditions to deteriorate and eventual cleanup costs to rise. Limitations on the extent of allowable removal actions similarly increased future cleanup costs. In some instances, aversion to addressing source control issues required repeat removals at a single site. The agency's Resource Conservation and Recovery Act program was also inefficient in a Superfund context. Lax policies with respect to inspection and enforcement at hazardous waste facilities with interim permits and with respect to issuing final permits raised the likelihood that many of these facilities would become future Superfund sites (U.S. General Accounting Office, 1981, 1983). The future cost of cleanup would far exceed near-term expenditures on control.

The Superfund enforcement program also promoted inefficiency. The agency's nonconfrontational voluntary compliance strategy was justified in part as a means to minimize transaction costs, in particular those associated with agency–responsible party conflict under an enforced compliance strategy. However, the agency's unwillingness to leverage an openness to negotiation with a timely use of its enforcement powers substantially diminished the incentive for responsible parties to negotiate and settle.[28] The inefficiency associated with this strategy was magnified through the granting of releases from future cleanup liability to responsible parties in exchange for their contributions to short-term cleanup actions. Anderson notes that "[c]ertain agreements, such as those involving Seymour in Indiana, General Disposal in California, and Chem-Dyne in Ohio drew severe criticism for their generosity to the responsible parties. These agreements involved large sites and major companies and portended permissive agreements to come unless the government adopted a more aggressive negotiating posture" (Anderson, 1985: 284).[29]

In granting release from future liability, the agency made the fund liable for any costs of cleanup not covered by the settlement. Given the impermanence of short-term remedies, future expenditures could be expected to more than offset any added transaction costs associated with a tougher settlement policy.

The Superfund program promoted inequity as well as inefficiency since both fund and enforcement strategies minimized polluting industry expenditures to the detriment of communities threatened by uncontrolled hazardous waste sites. The CERCLA mandate clearly articulated a consensus view that parties responsible for waste site problems should pay to protect public health and the environment from the consequences of the responsible party's past disposal practices.

Several factors help account for the inability of the Reagan administration to continue its plan for Superfund failure beyond mid-1983. First, public support for hazardous waste cleanup was at least as strong and broad-based in mid-1983 as it was in 1980. At the same time, public awareness of the frequency of hazardous waste emergencies and the scope of the site cleanup problem grew considerably after 1980 (Harris, 1982b, 1985). Greater awareness was due in part to EPA's inventory of the nation's hazardous waste sites. The inventory process involved participation by the states, localities, and the media as well as by the directly and potentially exposed public. By 1983 EPA had identified over 15,000 potentially hazardous sites nationwide. The promulgation of the National Priorities List also acted to expand the constituency for waste site cleanup as hundreds of communities were informed that they were home to the nation's worst toxic threats.

Second, the agency did not create a significant political constituency for its policies on the environment in general or on Superfund in particular. It alienated environmental groups that traditionally supported it in confrontations with industry. It alienated its own staff and contributed to information leaks to the press and Congress. At the same time, it failed to provide industry with a rational, predictable, and publicly supportable set of policies. Industries that invested heavily in pollution control or safe disposal were disadvantaged relative to those that had not acted in anticipation of Resource Conservation and Recovery Act or Superfund implementation. Further, as confrontations between congressional committees and the agency intensified, industry most likely came to fear that as an apparent beneficiary of EPA strategy, it would be required to bear a greater share of future environmental correction costs. J. Clarence Davies of the Conservation Foundation has suggested that the inability of the agency to develop a political constituency was rooted primarily in the political ineptness of Burford and the other political appointees at EPA: "Like a tragic figure from a classical Greek drama, [Burford], from her first day in office, began to sow the seeds of her own destruction. Each insult to Congress, each snubbing of an interest group, each refusal to listen or compromise formed a chain of events that could end only with the downfall of [Burford] and her associates" (Davies, 1984: 156).

Third, the Reagan administration sold Congress and the public on the benefits of deregulation in the context of an economic recovery program. However, its Superfund and environmental policies contradicted the tenets of the deregulatory movement. Many commentators noted that the Reagan administration neglected opportunities for statutory change in laws that were up for reauthorization as well as opportunities for designing market incentive systems and performance standards for efficient and effective environmental control.[30] But its sins of commission were more obvious than these sins of omission.[31] Administrator Burford's policy agenda for EPA advocated a better scientific foundation for agency decision making. In fact, the agency's research budget was cut by more than half and industry preferences were substituted for hard evidence and peer review. The agenda advocated strengthening federal-state-local relationships to support the president's New Federalism program. In fact, delegation of responsibilities to the states increased their administrative burdens while cuts in federal grants and revenue losses in the 1981–82 recession made the states unable to fulfill prior commitments to federal programs. The agenda advocated regulatory reform. In fact, it provided regulatory evisceration. The agenda advocated improved management and reduced budgets at all agency levels, with the former compensating for the impact of the latter. In fact, it only provided the latter.

Finally, congressional investigations and public exposure of the Superfund program made clear the substantial gap between what Reagan administration deregulation was achieving and what the public expected from the program. Public belief that top EPA administrators had acted unlawfully further discredited the argument that EPA Superfund strategy was intended to improve social welfare. Faced with a near total loss of public and industry support, the Reagan administration either had to free the Superfund program from its strong ideological guidance or face the possibility that its overall approach to regulation would lose legitimacy.[32]

The Superfund strategy instituted under EPA Administrator Ruckelshaus and continued after 1984 under his successor, Lee Thomas, was intended to reestablish the agency's legitimacy and to address the inefficiencies and inequities associated with the Burford EPA. The states and EPA regional offices would now play more active roles in the implementation of Superfund. Consideration of activity at the state and regional levels must precede evaluation of Superfund strategy and outcomes from mid-1983 through 1985.

Achievement of the nation's hazardous waste site cleanup goals depends substantially on the strength and funding of state environmental programs. While the Environmental Protection Agency has primary authority to set standards, write guidelines, and induce compliance, considerable implementation responsibility is left to the states. Federal and state programs are highly interdependent. Interdependence produces conflict over the distribution of hazardous waste control and cleanup costs at the state level that mirrors that at the federal level. Interdependence also produces conflict between federal and state governments over environmental program financing and responsibilities.

The perceived failure of state governments to promote environmental goals was central to the nationalization of environmental protection in the 1970s. Federal legislation established EPA authority to manage the generation and disposition of hazardous wastes while leaving considerable implementation responsibility to the states. During the 1970s federal government aid to state environmental programs increased as the states expanded their own commitments to environmental protection. Over the decade ending in 1980, EPA aid to state and local governments increased from 49 percent to 82 percent of total agency outlays. The New Federalism of the 1980s, emphasizing local responsibility for local problems, reversed this trend. EPA current-dollar outlays decreased by 18 percent between 1980 and 1987 while aid to state and local government fell to 64 percent of the agency's budget. Increased state and local government expenditures on natural resources and the environment made up for some of the loss in federal aid. Between 1980 and 1985 the ratio of state and local to federal government expenditures in this area increased from 10.9:1 to 12.4:1.

The shift in financial burden to the states elevated the significance of their resources as a constraint on environmental program achievements and consequently made the states a more important locus of conflict over hazardous waste control. Differential availability of public and private cleanup resources, variation in real and perceived hazardous waste threats, and uneven political pressure exerted by those with an interest in regulatory outcomes produced substantial variation across states in acceptance of hazardous waste control and cleanup responsibilities.[1]

This chapter begins with an overview of the Resource Conservation and Recovery Act (RCRA) in its relationship to Superfund, with particular emphasis on state control of existing hazardous waste facilities and state siting of new facilities. From a Superfund perspective, implementation of the Resource Conservation and Recovery Act is the major determinant of whether current hazardous waste management sites will become future Superfund sites. It is also a major determinant of whether adequate capacity exists to receive hazardous wastes generated by current production and by Superfund site cleanup. The chapter then shifts to a direct focus on state participation in the Superfund program. The strength of state legislative authority and the funding of state cleanup and enforcement programs are shown to determine both the extent to which the federal Superfund program can leverage a state's cleanup effort and the success of that effort. Next, variation across states in cleanup program authority, funding, and enforcement are examined and linked statistically to state and industry resources, hazardous waste site risks, and the political pressure exerted by those with a stake in program outcomes. The chapter ends with discussion of state hazardous waste regulation as it relates to the failure of the federal Superfund program. This investigation at the state level highlights the same complex of political and economic factors that affect Superfund design and implementation outcomes at the federal level.

RCRA AND SUPERFUND

The Resource Conservation and Recovery Act of 1976 mandates a cradle-to-grave program for the management of hazardous wastes and hazardous waste facilities. EPA authorizes state programs that meet RCRA requirements and delegates to these programs responsibility for tracking waste, promoting existing facility compliance, and siting new facilities. State failure to adequately oversee existing facilities and to enforce compliance with regulatory requirements increases the likelihood of ground water and other environmental contamination. A failed RCRA site may then become a Superfund site. State failure to site new hazardous waste facilities reduces the availability of economical waste management capacity and may exclude a state's uncontrolled sites from the Superfund program. By 1986 EPA had authorized RCRA programs in all but eleven states, leaving the achievement of hazardous waste facility regulation goals highly dependent on state efforts. [2]

Federal and state governments share in the cost of Resource Conservation and Recovery Act implementation. The states receive financial assistance from EPA for 75 percent of their program costs through annual matching grants. Constant-dollar federal grants to the states increased from about $26 million in fiscal year 1980 to about $73 million in fiscal year 1988. The increase reflects both the number of states administering all or part of the RCRA program and increasing state responsibilities. Over the same period, EPA constant-dollar RCRA expenditures fell from about $190 million in 1981 to less then $140 million in 1982, increased slightly to 1984, and then rose to nearly $260 million in 1988 (U.S. General Accounting Office, 1988a: 14–15). The 1981–84 reduction coincided with the Reagan administration efforts to eviscerate EPA hazardous waste management programs. The post-1984 growth reflects the agency's increasing responsibilities under RCRA's 1984 amendments.

The characteristics and strengths of state Resource Conservation and Recovery Act programs depend on the current activism and political power of affected interests as well as on historic patterns of environmental policy making and control. Generator industries prefer little government interference in their choice of least-cost technologies; desire adequate off-site treatment, storage, and disposal capacity; and advocate minimal regulation of their on-site facilities. The hazardous waste management industry generally supports comprehensive standards to avoid being placed in a noncompetitive position relative to proprietary on-site facilities. At the same time, their support for stricter state standards depends on the nature of out-of-state competition and the level of in-state facility sophistication. Owners of more technologically advanced facilities support stricter state standards to minimize competition from less environmentally sound facilities and to expand the market for their services. Local communities generally prefer stricter standards but may advocate minimal standards in an effort to support local generator industries or avoid industry flight to states with less stringent regulatory programs. State legislatures may also respond to the fear of industry flight, an application of the Gresham's Law principle that lax regulation in some jurisdictions drives out stringent regulation in competing jurisdictions (Goetze and Rowland, 1985: 117). Environmental organizations generally see state programs as a means to exceed federal standards and, under favorable political conditions, to acquire greater discretion in hazardous waste management. The structure of the state's environmental policy apparatus and the presence or absence of avenues for participation by competing interests affect the ability of industrial, environmental, and local community interests to shape state RCRA programs. A comparison of hazardous waste management programs in California and Texas illustrates the importance of several of these factors.[3]

California began regulation of land disposal facilities in the 1970s and devised the country's first cradle-to-grave hazardous waste manifest system. Soon after RCRA passage in 1976, California's waste management program was authorized by EPA to operate in lieu of the federal program. In 1981 California's Office of Appropriate Technology estimated that 75 percent of all hazardous wastes sent off-site for disposal could be treated using available and proven technologies. Acting on this projection, Governor Edmund G. Brown, Jr., directed the Department of Health Services—the lead agency in hazardous waste management—to prohibit land disposal of highly toxic wastes. The department was also directed to impose higher fees on land disposal until the ban took effect and to increase disposal site monitoring and enforcement. Petrochemical companies and other generators that had little contact with the Office of Appropriate Technology were shocked by this proposal to eliminate cheap land disposal and argued that "the governor's office had been captured by environmental zealots who had no comprehension of the realities of corporate economics" (Morell, 1983: 146). Following critiques by consulting firms, business, labor, and public interest organizations, increased communication between industry representatives and government proponents of the new policy resulted in a substantial revision to the proposal: the ban on land disposal would be enforced only to the extent that treatment technologies were actually available. Industry could not criticize this reasonable approach and deferred opposition until 1983, when decisions on the availability of treatment technologies were to be made.

The success of the land ban proposal rested on the ability of the state to site adequate treatment capacity. In anticipation of the ban, generators attempted to reduce their reliance on land disposal, and waste management firms proposed treatment and recycling facilities to profit from the expected growth in demand for these services. Several facilities eventually received permits to operate while others failed in the face of strong public opposition. California's efforts were successful in the sense that they focused attention on the need to develop alternatives to land disposal and forced industry and local communities to participate in this endeavor. This success can be attributed to the personal support of Governor Brown, to the high level of scientific competence within the state's regulatory and public health agencies, and to a regulatory structure and politics that allowed environmental interests to counterbalance generator industry interests. However, California's efforts did not produce treatment capacity sufficient to divert hazardous waste from land disposal. A 1985 report of the state's Commission for Economic Development estimated that 25 percent of California's hazardous waste cleanup costs are associated with the state's continued reliance on land disposal (*Hazardous Waste News*, August 12, 1985, p. 263). The report recommended an aggressive program to reduce waste generation, to increase private sector investment in treatment technologies, and to decrease the amount of land-disposed wastes. It also urged a more cooperative approach between business and government instead of the existing adversarial relationship.

Texas, like California, is among the nation's leading hazardous waste generators. Estimates available in 1983 ranked them fourth and sixth, respectively, while 1987 data rank them first and second, respectively.[4] The petrochemical industry accounts for an estimated 60 percent of the state's wastes and exerts a dominant influence on Texas waste management policy. Lloyd Bentsen, when U.S. senator from Texas, successfully pushed for 1980 amendments to RCRA exempting oil and gas waste from coverage under the law. This left regulation of these major petrochemical industry waste streams to the Texas Railway Commission, an agency with historically close ties to the oil and gas industries. The commission has been criticized for not enforcing its own rules on waste disposal and for allowing oil and gas operation wastes to contaminate land and drinking water supplies. The Texas Chemical Council, a chemical industry trade association, was influential in limiting the scope of the state's Solid Waste Disposal Act to the minimum required for EPA authorization of the Texas RCRA program. Industry favored delegation of RCRA authority to the state to avoid having to meet differential state and federal regulatory requirements. Industry also perceived that delegation would enhance their control over RCRA implementation in Texas. Generator industries and the waste management industry have successfully opposed stronger waste management regulations and a deemphasis of engineering criteria as a basis for regulatory decisions. Critics argue that state emphasis on engineering criteria for injection wells, landfills, and surface impoundments imply that these methods are environmentally sound if the criteria are met and that engineering criteria provide no incentive for waste reduction or development of more technologically sophisticated methods of waste management.

The ability of the petrochemical industry to dominate Texas waste management policy in the early 1980s is attributed to a set of interrelated factors: fragmentation of the state's regulatory response, barriers to citizen participation in a highly formalized process with a primary emphasis on engineering considerations, bureaucratic dominance of the regulatory apparatus combined with a weak governor's office and a legislature that ranks very low in evaluation of effective lawmaking, and the absence of sustained and extensive media coverage of hazardous waste problems. At the same time, industry political influence is being challenged by growth in the strength and resources of environmental organizations and by the preference of the commercial waste management industry for a uniform set of regulations that apply to on-site as well as off-site facilities.

State performance of Resource Conservation and Recovery Act responsibilities affects the likelihood that a facility will become a Superfund site. The California and Texas examples demonstrate that all states are not equally exposed to this likelihood and the related magnification of Superfund cleanup problems. However, when the states are viewed in the aggregate, the likelihood of RCRA failure is most substantial. In the early 1980s this fact resulted in extensive criticism of EPA and state actions on four primary RCRA responsibilities: ground water monitoring, closure and postclosure financial guarantees, inspections and enforcement, and permitting.[5]

RCRA mandates monitoring at land-based facilities to determine whether the facility is contaminating the ground water in the uppermost aquifer underlying the facility. General Accounting Office surveys of six states conducted in 1983–84 found that 78 percent of the facilities in Illinois and North Carolina were not in compliance with monitoring requirements, that a third of the facilities in New Jersey and Tennessee were not in compliance, and that Massachusetts and California did not know the extent of noncompliance because facilities had not been inspected. A March 1983 EPA finding of noncompliance in 109 out of 171 facilities reviewed showed that failure to satisfy ground water monitoring requirements was a nationwide problem (U.S. General Accounting Office, 1983, 1984a).

RCRA requires that facility owners or operators demonstrate their ability to finance closure and postclosure activities when the facility ceases operations. A facility that cannot cover these costs may become abandoned, may pose substantial risks to public health and the environment, and may consequently impose significant cleanup costs on the Superfund. A 1984 EPA study found that only 30 percent of 172 facilities sampled met closure plan requirements and only 33 percent met closure cost estimate requirements. It concluded that compliance with closure, postclosure, and financial responsibilities was also a nationwide problem. The General Accounting Office reported to Congress that states were not reviewing facility closure plans during inspections due to time constraints, limited staff resources, and lack of guidance and training for inspectors (U.S. General Accounting Office, 1983).

RCRA requires inspections of hazardous waste facilities as the primary means to detect and document health and environmental violations. The

General Accounting Office reported that only 12 percent of 7,056 interim status facilities[6] were inspected by 1981 and that few compliance orders were issued. Subsequent reviews in 1983 and 1984 found increased inspections of major facilities but a similar preference for warning letters and notices of violation over stronger compliance orders.

Finally, RCRA allows treatment, storage, and disposal facilities in operation on or before November 19, 1980, to continue to operate by complying with interim status requirements until a final permit is issued. The final permit imposes additional technical, design, and operating requirements to substantially lower the likelihood of facility failure. Although EPA considers facility permitting as one of the most important aspects of RCRA environmental protection and placed top priority on issuance of final permits to land disposal facilities, less than 2 percent of interim status facilities received final permits by early 1984.

Resource Conservation and Recovery Act implementation failure also applies to the small number of facilities that received Superfund wastes. EPA reported in late 1984 that fifty-seven commercial hazardous waste landfills were operating throughout the country. Of these, twenty-eight had received Superfund wastes, and sixteen of those facilities had significant violations of RCRA regulations. Further, five out of the sixteen facilities were leaking contaminants into the ground water. Were these commercial facilities to fail, EPA faced potential liability for the cost of cleanup since the agency was the legal generator of Superfund wastes. In November 1985 EPA formulated an off-site policy to prohibit disposal of wastes from Superfund sites at commercial facilities with significant RCRA violations. The following December the General Accounting Office informed Congress that some federal agencies (in particular the Department of Defense) were still sending cleanup wastes to commercial facilities that were in violation of RCRA regulations (U.S. General Accounting Office, 1985a: 1–3).

Against the background of extensive criticism of Reagan administration environmental policy, congressional debate in 1983 and 1984 emphasized EPA's limited progress in promulgating regulations under the Resource Conservation and Recovery Act. It also highlighted numerous incidents involving contamination at interim status facilities, a dramatic increase in estimated hazardous waste generation, and the extensive reliance on land disposal of managed hazardous wastes (U.S. General Accounting Office, 1988a: 24). Congressional concern that more RCRA facilities would become Superfund sites was highlighted by the fact that over fifty RCRA interim status facilities were already on the National Priorities List.

In November 1984 Congress reauthorized RCRA and enacted major amendments to discourage land disposal of hazardous waste and to encourage reduction in the volume and toxicity of hazardous waste being generated.[7] EPA's limited progress to date led Congress to set numerous statutory deadlines; a constraint on regulatory discretion subsequently followed in the 1986 reauthorization of Superfund. Among the RCRA deadlines was the requirement that the agency approve or deny final permits for interim status land disposal and incinerator facilities by the end of 1989. By January 1988, 956 out of 1,451 land disposal facilities nationwide had not certified compliance with ground water monitoring and financial responsibility requirements and therefore had to close. At the same time, EPA enforcement data revealed that despite agency actions at land disposal facilities, the percentage of operating facilities in compliance remained at about 50 percent between 1985 and 1987. EPA and the states had taken final permit action at only 42 percent of operating land disposal facilities and 27 percent of incinerator facilities. Further, although EPA estimated that about 2,500 facilities might be leaking and require corrective action, it made little progress in achieving the needed cleanup. The agency estimated that about 800 of these RCRA facilities might need to be transferred to the Superfund program (U.S. General Accounting Office, 1988a: 27–28).

The failure of state and federal efforts to manage RCRA facilities places the states in a double bind: on the one hand, the transfer of facilities to the Superfund program increases state financial responsibilities and the quantity of Superfund wastes; on the other, available treatment and disposal capacity is reduced. The reduction in capacity in turn threatens state participation in Superfund. The 1980 Superfund Act requires the states to guarantee access to permitted facilities for the treatment or disposal of Superfund wastes as a precondition to federal funding of priority site cleanup. The Superfund Amendments and Reauthorization Act of 1986 places additional pressure on the states to site new hazardous waste facilities. Section 104(k) requires that cleanup funds be withheld unless the state provides assurance of adequate capacity and access to facilities in compliance with RCRA for the treatment or disposal of all that state's hazardous waste for the next twenty years.[8]

The needs of industry and the requirements of Superfund both provide the states with a strong incentive to site new facilities. Siting, however, is generally at private initiative and conditional upon the issuance of an operating permit. The permit is issued under the Resource Conservation and Recovery Act and may also have to satisfy other federal, state, and local requirements. A 1987 survey found that thirty-seven states had established some form of siting procedure.[9] Procedures included preemption (nine states had power to select a site and authorize its use), override (nineteen states had power to intervene and override local decisions that blocked facility siting), local veto (eight states left primary power with local government), and procedural restraints (a few states placed restrictions on the exercise of local control). The survey identified 179 attempts to site new hazardous waste facilities (many for land-based disposal) between 1980 and 1986. Of these, 22 percent were successfully sited, 25 percent were not sited, and 53 percent were still pending. None of the various state approaches to siting proved to be a model of success. In 1988 the General Accounting Office found that EPA regional offices were aware of only nineteen treatment facilities in forty-two states that were sited and began operating after 1984 or were under consideration at that time (U.S. General Accounting Office, 1988b: 3). The limited success of these siting initiatives reflects political and economic factors as well as the perceptions and uncertainties that affect private and public decisions.

Local opposition to specific initiatives (the NIMBY, or not-in-my-backyard, phenomenon) presents the major political barrier to new facility siting. Opposition increases the time and cost of permit application and review. Efforts to site land disposal facilities are particularly vulnerable. Opposition has mounted with the increased certainty that landfills will leak and contaminate surface and ground water. It is buttressed by the failure of state and federal governments to effectively regulate existing facilities under RCRA or to clean up uncontrolled facilities under Superfund. Regulatory failure justifies local community perception that acceptance of an RCRA facility implies acceptance of a Superfund site.

Uncertainties regarding current capacity and future needs also reduced state resolve and ability to overcome political barriers to siting. In 1986 EPA reported that about 76 percent of an estimated 275 million tons of regulated wastes disposed of annually are treated at some 1,600 facilities nationwide. These estimates were based on a 1981 survey of generators and facilities. In 1987 the General Accounting Office concluded that national data on generation and disposition of hazardous wastes did not allow determination of whether the nation has sufficient capacity to manage current and projected hazardous waste volume (U.S. General Accounting Office, 1987a: 21). Uncertainty is compounded at the state level since each state must know not only its needs and capacity requirements but also the extent of out-of-state competition for available capacity. This uncertainty has been a major barrier to state compliance with Superfund capacity assurance requirements.

Uncertainty has increased with a shift in policy emphasis from land disposal to treatment. The 1984 Resource Conservation and Recovery Act amendments state that land disposal is the least favored method of hazardous waste management and prohibits land disposal unless wastes are treated to substan-

ce toxicity or it is demonstrated that the hazardous constituents are
y to migrate for as long as they remain hazardous. The Superfund
ndments and Reauthorization Act of 1986 builds on this belief that land
sposal facilities are not capable of assuring long-term containment of hazardous waste. It mandates that permanent treatment be preferred over land-
based disposal in managing Superfund wastes. The emphasis of these acts on
the desirability of treatment facilities contributed to a relative decline in land-
based facility siting proposals. Although treatment facilities may be more
acceptable to communities than land disposal facilities, they too face local
opposition. The permitting process allows local communities to express concerns over the effects of treatment facility siting on drinking water supplies and
air and water quality; on property values; on the likelihood of accidents during
the transportation and treatment of wastes; on operator adherence to permit
conditions; and on the diligence of the state or EPA in enforcement. A 1987
New York State legislative commission survey found that twenty of fifty
applications for commercial facilities (including incinerators) either failed to
win approval or were withdrawn (U.S. General Accounting Office, 1988b: 20–
21). The General Accounting Office speculates that fear of public opposition
has deterred some companies from proposing projects.

Private initiatives are also deterred by regulatory and economic uncertainties. As of 1988 EPA had neither fully defined all types of hazardous waste
under RCRA nor set treatment standards. At the same time, the economic
attractiveness of landfills to the commercial waste management industry has
declined as large quantity generators began to emphasize source reduction and
on-site management as a means of minimizing site cleanup liability under
Superfund. Generators have delayed decisions to add to capacity. Their delay,
combined with the availability of alternative waste management options,
makes estimates of demand for off-site treatment capacity virtually impossible
and deters construction of added capacity by the commercial hazardous waste
management industry (U.S. General Accounting Office, 1988b: 17–19). The
latter industry faces additional uncertainties since EPA does not know the
quantity of Superfund wastes requiring treatment.

FEDERAL/STATE INTERDEPENDENCE

The federal/state government relationship in controlling hazardous waste site
conditions and in promoting hazardous waste site cleanup is marked by both
symbiosis and tension. The following discussion of interdependence serves as a
backdrop to an examination of state participation in the nation's cleanup effort.

With interdependence, failure at one level substantially constrains accomplishments at the other.

Superfund, like RCRA, imposes substantial responsibilities on the states. The states are expected to identify problem sites and to participate in determining whether the site is eligible for Superfund-financed cleanup. If the site is eligible and if cleanup is not financed by a private responsible party, the state is required to provide 10 percent of the cost of cleanup for privately owned sites and 50 percent for state- or municipality-owned sites. The state is required to provide long-term operation and maintenance once a cleanup remedy is completed and functioning as planned. The state is required also to assure that approved facilities are available to store, treat, or dispose of any hazardous waste transported off-site. As discussed above, the latter requirement expands state responsibilities under RCRA and forces the state to site new hazardous waste facilities. Further, states with authorized hazardous waste management programs are expected to take the lead role in managing a portion of Superfund-financed cleanups. The agency transfers federal money to the state and the state develops the remedial cleanup plan, schedules the work, and hires contractors. Although EPA cannot delegate its statutory enforcement authority to the states, the latter are expected to take a lead role in pursuing responsible party contribution at some enforcement sites. When a state program does not meet EPA standards or state management resources are limited, EPA takes the lead role. Since Superfund is not available to finance cleanup at sites not listed on the National Priorities List (so-called non–priority list sites), total responsibility at these sites falls upon the states. Many sites that are not on the NPL pose considerable environmental risk and necessitate state action. In the absence of a voluntary or state enforcement-induced responsible party response, cleanup only occurs if financed solely through state funds.

From the states' point of view, Superfund can provide substantial leverage to state cleanup efforts. Federal funds provide the maximum leverage when a site is on the priority list and privately owned: the state achieves a 9:1 federal/state expenditure ratio. Federal expenditures leverage state efforts when the agency conducts a short-term removal since these actions do not require state cost-sharing.[10] Further, Superfund leverages state discretion by allowing each state to designate one site as its top priority and have it placed among the first 100 sites on the National Priorities List. The site may be the worst in the state or be one cast as a bellwether of state program efficiency. Finally, federal expenditures can leverage state efforts at priority sites when state environmental quality standards exceed federal standards and postcleanup site conditions must satisfy the former. Prior to 1986 a state was required to pay the added cost of cleanup to achieve a standard that was not satisfied by EPA's choice of a cost-effective remedy. Revisions to the agency's National Contingency Plan that were codified in the 1986 Superfund amendments now require that cleanup satisfy promulgated state requirements when the latter are more stringent (U.S. General Accounting Office, 1989a: 14).

The federal Superfund program also leverages state enforcement. Responsible party cleanup and cost recovery resulting from federal enforcement actions reduce the number of sites requiring state enforcement, thereby freeing state resources for enforcement at other sites. Further, cleanup costs incurred by the state as a result of responsible party recalcitrance can be recovered under section 107 of the Superfund law if the state brings suit in federal court and if the cleanup is consistent with the National Contingency Plan. Finally, for nonpriority sites, the threat of placing the site on the National Priorities List may provide a substantial inducement to responsible party settlement. Nonpriority site cleanups may be less expensive in that they do not have to follow Superfund procedures or satisfy Superfund standards.

For public and privately financed cleanup at both priority and nonpriority ʃsites, EPA leverages state efforts through provision of information, guidelines, and technical assistance. Decisions on cleanup levels require extensive scientific information on the public health and environmental risk posed by the thousands of chemicals found at hazardous waste sites. Decisions on cleanup remedies require extensive technical information on the cost, efficacy, availability, and applicability of alternative remedies to site specific contamination problems. The states benefit from the centralization of scientific and technical information production at the federal level; centralization is more efficient due to scale economies and avoidance of redundant expenditures. For the vast majority of states, the cost of developing needed information is prohibitive.

EPA leverage of state cleanup efforts through provision of information, guidelines, and technical assistance has increased since the mid-1980s. In the early years of the Superfund program, political turmoil retarded development of guidelines while the agency's case-by-case approach to cleanup mitigated against development of cleanup standards. The states received minimal guidance in their cleanup lead responsibilities at priority sites. With the development of guidelines and standards, state lead responsibilities at priority sites are clearer and state cleanup decisions at nonpriority sites are better informed. Despite these developments, states program officials feel that more agency assistance is necessary. In response to a recent General Accounting Office survey of nonpriority site cleanup activity, forty-three out of fifty states said their cleanup efforts would benefit from more assistance with health effects data for conducting risk assessments, reports on new treatment technologies, training for state personnel on treatment technologies, and training on choosing remedies. Most states also said more training for state personnel on identifying cleanup standards would be helpful (U.S. General Accounting Office, 1989a: 54–55).

Much of the tension between federal and state hazardous waste programs is a direct product of their interdependence. Inaction at either level of government limits achievements at the other. In early 1985 the head of the federal Superfund program criticized some states with the largest number of priority sites for not shouldering their fair share of cleanup costs and for shirking their responsibilities to site-approved facilities for disposal of waste within their borders (Frank and Atkeson, 1985: 18). From this federal perspective, program failure is in large part attributable to inaction at the state level. The states in their turn criticize the delay, uncertainty, and loss in discretion associated with dependence on federal funds and federal enforcement to achieve cleanup. In a 1987 survey for the Association of State and Territorial Solid Waste Management Officials, states attributed some of the delay in program achievements to the fact that EPA's Superfund process and coordinating procedures are often too long, bureaucratic, inefficient, and cost-ineffective; to a lack of clear standards and guidance; to the time and resources spent in meeting federal cost recovery requirements; and to the level and uncertainty of federal funding. They recommended changes to streamline the federal program: reduction or elimination of some of the lengthy studies and reviews associated with site investigation and remedy selection, reduction in excessive federal oversight and redundancy to state efforts, and delegation of more responsibility to states willing to take a lead role (Association of State and Territorial Solid Waste Management Officials, 1987: 42–44). Similarly, in response to a General Accounting Office survey, some states criticized the long delay between site discovery and placement on the National Priorities List, noting that years elapse before cleanup actually begins. Others said that state cleanup proceeds more quickly, more cost-effectively, and with very reduced oversight costs. A state with cleanup standards in some respects more stringent than Superfund standards protested that responsible parties can shop around for the best deal among federal and state agencies (U.S. General Accounting Office, 1989a: 61–62).[11]

STATE AUTHORITY AND FUNDING

A comprehensive and well-funded state program can achieve maximum leverage from a comprehensive and well-funded federal program and can substitute, to some extent, for a weak or underfunded federal program. In contrast, a fragmented or underfunded state program leaves state-level achievements dependent on the vagaries of federal policy. Discretion and program achievements at the state level thus depend crucially on the nature of the state's legislated authority and the extent of its program funding. As demonstrated in this section, fiscal capacity to address hazardous waste site cleanup varies substantially across states.

Many states authorized cleanup programs and established state superfunds within a few years after passage of Superfund. Program authority and/or cleanup funding in some states with substantial waste site problems, such as New Jersey, Illinois, and Massachusetts, preceded or coincided with Superfund passage. By 1986 some thirty-six states and territories had authority and funds to conduct site assessments and remedial actions while thirty-two of these had enforcement authority to ensure that responsible parties would assess site conditions and undertake remediation.

The range of program characteristics and the basis for state program strength or weakness is revealed in a 1988 General Accounting Office review of hazardous waste site cleanup programs in seven states: three with older, more active programs (New Jersey, Massachusetts, California) and four with newer programs (Indiana, Oregon, Montana, Virginia) (U.S. General Accounting Office, 1989a: 29–35). The study attributes the increased progress of the three larger programs to several factors.

First, these programs have specific state authority to clean up hazardous waste sites and state superfunds to address sites without responsible party funding. All three programs were established and funded by 1983. New Jersey has generated about $143 million as of December 1988 through a tax on transfer of certain hazardous substances and petroleum products and is authorized to sell $300 million in bonds. Massachusetts appropriated $26 million and authorized $85 million in bonds. Revenue to pay back the bonds and cover additional operating expenses comes from hazardous waste transporter fees, cost recoveries, and certain fines and fees. California's superfund program is funded through a tax on hazardous waste generation and a $100 million bond authorization.

Second, these programs have strong and effective legal provisions to ensure responsible party cleanup. All three hold responsible parties to a standard of strict, joint and several liability and are authorized to charge a recalcitrant responsible party triple damages for any action taken by the state. Although none of the three have recovered the latter damages, they report that this potential is a significant threat in encouraging responsible party action. Further, both New Jersey and Massachusetts can recover costs through imposition of priority liens on properties held by responsible parties. Priority liens make sale of these properties more difficult and create problems in obtaining mortgage finance.[12] New Jersey also has a real estate transfer law that requires a careful review of certain types of property before ownership is transferred to determine whether hazardous substances have been improperly disposed of on the property.

Finally, these programs have sufficient staff with suitable skills to oversee cleanups. At the time of the survey, New Jersey had a staff of nearly 200 overseeing responsible party cleanups and 260 handling publicly funded cleanups. Case management teams with primary responsibility at major sites include a manager, an attorney, a scientist, a geologist, and a public relations person. Massachusetts had a staff of 140 working in its cleanup program and an additional 110 providing legal, toxicological, and administrative support. California assigned a staff of about 160 to site cleanups with skills including law, chemistry, hydrology, toxicology, accounting, hazardous materials, geology, and engineering. Technical assistance and other support is provided by an additional seventy people. All three states had established systems for keeping an inventory of sites and for assigning priorities and responsibilities for site cleanup.

In contrast, the programs in the other four states are more recent, lack sizable staff and funding, and have only begun to establish operating policies and procedures. Prior to program authorization, site remediation was done by units with primary responsibility in some other area such as water quality or solid and hazardous waste regulation. At the time of the survey, cleanup funds were relatively small: Indiana's trust fund had $5.6 million, Montana's mini-superfund had received $100,000, Oregon had collected $3.6 million in disposal fees, and Virginia's fund balance was $43,000. Enforcement tools are fewer and weaker: Montana and Virginia do not specifically provide for strict or joint and several liability while Oregon only provides for strict liability. Indiana and Oregon can recover triple damages and Montana can recover double damages. Indiana can recover actual costs incurred. None of these states has a real estate transfer law or can impose priority liens. The operating budgets of all four programs allow for only a small staff: Oregon leads with twenty-one staff members while Montana has only one, the program director.

As suggested above, funding levels clearly determine program capacity to cover cleanup costs as well as program capacity to hire sufficient staff to utilize legislated powers. Funding levels are a basic index of state program potential. They are unequal among the states. Data on the distribution of cleanup funds for thirty-three states are presented in table 5.1. The first column reports the sum of cleanup funds authorized by 1983 and projected for 1984–85 (totalling about $293 million) while the second gives a cleanup fund balance available in

January 1988 (totalling about $249 million). These data, though informative, provide a misleading picture of relative program potential since no adjustment is made for such factors as the cost of remediation, the number of hazardous waste sites that need to be addressed, cleanup standards, technology preference, or the extent of federal enforcement.[13] These factors determine the funding the states need to cover their share of the cleanup burden. Furthermore, the priority list grew from 539 sites in late 1983 to 858 sites in 1986 and to 1,174 sites in 1988. EPA estimates of average cleanup costs increased from $7.2 million in 1983 to $8.1 million in 1986 due in part to a change in applicable standards.[14] More aggressive enforcement after mid-1983 increased the share of cleanup costs coming from responsible parties. When these considerations are factored in, the funds required for state participation in cleanup at all priority list sites decreased slightly between 1983 and 1986 from an estimated $326 million to an estimated $322 million.[15] State cost-share needs then increased substantially after 1986 due primarily to requirements of the Superfund Amendments and Reauthorization Act of 1986. The act mandated use of existing environmental standards and stated a preference for permanent remedies over off-site transport and disposal (U.S. General Accounting Office, 1989a: 15). With the average cost of remedial action recently estimated at between $21 and $30 million (U.S. General Accounting Office, 1989a: 12), the aggregate state cost-share requirement associated with a 1,174-site priority list increases to an estimated $1.37 to $1.96 billion.[16]

Viewed in the aggregate, these data suggest that the states were relatively well positioned in the early 1980s to address their Superfund cost-share responsibilities; the $293 million appropriated was equal to about 90 percent of their $326 million potential cost-sharing needs. When funds and needs are examined on a state-by-state basis, however, a wide variation in program potential emerges. At root is the fact that the distribution of program funds is not proportionate to the number of priority sites by state. The wide disparity in program potential can be demonstrated through examination of state program funding as a percentage of cost-share requirements. This exercise shows that in 1983 five states could meet 100 to 400 percent of their needs, eight states could meet 50 to 99 percent of their needs, ten states could meet 10 to 49 percent of their needs, and six states could meet less than 10 percent of their needs.

When nonpriority as well as priority sites are considered, the aggregate shortfall expands substantially. By 1988 the states identified 28,192 nonpriority sites needing attention (U.S. General Accounting Office, 1989a: 92–93). State financial burden at nonpriority sites is somewhat reduced by the fact that responsible party cleanups at these sites are more frequent than at priority sites. Regardless, limited data on the cost of cleanup at nonpriority sites suggest the

Table 5.1. Funds Available for State Hazardous Waste Response

Fund Range	1983[a] (Number of states)	1988[b] (Number of states)
Under $50,000	3	3
$50,000–$99,999	2	2
$100,000–$499,999	9	3
$500,000–$999,999	1	3
$1,000,000–$4,999,999	8	11
$5,000,000–$9,999,999	5	5
$10,000,000–$24,999,999	2	3
$25,000,000–$49,999,999	2	2
$50,000,000–$119,999,999	0	1
$120,000,000	1	0

Sources: U.S. Environmental Protection Agency, 1984c: 3-2; U.S. General Accounting Office, 1989a: 36.
[a]Actual and projected cleanup program funds, 1983–85
[b]Response fund balance as of January 1988

states may need as much as an additional $38 billion in cleanup funds.[17] Since the distribution of nonpriority sites across the states is roughly proportionate to that of the priority sites, it is clear that even the best funded state programs are substantially underfunded.[18]

CONFLICT OVER FUNDING AND ENFORCEMENT

The interdependence of federal and state hazardous waste programs produces conflict over payment of the toxic debt at both state and federal levels. Chapter 4 related legislative and implementation outcomes to economic and environmental factors and to political pressures exerted by affected interests. This section examines the interplay of these same factors as a source of variation in state cleanup program funding and state enforcement action. It builds on a statistical analysis of state decisions in 1983 as described in an appendix to this chapter. Comparison of 1983 and 1988 data suggests that the same complex of factors that explain state decisions in 1983 can explain state decisions at the end of the decade.

From an economic perspective, a state's commitment of funds to a cleanup program can be judged efficient if it provides a balance between the costs and benefits of cleanup. The more extensive is the environmental threat posed by hazardous waste sites, the greater should be that commitment. The commitment should also expand with the state's budget: the richer the state, the smaller the sacrifice in other public programs to achieve a given level of environmental protection. At the same time, the state need commit less to publicly funded cleanup if private parties can be expected to provide environmental protection either voluntarily or through enforcement program inducement. Political action by affected interests can promote or constrain achievement of an efficient balance.

From a policy perspective, it is essential to determine the degree to which economic versus political factors explain the level of state cleanup activity. If state fiscal capacity (i.e., the state budget) clearly constrains the size of a state's cleanup program, placing an increased financial burden on the states must limit both state and federal cleanup progress. Shifting the burden to the federal government will promote progress at both levels. Alternatively, if the size of state cleanup programs bears little relationship to the magnitude of state fiscal capacity, governors and state legislators rather than federal decision makers must accept a greater share of the blame for limited progress. Finally, if state program funding and effectiveness is constrained by generator industry political pressure, less demanding requirements for state participation in the national cleanup effort can limit the ability of industry to forestall progress.

Not surprisingly, the size of a state's budget is a primary determinant of cleanup program funding; the two grow in near proportion. At the same time, states that suffered more during the 1981–82 recession allocated less to cleanup programs. Taken together, these relationships demonstrate that as state fiscal capacity expands and becomes more certain, a state will expand its commitment to environmental protection. In contrast, program funding is only half as responsive to the size of the state's population at risk of exposure as to the size of the state budget. On efficiency grounds, an expansion in expected damages would justify state acceptance of a proportionate increase in cleanup costs. That this has not occurred suggests that state programs are underfunded and operate at an inefficient level. The inadequacy of state funding could result from decision makers placing a lower priority on the long-run consequences of uncontrolled hazardous waste sites than on the more immediate sacrifice associated with expanding the state budget or contracting support for competing public programs. To the extent that neither is a viable option, state fiscal capacity again becomes the primary constraint on efficiency. Alternatively, states may have hesitated to more fully fund cleanup programs due to uncertainty regarding federal government commitment to environmental protection in general and to Superfund in particular. As already discussed, EPA was subject to substantial criticism between 1981 and 1983 for its lack of commitment to Superfund cleanups and its efforts to raise the cost of state participation. Consequently, a state would be less willing to appropriate funds when federal leverage is likely to be reduced or withdrawn. Uncertainty regarding federal implementation provides a rationale for inaction on the part of budget conscious legislators.

Public funding of cleanup programs is generally lower in those states where voluntary or cooperative generator industry expenditures account for a higher percentage of total private and public pollution control expenditures. In these states, decision makers have reason to believe that private sector actions will substitute for public sector cleanup efforts. However, states with a higher percentage of large, financially viable generator industry firms allocated no less to cleanup programs than did similarly situated states with fewer such generator firms. This suggests either that legislators were not convinced that generator industry resources could be drawn into the cleanup effort through use of enforcement powers or that they were unwilling to fully support an aggressive application of these powers.

Beyond consideration of damages and of the availability of public and private resources, state decisions are influenced by the actions of parties with an interest in distributional outcomes. As argued in chapter 3, business support or opposition to state cleanup programs is based on expectations of distributional consequences. There is, of course, every reason to expect that generator industries will support a state cleanup program if it results in a substantial socialization of cleanup costs via the tax base. However, state programs leverage federal Superfund expenditures and increase the exposure of generators to subsequent cost recovery efforts. Consequently, generator industries have little reason to believe that state program funding can facilitate socialization and would tend to oppose expanded state programs.

Consistent with this view, state program funding is generally lower when the potential political influence of chemical and petroleum industry corporations is greater. Petrochemical industry firms, understandably, are among the most active opponents of state hazardous waste programs. The petrochemical industry was the dominant industrial opponent of the federal Superfund and also a strong advocate of maximizing state responsibilities under the program. During the Superfund debate, the petrochemical industry fought for federal preemption of certain state powers, in particular the power to tax generator industries that were subject to the federal feedstock tax. Subsequently, five oil and chemical companies spearheaded an effort to have the New Jersey Spill Compensation Fund taxing authority declared unconstitutional under the Superfund section 114(c) preemption clause.[19] Petrochemical industry firms account for some three-quarters of hazardous waste generation and are the most exposed among responsible parties to suits for cost recovery. Petrochemical industry firms could substantially reduce their exposure to liability by weakening state programs.

Labor employed in the petrochemical industry also attempts to influence state program decisions. If employees of petrochemical firms are predominantly concerned with wage levels and short-term job security, they will follow their employers' lead and attempt to weaken state programs. However, if environmental protection ranks high among employee goals, they will support aggressive state action regardless of employer projections of the consequences. The latter appears to be the case: state program funding is generally higher when the potential political influence of petrochemical industry labor is greater. In fact, labor efforts to expand state commitment to cleanup essentially counterbalance the efforts of capital to constrain this commitment.

Interviews conducted by the author with officials of the Chemical Workers Union and the Union of Oil, Chemical and Atomic Workers clearly indicate that organized labor is more likely to support an aggressive state program than to stand in opposition.[20] First, these unions were actively involved in lobbying for right-to-know legislation, a goal which generally places them in opposition to their employers. An analysis of House of Representatives voting on a right-to-know amendment to the 1986 Superfund law found greater support coming from districts with heavier employment in the chemical industry (Waldo and Griffiths, 1986: 20). The petrochemical industry opposed this legislation. Second, union officials expressed their desire to promote the perception of their industries as good citizens. While industry is also concerned with promoting this perception, it is less inclined to achieve this end through a general acceptance of financial liability for cleanup. Union support for state programs that increase generator liability does not reflect their indifference to job security. The opinion was expressed that responsible action by industry in the short run was likely to yield job security in the long run. An unwillingness on the part of industry to take action in the short run would magnify long-run liability and thus reduce economic viability. Finally, union support for strong state programs emerges from the fact that employees of the chemical and petroleum industries are often substantially represented among people at risk from exposure.[21]

Generator industry capital and labor can often anticipate concentrated costs or benefits from state cleanup programs. In contrast, a population at risk from hazardous waste site exposure can generally anticipate only diffuse benefits and generally does not define a cohesive political force. Environmental advocacy groups can serve as an organizational locus for these populations and can act to promote their interests in legislative and enforcement decisions. Environmental groups support strong, well-funded state cleanup programs and advocate that a maximum share of cleanup costs be imposed on industry out of conviction that those who create an environmental problem should pay for its correction. As in the federal Superfund debate, environmental groups attempt to make state legislators aware of the true extent and severity of the hazardous waste problem. Their projections serve as a counter to those offered by generator industries.

Environmental groups stand in sharp contrast to generator industry capital and labor in that the size of their membership is not independent of hazardous waste site issues. Environmental group membership will grow in response to the need to exert political pressure to achieve environmental action goals. The statistical findings reported in the appendix demonstrate that environmental groups attract fewer members when the private sector is likely to address environmental problems in the absence of public sector pressure. They attract more members, however, when the petrochemical industry has a place of greater prominence in the state's economy. The presence of concentrated generator industry power results in a greater perceived need for organization on the part of those concerned with environmental quality. At the same time, environmental group membership is lower when the representation of petrochemical industry employees in total manufacturing industry employment is greater. Where petrochemical industry labor supports strong state action, unions serve as a political substitute for environmental groups. Environmental group membership and the priority placed on environmental issues both increase when unemployment diminishes as a cause for popular concern.

As noted above, petrochemical industry capital and labor appear to have a substantial impact on program funding decisions: state funding expands with the influence of labor and contracts with the influence of capital. While the relative power of either group to affect program funding may be greater in some states and less in others, on average the political influence of the one appears to counterbalance that of the other. In contrast, although environmental group membership expands with the perceived need for environmental action, these groups do not appear to have any direct influence on the magnitude of state cleanup program funding. As suggested below, this may reflect the fact that environmental group activism is more effective at publicly visible stages of the regulatory process (e.g., enforcement) than at more hidden stages (e.g., funding).

An aggressive enforcement program can induce financially viable responsible parties to underwrite an expanded cleanup effort. Here, as before, state fiscal capacity is a primary determinant of progress. Growth in state budget revenues produces a near proportionate growth in the number of enforcement actions undertaken at hazardous waste sites. In contrast, the number of enforcement actions is almost twice as responsive to the availability of generator industry resources, suggesting that state enforcement programs have aggressively pursued financially viable corporations that bear responsibility for waste site problems. The interrelationship between state fiscal capacity and the size of a state cleanup fund is essentially different from that between the former and state enforcement activity, in that enforcement can substitute for publicly funded cleanup. At the same time, the potential for enforcement to achieve this substitution and to reduce the cleanup burden imposed on state taxpayers is limited by state funding. It is unclear whether governors and legislators have imposed funding constraints on enforcement activism, for example, out of fear that the state will achieve a reputation for being antibusiness. It is interesting to note that enforcement is no more aggressive with uncooperative polluting industries than with cooperative industries.

Enforcement assigns liability for cleanup to responsible parties. Consequently, petrochemical industry capital and labor have as great an interest in the aggressiveness of state enforcement programs as in the level of state program funding in general. Interestingly, they appear to have no direct impact on the extent of state enforcement activity. In contrast, although environmental groups have no clear impact on overall program funding, they do exert a considerable influence on the extent of state enforcement. This indicates an unequal ability or effort to influence environmental legislation versus implementation. Industry-based pressure groups may be more oriented toward lobbying legislators, most likely have greater financial resources to underwrite electoral campaigns of friendly legislators, and are more likely credible in their threats or promises to sway the electorate. Environmental groups certainly lobby legislators and attempt to sway the electorate. Their greatest strength at the state level appears to be oversight of program implementation and the application of pressure on state program administrators and staff to carry out legislative mandates and to implement enforcement programs. The noted aggressiveness of state enforcement suggests that environmental groups can promote actions that are more than merely symbolic.

The clear implication of these findings is that state fiscal capacity constrains the size of a state's cleanup fund as well as the ability of a state enforcement program to aggressively pursue those responsible for hazardous waste site problems; both grow in rough proportion to the size of a state's budget. Consequently, federal decisions to impose a greater financial burden on the states can only limit the achievement of these programs and in turn constrain cleanup at the national level. However, the fact that state program funding is less responsive to the risks posed by waste sites than to fiscal capacity suggests that a degree of underfunding reflects conscious political decisions by governors and legislators. It is therefore unclear how the states would respond to a reduction in their Superfund financial burden. If state funding remained unchanged, total state plus federal funding would increase. Alternatively, if the states reduced their funding in response to a reduction in the federally imposed fiscal burden, total funding would remain constant. Given that funding and enforcement do respond to the magnitude of cleanup problems and that labor counterbalances capital's ability to limit funding, I would expect a reduction in federal financial burden to yield an increase in total funding.

INTERDEPENDENCE AND FAILURE

The interdependence of federal and state programs and the conflicts emerging from interdependence have conditioned progress at both levels of government. Each is dependent on the resources and efforts of the other. Each attempts to conserve resources by shifting financial responsibility to the other while retaining discretion over expenditures and program decisions. EPA has a dominant role in this relationship with its power to set conditions for state participation, including national standards, and its ability to leverage state expenditures and enforcement actions. EPA also has a fiscal advantage: the federal government can draw from a larger and more stable pool of public and private cleanup resources and can redistribute them among the states. As to the relative stability of this national pool, one need only recall that the recession of 1981–82 had its greatest impact on midwestern states, the collapse of the energy market in the mid-to-late 1980s had its greatest impact on oil patch states, and the recession of 1990–92 had its greatest impact on states in the northeast.

Despite the fiscal advantage held by the federal government and the fact that management of hazardous waste is a national problem, EPA has consistently attempted to shift fiscal responsibility to the states. These efforts have generally been supported by the White House. Under Administrator Burford, EPA set a hazard ranking system cut-off score intended to limit the size of the National Priorities List to 400 sites, the minimum number mandated by the Superfund Act. The remaining sites became the fiscal responsibility of the states. EPA also required the states to share in the high cost of precleanup remedial investigation/feasibility studies, a requirement that went well beyond the minimum participation mandated by the act. In the late 1980s EPA proposed a deferral policy that would leave states responsible for cleanup at sites that could qualify for the National Priorities List (see chapter 9). These efforts were rationalized as methods to conserve the Superfund and to address the federal government's fiscal crisis. They were also rationalized on efficiency grounds. In the absence of a significant financial burden, it was argued, state governments would not need to ask whether the benefits of cleanup are justified by costs and would consequently be willing to promote excessive and inefficient cleanups.

Efforts to increase the states' financial burden renders the nation's progress in hazardous waste site management even more dependent on state fiscal capacity. It also affords opponents of control and cleanup the opportunity to impose state-level constraints that further compromise the national effort. Major generators that are exposed to Superfund liability can diminish that exposure by successfully limiting state participation in Superfund. Regulatory battles that are lost at the federal level can be won at the state level.

Variation across states in the circumstances and forces that condition hazardous waste management decisions have resulted in differential state progress in both RCRA and Superfund programs. At one extreme, a constellation of economic and political forces have allowed some states to draw successfully on federal and state resources to reduce toxic threats to public health and the environment and have contributed to national success in these endeavors. At the other extreme, some states that are constrained by economic and political factors and face a large share of RCRA and Superfund sites have neither served their citizens nor contributed to national hazardous waste management goals.

Limited state progress in establishing strong, effective RCRA facility management is contingent on the same factors that set limits on state progress in establishing strong, effective Superfund programs: inadequate budgetary resources, unrealistic perceptions of the need for control, and the relative political strength of adversely affected interests. Progress in both areas is also limited by shifting national priorities: a reduced flow of resources and guidance from the federal government in the early 1980s and its wavering commitment to RCRA and Superfund implementation reduced state resolve to allocate funds to these programs and magnified local community fears that a new RCRA facility would become a Superfund site. The deemphasis on land disposal facilities also constrained state progress in siting new facilities. The shift in federal policy was desirable given the high contamination risks associated with land disposal but problematic in that it fed the perception that federal government guidance was often shortsighted.

Federal/state interdependence allows actions at the state level to diminish the efficiency and equity of the nation's hazardous waste management efforts. The failure of some state RCRA programs significantly increases the number of hazardous waste sites that ultimately will need to be addressed by Superfund. In deferring to these states, federal policy has tolerated decisions that shift hazard waste management costs from the present to the future, often with the intention of promoting the profitability of local industry. This shortsighted preference to save now and spend considerably more later perpetuates the syndrome that created a need for Superfund's multibillion dollar cleanup program in the first place. It contributes to the combined inefficiency of the RCRA and Superfund programs.

The efficiency of the cleanup effort also is compromised by its dependency on state financial resources.[22] At nonpriority sites, budgetary constraints leave the states highly dependent on generator industry contributions to accomplish cleanup. Nevertheless, state enforcement does produce results at nonpriority sites that compare favorably to those at the priority sites. By the end of 1988, responsible parties financed 60 percent of response actions at a sample of 314 nonpriority sites in contrast to 24 percent of response actions at 821 priority sites (U.S. General Accounting Office, 1989a: 29). However, some of these cleanups may not be as protective of public health and the environment as priority site cleanups. Further, some may be of limited scope; EPA would characterize them as removal actions (U.S. General Accounting Office, 1989a: 28). To the extent that generators have been induced to participate in nonpriority site cleanups in exchange for state acceptance of inferior remedies, the protectiveness and efficiency of these state actions is diminished. EPA also has been criticized for its willingness to negotiate inferior remedies (see chapter 9). Given its fiscal and enforcement advantages, it is possible that EPA would need to make fewer concessions to secure responsible party settlement.

At priority sites, the federal program's dependence on state fiscal capacity also constrains cleanup progress. To accommodate a state's limited resources, the federal program must address fewer sites in that state or recommend less expensive remedies. When state resources are limited, EPA cannot use the threat of a fund-financed cleanup in negotiation and may be constrained to accept an inferior privately financed cleanup (as discussed in chapters 6 and 7). In the absence of state cost-sharing requirements, EPA could prioritize sites on the basis of risk posed and choose cost-efficient remedies to correct these problems. With state cost-sharing requirements, EPA is forced in some in-stances to exclude high-risk sites from consideration or to accept inferior remedies. Through all of these avenues, state budgetary constraints diminish the cleanup benefits derived per dollar of federal cleanup expenditure. The efficiency of the federal program suffers.

Dependency on state resources produces parallel inequities. The promise of equal protection from environmental threats becomes conditional upon the relative size of these resources. The cost of inaction at hazardous waste sites ends up falling more heavily on communities at risk in economically disadvantaged states while the corresponding benefits of inaction are conferred upon corporations responsible for site conditions in these same states.

It is difficult to brush aside the argument that the imposition of a fiscal burden on the states supports financial discipline. However, when the cost of state participation is excessive or when the opponents of cleanup can dominate state decision making, the efficiency gain from imposing such discipline on the states is more than off-set by the efficiency loss associated with not being able to respond when benefits exceed costs. In such circumstances, the financial burden placed on the states produces inefficient and inequitable results and exacerbates Superfund failure.

APPENDIX: FUNDING AND ENFORCEMENT

This appendix examines variation across states in two measures of program strength: funding and enforcement.[23] The 1983 Association of State and Territorial Solid Waste Management Officials (ASTSWMO) survey of state cleanup programs provides funding and enforcement data for thirty-three states. Estimation of a program funding equation is based on a sample of twenty-six states since data for all independent variables is not available for seven of the thirty-three states. Estimation of an enforcement equation is based on a sample of thirty-one states since data for all independent variables is not available for two of the thirty-three states.

State Funding

State program funding levels determine the potential to participate in the Superfund program and to take independent action at non–National Priorities List (non-NPL) sites. The analysis focuses specifically on funds available to state cleanup programs in 1983 (the dependent variable STFUND).[24] This year is chosen for two reasons. First, it is the only year in which ASTSWMO surveys report total state program funding levels. A 1988 survey reports an available balance, that is, the difference between total funding and total funds expended.[25] Second, the availability of funds in 1983 appears to predict the level of subsequent funding: 90 percent of the variation in non-NPL site progress as of 1988 is explained by variation in 1983 funding levels.[26] As direct a relationship between funding and progress is not observed at NPL sites. In contrast to the former relationship, the latter involves decisions at the federal as well as the state.level.

A state's optimal program funding level depends on environmental factors that determine the opportunity cost of inaction and economic factors that determine the opportunity cost of action. Greater funding is justified on efficiency grounds by more extensive threats to public health and the environment. Greater funding is also justified by a less binding state budget constraint. Conflict over distributional outcomes results in differences between actual and optimal funding levels that exceed those attributable to limited information and uncertainty. Actual funding levels reflect the relative political power of industry, labor, and environmental interests.

The environmental and public health costs associated with an absence of public funding depend, first, on the expected damage to population and sensitive environments associated with hazardous waste sites within state borders. Expected damage resulting from inaction increases with the number of NPL and non-NPL sites, the quantity and toxicity of waste, the likelihood of uncontrolled release, the multiplication of pathways linking released waste to receptor populations and sensitive environments, and the size of the population at risk. Expected damage is indicated by site characteristics contained in EPA's hazard ranking system (HRS) data base. EPA uses HRS data to score sites in terms of the potential risk faced by receptor populations via three media: contaminated air, surface water, and ground water. The scores are not absolute measures of expected damage and, therefore, cannot be summed over sites in a given state to determine total expected damage. However, the size of the population potentially exposed through each media is used by EPA to compute HRS scores and is used here to estimate the first component of the opportunity cost of inaction. The variable PRISK[27] is the percentage of each state's population potentially at risk from NPL site contamination, for those NPL sites known as of 1983. PRISK is a measure of expected damage generally available to each state at the time of program funding debates. Since the number of NPL sites is roughly proportionate to the number of non-NPL sites by state, PRISK approximates expected damage to state population from both NPL and non-NPL sites. The HRS data base does not contain an absolute measure of expected damage to sensitive environments.

The environmental cost of public inaction is reduced if potentially responsible parties (PRPs) will voluntarily undertake site cleanup. The likelihood of voluntary or cooperative private remedial action given existing state law is indicated by the extent to which state environmental protection is historically provided for by polluting industry expenditures. This likelihood is measured by the variable PVTPUB,[28] the ratio of private pollution control to public pollution control expenditures. With a highly responsive private sector, a given degree of cleanup activity can be achieved with a smaller allocation of public funds to cleanup and enforcement.

The environmental cost of inaction is also lower where a greater percentage of a state's NPL sites are owned by the federal government since the latter is expected to take full responsibility for these sites. As of 1983 approximately 7 percent of sites on the NPL were federal facilities. In 75 percent of the states, federal facilities account for more than 10 percent of NPL sites. A qualitative variable (FEDOWN)[29] distinguishes between these states and those for which federal facilities account for less then 10 percent of NPL sites. The former states will face a lower opportunity cost of inaction for a given size NPL and will need to allocate fewer funds to cleanup.

The opportunity cost of state action depends on the size of the state budget relative to cleanup needs. The higher are state revenues, the smaller is the sacrifice required in other state programs to satisfy given cleanup obligations, other factors remaining constant. State budget revenues in 1983 (the variable REVENUE)[30] measure the availability of public resources. Underlying weakness in the state's economy may make legislators less willing to expand state obligations and risk not being able to cover preexisting obligations. The major recession of 1981–82 makes this a particularly important consideration when focusing on legislative decisions in 1983. A qualitative variable (ECONOMY)[31] measures the degree to which each state suffered during the recession. It has a value of one for states experiencing no employment decrease over the 1980–82 period and a value of zero otherwise.

Enforcement-induced, involuntary private contributions to cleanup can substitute for publicly funded cleanup. The availability of these private resources depends on a firm's exposure to liability and its financial viability. The former depends substantially on the firm's contribution to waste generation. Firms in seven industries account for some 91 percent of hazardous waste generation in 1981: chemicals, petroleum and coal products, primary metals, fabricated metals, electric and electronic equipment, transportation equipment, and paper (see chapter 2). Under a strict, joint and several liability standard, large, financially viable firms in these industries are the most attractive targets for enforcement.

Financial viability is defined as the capacity to absorb cleanup costs out of current profits. Payment of one year's profits to finance cleanup is painful to the firm but will not generally threaten its long-term existence. Using this definition, and assuming an average $8.1 million cleanup cost, examination of *Census of Manufacturers* data on firm size suggests that a financially viable PRP is a firm with 500 or more employees.[32] The potential availability of PRP resources is measured by the percentage of firms in major generator industries, by state, that have 500 or more employees (the variable PRP).[33] The greater this percentage, the greater is a state's potential to achieve enforcement-induced privately financed cleanup and the smaller the state's need to provide for publicly financed cleanup.

Interested parties participate in funding and enforcement decisions in support of preferred distributions of program costs and benefits. Among generator industries, firms engaged in chemical and petroleum product manufacture (i.e., petrochemical industry firms) will be among the most active opponents of state hazardous waste program funding and enforcement since both hold out the potential to impose the cost of cleanup on these firms. The potential for firms in the chemical and petroleum industries to affect state funding and enforcement decisions is indicated by their share of total value added in each state's manufacturing industries (the variable INDUSTRY).[34]

Labor employed in the petrochemical industry may also attempt to influence state funding and enforcement decisions. The potential political influence of chemical and oil industry employees is indicated by their share of total employment in each state's manufacturing industries (the variable EMPLOY).[35]

Environmental advocacy groups serve as an organizational locus for the population at risk and act to promote their interests in legislative and enforcement decisions. The potential political influence exerted by environmental groups is indicated by total membership in four national environmental organizations (the Audubon Society, the Environmental Defense Fund, the Natural Resources Defense Council, the Sierra Club) as a percentage of state population (the variable ENVGRP).[36]

The size of environmental group membership is not independent of hazardous waste site issues. Environmental group membership grows in response to the need to exert political pressure to achieve environmental action goals. This implies that variation across states in membership per capita depends on some of the same factors that explain variation in program funding.[37] To test this hypothesis, environmental group membership is regressed on the proposed determinants of state funding with the exception of three variables not expected to affect membership: REVENUE, FEDOWN, and PRP.[38] The results are reported in table 5.2. Note that the low absolute values of the coefficients are due to the fact that the dependent variable is measured in per capita terms. The negative coefficient of PVTPUB suggests that environmental groups attract fewer members when the private sector is likely to address environmental problems in the absence of public sector pressure. The positive coefficient of INDUSTRY suggests that a greater representation of petrochemical industry firms in the state economy results in a greater perceived need for organization on the part of those concerned with environmental quality. The negative coefficient of EMPLOY suggests that environmental group membership will be lower when the representation of petrochemical industry employees in total manufacturing industry employment is greater. This result, in conjunction with the expectation that petrochemical industry labor supports strong state

Table 5.2. Determinants of Environmental Group Membership

	ENVGRP
Intercept	0.004 *** [7.82]
PRISK	0.002 [0.84]
PVTPUB	–0.045 ** [–1.87]
INDUSTRY	0.012 * [1.44]
EMPLOY	–0.041 ** [–2.00]
ECONOMY	0.001 * [1.39]
Adj. R^2	0.32
F	3.37
Condition Number	14

*Significant at .10   **Significant at .05   ***Significant at .01

action, indicates that unions serve as a political substitute for environmental groups. The positive sign on ECONOMY indicates that the priority placed on environmental issues increases when unemployment diminishes as a cause for popular concern. The coefficient of PRISK is not statistically significant. This is consistent with the argument that population at risk does not define an organized interest group.

The influence of environmental and economic costs and of political pressure on state funding decisions (STFUND) is estimated using ordinary least squares. Variables are expressed as natural logs, with the exception of the qualitative variables FEDOWN and ECONOMY.[39] This allows the coefficients of quantitative variables to be interpreted as elasticities (i.e., as a ratio of percentage change in dependent variable to percentage change in independent variable). Coefficients, therefore, indicate the relative responsiveness of change in dependent variable to change in an independent variable. Funding equation results are reported in table 5.3.[40] These results reflect central tendencies across states. The impacts of opportunity cost and political power are discussed in turn.

Growth in state budget revenues (REVENUE) produces a near proportionate growth in program funding. In contrast, program funding is only half as responsive to an expansion in the population at risk (PRISK). This implies that state program funding is generally inefficient. On efficiency grounds, an expansion in the opportunity cost of inaction (i.e., greater expected damages) justifies a proportionate expansion in the opportunity cost of action (i.e., a greater reduction in other goods and services to fund a public response).

Program funding is reduced when voluntary private action is more likely (as indicated by the negative relationship of STFUND to PVTPUB), when site problems are likely to be addressed by responsible federal agencies (as indicated by the negative relationship of STFUND to FEDOWN), and when recession makes state revenue growth less certain (as indicated by the positive relationship of STFUND to ECONOMY). The first two factors lower the cost of inaction while the last raises the cost of action. The availability of generator industry resources (PRP) does not bear a statistically significant relationship to the level of program funding. This suggests that, given the uncertainty involved in enforcement-induced contribution, state legislators do not consider the availability of private resources to be an easy substitute for budgeted cleanup revenues.

The funding equation suggests that both petrochemical industry capital (INDUSTRY) and labor (EMPLOY) have a substantial impact on program funding decisions. Although responsiveness to the efforts of labor is greater than to capital, the coefficents are close enough in value to indicate an effective counterbalance of political influence on average. At the same time, the relative ability of either interest to affect program funding decisions may be greater in some states and less in others. The measure of potential environmental group influence (ENVGRP) is not statistically significant.

State Enforcement

Enforcement actions are directed at increasing responsible party cleanup. The relative strength of state enforcement is measured by the number of hazardous waste sites (NPL and non-NPL) subject to enforcement actions taken between 1981 and 1983 per NPL site (the dependent variable ENFORCE).[41] The number of NPL sites is used in the denominator of ENFORCE for consistency with other data considered in the present analysis. ENFORCE is highly correlated with the number of responsible party negotiations and enforcement actions underway or completed at non-NPL sites by the end of 1988.[42]

Expected damage to public health and the environment will have an indirect impact on enforcement actions to the extent that greater damage justifies a larger program and a larger program supports more enforcement. However,

Table 5.3. Determinants of State Funding and Enforcement

	STFUNDS	ENFORCE
Intercept	8.92 [0.89]	12.07 * [1.79]
REVENUE	0.83 *** [3.46]	0.99 *** [3.41]
PRISK	0.52 ** [2.42]	
NPL83		0.57 ** [2.14]
PVTPUB	−0.59 * [−1.54]	0.23 [0.74]
FEDOWN	−1.79 *** [−2.64]	
PRP	−0.6 [−0.85]	1.94 ** [2.41]
ECONOMY	0.97 ** [1.80]	
INDUSTRY	−5.65 *** [−3.83]	−0.19 [−0.22]
EMPLOY	6.35 *** [3.70]	0.69 [0.71]
ENVGRP	0.58 [0.49]	2.11 *** [3.00]
Adj. R^2	0.62	0.64
F	5.63	8.77
Condition Number	175	120

*Significant at .10   **Significant at .05   ***Significant at .01

since the number of enforcement actions is more directly related to the number of sites than to the size of population at risk, the former is used to explain variation in the level of state enforcement effort. The variable NPL83[43] is the number of NPL sites, by state, as of 1983.

State budget revenues determine the potential to allocate state resources to enforcement while responsible party resources determine the potential to affect privately funded remedies. Conflict over the preferred distribution of cleanup costs between taxpayers and responsible parties also affects enforcement effort.

The variable REVENUE is preferable to STFUND as a measure of enforcement resource availability since not all states authorize the use of cleanup funds for enforcement purposes. As above, the variable PRP measures the private resources that can be attached through enforcement actions. The willingness of polluting industries to voluntarily contribute to the solution of environmental problems (indicated by the variable PVTPUB) can reduce the need for enforcement actions. The variables INDUSTRY, EMPLOY, and ENVGRP measure the ability of polluting industries, their employees, and environmental groups, respectively, to influence the level of enforcement activity.

The influence of environmental and economic costs and of political pressure on enforcement decisions (ENFORCE) is estimated using ordinary least squares. All variables are expressed as natural logs. Enforcement equation results appear in table 5.3.

Growth in state budget revenues (REVENUE) produces a near proportionate growth in enforcement actions. At the same time, enforcement actions are twice as responsive to the number of large, financially viable generator industry firms (PRP) and only half as responsive to expansion in the number of NPL sites (NPL83). Like funding decisions in general, enforcement activity is more responsive to available funds than to cleanup needs. The likelihood of voluntary industry contribution to cleanup does not appear to affect the level of enforcement action; the variable PVTPUB is not statistically significant. In contrast to the findings with respect to state program funding decisions, the enforcement equation suggests that environmental groups exert considerable influence on enforcement program activity while petrochemical industry capital and labor have no statistically significant impact.

EPA headquarters in Washington, D.C., is the locus of political-economic conflict over the direction and achievements of Superfund implementation. EPA regional offices are the locus of conflict over implementation at the site-specific level. Authority runs from Washington to the regions; accomplishments run from the regions to Washington. The more successful are the regions, the closer EPA comes to meeting its cleanup goals. There is variation across regional offices in their implementation of the Superfund mandate and in their corresponding accomplishments that in turn contribute substantially to Superfund progress at the national level.

Cleanup at Superfund sites is an outcome of decisions made by EPA headquarters and the regional offices in conjunction with decisions made by the states, affected communities, and responsible parties. Once a site is added to the National Priorities List, the region applies agency guidance to determine where lead responsibility for cleanup will reside. As discussed in more detail below, if no responsible parties are identified, lead responsibility is placed in the region's fund program and cleanup is financed out of the fund. If responsible parties are identified, lead responsibility is either placed in the region's enforcement program or delegated to a state enforcement program. Once lead responsibility is determined, the site proceeds through a number of stages outlined in the National Contingency Plan and elaborated upon in agency guidance documents: site conditions are investigated and the feasibility of alternative remedies are evaluated; a remedy is designed and implemented.

Cleanup decisions proceed under legislative and agency guidance on how clean is clean. Appropriate cleanup standards are selected and feasible remedies are examined that satisfy these standards. The role of cost considerations in choosing among alternative remedies is a source of substantial controversy. The cleanup selection procedure is to apply whether a site is placed in a fund- or enforcement-lead program.

Negotiations with responsible parties for cleanup at sites placed in an enforcement program are guided by agency settlement policy. Settlement policy stipulates the goals the region is to pursue in negotiations and the use of enforcement powers to achieve these goals.

This chapter begins with discussion of the regional office role within the web of decision making. I then examine two regional outcomes that are important for understanding overall Superfund progress. The first is regional office determination of whether cleanup at each site will proceed under the lead of the federal fund program, the federal enforcement program, or a state enforcement program. As demonstrated in the next chapter, this decision has far-reaching implications in terms of the ultimate cleanup remedy selected at each site. I argue that lead responsibility decisions are conditioned by the allocation of EPA resources to the regions, the availability of state and responsible party resources, and the risk posed to human health and the environment. The second outcome is regional office progress in execution of cleanup at fund-lead sites and regional office progress in effectuating settlement at federal enforcement-lead sites. I discuss guidance on how clean is clean and on settlement policy as constraints on regional discretion and then argue that variation in progress is related to regional interpretation and implementation of settlement policy and to the availability of state cleanup resources. The analysis in chapter 7 demonstrates that regional progress is a primary factor in fund and enforcement outcomes at the site-specific level.

The analysis in this chapter concentrates on the first five years of the Superfund program, 1981–85. It provides a lead into the more general discussion of Superfund success and failure over this same time period in the following chapter. It also highlights agency strategy on the eve of the Superfund reauthorization debate as discussed in chapter 8.

THE REGION'S WORLD

The agency's world is dominated by Congress, the Office of Management and Budget, industrial and environmental interest groups, and the courts. The region's world is dominated by the agency, the states, localities, and those who are potentially liable for the costs of cleanup. The regional offices can be viewed conceptually as mini-agencies; they pursue a set of objectives subject to legal, policy, and resource constraints. Their mandate is essentially the same as

EPA's: to minimize threats to public health and the environment and to maximize responsible party contributions to cleanup.

The regions mirror the agency in pursuing a degree of autonomy and discretion. Like the federal/state government relationship, the agency/ regional-office relationship produces both symbiosis and tension. The regions are dependent on the agency for guidance and resources. Their power derives, in part, from the strength of agency support for their decisions and actions. The agency is dependent on the regions for converting often vague guidelines into effective site-specific accomplishments. Regional staff often perceive the agency as an essentially political creature. They criticize Washington policy decisions as out of touch with implementation realities and top Washington administrators for allowing responsible parties to go over the heads of regional administrators. Washington staff in turn differentiate regions in terms of their aggressiveness, ability to innovate, and effective use of agency resources. In an uncharacteristic public critique, the director of EPA's Office of Waste Program Enforcement once accused regional staff of too slavishly adhering to agency enforcement guidance despite headquarters efforts to implement a new policy direction (Lucero, 1988: 9–10). While acknowledging problems with agency policy, the director laid substantial blame for program failure at the door of the regional offices.

The relationship between EPA headquarters and the regional offices has undergone considerable change. During the first two years of the program, regional autonomy was severely restricted by centralization of decision-making power in Washington. The absence of strong agency support forced regional staff to make their own accommodations in the web of relationships at each site (Anderson, 1985: 307, n. 173). Following the replacement of Administrator Burford, decentralization provided the regions with considerable discretion, in particular with respect to enforcement decisions. By 1989 critical studies were attributing Superfund failure in part to excessive regional flexibility.

Despite decentralization and enhanced flexibility, the regions are far from autonomous. On the one hand, regional action is constrained by the remedial and removal guidelines contained in the National Contingency Plan and by supplemental headquarters guidance on major aspects of fund-financed and enforcement decision making. On the other hand, regional action is constrained by state funding and enforcement decisions; by the resources and cooperation/recalcitrance of potentially responsible parties; by community pressure for swift and effective cleanup actions; and by the environmental conditions and available technologies that shape cleanup decisions. While guidance from Washington pushes the regions toward uniformity in their fund and enforcement programs, the diversity of pressures operating at the regional level pushes them toward selection of strategies which can achieve agency expectations within unique regional political-economic contexts.

SITE LEAD RESPONSIBILITIES

As of March 1986, 813 nonfederal sites were added to or proposed for the National Priorities List. Region 2 (New York, New Jersey, and Puerto Rico) and Region 5 (the Great Lakes states) account for 45 percent of these NPL sites. In contrast, Region 7 (Iowa, Kansas, Missouri, and Nebraska), Region 8 (Utah, Colorado, and the Northern Plains states), and Region 10 (the Pacific Northwest) account for only 12 percent. Viewed geographically, nearly 75 percent of priority sites are east of the Mississippi River.

Once a site is added to the priority list, the region must determine where lead responsibility for cleanup will reside. If cleanup is to be financed solely through the fund, the site is designated a *fund-lead* site and is the responsibility of the region's fund program. If responsible parties are targeted to conduct cleanup, the site is designated an *enforcement-lead* site and is the responsibility of the region's enforcement program. If enforcement action is to be undertaken by a state agency, the site is designated a *state-lead enforcement* site. Responsibility resides with the state program, although EPA retains an oversight role.

This section discusses the criteria the regions apply in determining lead responsibility. Based on these criteria I place each National Priorities List site into one of the above lead categories or into a residual *no action* category. Using this categorization I then identify major factors that influence whether any cleanup activity was initiated prior to 1986 and whether the lead for enforcement resides with a regional program or a state. In the next section, lead responsibility categorization provides the basis for examining regional progress in fund and enforcement programs.

Under EPA's initial fund-conserving strategy, the presence of at least one financially viable responsible party required that a site be placed in the enforcement program. This strategy resulted in most sites being classified as enforcement sites. Combined with the agency's nonconfrontational, voluntary compliance enforcement strategy, it also resulted in minimal progress. At the regional level it often produced frustration. For example, a Region 9 project manager reported that the Mountain View Mobile Home site (Globe, Arizona) first had to be addressed as an enforcement site even though the sole owner was known to be bankrupt. The site was subsequently (and with implementation delay) transferred to the fund program.[1]

In 1982 EPA experimented with a dual-track system involving both fund and enforcement program staff activity at a given site. This approach resulted in considerable duplication of effort. In June 1983 EPA adopted its current site classification system. Sites are divided into four categories based primarily on the strength and likelihood of success of the enforcement case, the need for prompt response, and the ability of the states to provide the necessary statutory assurances to begin fund-financed actions (U.S. Environmental Protection Agency, 1984a: 4-3).

Category I includes sites where no financially viable responsible parties are identified. Only fund-financed activity is to be conducted at these sites. As of late 1984, 15 percent of priority sites were placed in the fund-lead category. Category II includes sites where the case against responsible parties is strong and there is no urgent need to begin remedial action. Negotiations are initiated and if no settlement is reached, the regions are directed to use civil or administrative authority to compel responsible party action. Generally, fund money will be spent only on a site remedial investigation/feasibility study that can serve as a basis for negotiation. As of late 1984, 32 percent of priority sites were classified as Category II enforcement-lead. EPA directed the regions to place their best enforcement sites in this category. Category III includes sites where the need for action is urgent and there is only limited time for negotiations before response action must begin. If no settlement is reached within a specified time frame, the region may issue a unilateral order to compel responsible party cleanup. If responsible parties fail to comply, the region can proceed with a fund-financed cleanup and then seek to recover response costs and impose treble damage penalties. In late 1984, 28 percent of priority sites were classified as Category III enforcement sites. Category IV includes state-lead enforcement sites where the region's role is limited to oversight and technical enforcement. The remaining 25 percent of NPL sites were placed in this category in late 1984.

Placement of sites into the first three categories is at the region's discretion. In contrast, placement of sites into the state-lead enforcement category depends on communication, information sharing, and coordination between regional offices and the states. EPA has lamented the absence of consistent regional efforts to consult with the states (U.S. Environmental Protection Agency, 1984g: 7). While EPA favors state-lead enforcement activity to free up regional enforcement resources, it also recognizes that state enforcement resources are generally inadequate. EPA's late-1984 site classifications clearly demonstrate the importance of federal and state enforcement to the achievement of Superfund goals. The regional offices were expected to achieve responsible party–financed cleanup at 60 percent of priority sites while the states were expected to achieve responsible party–financed cleanup at an additional 25 percent of these sites.

EPA does not publish a list of site-specific categories since the classification of each site may change over time. Examination of regional action therefore requires development of a comparable classification scheme. Following the logic of EPA's scheme, I have placed nonfederal National Priorities List sites into four categories. A site is categorized as *fund-lead* (34.4 percent of the total) if the region has obligated the fund to finance one or more phases of the cleanup process[2] and if precleanup studies at the site are not designated as in support of a subsequent enforcement action (i.e., they are not enforcement-lead studies as in EPA's categories II and III). These sites have no recorded federal enforcement action, although some do have state enforcement activity. A site is categorized as *enforcement-lead* (34.3 percent of the total) if there are recorded federal enforcement actions or if the fund has been obligated to conduct investigations in support of subsequent enforcement activity (e.g., negotiation). State as well as federal enforcement activity may be conducted at these sites. A site is categorized as *state-lead enforcement* (13.2 percent of the total) if there are recorded state negotiations, settlements, or litigation activity. In contrast to sites placed in the above categories, these sites have no obligations from the fund nor do they have a recorded federal enforcement activity. Finally, a site is placed in a residual *no action* category (18.1 percent of the total) if there is no recorded fund, federal enforcement, or state enforcement activity. Some of these sites may have on-going though unreported federal negotiations which have not yet resulted in a settlement or a unilateral order or may be in a prelitigation planning stage.[3]

There is significant variation in the percentage of sites in each region falling within these categories (see figure 6.1).[4] For example, Region 6 (where Texas accounts for over half of the region's priority sites) has 51 percent of its sites in the fund program and 44 percent in the enforcement program. There are no state-lead enforcement sites and only 4 percent are no action sites. In contrast, Region 5 has 24 percent of its sites in the fund program and 33 percent in the enforcement program; 16 percent are state-lead enforcement and 28 percent are no action sites.

In the remainder of this section. I examine four factors that affect whether or not a site falls within the no action category and whether the region or a state takes the lead in enforcement activity. These factors are federal resource constraints, state resource constraints, the presence of financially viable responsible parties, and priority site conditions.[5]

Federal Resources

Allocations of personnel and fund resources to the regions set a limit on the number of sites that can be passed through the cleanup pipeline. Allocations

Figure 6.1. Regional Site Classification

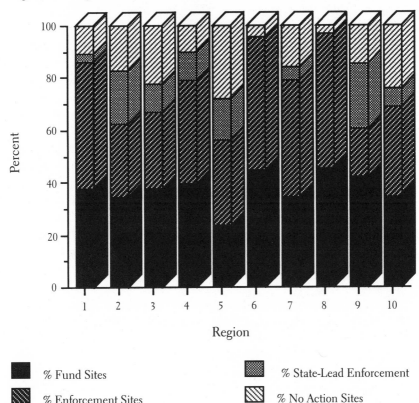

% Fund Sites

% Enforcement Sites

% State-Lead Enforcement

% No Action Sites

Source: Author's computations from U.S. Environmental Protection Agency data.

are based on the planned activities contained in each region's Superfund Comprehensive Accomplishment Plan (SCAP) submittal to the agency. The SCAP specifies planned activities at fund- and enforcement-lead sites. Personnel for fund-lead sites are allocated on the basis of the number of priority sites involved and the number of staff necessary to conduct specified activities.

The allocation of staff to enforcement-lead sites involves a more speculative procedure than that required for fund-lead sites. Early in the program, these allocations were made simply on the basis of the number of priority sites in the region. As EPA acquired more experience with the enforcement process, a work load model was developed for the allocation of enforcement staff. Using national data, EPA estimated the percentage of enforcement-lead sites which would require specific activities and the number of staff required to conduct each activity. The work load model was then applied to the plans contained in the SCAP to determine each region's staff requirement.[6]

There are several reasons to expect that the allocation of enforcement staff positions to the regions will produce variation in regional lead responsibility. First, if regional aggressiveness in completing work or in taking legal action does not fit the national pattern, the region can face an unequal resource constraint. Second, the work load model assumes that enforcement resources can expand to meet regional needs. When this is not the case, limited agency enforcement resources must constrain regional action. If the agency is compelled to fund some minimal level of enforcement in all regions, regional offices that are more aggressive or that have a larger number of priority sites will face a relatively more restrictive enforcement resource constraint.

A differential regional enforcement staff constraint seem most likely given EPA's continuous problems of understaffing and turnover. Outlays for enforcement increased from $1.6 million in 1981 to $5.4 million in 1984 and then jumped to $22.1 million in 1985 and $45.4 million in 1986. However, growth in enforcement outlays relative to outlays for cleanup expenditures reveal a less impressive pattern: the ratio increased from 5.4 percent in 1981 to 9.3 percent in 1983, then decreased to 4.5 percent in 1984 and rose to 11 percent in 1985 (Acton, 1989: 37). Regional enforcement staff requests to the agency generally have exceeded EPA requests to the Office of Management and Budget. While Congress has replaced positions, the final number of regional enforcement staff still falls short of regional estimates. For example, the regions requested 463 staff positions for fiscal year 1986. The agency, in turn, requested 423 and the Office of Management and Budget approved 379. Congress then approved 426, leaving the regions about 8 percent short (U.S. General Accounting Office, 1986a: 9).

In response to congressional concern over the impact of a staff constraint on the level of enforcement activity, the General Accounting Office documented the consequences of understaffing in the Office of Regional Counsel (U.S. General Accounting Office, 1986a: 14–17). Region 1 (New England) reported reductions in legal support for responsible party searches, removals, and oversight of cleanup studies. It also reported that in four of thirty-seven ongoing negotiations, responsible parties had agreed to conduct studies, but no attorney was available to sign the necessary documents so that work could begin. Another region reported that an enforcement decision document could not withstand legal scrutiny—the attorney lacked time to review the work plan, which did not contain a necessary wetlands and flood plan assessment. Most regions reported backlogs and delays in processing administrative orders or substantial overtime by attorneys. At the beginning of fiscal 1985, Region 2 had a backlog of sixty-two unresolved administrative orders.

A subsequent General Accounting Office report highlighted project manager work load and attrition as factors in inadequate oversight of responsible party cleanup (U.S. General Accounting Office, 1986b). Each fund-lead and enforcement-lead site is assigned to a project manager who has considerable latitude in selecting and establishing methods for resolving complex waste site problems and in determining individual work priorities:

> [Enforcement-lead site] project managers have numerous duties and responsibilities that place competing demands on their time. In addition to settlement oversight, they are responsible for coordinating the technical development of enforcement actions and other related activities. These activities can include collecting and evaluating data on responsible parties and informing them of their liabilities; preparing reports supporting recommendations for enforcement actions; participating in or leading technical negotiations in attempts to obtain responsible party cleanups; preparing and coordinating civil and administrative enforcement actions; conferring with EPA and Department of Justice attorneys; participating in formal hearings and trials, and internal meetings to discuss enforcement cases; directing contractors to perform technical-engineering studies supporting enforcement actions; evaluating state enforcement response to hazardous waste site problems; attending public meetings and responding to inquiries from citizens, state and facility officials, the Congress, EPA, and the press concerning enforcement efforts. (U.S. General Accounting Office, 1986b: 25)

Many of these responsibilities also fall on fund-lead site project managers.

The study found that twenty-four out of twenty-six project managers interviewed in three regions were responsible for multiple sites. Ten were responsible for six to ten sites, four were responsible for eleven to fifteen sites, and one was responsible for sixteen to twenty sites. Heavy work loads caused delay and contributed to incorrect decisions. Further, unstable work environments reduced the effectiveness of these key personnel. Regional officials told the General Accounting Office that EPA's program "has been characterized by regional reorganizations, project manager attrition, project manager rotation among priority sites, and an influx of new and inexperienced project managers" (U.S. General Accounting Office, 1986b: 28).[7] The problems posed by attrition and rotation were magnified by the poor condition of settlement records and files. A new project manager would have only a limited basis for reconstructing a site's action history.

EPA's enforcement staffing problems are manifest in the ability of the regions to take action at their priority sites. A statistical analysis of site classification shows that attorney and enforcement staff allocations to the regions are

Figure 6.2. Probability of No Action

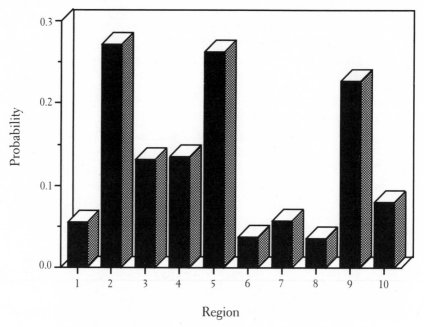

Source: Author's computations from U.S. Environmental Protection Agency data.

a primary determinant of whether any action has been initiated at a region's priority sites (see the appendix to this chapter). A site located in a region with a high ratio of attorneys to priority sites (for example, Region 8) has less than a 10 percent chance of being a no action site while a site located in a region with a low ratio of attorneys to priority sites (for example, Regions 2 and 5) has around a 30 percent chance. Since classification as fund- or enforcement-lead requires a responsible party search, limits on enforcement personnel restrict the assignment of sites to either category.[8] The probability of a site in each region being a no action site is presented in figure 6.2.

Attorney and enforcement staff levels are also a primary determinant of whether enforcement-lead responsibilities are federal or state. A site located in a region with a high ratio of attorneys to priority sites has about an 85 percent chance of being a federal enforcement-lead site while a site located in a region with a low ratio of attorneys to priority sites has around a 45 percent chance of being a federal enforcement-lead site. The probability of a site in each region being a federal enforcement-lead site is presented in figure 6.3.

Figure 6.3. Probability of Federal Enforcement

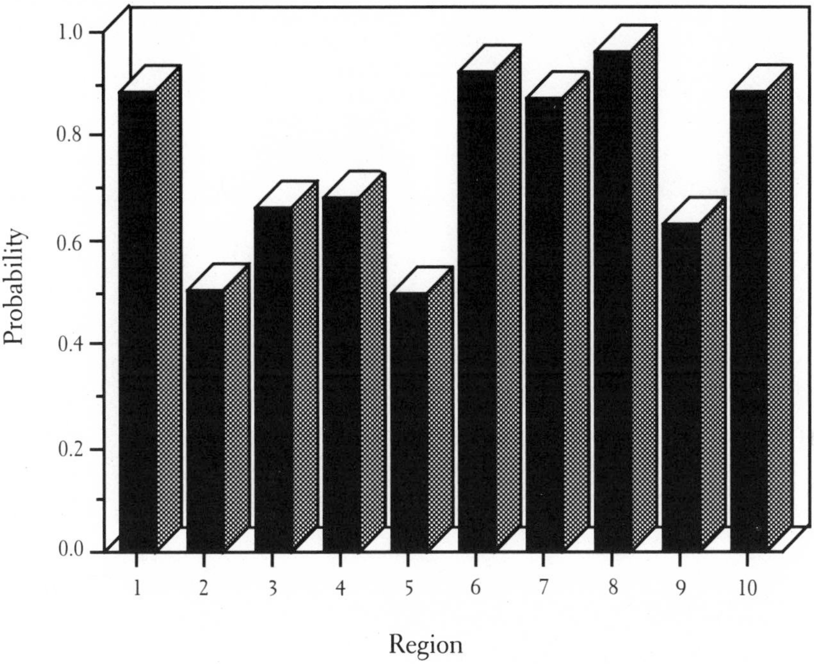

State Resources

State priorities and the availability of state resources also affect the determination of lead responsibility. As discussed in chapter 5, a state's capacity to share in the cost of cleanup and to run an effective enforcement program is primarily determined by state funding decisions. Given funding, a state can choose the fund-lead sites where it will guarantee to share costs and, within limits imposed by the regional office, can choose sites as state-lead enforcement. EPA guidance recommends that if it is unlikely that a state can cover its share of remedial action costs at a site, the region should not classify that site as fund-lead. Region 5 reports that municipal 50 percent cost-share sites are placed in the enforcement-lead category when state resources are limited.[9]

A statistical analysis reported in the appendix shows that the availability of state resources per state priority site affects the classification of a region's sites as federal- or state-lead enforcement. Where states have adequate financial resources, a larger percentage of a region's enforcement sites are state-lead enforcement. In these regions, state enforcement activity substitutes for federal activity and, in the process, frees up federal enforcement resources.

Industry Resources

The financial viability of responsible parties affects the potential for regional enforcement program accomplishments. Under EPA's site classification system, a site will only be designated fund-lead if no viable responsible parties are identified. In contrast, the classification presented in figure 6.1 assigns sites to the enforcement-lead category if an enforcement action was recorded by early 1986. Statistical analysis shows that responsible party financial viability is the second most important determinant of whether any action is taken at a region's priority sites. A site located in a region with a large pool of generator industry resources per priority sites (for example, Region 4) has about a 12 percent chance of being a no action site while a site located in a region with a small pool of generator industry resources per priority sites (for example, Region 8) has around a 19 percent chance of being a no action site.

Site Conditions

The nature of uncontrolled release problems at priority sites also affects classification. Hazard ranking system (HRS) scores are an important factor in regional selection of sites for study and remediation; EPA considers higher scores as indicative of a greater threat to public health and the environment.[10] The total HRS score reflects the threat of contamination posed via air, surface water, and ground water pathways. A statistical analysis shows that a site is somewhat less likely to be a no action site if it has a higher total HRS score. At the same time, a site is somewhat more likely to be a no action site if it has a higher ground water score. As discussed in chapter 7, the latter finding reflects agency preference for addressing surface over subsurface contamination problems and the tendency of host communities to exert more pressure for action when the threat is visibly on the surface, rather than hidden below the surface.

PROGRESS AT FUND AND ENFORCEMENT SITES

Evaluation of regional office progress requires measures of contribution to primary Superfund goals: the minimization of risk posed to human health and the environment and the maximization of responsible party cleanup activity. Measuring progress relative to the first goal is complicated by disagreement on the appropriateness of alternative cleanup standards, the role of cost in choosing among alternative remedies, and the degree of preference to be accorded permanent versus short-term containment remedies. Measuring progress relative to the second goal is complicated by the above considerations as well as by disagreement on the appropriate incentives to offer responsible parties in exchange for a settlement and the use of threats to induce settlement in face of recalcitrance.

Ideally, a measure of progress toward the first goal would quantify the degree to which cleanup affords protection to exposed populations from hazardous waste site risks. A measure of progress toward the second goal would quantify the contribution of responsible parties to risk minimization at sites where there are private responsible parties. Unfortunately, data does not exist to construct either measure. After consideration of several alternatives, [11] I have chosen to measure progress toward risk minimization in terms of phases of the cleanup process that are initiated. [12] This narrow measure is applied at sites within the region's fund and enforcement programs.

Regional progress toward the second goal, maximization of responsible party cleanup, involves a further distinction. The intent of EPA settlement policy is to achieve negotiated, voluntary, private party cleanup through application of incentives and threats. Responsible party recalcitrance necessitates stronger enforcement actions including litigation. Settlements achieved through voluntarism are preferable to those achieved through protracted conflict to the extent that the latter can involve greater delay and higher transaction costs. Enforcement sites are therefore divided into those with voluntary settlements and those with additional conflict. Progress is then measured at sites within each category.

In the remainder of this section I discuss the construction of progress indices and examine several reasons for variation in progress across regions. In the next chapter, relative regional progress is shown to be a major determinant of program achievements at the national level.

Cleanup follows a sequence of phases outlined in the National Contingency Plan. [13] A detailed remedial investigation/feasibility study (RIFS) is conducted to determine the nature of contaminant constituents, pathways, and risks at the site and to propose alternatives for cleanup. A record of decision (ROD) is published that summarizes site conditions and alternative remedies and reports the basis for choosing a specific remedy. The development of cleanup alternatives involves selection of a set of standards that are likely to satisfy legislative and agency guidance on how clean is clean and selection of cleanup technologies that will meet these standards. It also involves evaluation of alternatives relative to their cost. The selected remedy is designed in the remedial design (RD) phase and implemented in the remedial action (RA) phase. At any point during this process, a short-term removal action may be undertaken when a release or threatened release occurs. A more extensive emergency interim remedial action (IRM) may be conducted before a permanent remedy is selected if it is necessary to limit exposure to a significant health or environmental hazard.

For the purposes of this study, a phase is considered to be initiated at a fund-lead site if EPA has obligated funds for that specific activity.[14] For enforcement-lead sites, a phase is considered to be initiated if EPA has obligated funds or if the activity is stipulated in a signed agreement or decree, a unilateral order, or in a case filed by the Justice Department. While obligations at fund-lead sites generally imply that a specific phase of work has begun, the issuance of a unilateral order or the filing of a case by the Justice Department may involve some lag time before responsible parties begin the required work. Where litigation is involved, the lag can be substantial.

To summarize progress in initiating phases of the cleanup process, I have calculated fund and enforcement scores for each region. The score is the weighted value of work initiated as a percentage of the work that needs to be completed. The weights are based, in general, on the cost of each phase relative to the total cost of cleanup. The exception is the weight placed on remedial action. While this phase is expected to comprise about 80 percent of the total cost of cleanup (prior to reauthorization in 1986), construction may take about as long as to complete as the remedial investigation/feasibility study (Association of State and Territorial Solid Waste Management Officials, 1987: 27–40). Remedial action, therefore, is assigned a weight some 4.5 times that assigned to these studies, in contrast to the 9:1 ratio implied by expected cost. The scores therefore measure progress in terms of both time and money.[15] The average regional fund score (.17) suggests that 17 percent of necessary cleanup activity was initiated at 280 final or proposed fund-lead priority sites by early 1986. The average enforcement score (.38) suggests that 38 percent of necessary cleanup activity was initiated or required at 279 final or proposed enforcement-lead priority sites by this date.

The regional fund and enforcement scores (presented in figure 6.4) indicate considerable variation in progress across regions. There is greater variation for fund-lead sites than for enforcement-lead sites. For the former, regions which have progressed further in initiating remedial design and remedial action generally have higher scores. There is less variation in initiation of studies and removals. For enforcement sites, there is no clear relationship between scores and initiation of a specific phase.

Regional enforcement scores do not distinguish between actions resulting in

Figure 6.4. Regional Fund and Enforcement Scores

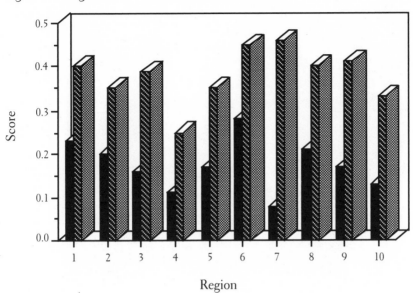

Source: Author's computations from U.S. Environmental Protection Agency data.

voluntary settlement and actions where compliance results from additional coercion. As discussed above, voluntary settlements are likely to involve less delay and lower transaction costs than those achieved through conflict. EPA considers actions that result in signed administrative orders or consent decrees to be voluntary settlements. In contrast, actions that result in the issuance of unilateral orders or in case referrals to the Justice Department involve conflict. The threat of a treble damage penalty may be required to induce responsible party action. Some responsible parties are reported to prefer unilateral to signed orders; they wish to appear forced into action by EPA to demonstrate subsequently that they did not accept liability for site conditions.[16]

To draw this distinction, settlement and conflict scores are calculated for each region using the method described above and are presented in figure 6.5. The total number of enforcement sites appears in the denominator in computing scores. The settlement score represents the weighted percentage of necessary cleanup activity at enforcement-lead sites which is voluntarily agreed to by responsible parties. The conflict score represents the weighted percentage of

Figure 6.5. Regional Settlement and Conflict Scores

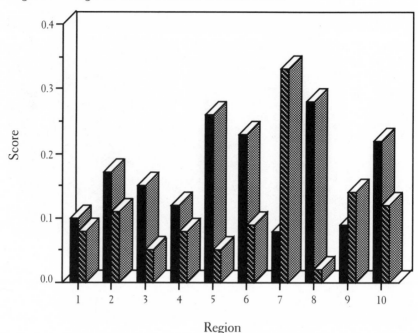

Region

■ Settlement Score   ▨ Conflict Score

Source: Author's computations from U.S. Environmental Protection Agency data.

necessary cleanup activity at those sites where responsible party contribution requires added coercion. The scores indicate that responsible parties on average have agreed to fund or perform 17 percent of necessary cleanup activity and are involved in active or passive conflict over an additional 11 percent.

Variation in regional fund and enforcement outcomes reflects a complex of factors discussed below: the discretion inherent in agency remedy selection and settlement policy guidance to the regions, state and responsible party resources and decisions that constrain regional action, and the approach each region adopts to balance agency expectations against state and responsible party goals.

How Clean Is Clean?

Guidance on evaluation of cleanup remedies applies to all sites whether assigned to a region's fund or enforcement program and is at the heart of the how-clean-is-clean debate. In a departure from environmental legislation of the 1970s, the Superfund Act neither stipulated standards for cleanup at hazardous waste sites nor required that standards in other environmental laws be applied to Superfund cleanups. Congress did require that a plan for implementing Superfund cleanup authority be incorporated into the National Contingency Plan (NCP) and that EPA cleanup response be consistent with the plan. However, when issued in 1982, the National Contingency Plan did not provide cleanup standards. It simply stipulated that the Superfund remedial action chosen at any hazardous waste site be "the lowest cost alternative which effectively mitigates and minimizes damage to and provides adequate protection of public health, welfare and the environment" (U.S. Environmental Protection Agency, 1982b: 31182). The range of alternatives included no action, on-site containment of waste, and total site cleanup. No level of cleanup was stipulated for wastes remaining on site in the form of contaminated soil or ground water.

The 1982 National Contingency Plan provided considerable flexibility in the selection of cleanup remedies, but little effective guidance. In a 1983 report, the Office of Technology Assessment noted that "Superfund cleanups under the NCP's flexible standards of protection may not result in removal of toxic substances from the site. . . . Each decision will be made on an ad hoc basis; each site will be treated as unique."[17] The report went on to say that while the NCP requires cost-effectiveness and the minimization of damages, it does not define how the effectiveness of the alternative is measured or what level of protection of the public and the environment is adequate. The report also drew attention to the fact that "[u]nder NCP, existence of contaminant levels that would require corrective action at permitted land disposal facilities under [Resource Conservation and Recovery Act] regulations could, conceivably, be allowed to continue after remedial response actions or without any remedial action being taken." Finally, the report pointed out that the NCP did not specify the time period over which the remedy must be effective and, consequently, created a conflict between the federal and state governments over aggregate cost shares. State governments were concerned that "EPA may select less expensive, incomplete remedial actions that leave the states open to substantially greater costs in the long run, instead of a more expensive permanent remedy that removes or completely cleans up the problem caused by the hazardous substance."

As EPA cleanup activity increased after the replacement of Administrator Burford, congressional concern over cleanup decisions also increased. In several of its reports to Congress, the General Accounting Office pointed to the absence of environmental standards as a major problem in making cost-effectiveness determinations. The director of the Superfund program was quoted as stating that choosing site cleanups where there are no applicable numerical standards—mostly where there is extensive ground water or soil contamination—is the most difficult Superfund policy decision facing EPA (reported in U.S. General Accounting Office, 1985c: 40). The Region 2 Hazardous Waste Site Branch chief told GAO that if cleanup standards existed, a consultant's scope of work could include identifying and determining the cost-effectiveness of a range of alternatives that would accomplish those levels of cleanup. In the absence of such standards, consultants identify remedial alternatives that accomplish various levels of problem mitigation and then decide on which alternative provides the most mitigation for the cost involved. He characterized this approach as more cost-benefit than cost-effectiveness analysis (U.S. General Accounting Office, 1984d: 15).

The Office of Technology Assessment reviewed remedies at four Superfund sites for its 1985 *Superfund Strategy* report and found that all remedial strategies were based primarily on waste containment and ground water treatment rather than on waste removal and treatment.[18] The cost of a complete site cleanup appeared to be a factor at the Love Canal (Niagara Falls, New York) and Seymour (Seymour, Indiana) sites. At the Stringfellow site (Glen Avon Heights, California), incorrect assumptions formed the basis for a remedial action decision that proved to be ineffective. OTA noted that "[l]ittle consideration was given to the long-term effectiveness of containment, continually increasing operating and maintenance costs, possibilities of containment failures and continuing ground water contamination, and practical problems resulting from the very long times (hundreds to thousands of years) required to manage these hazardous waste sites." The Sylvester site (Nashua, New Hampshire) was the only one where environmental goals were set prior to remedial action. The report concluded that EPA's "current ad hoc, highly flexible, and nonspecific approach" was not satisfactory and that more explicit attention was warranted for this issue at the highest policy levels. It emphasized that "[w]ithout clear and well-supported cleanup goals the selection of cleanup technologies and the ultimate evaluation of cleanup performance will remain contentious" (U.S. Office of Technology Assessment, 1985: 17).

In 1984 EPA reached settlement of a 1982 lawsuit brought by the Environmental Defense Fund and the state of New Jersey that challenged the National Contingency Plan in federal court. At issue was the failure of the NCP to specify cleanup to appropriate health and environmental standards. EPA agreed to propose amendments to the plan so that relevant quantitative health and environmental standards and criteria developed by EPA under other programs could be used in determining the extent of remedy at hazardous waste sites. The cornerstone of the agency's 1985 revision to the plan was the stipulation that response actions attain or exceed applicable or relevant and appropriate federal requirements (ARARs). Applicable requirements are federal standards that guide a response action if not taken under Superfund authority. Relevant and appropriate standards are federal requirements that are designed to apply to problems sufficiently similar to those encountered at Superfund sites that their application is appropriate. The determination of standards would be made on a case-by-case basis (U.S. Environmental Protection Agency, 1982b: 47918–19).

Comments on the draft version of the 1985 National Contingency Plan revision recapitulated the on-going controversy over cleanup costs and cleanup effectiveness. Critiques delivered to the agency were also presented in congressional hearings on Superfund reauthorization issues. Responsible parties and their representatives, desiring minimal standards as a means to reduce settlement costs, argued that the revised policy was too stringent. Local community and environmental advocacy groups, desiring maximum standards as a means to protect public health and the environment, argued that flexibility would lead to excessive leniency. The revision was criticized by the states and other commentators (for example, the Office of Technology Assessment) for not requiring that state as well as federal standards be considered, in particular when the former were more stringent. EPA stated that state standards would be seriously considered and argued that it should not be bound by stricter state standards nor should the fund necessarily bear the additional cost of attaining these standards (U.S. Environmental Protection Agency, 1982b: 47923). If a state desired that its stricter standards apply, it could cover the increased cost of cleanup when the agency chose to apply less strict federal standards.

The absence of clear guidelines in the 1982 plan enhanced the scope for regional discretion at the site-specific level and reduced the likelihood of consistency in remedy selection. The regions were essentially expected to conduct cost-benefit analyses under a set of guidelines couched in terms of cost-effectiveness. Early records of decision manifest the absence of guidance in their litanies of a selection methodology. The language of EPA's vague guidance appears as the reason for selecting a preferred remedy. The 1985 plan provided a basis for a cost-effectiveness evaluation of alternatives that would afford protection to public health and the environment. The regions still could exercise discretion in selection of standards on a case-by-case basis. They still would have to contend with the inadequacy of federal standards for safe levels of exposure to a multitude of hazardous substances and with a wide variance in formal and informal state standards.

Settlement Policy

EPA's settlement policy defines its strategy for achieving responsible party contribution to hazardous waste site cleanup and its conditions for settlement.

The agency desires maximum control over settlement terms and the cleanup process since it bears ultimate responsibility for program outcomes. In contrast, responsible parties desire latitude in the range of issues subject to negotiation, the potential to settle at minimum cost, and the finality of release from future liability.

Settlement policy has undergone several substantive revisions over the life of the program. Under the initial fund-conserving strategy (1981 to mid-1983) discussed in chapter 4, the agency was willing to negotiate every cleanup issue but provided little motivation for negotiation or settlement. While a number of major settlements were secured, the agency was severely criticized for its generosity to responsible parties, in particular for granting release from future liability in exchange for short-term cleanup actions.[19] The strategy centralized enforcement decisions in Washington and left the regions with minimal discretion. Less than 25 percent of the actions recorded by early 1986 were initiated during this period.

In 1983, in the wake of Sewergate, EPA abandoned this discredited settlement policy and formulated one that was more aggressive. The agency stated that it would not entertain settlements for less than 100 percent of site cleanup costs, although this was modified to an 80 percent threshold by late 1983. Responsible parties could perform site studies only if they would agree to implement the selected remedy. The agency would not use the fund to cover orphan shares (i.e., the share not attributable to known and financially viable responsible parties) and shied away from granting a release from future liability. This policy drew substantial criticism from responsible parties who claimed that it fostered litigation and discouraged voluntary cleanup. The policy did not necessarily make settlement a less costly alternative to accepting the high transaction costs of litigation.

In 1984, in response to this criticism, EPA proposed a new settlement policy emphasizing use of the fund as an incentive for responsible party financial contribution and cleanup.[20] The agency characterized this policy as more conciliatory and a reflection of the government's growing flexibility in negotiation. While the accompanying decentralization of enforcement decisions afforded the regions a greater role in the settlement process, the settlement issues over which they could exercise discretion were narrowly circumscribed. The agency wished to avoid settlements which would subject it to renewed congressional criticism (Anderson, 1985: 298). Responsible parties found the policy to be more flexible in principle than in practice.

Negotiations could proceed only if the initial responsible party offer represented a substantial portion of cleanup costs or of the remedial action that needed to be undertaken.[21] The agency emphasized that recent court decisions reinforced its position that responsible party liability was strict, joint and several. The objective of negotiations, therefore, should be to collect 100 percent of cleanup costs or to achieve complete cleanup. The regions were to evaluate proposals for less than total settlement in light of several factors: the extent of responsible party contribution to waste at the site; the strength of the evidence linking waste to settling parties; ability to pay; litigative risks in proceeding to trial; public interest considerations (i.e., the ability of the government to clean up the site); precedential value; the value of obtaining a certain present sum through settlement versus the value of a large future sum through litigation; inequities and aggravating factors; and the nature of the case remaining after settlement.

Attorneys representing targets of EPA enforcement considered the abandonment of an arbitrary 80 to 100 percent threshold as positive but claimed that the regions and the Justice Department were still clinging to the 100 percent principle in practice. Further, they argued, EPA negotiators were still reluctant to use the fund to cover orphan shares. Finally, while the new policy allowed minor contributors[22] to cash out and avoid high transaction costs, a procedure for effectuating this idea was absent and little agency follow-up was in evidence (Stoll and Graham, 1985: 8).

The new settlement policy directed the regions to consider offers to pay for or perform one phase of site cleanup (for example, surface removal) without committing to any other phase of cleanup. Since a partial settlement reduced responsible party near-term cost commitments, it provided an incentive to settle. The regions could also consider offers to perform only the remedial investigation/feasibility study if the responsible party had the financial and technical capabilities to conduct this work in conformity with agency guidelines (U.S. Environmental Protection Agency, 1984h). Performing these studies was in a responsible party's interest since it afforded greater potential influence in the selection of a least-cost remedy. Attorneys acknowledged that this was a substantial inducement to settlement but noted great frustration in practice; by fall of 1985 EPA had yet to issue its guidance document on the performance of these studies, although it had been promised for summer of 1984. The agency tended to jump ahead and initiate studies without giving responsible parties a reasonable chance to develop a proposal for EPA consideration (Stoll and Graham, 1985: 45).

As an additional inducement to settlement, the regions were directed to consider providing contribution protection to settling parties. With joint and several liability, it was possible that settling parties would be sued by nonsettling parties that the agency had sued for the remaining cleanup costs. Since settling parties could then end up paying a larger share of cleanup costs, this threat was a disincentive to settlement. Contribution protection in a consent decree meant that the agency funded the settling party's liability to nonsettling third parties. EPA's willingness to provide this incentive to settlement was linked to the extent of cleanup agreed to by settling parties.

The agency's stance on the release of settling parties from subsequent liability for recurring endangerments and unknown site conditions was less generous. Desiring finality in settlement, targets of EPA enforcement wished to negotiate a release from liability or a covenant not to sue as part of the consideration for payment or cleanup. EPA, wishing to avoid the need to commit the fund to address any as yet unknown future cleanup needs, allowed the regions to negotiate covenants not to sue only in very limited circumstances. The stringency or expansiveness of the covenant depended on the agency's faith in the effectiveness and reliability of the remedy. Since land disposal, the least reliable remedy, was the remedy most frequently selected, expansive covenants were generally not appropriate. More reliable remedies, such as incineration, were often rejected as too costly (U.S. General Accounting Office, 1986c: 28–32), suggesting that responsible parties were not necessarily willing to increase their near-term cost commitments to secure a more expansive liability release.

Covenants not to sue could be negotiated in association with less reliable remedies if performance standards were specified in the agreement or if reopener clauses were included. The latter made the covenant more stringent. The region could use covenants not to sue as an inducement to settle for a more extensive cleanup. As suggested above, responsible party concern with near-term costs would minimize the value of this incentive. Finally, in extraordinary circumstances, the region could offer a more stringent or expansive covenant if it was in the public interest to do so. However, agency concurrence would need to be obtained before negotiation. In light of these limitations, covenants not to sue did not provide the regions with a flexible incentive to settlement. When overall agreements were reached, a partial release from liability was ordinarily granted. However, the most important release—that from later emerging ground water contamination—was usually denied (Anderson, 1985: 286). Attorneys representing responsible parties characterized this aspect of EPA policy as designed to promote a reluctance to settle (Stoll and Graham, 1985: 9).

If initial offers precluded negotiation, or if negotiation did not yield an acceptable offer, the region could issue a unilateral order or refer the case to the Justice Department for litigation. In selecting targets for litigation, the regions were directed to give highest priority to cases involving cost recoveries where all cleanup costs had been incurred by the fund and to cases where responsible parties were recalcitrant and the fund would not be used to finance the identified cleanup phase. Under joint and several liability the government was not obligated to bring enforcement actions against all parties at a site. Therefore, the primary concern of the regions in identifying targets for litigation was to bring a meritorious case against responsible parties who had the ability to undertake or pay for response action. The regions were also to consider the willingness or recalcitrance of parties to settle in identifying a manageable number of parties for litigation. If settlement was reached for one phase of cleanup, the region could choose to sue only financially viable nonsettling parties for the next phase. Regional latitude in selecting targets for litigation provided potential leverage in achieving productive negotiation and settlement.

The regions were advised to limit the time allowed for negotiation prior to taking enforcement action. After the region planned to obligate funds for the remedial investigation/feasibility study, responsible parties had sixty days to agree to fund or conduct these studies themselves. They also had sixty days after the selection of a remedy to agree to finance or perform cleanup. As noted above, these time frames were considered restrictive, in particular when site issues were complex and large numbers of parties were involved. It was not uncommon for 100 or more companies to be identified as responsible parties. They had the responsibility to organize themselves into a negotiating committee for their dealings with the region. Agency policy directed the regions to facilitate this process by providing responsible parties with the names of other identified parties and the volume and nature of waste sent to the site. Waste volume data provided targeted parties a basis for apportioning liability among themselves, a first step in formulating an offer to the region. Responsible party attorneys argued that the regional offices were failing to provide this relevant information on an expeditious basis. Proposals were therefore less likely within the time allotted (Stoll and Graham, 1985: 45). Further, the agency's refusal to participate in apportionment, based on a desire to protect its litigative position, was viewed as delaying and deterring negotiation (Anderson, 1985: 299).

In general, the targets of EPA enforcement and those with faith in the efficacy of negotiation considered agency settlement policy to contain stronger disincentives than incentives—it was "replete with the vocabulary of the litigator and the courtroom" (Anderson, 1985: 299).

Regional Strategy: Removals

EPA settlement policy includes goals, principles, and guidelines. It does not, however, include a detailed set of implementation steps for the regions to follow. For example, it is silent on the weight to be placed on the various factors used to evaluate a settlement offer. Rather, each region is left to develop a version of the strategy that is consistent with its own interpretation of agency documents. Under these circumstances, variation in regional application of settlement policy is to be expected. A review of enforcement strategies for sites requiring a removal action, based in part on my interviews at several regional offices, illustrates that the regions in fact adopted a range of interpretations. After 1983 removals were accorded increased importance as an initial phase of remedial action (U.S. Environmental Protection Agency, 1984i). They account for about a quarter of actions initiated by the regions through 1985.

Region 2 (primarily New York and New Jersey) appears to have developed the most formalized approach to achieving responsible party removal actions. This strategy, evolved over several years, is applied at sites involving large numbers of parties when some lead time exists before removal must begin. It builds on the settlement policy statement that the government will consider the willingness of parties to settle, as demonstrated in the negotiation stage, in choosing targets for litigation.[23]

The first major element in the Region 2 approach is to identify all responsible parties connected with a site, rather than limiting the search to identification of a few deep pocket corporations. The volume and nature of waste contributed by each party is computerized, allowing the region to provide a volumetric basis for cost allocation arrangements. The region invites all identified responsible parties to a mass meeting at which they are informed of the Superfund mandate, site conditions, the agency settlement policy, settlement options, and the time schedules which apply. They are told that EPA will only negotiate with a committee and are advised of the incentives to be offered settlors and the disincentives offered the recalcitrant. Incentives may include a limited liability release or acceptance of less than 100 percent of cleanup or cost recovery. The balance of costs will be sought from nonsettlors. Disincentives for nonsettlors include the use of unilateral orders requiring the nonsettlors to participate in cleanup and threats of enforcement targeted against nonsettlors for recovery of EPA's costs and/or for future phases of site response. Responsible parties are informed that unilateral orders carry severe sanctions for noncompliance (including $5,000 per day civil penalties and punitive treble damages). The region applies pressure by holding to short and fairly rigid deadlines and by informing responsible parties that government funds will be spent if settlement is not reached by the specified deadline. It is anticipated that these parties recognize that they can carry out cleanup more cheaply than can the government.

Settlement outcomes obtained over time by this approach have convinced

Region 2 officials of its efficacy. In late 1984 New Jersey asked EPA to conduct a removal at the Renora site (Edison Township, New Jersey) after its negotiations had proved unsuccessful. Since more than seventy parties were already identified, EPA was required to use enforcement before committing the fund. Responsible parties were informed that a unilateral order was issued. They were taken aback that no time was given to negotiate. After threatening a court challenge, they asked for a week to allocate cost and then about half of the group agreed to comply with the order. By spring of 1985 a large number also agreed to voluntarily sign a consent order for the next phase of cleanup after the region threatened prospective nonsettlors with unilateral orders. Promptly after settlement the remaining nonsettlors were advised that the agency was seeking from them all of its oversight and response costs. This approach was next tried at the New Jersey Duane Marine site to bring about a several-million-dollar removal. Again, forty to fifty parties, though irritated by EPA's high-handed manner, agreed to comply with the order.

Large groups of responsible parties having been induced to comply with unilateral orders under duress, Region 2 perceived that similar groups might be induced to sign a consent order if allowed sufficient time. Early in 1985 some 132 parties were sent a draft administrative order for a $3.5 million removal at the Scientific Chemical Processing site (Newark, New Jersey). They were informed that they could sign the order or be issued a unilateral order. EPA would allow limited negotiation on terms and intended to treat nonsettlors worse than those who would shoulder their legal burden. Within five weeks, seventy companies (including deep pockets) signed. Of the forty-five nonsettlors who received unilateral orders the next day, about half subsequently agreed to cooperate. The remainder were mostly small and/or bankrupt companies.

After these settlements, Region 2 believed that it had demonstrated to the regulated community that it could provide them with information necessary for a fair apportionment of costs and that it would act on its threats by the stipulated deadlines. This expectation was confirmed later in 1985 at the New Jersey Quanta Resources site. The vast majority of responsible parties signed a consent order for a $9 million removal. A notable and culpable financially viable company was among the nonsettlors. Region 2 issued a unilateral order to this company in which they carved out three specific removal tasks. If the company did not comply, EPA would do the work and sue for cost recovery, penalties, and treble damages—clearly a costly threat.

Through 1986 Region 2 used this approach at about ten sites involving more than 500 companies. As indices of their success, regional staff point to the fact that the percentage of settlors has increased in subsequent applications and to the fact that Region 2 accounts for 70 percent of national privately funded removal action costs. However, they are quick to point out that the efficacy of this approach may be greatest when applied to multiparty removals. First, the issues involved in removals are far less complex than those involved in site studies or remedial actions. Second, it is common in these cases to have 10 percent of companies responsible for 90 percent of waste and 90 percent of companies responsible for the remaining 10 percent. Many of the latter are minor contributors (in the extreme, accounting for a can of paint). In bargaining, the majority of small contributors are willing to pay a premium to avoid the high cost of litigation. The minority of large contributors, knowing they will eventually have to pay (and that they are liable for more than their share), will try to get the most out of the majority group without driving them away. The Region 2 approach plays to these different interests and promotes a movement toward settlement.

Region 2 also emphasizes that this approach requires extensive effort and devotion of meager staff resources. Further, they note that they have been least successful in the promptness of their follow-up cost recovery actions, a problem they attribute in part to Justice Department caseloads. Finally, they point out that their policy of providing waste volume printouts to responsible parties is in opposition to the natural inclination of litigating attorneys to withhold information. As noted above, attorneys representing responsible parties argue that most regions have not overcome this inclination.

The enforcement approach for removals adopted in Region 2 is unique in its efforts to facilitate negotiation among responsible parties to promote their voluntary cooperation with EPA. In contrast, Region 5 (the Great Lakes states) reports that they generally will not take time for negotiation in removal cases.[24] Unilateral orders are issued to all or a select group of parties. If they do not comply, the removal will be financed out of the fund. The use of the fund is relied upon as the highest incentive to compliance. In targeting responsible parties for litigation, the financial viability of nonsettlor companies and the strength of the evidence linking them to the site in question are of primary importance. Region 5 considers unilateral orders as most effective in removal cases: compliance is most likely, the issues are the least complex, and a showing of imminent and substantial endangerment is the most straightforward. Since removals are to address emergency situations, a fast response is crucial; a fund-financed response is the quickest response. Settlement through negotiation is less rapid while litigation is the least rapid.

A similar perspective is articulated in Region 9 (California, Nevada, and Arizona).[25] Following agency guidelines, a responsible party search is conducted. The decision whether to allow time for discussion with these parties or to issue a unilateral order is based on the immediacy of the problem, its magnitude, the nature of action required, evidence, the viability and technical expertise of responsible parties, and the likelihood of compliance. In most instances, unilateral orders are issued. Orders on consent are not deemed to be generally appropriate for removals.

The approaches taken by these three regions demonstrate variation in interpretation and application of agency settlement policy. When the need for response is immediate (action must begin in less than a week), all regions are expected to conduct a fund-financed removal and then seek recovery of costs. The uniqueness of the Region 2 approach emerges where several weeks are available prior to initiation of the removal and where there are a large number of responsible parties. In this situation, Region 2 is more willing to devote enforcement resources to up-front negotiation with all parties. Regions 5 and 9 are more likely to issue unilateral orders to a limited number of parties and then proceed with a fund-financed action followed by cost recovery.

Further insight into the diversity of regional strategies is provided by a recent Clean Sites report (Church, Nakamura, and Cooper, 1991). Based on several case studies, the authors found that Region 2 and Region 5 emphasized a prosecutorial, litigation-based strategy; Region 3 (Middle Atlantic states) and Region 10 emphasized a settlement-oriented, accommodation approach; and Region 4 (most of the Deep South states) emphasized a strong public works, fund-financed cleanup approach. The study found that any of these strategies can be effective at simple sites. At complex sites, none of the strategies were wholly successful. For these sites, alternative strategies involved trade-offs between speed of cleanup, transaction costs, and the distribution of cleanup costs and risk between government and responsible parties.

Studies by the Office of Technology Assessment and the General Accounting Office consistently demonstrate differences in regional outcomes and, with less frequency, differences in approach across regions. For example, a 1986 GAO report on oversight of responsible party cleanups found variation in the use of a quality assurance office to examine project submittals (U.S. General Accounting Office, 1986b: 27). Variation was attributable in part to the vagueness of agency guidance. Whether or not vague guidance will induce or allow a region to forge a consistent approach to its work is uncertain. What is certain is that vague guidance will allow discretionary action which in turn will appear as differential outcomes in specific areas of the region's mission.

Regional approach, strategy, and allocation of staff resources contribute to regional enforcement success. Region 2 points to its disproportionate share of total privately funded removal action costs. However, it falls behind in some other measures of relative regional progress. As figure 6.5 indicates, Region 5 is slightly short of achieving the highest settlement score, Region 2 has an average score, and Region 9 has the second lowest score. At the same time, the average dollar value of enforcement actions is highest in Region 9. As innovative as the regions are in their exercise of discretion for the promotion of settlement, their success in these endeavors is constrained by the actions of other participants in the site cleanup process.

State Resources and Regional Leverage

The options available to the regions at fund-lead and enforcement-lead sites depend in part on state allocation of resources to their hazardous waste programs. The availability of state resources appears to constrain progress at fund-lead sites; regions with less ample state cost-share resources tend to have lower fund progress scores.[26]

At enforcement-lead sites, if a state has ample resources relative to site cleanup needs, the region is in a position to demand tougher terms for settlement and is subject to less pressure to make concessions. If responsible parties will not settle, the region can conduct a fund-financed remedial action and then sue for cost recovery and treble damages. It can also threaten to turn the site over to the state, if the state has a reputation for aggressive enforcement. Alternatively, if a state has more limited resources relative to site cleanup needs, the region cannot place as great a reliance on the fund option if settlement is not reached. This forces the region to achieve greater progress via settlement and, at the same time, provides the region with less freedom to present responsible parties with a cost recovery/treble damage threat. A diminished capacity to invoke the fund option threat—the generally acknowledged highest incentive to settlement—will induce the region to demand more while constraining it to accept less. While EPA settlement policy does suggest minimum acceptable offers, it also states that "if the state cannot fund its portion of a fund financed cleanup, a private party cleanup proposal may be given more favorable consideration than one received in a case where the state can fund its portion of cleanup costs, if necessary."[27]

Statistical analysis provides evidence of a relationship between state resources in each region and the characteristics of settlements achieved. Regions in which states have greater hazardous waste program resources per priority site have achieved settlement for less extensive but more costly cleanup actions (see appendix). For example, these may involve phased settlement for a thorough site investigation with negotiation of subsequent cleanup phases to be conducted once preliminary work is completed. They may also involve phased settlement for a major removal action or for a complete surface cleanup with the expectation that settlement on other cleanup phases will follow. In contrast, regions in which states have fewer hazardous waste program resources per priority site have achieved settlement for more extensive but less costly actions. For example, these may involve settlement for study and subsequent cleanup that simply stabilizes site conditions or contains waste without addressing the source of the problem.

These results may be explained by the fact that, first, the regions are more likely to designate smaller, less costly, or less contentious sites as state-lead enforcement.[28] Consequently, the region's federal enforcement-lead sites will be more expensive to clean up and more likely to involve conflict. The states would concur with this regional decision so as to conserve their own enforcement resources and increase their chance of favorable enforcement outcomes. As argued in chapter 5, more ample state resources allow an increase in state enforcement activity. As states with greater fiscal capacity are assigned a larger percentage of the total number of enforcement sites, the number of sites remaining in the region's enforcement program decreases but the complexity and cleanup costs associated with these sites increases. In other words, the region ends up with a smaller number of tougher cases to settle.

Second, responsible parties are less likely to settle the more expensive is the remedy the region demands. Therefore, to bring about settlement at sites that require more complex and more expensive remedies, the region would be more inclined to compromise on the scope of the settlement to conserve its own resources and to raise the likelihood of agreement. The fact that settlements in regions with more ample state resources tend to be for more costly but less extensive cleanup actions suggests that these regions achieve settlement in part through adopting a phased approach which reduces responsible party near-term costs (see the discussion of settlement policy). The region must then conduct further negotiations to achieve settlement on subsequent cleanup phases (as in the examples above).

Financial Viability and Settlement

Regional achievements in securing settlement are ultimately contingent on the financial viability and cooperation or recalcitrance of private parties. Financial viability affords the capacity to contribute to site cleanup as well as the capacity to absorb the potentially high costs of litigation. The ability of the regions and the responsible party community to marshal their resources and to forge effective strategies determines which side will dominate enforcement outcomes.

Federal court rulings in support of strict, joint and several liability afford the regions substantial leverage in negotiations and a clear potential to dominate outcomes. Agency settlement policy with its various incentives and disincentives to settle can only be effective if the regions use this leverage skillfully, consistently, and aggressively. At the same time, aggressive enforcement action is constrained from within by the availability of attorneys and without by state resources. Responsible parties, attempting to minimize their share of cleanup costs, negotiate around perceived regional strengths and weaknesses. Which party has achieved dominance is not apparent at the regional level. There is no clear relationship between the extent or value of settlement and conflict outcomes and the size of the pool of financially viable parties. The analysis of enforcement outcomes presented in chapter 7 demonstrates that, in general, the regions are able to exert a position of dominance.

REGIONAL DISCRETION AND CONSTRAINT

Conflict over implementation on a site-by-site basis focuses primarily on the regions. Regional capacity to act in turn reflects the resolution of conflict at the national and state levels. Agency resource allocations constrain regional action while agency policy both directs and constrains action. Within the limits of discretion, the regions adopt strategies which they believe are likely to meet agency objectives. Regional strategies reflect the unique perspectives of regional administrators and staff and the resources, decisions, and behavior of other participants in the implementation process, in particular the states and responsible parties. The interplay of discretion and constraint yields variation in implementation success across regions.

Conflict over the National Contingency Plan and agency settlement policy affects regional discretion and the burden placed on regional decision makers. The discussion of agency behavior in chapter 3 suggests that regional offices, like the agency, prefer a degree of discretion in pursuit of the Superfund mandate. The exercise of discretion in enforcement promotes agency goals when it affords the latitude to create strategies that work within the region's world and when the agency can learn from the regions. A recent article by EPA's director of the Office of Waste Programs Enforcement alludes to the Region 2 removal strategy as a potentially promising technique that could be integrated into settlement policy (Lucero, 1988: 10). At the same time, discretion that emanates from a lack of direction burdens the regions and undermines program goals. The 1982 National Contingency Plan with its emphasis on cost and its silence on standards forced the regions to resolve issues that should have been resolved in Washington and presented the agency with inconsistent and often indefensible remedies.

While appropriate guidance and an effective exercise of discretion contribute to program success, resource constraints on regional action limit achievements. In authorizing a $1.6 billion response fund to solve a multibillion-dollar problem, EPA projections led Congress to anticipate that a substantial portion of cleanup activity would be funded by private parties. After mid-1983 EPA policy emphasized fund expenditures and aggressive enforcement as a means to this end. The exhaustion of the fund by late 1985 (see chapter 7) slowed progress at fund-lead sites in the aggregate and weakened the fund option threat. Limits on attorney resources further restricted regional pursuit of agency enforcement goals in general and the actions of the more aggressive regions in particular. As argued above, sites in Region 2, Region 5, and Region 9 were most likely to be no action sites and least likely to be federal enforcement-lead sites due primarily to an inadequacy of attorneys. Structural, symbolic action models of state behavior emphasize the contradiction between legislation that grants strong powers to an agency and funding decisions that constrain an agency's exercise of these powers (see chapter 3). In this regard it is clear that agency staffing decisions by the executive branch and Congress substantially constrain actions to minimize risk and to maximize responsible party contribution to cleanup.

Decisions at the state level determine the adequacy of state hazardous waste program resources and affect both fund-lead and enforcement-lead activities. Limited state resources constrain fund-lead progress and increase the number of federal enforcement-lead sites. State-lead enforcement substitutes for federal enforcement and increases the level of responsible party contributions. At the same time, active state enforcement affects the characteristics of regional caseloads. As discussed above, where states have greater capacity to pursue enforcement activity, regional enforcement programs face more complex and/or costly cleanup problems and are forced to compromise to achieve settlement. The New Federalism has made federal program outcomes more sensitive to state-level funding decisions and the relative political leverage available to a state's cleanup advocates and opponents.

The regional offices are more mini-agencies than mere reflections of EPA. Variation in their accomplishments stems from differential political and economic forces operating at the regional level and the strategies they adopt to contend with these forces. In the next chapter, variation in regional progress is seen to have a substantial impact on the program's overall fund and enforcement outcomes.

APPENDIX: REGIONAL OUTCOMES

This statistical appendix addresses two issues: the factors that differentiate sites by lead responsibility and the relationship between state resources and enforcement outcomes.

Determinants of Lead Responsibility

As discussed above in the text, the regions categorize each site as fund-lead, federal enforcement-lead, or state-lead enforcement. For this study, sites are categorized as no action sites when the region has taken neither fund nor enforcement action and when the site is not listed by EPA as a state-lead enforcement site. Two dimensions of regional choice are examined: the choice of action versus no action at 768 nonfederal National Priorities List (NPL) sites and the choice of federal versus state-lead enforcement responsibility at 395 nonfederal NPL sites.[29]

Designation of lead responsibilities depends on regional, state, responsible party, and site-specific characteristics. The most important variable at the regional level is the availability of staff resources. Given the emphasis placed on enforcement, the number of attorneys per NPL site (the variable AT-TORNEY) is used as a general measure of regional capacity to move sites into the fund or federal enforcement programs and to address sites in the federal enforcement program.[30] Since the size of the NPL has grown more rapidly than have program resources, the date at which a site was added to the NPL should affect whether it becomes a target for federal action. The variable UPDATE specifies the revision of the NPL when each site was proposed for listing.[31] A higher update number indicates a more recent date of proposal and listing.

The state resource constraint is measured by state hazardous waste program funds per state NPL sites proposed or listed as of 1983 (the variable STFDNPL).[32] Recall that the measure of state funds also uses 1983 data (see chapter 5). Each state can designate one site as its top priority for action (the qualitative variable TPS)[33] and expect the region to give priority to this site. State cost-share requirements depend on whether the site is owned by the state or a municipality. In contrast to privately owned sites, the state is required to cover 50 percent of fund-financed cleanup costs at state-owned sites. To conserve resources, states prefer that these sites be addressed under regional removal authority (cost-sharing does not apply for immediate removals) or under an enforcement program. The qualitative variable STOWN[34] identifies state-owned sites.

The availability of private resources is measured at a state level of aggregation. The variable PRP is the percentage of establishments, by state, with 500 or more employees.[35] As discussed in chapter 5, an establishment of this size has average profits sufficient to cover the cost of a site cleanup.

Site characteristics include measures of risk posed and cleanup costs. Estimates of risk to public health and the environment utilize EPA hazard ranking system (HRS) scores. EPA scores each site on a scale of 0 to 100 to indicate the potential risk faced by receptor populations via three media: air, surface water, and ground water. The total score (the variable TOTAL) is based on the square root of the sum of the media scores for each site and has a maximum value of 100.[36] Given both the emphasis Congress placed on addressing ground water problems in debating Superfund and the long-term threat posed by contaminated ground water, each site's ground water score is included as an explanatory variable (the variable GW).[37] The use of HRS scores as indices of risk is controversial.[38] The variable COST is an estimate of cleanup costs by site type. Generic site types are landfills, wells, industrial dumps and treatment facilities, chemical plants and refineries, manufacturing plants, water bodies, pure lagoons, radioactive sites, and city contamination.[39]

The dependent variable ACTION has a value of one if action has taken place at the site and a value of zero otherwise. The dependent variable FEDERAL has a value of one if federal enforcement action is undertaken at a site and a value of zero if only state-lead enforcement action is indicated.[40] The ex-post probability of a site being an action versus a no action site or a federal versus a state-lead enforcement site is a dichotomous variable. An ex-post difference cannot be observed between sites where conditions are just sufficient for action or federal enforcement-lead and sites where conditions are more than sufficient. Similarly, an ex-post difference cannot be observed between sites where conditions are just insufficient and sites where conditions are far from sufficient. The underlying relationship between the probability of action or federal enforcement-lead and the explanatory variables is therefore nonlinear. To capture this nonlinearity, the probability of a specific categorization is estimated using logit.

The logit estimates of factors accounting for action versus no action and federal versus state-lead enforcement categorizations are presented in table 6.1. For the action versus no action estimates, both regional variables (ATTORNEY and UPDATE) are significant at the 1 percent level and have expected signs. None of the state-level variables are statistically significant. As indicated below, the absence of a significant role for STFDNPL most likely reflects the fact that this variable distinguishes between whether a site is categorized as federal or state-lead enforcement. PRP is significant at the 5 percent level. Its positive sign reflects the importance of PRP financial viability in assigning sites to either federal or state-lead enforcement. TOTAL has a positive sign and is significant at the 5 percent level while GW has a negative sign and is significant at the 1 percent level. The low coefficients of both these variables indicate that they are secondary considerations in the decision to take action. The use of the total HRS score as a factor in choosing sites for regional

Table 6.1. Action versus No Action and Federal versus State Enforcement

	ACTION	FEDERAL
Intercept	−0.13	−0.163
	[0.17]	[0.15]
UPDATE	−0.65 ***	−0.625 ***
	[8.40]	[5.24]
STFDNPL	−0.0000861	−0.000372 *
	[0.06]	[1.90]
TPS	16.09	0.00179
	[0.01]	[0.01]
PRP	8.79 **	−3.03
	[2.47]	[0.61]
ATTORNEY	6 ***	7.05 ***
	[6.98]	[5.54]
STOWN	−0.0253	−0.0512
	[0.11]	[0.14]
TOTAL	0.0323 **	0.024
	[2.01]	[1.32]
GW	−0.0235 ***	−0.0107
	[3.11]	[1.40]
COST	0.0131	0.0711
	[0.63]	[1.55]
χ^2	199.49	108.24
d.f.	9	9
Sig. level	0.32e–13	0.32e–13

*Significant at .10   **Significant at .05   ***Significant at .01

action is consistent with EPA policy.[41] The tendency to choose action at sites with less severe ground water problems is not.[42] As discussed further in chapter 7, hesitancy to confront ground water problems may reflect local pressure to address more visible surface problems, agency tendency to address short-term versus long term problems, and/or agency tendency to address less costly versus more costly cleanup problems. The variable COST is not statistically significant, suggesting that anticipated cost, per se, is not a factor in choosing sites for action versus no action.

Table 6.2. Probability of No Action

Attorney Values	PRP Values		
	0.086	0.116	0.146
0.201	0.65	0.71	0.76
0.336	0.81	0.85	0.88
0.471	0.9	0.93	0.94

The coefficient of a variable in a logit estimation determines the direction of the effect.[43] Effects tend to be larger, the larger is the coefficient and the larger is the derivative of the independent variables with respect to the dependent variable. However, the magnitude of the effect varies with the values of the exogenous variables. This can be observed in table 6.2, where the probability of no action is estimated for alternative values of ATTORNEY and PRP. The values are mean values and mean values plus and minus one standard deviation. Population means are used for the remaining variables. Examination of the derivatives for the variables in the ACTION estimate shows that variation in ATTORNEY and PRP have greater effects than do the other variables by an order of magnitude (e.g., the derivative of ATTORNEY [0.78] is smaller then the derivative of PRP [1.15] and is ten times that of the next highest variable, UPDATE [0.08]). The probability of a site receiving no action is estimated for each region using appropriate regional values of ATTORNEY and PRP[44] and population means for the remaining variables. The results, presented in figure 6.2, suggest that these two factors generate considerable variation in a region's capacity to initiate action at its NPL sites.

The federal versus state-lead enforcement estimates reported in table 6.1 show that regional variables are the most important determinants of whether federal enforcement action occurs at an NPL site. Both ATTORNEY and UPDATE are significant at the 1 percent level and have expected signs. While the positive sign on ATTORNEY suggests an explicit decision to assign sites to federal enforcement-lead when attorney resources are available, the negative sign on UPDATE suggests that more recently added sites receive enforcement action if state resources are sufficient to take up the slack. The negative sign on STFDNPL lends itself to a similar interpretation: a site is more likely to be state-lead enforcement, given regional resources, the greater are state hazardous waste program resources. Although the coefficient of COST is not significant at the 10 percent level, the t-statistic is great enough to indicate some faith in its positive sign. It suggests that the regions assign sites with lower cleanup costs to state-lead enforcement. The significance of this choice for regional enforcement progress is discussed in the text.

Table 6.3. State Resources and Regional Enforcement
(Rank Order Correlations)

	State Resources
Score	
Settlement	−0.71 **
Conflict	0.72 **
Average Value of Cleanup Action	
Settlement	0.75 ***
Conflict	0.58 *
Total Value of Cleanup Action	
Settlement	0.48
Conflict	0.65 **

*Significant at .10   **Significant at .05   ***Significant at .01

Examination of the derivatives of the explanatory variables with respect to FEDERAL show ATTORNEY to have the greatest impact. Its derivative is 1.52 compared to 0.14 for UPDATE and $8.1e-5$ for STFDNPL. The probability of a site being categorized as federal enforcement-lead is calculated for each region using appropriate regional values for ATTORNEY and population means for the remaining variables. These estimates are presented in figure 6.3. Variation in attorney resources across regions yields substantial variation in the probability that a site will be addressed in the federal enforcement program.

State Resources and Enforcement

Table 6.3 reports rank order correlations between state resources aggregated to the regional level[45] and regional enforcement outcomes. Outcomes evaluated include the settlement and conflict scores (discussed in the text) as well as a calculation of the average and total value of work stipulated in settlement and conflict actions based on EPA estimates.[46] The total value of work agreed to at all settlement sites is $254 million and the total value of work at issue at all conflict sites is $131 million. The average value of work at settlement sites is about twice that at conflict sites.

The correlation of state resources with settlement and conflict scores are negative and positive, respectively, and significant at the 5 percent level. The correlation with mean settlement and conflict values of cleanup action are both positive, although the statistical significance of the former relationship is greater than that of the latter. State resources are positively correlated with the total value of work required at conflict sites (significant at the 5 percent level) but are not significantly correlated with the total value of work agreed to at settlement sites. The interpretation of these results appears in the text.

CHAPTER 7

The first half of the 1980s witnessed substantial conflict over Superfund implementation. Through 1983, events at the national, state, and regional levels were dominated by Reagan administration efforts to eviscerate the program and guarantee that there would be no Son of Superfund. During 1984 and 1985, conflict over Superfund implementation was played out against the backdrop of congressional hearings on reauthorization. EPA revised its cleanup and settlement strategies while Congress scrutinized its actions.

The purpose of this chapter is to evaluate Superfund through 1985 to highlight the roots of its failure. This involves telling three versions of the Superfund implementation story. The emphasis of the first summary version is on aggregate measures of progress. The emphasis of the second version is on fund-financed cleanup and the selection of cleanup remedies. The emphasis of the third version is on enforcement strategy and responsible party cleanup. The common theme running through these versions is that the failure of Superfund is rooted in four intertwined program characteristics: the absence of cleanup standards, the preference for containment versus permanent treatment technologies, the strategies applied to promote fund- and responsible party–financed cleanup, and the program's budget constraints.

The first root emerges from resolution of the how-clean-is-clean controversy. At issue is whether the adequacy of cleanup is to be judged on a case-by-case basis or with reference to explicit cleanup standards. EPA's rejection of the latter option generally lowered the cost of cleanup and the protection afforded exposed communities and the environment.

The second root emerges from economic and technological factors. Containment technologies are less expensive in the short run than are permanent treatment technologies but, due to their impermanence, are often more expensive in the long run. The agency's preference for minimizing short-term costs and for selecting remedies with known track records translated into a preference for containment technologies. Since technological development often follows profitability, agency preference for containment discouraged needed research and development into more permanent alternatives.

The third root emerges from the dominance of early Superfund implementation by the Reagan administration's deregulatory ideology. The 1982 National Contingency Plan made cost the primary consideration in remedy selection and generally directed the agency to select the lowest cost remedy whether cleanup was paid for out of public or private funds. Although the Burford administration's fund-conserving strategy was replaced by the more active Ruckelshaus/Thomas fund-first strategy, the National Contingency Plan still mandated a preference for containment technologies. The Burford strategies of fund conservation and nonconfrontational voluntary compliance were driven by the desire to minimize public and private expenditures. They retarded progress in both the fund and enforcement programs.

The final root emerges from the political and economic considerations that surrounded executive branch and congressional funding decisions. The inadequacy of the Superfund to support a needed level of expenditures constrained the efforts of the Ruckelshaus/Thomas administrations to use the fund to finance cleanup and to pursue a fund-first inducement to responsible party contribution. The inadequacy of program staff constrained efforts to undertake and carry through a policy of more aggressive action against recalcitrant responsible parties.

MEASURING SUPERFUND PROGRESS

The ultimate goals of Superfund are cleanup of hazardous waste sites that pose significant risk to public health and the environment and assignment of liability for the toxic debt to parties responsible for conditions at these sites. The search for and initial evaluation of sites culminates in selection of a National Priorities List. Cleanup at these sites, whether financed through public or private funds, then involves some combination of removal and/or remedial actions. A removal is a short-term, emergency action intended to address imminent and significant hazards and to stabilize site conditions. In contrast, a remedial action is a long-term and far more expensive process that involves study of site conditions, development of feasible cleanup technologies, and, finally, design and construction of the chosen cleanup remedy. This section provides an overview of Superfund progress toward its goals.

Aggregate measures of Superfund progress summarize many of the problems discussed in previous chapters and highlight oft-repeated critiques of the program. Data on appropriations and expenditures reveal the limitations imposed by EPA Administrator Burford and the accelerated, though sluggish, progress made under EPA Administrators Ruckelshaus and Thomas. By the termination of Superfund taxing authority in 1985, EPA had appropriated 86 percent of the fund authorized by Congress but spent only 52 percent.[1] The lion's share of allocations and expenditures were for general management and support and for annual laboratory support. Removal and remedial activity account for the next largest share while enforcement and research and development account for the smallest shares. The minimal allocation to research and development is striking considering the paucity of hard information on hazardous waste characteristics and waste site cleanup technologies. The ease with which the agency could spend these funds suggests that larger allocations would have promoted greater efficiency in cleanup activities, a view shared by oversight agencies and EPA staff (see, for example, U.S. Office of Technology Assessment, 1985: 54). A low ratio of expenditures to appropriations for remedial and enforcement activities also bears a striking contrast to a high ratio for removals. The latter reflects the relatively streamlined nature of the emergency removal program in contrast to the cumbersome procedures involved in remedial cleanup and enforcement. The removal program is generally considered the most successful component of Superfund.

The search for additional uncontrolled hazardous waste sites in combination with the program's slow start-up and sluggish pattern of expenditures generated a large backlog of sites requiring further examination and cleanup activity. EPA's inventory of potential priority list sites grew by nearly 40 percent from 16,309 in 1983 to 22,621 in 1985 even though a low priority was placed on site discovery by both EPA and the states. Preliminary assessments of threats to public health and the environment were conducted at an increasing percentage of these newly discovered sites. However, the more extensive inspections required to determine whether a site should be classified as a cleanup priority lagged behind preliminary assessments, resulting in an increasing backlog of sites needing attention but unexamined for placement on the National Priorities List. By 1985 nearly 13,000 sites that required an inspection had not been examined.

The National Priorities List increased by 57 percent between 1983 and 1985, a rate of increase far below that for preliminary assessments. The priority list included 857 sites by the end of this period. The percentage of sites deemed eligible for Superfund remedial action expenditures declined. In contrast, the percentage of sites selected for emergency removals increased by 350 percent

Figure 7.1. Fund Obligations at Priority Sites, March 1986

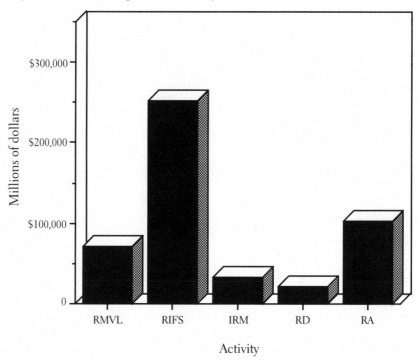

Key:

RMVL	Removal	IRM	Interim Remedial Action
RIFS	Remedial Investigation/ Feasibility Study	RD	Remedial Design
		RA	Remedial Action

Source: Author's computations from U.S. Environmental Protection Agency data.

between 1983 and 1985, reaching a total of 768 by the end of 1985. Approximately 80 percent of these removals were at sites that did not qualify for the priority list.

For sites added to the National Priorities List, Superfund progress was most pronounced in the execution of remedial investigation/feasibility studies to determine an appropriate remedial action. These studies were conducted at only 31 percent of priority sites by the end of 1983 in contrast to 58 percent by the end of 1985. Progress in conducting subsequent remedial design and remedial cleanup was even less impressive. The number of sites with remedial

Figure 7.2. Fund Activities at Priority Sites, March 1986

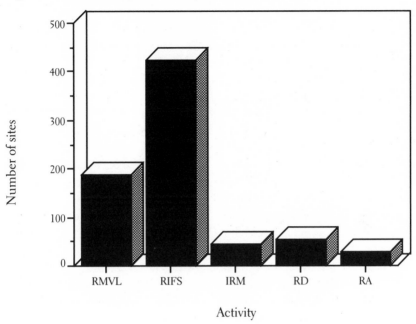

Key:

RMVL Removal   IRM Interim Remedial Action

RIFS Remedial Investigation/   RD   Remedial Design
      Feasibility Study
                                         RA   Remedial Action

Source: Author's computations from U.S. Environmental Protection Agency data.

design activity increased from thirty in 1983 to sixty-one in 1985 while the number of sites with remedial action activity (including initial removals) increased from twenty-one in 1983 to eighty-eight in 1985. EPA reported the completion of cleanup at sixteen priority list sites, a number disputed by many outside experts (see for example, U.S. Office of Technology Assessment, 1985: 237).

Data on allocations from Superfund to support activities at priority sites through March 1986 show that over 50 percent of the funds obligated ($251.4 million) were for the conduct of remedial investigation/feasibility studies at 423 sites (see figures 7.1 and 7.2). Remedial cleanup activity at thirty sites absorbed another 21 percent of obligated funds ($102.3 million). Removals at

187 sites absorbed $70.6 million while interim remedial measures at forty-six sites absorbed an additional $33.8 million. (Note that an interim remedial measure is essentially a more extensive emergency removal.) These figures confirm the general criticism that EPA was far more effective in executing emergency and interim actions and studying site problems than it was in actually responding to long-term hazardous waste site conditions through remedial cleanup.

Accomplishments in the Superfund enforcement program reflect a pattern of activities similar to that of the fund program; the majority of cases involve voluntary settlements with responsible parties for the conduct of removal actions or remedial investigation/feasibility studies or agency demands that responsible parties take these actions (see figure 7.3). The agency was far more successful in negotiating responsible party agreements to conduct remedial investigation/feasibility studies than in negotiating responsible party agreements to conduct removals.[2] The difference in enforcement achievements before and after Sewergate is also striking. Under the Burford administration, the agency settled twenty-nine cases for work valued at some $200 million and was involved in conflict in twelve cases for work valued at $33.4 million. Under the Ruckelshaus/Thomas administrations, the agency settled 104 cases valued at $375.7 million and was involved in conflict in eighty-two cases for work valued at $124.7 million. Some 85 percent of cases involving remedial investigation/feasibility studies and removals were initiated after Sewergate and about 70 percent of cases involving remedial design and remedial action were initiated in this later period. An even smaller percent of cases involving remedial design and remedial action were settled in the later period.

PROGRESS IN FUND-FINANCED ACTIVITY

For sites included in EPA's fund-lead program, short-term emergency removals and long-term remedial cleanups are financed by the Superfund. Sites are targeted for fund-financed cleanup when financially viable responsible parties cannot be identified or when the need for immediate action leaves insufficient time for negotiation. After Sewergate, Congress launched a number of major studies to determine the extent of change in EPA cleanup activity and to evaluate the need for legislative action upon termination of Superfund taxing authority in late 1985. Critics in the House of Representatives were particularly sensitive to continuing Reagan White House interference in Superfund implementation. An absence of desired change in EPA cleanup decisions would justify legislative constraint on agency discretion.

In this section, I discuss critical studies of the removal and remedial pro-

Figure 7.3. Enforcement Activities at Priority Sites, March 1986

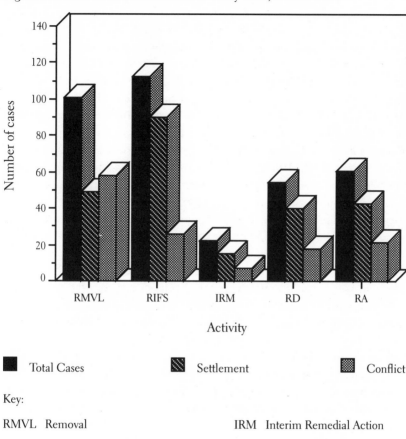

Total Cases   Settlement   Conflict

Key:

RMVL Removal   IRM Interim Remedial Action

RIFS Remedial Investigation/   RD Remedial Design
      Feasibility Study
                                       RA Remedial Action

Source: Author's computations from U.S. Environmental Protection Agency data.

grams, report the findings of a statistical investigation into resources and site conditions as constraints on relative cleanup progress at fund-lead sites, and evaluate the efficiency and equity implications of these findings.

Removals

The removal program is generally considered the most successful of Superfund cleanup efforts. Removal actions are undertaken to address imminent and significant hazards to public health and the environment and are intended to remove these hazards and stabilize site conditions. These actions include installing fences around sites to prevent access, removing drums and tanks, draining lagoons and ponds, treating liquids and sludge, placing drums in larger containers and storing them elsewhere on the site, covering contaminated soil with clay caps, and building dikes around hazardous waste lagoons and tanks to prevent runoff (U.S. General Accounting Office, 1985c: 32).

In 1984 Representative Florio's House Committee on Energy and Commerce asked the General Accounting Office to examine the accomplishments of EPA's removal program, its contribution to long-term cleanup, and whether more comprehensive removals could be conducted under existing legislation. The report, published in early 1985, was highly critical of the inefficiency attendant upon conducting limited initial removals that left subsurface contamination sources on site and required expensive repeat removals (see U.S. General Accounting Office, 1985b). Removals were relatively more thorough in addressing hazards posed by drums and containers and hazards posed by soil and hazardous substances at or near the surface. Roughly half of these sources were removed. In contrast, roughly 80 percent of the hazards posed by lagoons, pits, and tanks remained after removal. A total of fifty-four repeat removals were subsequently required at twenty out of thirty-eight sites where hazardous waste substances remained on the surface after the initial removal. Lagoons and pits required the most frequent repeat actions. Typically, a removal at a lagoon would stabilize the hazard by pumping out the contents to a lower level or by increasing the height of the walls or dikes surrounding the lagoon. EPA would then need to return to the site when rain refilled the lagoon and released its hazardous contents. One high priority site, American Creosote (Pensacola, Florida), required six removal actions (U.S. General Accounting Office, 1986d).

The General Accounting Office pointed out that feasibility studies at priority sites often concluded that initial elimination of the contaminant source would reduce the overall cost of cleanup. It also emphasized that the agency's 1982 National Contingency Plan imposed restrictions on the scope of removal actions that extended beyond those mandated by Superfund legislation. Under Administrator Burford, more extensive removals were seen as an encroachment on the responsibilities of the remedial cleanup program (U.S. General Accounting Office, 1986d).

In 1986 the General Accounting Office published a follow-up study that examined forty-two priority sites with completed removal actions conducted between February 1984 and December 1985 (see U.S. General Accounting Office, 1986d). Improvement was anticipated. The agency had changed its fund management strategy with the replacement of Administrator Burford by

William Ruckelshaus and had begun to emphasize removals as a first step in the overall cleanup process. Further, the agency had recognized some of the bureaucratic impediments to more rapid and thorough removal actions in its February 1985 revision to the National Contingency Plan. The revised regulations would not be effective, however, until February 1986.

The seventy-two removals completed prior to February 1984 were compared to those completed after this date. Slightly more than half of the later removals required additional cleanup, in contrast to all of the earlier removal actions. The greater thoroughness of the more recent actions resulted in substantial cost savings to the Superfund. The initial cost of the pre–February 1984 removals was $22.5 million while repeat actions added another $22 million. In contrast, repeat removals at the sites first acted upon after February 1984 added only $600,000 to an initial cost of $8.6 million. Inadequate elimination of the hazards posed by soil and by lagoons still remained a major shortcoming of the removal program. Discussion with EPA staff suggested that cleanup of the hazardous substances present at the bottom of a lagoon, once drainage was completed, required technologies and expenditures that exceeded those possible under the emergency removal program.

The General Accounting Office reported that evaluation of EPA's more recent removal actions was complicated by delays in Superfund reauthorization (see chapter 8). Cleanup actions were curtailed to retain resources and EPA was forced to revert back to its approach under Administrator Burford and only conduct removals at sites with true emergencies, that is, where a response was required in a matter of hours or days. EPA emergency response officials told GAO that the delays "generally resulted in prolonged risk of hazardous exposure to the public and environment, less efficient cleanup work in instances where work was demobilized, and the possible need for future repeat action" (U.S. General Accounting Office, 1986d: 28).

Remedial Action

The ultimate goal of Superfund cleanup is elimination, through remedial action, of risks posed to human health and the environment. The remedial cleanup process is long and expensive. Work, performed by outside contractors with agency oversight, begins with a remedial investigation to determine the type and extent of contamination and a feasibility study to analyze possible cleanup remedies. Potential remedies are subjected to a detailed evaluation to develop cost estimates, determine engineering feasibility, and compare alternatives in terms of their effectiveness in protecting public health, welfare, and the environment and in mitigating and minimizing damages. Due to the extensiveness and complexity of these studies, two to three years may pass before EPA selects the most cost-effective alternative(s) and presents its choice in a record of decision.

Systematic studies of the remedial action process through the first five years of the program are highly critical of EPA's cleanup decisions. In its 1985 *Superfund Strategy* report, the Office of Technology Assessment identified serious flaws in the remedial investigation/feasibility studies that formed the basis for remedy selection.[3] Its examination uncovered technical shortcomings, with poor quality work on ground water contamination and site hydrology appearing as the most serious recurring problem. Site assessments, in general, were found lacking in terms of their adequacy, completeness, cost-effectiveness, and timeliness. The report attributed these problems in part to the diffuse nature of the site assessment process, in particular to the conduct of multiple studies at a single site by multiple contractors. OTA also argued that the inexperience and high turnover rates of EPA technical staff compromised the technical direction, oversight, and continuity of cleanup supervision and reduced the effective management of contractors.

The Office of Technology Assessment examined records of decision completed by mid-1984 to determine the extent to which EPA was selecting partial and impermanent containment remedies versus permanent treatment remedies. *Containment remedies* are intended to seal hazardous wastes on-site or off-site, restrict the movement of contaminants and prevent further ground water contamination, and reduce community and environmental exposure. They do not address the source(s) of contamination. They generally involve relatively low capital costs and require substantial operation and maintenance costs which are borne by the states for as long as thirty years. *Permanent treatment technologies*, in contrast, are intended to permanently change or destroy the hazardous composition of waste through chemical, biological, thermal, or physical means and to reduce toxicity, mobility, or volume. They generally involve high capital costs and low or no long-term operation and maintenance costs (U.S. General Accounting Office, 1986c: 7–9).[4]

The OTA review identified only eight sites (one-third of the total) where a final or permanent remedial action was underway (U.S. Office of Technology Assessment, 1985: 238). Further, it found that 60 percent of the actions undertaken involved removal and off-site disposal, 21 percent involved provision of an alternative water supply, and 8 percent involved ground water pumping and treatment. The Office of Technology Assessment faulted EPA's "consistent bias toward containing waste on the site rather than rendering them harmless through treatments such as detoxification, conversion, or destruction." Containment was preferred by EPA "because it is often seen as a cost-effective remedy" (U.S. Office of Technology Assessment, 1985: 226). The report questioned the adequacy and reliability of containment technologies and pointed to the significant risk that containment barriers will eventually fail, allowing migration of hazardous substances into the ground water and the environment. It argued that if long-term operation and maintenance costs and the likelihood of containment failure were included in cost-effectiveness comparisons, treatment technologies may be found to be relatively more cost-effective.

Several factors were identified as contributing to a preference for partial and impermanent remedies and limited consideration of treatment technologies by EPA and its contractors. First, case studies revealed a pervasive preference for containment based on an "optimistic assumption of doubtful validity about the long-term effectiveness of this technology" (U.S. Office of Technology Assessment, 1985: 229). Alternative technologies were evaluated against this presumption of effectiveness. Second, the lack of explicit cleanup standards made evaluation of the suitability of alternative treatment and destruction technologies extremely difficult. In the absence of reliable performance standards or risk assessment methodologies, a contractor could not determine whether a particular technology performed well enough to be applied at a specific site. Limited information further biased the case for containment. Third, a preference for least-cost remedies was implied by the Superfund cost-balancing test for remedial actions. The contractor was required to balance cleanup criteria against the availability of funds to address remedial needs at other sites. Since containment technologies were the least-cost alternative in terms of Superfund outlays, they were selected even though the states would need to absorb the long-term costs of operation and maintenance. The Office of Technology Assessment found that certain remedial alternatives were excluded from consideration primarily on the basis of their cost to Superfund. Finally, policy uncertainties created market uncertainties that in turn limited development of performance and cost data for permanent treatment technologies. With Superfund as a major potential client, an engineering firm would shy away from investment in research and development on innovative treatment technologies when agency policy indicated a low probability that speculative (and potentially expensive) alternatives would be acceptable for site cleanup. The need to authenticate a new technology, to acquire testing materials, and to obtain permits for testing also posed barriers to research and development. In the absence of sufficient research and development to generate necessary performance and cost data, the bias toward established technologies would prevail.

The Office of Technology Assessment's critical evaluation of the remedial action program as of mid-1984 can best be summarized with two of its observations: "Experience to date suggests that there has been overdesign and overemphasis on extensive, high-cost, time-consuming site investigations and feasibility studies for impermanent partial remedies such as temporary containments, removals, and alternative water supplies" (U.S. Office of Technology Assessment, 1985: 227). "Spending large sums before specific cleanup goals are set and before permanent cleanup technologies are available leads to a false sense of security, a potential for inconsistent cleanups nationwide, and makes little environmental or economic sense" (U.S. Office of Technology Assessment, 1985: 4).

A number of reports published in 1985 reiterated and documented the problems that the Office of Technology Assessment argued were associated with EPA preference for land-based containment remedies. A ground water monitoring survey for the House Committee on Energy and Commerce found that 75 percent of permitted land disposal facilities required to meet EPA's ground water monitoring requirements were not in compliance, were leaking, or were in a condition unknown to the agency (U.S. Congress, House, 1985c). Echoing Office of Technology Assessment concerns about transferring risk through removal/off-site disposal, the study found that 87 percent of landfills that had received Superfund waste were in unacceptable condition. EPA released its own estimate that most landfills would likely attain high failure rates shortly after fifty years of operation. Subsequent agency memorandums stated that several major landfills could no longer accept waste from Superfund sites due to compliance problems and that EPA's policy was now to pursue response actions that used treatment, reuse, or recycling over land disposal to the greatest extent practicable (U.S. General Accounting Office, 1986c: 9). The ban on land disposal contained in the 1984 amendments to the Resource Conservation and Recovery Act motivated EPA to seek alternatives to off-site disposal in both removal and remedial actions.

Soon after the publication of the Office of Technology Assessment report, the General Accounting Office was asked to determine the extent to which EPA was now choosing permanent treatment technologies to clean up Superfund sites. Over a year had passed since presentation of the last record of decision included in the OTA study and more then two years had passed since the replacement of EPA Administrator Burford. EPA was issuing records of decision at an increasing rate. It would issue sixty-six decisions in 1985 in contrast to seventeen issued in 1982–83 and thirty-eight issued in 1984. If the agency was shifting its emphasis from containment to permanent remedies, the change would be observable in more recent cleanup decisions.

To assess whether EPA preferences had changed, the General Accounting Office examined the 121 records of decision issued by September 1985. The review found that permanent treatment technologies were considered as remedies almost as frequently as off-site disposal and on-site containment when a hazard was posed by drummed, containerized, and bulk waste. They were selected in only 35 percent of these decisions in contrast to a 70 percent selection rate for off-site disposal and a 51 percent selection rate for on-site containment. Incineration was the most frequently selected among the permanent remedies considered. Ground water pumping and treating was considered as a remedy for the ground water contamination present at all 121 sites and was selected 50 percent of the time. (Ground water pumping and treating does not address the source of ground water contamination.) Alternative water supplies were the selected remedy at 8 percent of the sites examined. Although the study results suggested a continuing reliance on containment technologies, examination of annual data showed that EPA had increased its reliance on permanent treatment technologies. These technologies were not selected in any of the four records of decision issued in 1982. They were selected in 15 percent of the thirteen decisions issued in 1983, 21 percent of the thirty-eight decisions issued in 1984, and 26 percent of the sixty-six decisions issued in 1985.[5]

Interviews with EPA officials, EPA contractors, and state officials involved in the Superfund program suggested, not surprisingly, that cost considerations and expectations of effectiveness were the primary reasons for not selecting permanent technologies. The requirement to select the most cost-effective remedy was seen as the major obstacle. Cost-effectiveness was generally interpreted in terms of lowest cost, and traditional land-based containment technologies were the least expensive remedy. For all records of decision examined, permanent treatment technologies were rejected as too costly compared to other alternatives in 70 percent of the cases where they were considered. In 50 percent of the cases where a permanent remedy was considered, it was rejected by EPA as unproved. Confirming earlier findings by the Office of Technology Assessment, the General Accounting Office found the lack of reliable and comparable performance data and lack of standardized cost data to be the two major reasons for rejection of a remedy as unproved. Any comparison of cost and effectiveness was rendered subjective by the absence of this information, by the absence of explicit cleanup standards for setting remedy objectives, and by the presumed effectiveness of containment. By default, least cost was the only applicable criterion.

The bias against selection of permanent remedies provided a negative incentive to commercial development of performance and cost data. Commercial development was also constrained by permitting requirements, delisting requirements, and procurement requirements when an innovative technology was propitiatory and thus only available from a sole source contractor. Further, community resistance to alternative treatment technologies posed a significant barrier, according to EPA officials. Local communities preferred waste management at distant locations and objected to being used as guinea pigs. Finally, the growing unavailability of liability insurance posed a barrier since cleanup contractors were strictly and indefinitely responsible for any harms or accidents associated with cleanup, disposal, and management of Superfund wastes. If insurance was available, its cost escalated due to the tendency of the insurance industry to impute an increased probability of failure to alternative technologies (U.S. General Accounting Office, 1986c: 18–27).

The General Accounting Office did express some optimism that the recent tendency to select permanent solutions would accelerate and that some of the identified barriers would be modified. In particular, the emphasis placed on cleanup standards in the 1985 National Contingency Plan and in the pending reauthorization of Superfund both reflected and encouraged revisions to agency remedy selection.

Resource Constraints

The descriptive statistics presented earlier in this chapter clearly illustrate how few sites progressed beyond remedial investigation/feasibility studies as well as the large percentage of Superfund resources devoted to these studies. Critiques of the program emphasized the low quality of removal and remedial response and consistently returned to cost considerations as a primary reason for selection of impermanent measures. The elevation of cost-effectiveness as a primary agency selection criteria in turn reflects the resource constraints under which Superfund operated. Congress effectively constrained program potential in authorizing a $1.6 billion public program and the Reagan administration magnified this constraint through its initial fund-conserving strategy. The Superfund mandate left room for the Reagan administration to balance cleanup standards against costs in its initial version of the National Contingency Plan. The rejection of this option on ideological grounds limited program potential through 1985.

In this context, I interpret the low priority placed on permanent remedies as essentially a product of the need and political desire to conserve limited resources. If the program cannot afford permanence, then it must establish a set of policies that allow selection of remedies that it can afford. The availability of agency staff, also a reflection of funding, further contributes to selection of low quality remedies since more permanent remedies require greater oversight and technical direction. Finally, the limited resources available to the states to share in the cost of cleanup constrains the choices available to the agency. While states assuredly prefer permanent to stopgap measures, they can in many cases afford only the latter.

A statistical analysis of fund-financed actions presented in the appendix to this chapter illustrates several of the avenues through which limited resources constrained cleanup progress. As in chapter 6, progress at each of the sites considered is measured in terms of the number of phases in the cleanup process initiated.

The overall progress of regional offices in executing cleanup at their priority sites has a substantial impact on whether a removal is conducted and/or whether a remedial study is initiated. Regional office progress is less important in determining the extent of remedial action that follows upon a remedial study. Regional capacity to organize and implement emergency response actions and remedial studies can overcome staffing and fund resource constraints to an extent not possible in the execution of remedial cleanup. The limitations on action imposed by agency guidance and the size of the Superfund minimize differences in cleanup progress among the most and least efficient of the regional offices.

The availability of state resources to finance a share of cleanup costs also constrains progress. A doubling of state resources per National Priorities List site results in an 8 percent increase in site-by-site cleanup progress. The high cost of remedial cleanup, even when limited to containment measures, therefore requires a great increase in state resources to achieve a small increase in the number of sites receiving a remedial response. Consequently, the response where states have less ample resources is more likely to involve removals only and the response where states have greater resources is more likely to progress to remedial studies and remedial action. The availability of state resources also affects progress at sites owned by the state or one of its municipalities. A state must cover 50 percent of remedial action costs at these sites in contrast to the 10 percent requirement at other sites. The degree of progress at state-owned sites is some 74 percent below that for all sites examined. The regions are forced to limit action at state-owned sites to removals (where states are not required to share costs) given the inability or unwillingness of the state to accept the greater costs imposed if remedial actions are initiated. Through these two avenues, limited state resources magnify the constraint on cleanup progress imposed by the Superfund and EPA's fund-conserving policies.

Analysis of the fund program also confirms EPA tendency to avoid the high costs associated with addressing pervasive ground water contamination problems. Progress at sites that have reached the remedial study phase is greater when the total risk the site poses via air, surface water, and ground water avenues is greater. At the same time, progress at sites with a higher risk of ground water contamination is virtually identical to that at sites with a lower risk of ground water contamination. The implication is that agency cleanup response is more sensitive to surface problems than to ground water (subsurface) problems.[6] Further, while greater cleanup progress results in a proportionate increase in planned expenditures, these obligations are six times more responsive to total risk than to the risk posed by ground water contamination. The presence of ground water contamination problems therefore neither results in more extensive remedial studies nor in agency commitment to more expensive remedial actions.

Efficiency and Equity

The factors that guide and constrain fund-financed cleanup substantially affect the efficiency and equity of the Superfund program. EPA's emphasis on least-cost technologies and its rejection of cleanup standards downplays the importance of risk in the selection of remedies and contributes to allocative inefficiency. Although cleanup decisions are to be made on a cost-effectiveness basis as opposed to a cost-benefit basis, the absence of standards in effect requires EPA contractors to choose among alternatives through a balancing of cost and benefits. To promote efficiency, the contractor needs to recommend more permanent and expensive remedies when the resulting reduction in risk justifies rejection of impermanent, lower cost remedies that are expected to yield proportionately less protection to public health and the environment. Since contractors are constrained by agency policy to generally choose the least-cost technique, they will systematically reject more expensive remedies that are more efficient when judged in a cost-benefit context. Agency policy promotes inefficiency.

The remedy selection process is also inequitable. Strong public sentiment that risk be accorded prominence in Superfund cleanup decisions in conjunction with support for the use of standards implies a social judgment that postcleanup exposure to contamination be equivalent at all sites receiving remedial action. In rejecting the use of standards, the agency also sacrifices equity to pursuit of least-cost solutions.

Federal resource constraints magnify the inefficiency and inequity of the program. The limited size of the Superfund encourages the emphasis on least-cost remedy selection. Agency staff deficiencies compromise effective contractor oversight and make selection of efficient remedies less likely.

The inadequacy of state resources also contributes to inefficient and inequitable outcomes. When a state cannot meet its share of cleanup costs, cleanup cannot proceed even if the exposure and cost characteristics of a site imply a highly favorable ratio of cost to risk reduction benefits. EPA aggravates this constraint through its preference for containment technologies that impose high operation and maintenance burdens on the states. State ability to expand cleanup funding is generally inferior to that of the federal government. Consequently, the potential for progress diminishes as the state share of the total cleanup burden increases. State preference for cleanup at privately owned sites also restricts application of a cost-benefit calculus in selecting among sites for cleanup. To the extent that equity demands equal treatment regardless of the state in which a site is located, unequal state allocations to hazardous waste programs and state preference for cleanup at privately owned sites produces inequitable outcomes.

PROGRESS IN ENFORCEMENT ACTIVITY

Since initial authorization in 1980, EPA has projected that private parties would perform or finance from 40 to 60 percent of site cleanups. Agency success in inducing responsible party action is thus integral to the achievement of Superfund goals. The Sewergate scandal highlighted the contradiction between the Burford administration enforcement strategy and overall program goals. In its wake, EPA formulated a fund-first strategy that promised a more aggressive approach to enforcement. Congress scrutinized agency accomplishments under the new strategy as it debated reauthorization of the Superfund mandate. Oversight evaluations of the EPA enforcement through 1985 identified many of the same shortcomings that characterized fund-financed cleanups and pointed to many of the same reasons for failure.

In this section I discuss critical studies of the enforcement program and then report the findings of a statistical analysis of the settlement process. As in the previous section, I then evaluate the efficiency and equity implications of these findings.

In 1985 Representative Florio's House Energy and Commerce Committee asked the General Accounting Office to examine Superfund enforcement activity (see U.S. General Accounting Office, 1986b). GAO found that by the end of June 1985 EPA had negotiated 158 responsible party settlements worth an estimated $417 million.[7] Of these settlements, seventy-two required responsible parties to conduct remedial action activities, nineteen required activities such as sampling, and forty required removal activity only. The remaining twenty-seven settlements were split between private party cashouts (i.e., private party payment to settle agency claims) and private party cost recovery (i.e., private party reimbursement for work done by EPA). Nearly 90 percent of the estimated worth of these settlements involved remedial action activities.

Upon further examination of the seventy-two remedial action settlements, the General Accounting Office found that thirty settlements (42 percent) were for investigation and study of site problems only, nineteen settlements (26 percent) were for partial cleanup with additional study anticipated, twenty-one settlements (29 percent) were final remedies with no additional study antici-pated, and two settlements (3 percent) were for sampling and ground water monitoring. Additional review of thirty-nine settlements negotiated by three of EPA's more active regional offices revealed that the work involved in only one settlement had been completed (this was for one of five partial cleanup agree-ments) and that the work agreed to in nine out of fourteen settlements for final cleanup had not started. The work involved in the remaining twenty-nine settlements was in process. Some two-thirds of these settlements were for study only.

The report clearly demonstrated that EPA's enforcement program mainly had achieved settlements for expensive site investigations and studies and, to a lesser extent, had achieved settlements for partial cleanups. In this respect, enforcement outcomes were similar to outcomes achieved in the agency's fund-financed response program. At the same time, the report offered no reason to believe that the quality of these removal and remedial actions were superior to those observed in the fund-financed program.

Because the criteria contained in the National Contingency Plan for select-ing remedial action measures apply whether the action is financed by responsi-ble parties or by the Superfund, remedial action recommendations in an enforcement decision document (the enforcement program equivalent of a fund-financed record of decision) are therefore guided by cost-effectiveness as a primary criterion and by its interpretation as the least-cost remedy. The prefer-ence for containment versus permanent treatment technologies applies to responsible party–financed as well as fund-financed remedies.

The potential effectiveness of the proposed remedies examined by the Gen-eral Accounting Office were also uncertain. Performance problems were iden-tified in the majority of thirty-nine settlements that GAO scrutinized in detail. Half of these involved submittals deemed inadequate by the project manager, with inadequate preliminary plans being the most frequent problem area. Since the preliminary plan specified how the site studies would be conducted, a poor quality plan resulted in an inaccurate assessment and a rejected plan delayed field investigation and prolonged cleanup. In some cases, the responsi-ble party was allowed to proceed with a potentially flawed remedial investigation to expedite cleanup. A number of instances also were observed where EPA found the responsible party's remedial investigation to present unacceptable field investigation data. Project managers told GAO they believed that responsible parties intentionally biased the reports by misrepresenting the extent of site contamination in an effort to obtain less extensive, and probably cheaper, remedies.

Some quality and delay problems were attributed to the inadequacy of agency and regional office guidance and to the inadequacy of staff resources.[8] As noted in chapter 6, EPA's Interim Superfund Settlement Policy did not provide guidance on procedures and decisions necessary for its implementation. Implementation therefore relied heavily on the judgment of individual project managers, many of whom were inexperienced and responsible for heavy caseloads. Due to poor record keeping, some project managers could not track settlement history and could not determine effective settlement dates and the related due dates for responsible party submittals. Vague agency guidance resulted in subjective project manager determination of whether or not a responsible party was in compliance with the terms of a settlement. The project manager was required to determine, on a case-by-case basis, whether responsible parties were making a good faith effort or living up to the spirit and intent of the order. With heavy work loads and minimal guidance, project managers avoided assessing penalties as a time-saving strategy. Penalties were assessed in only two out of twenty-five settlements where performance problems were attributable to the responsible party. In a subsequent report, the General Accounting Office noted that a shortage of remedial project managers created a bias in favor of fund-financed activities. The project managers felt that it required less effort to supervise EPA contractors than to supervise a responsible party (U.S. General Accounting Office, 1987b).

Settlement outcomes also reflected the leverage EPA could exert under its evolving enforcement strategy. The following section examines settlement strategy and identifies reasons for enforcement failure.

Negotiation and Settlement

EPA settlements are negotiated agreements with private parties who bear responsibility for conditions at hazardous waste sites. The number of settlements the agency can conclude and the terms of these settlements depends in general on agency strategy and resources and on regional office implementation.

The agency's ability to prevail in negotiations is contingent on the resources of potentially responsible parties and whether the agency or these parties can dominate the negotiation process. Agency domination means that responsible parties have little choice but to settle on EPA's terms. If the latter are recalcitrant and choose confrontation over settlement, subsequent agency actions can impose costs on them in excess of those resulting from settlement (see the discussions of settlement policy and regional removal strategy in chapter 6). Responsible party domination, in contrast, means that the agency must make major concessions to achieve settlements. Responsible parties can dominate the negotiation process if they have sufficient resources to finance confrontation with EPA and have reason to expect that the agency is either unwilling or unable to carry through on its threats.

Judgments on dominance are implicit in public and private sector evaluations of agency settlement policy. Under EPA Administrator Burford, the agency's nonconfrontational voluntary compliance strategy was criticized for allowed excessively lenient terms in exchange for responsible party contributions to cleanup. The agency was also faulted for the small number of enforcement actions initiated and concluded. In contrast, the more aggressive fund-first strategy applied under the Ruckelshaus/Thomas administrations was criticized for providing too few incentives for settlement. Under fund-first, EPA stood ready to conduct fund-financed site studies in the face of responsible party recalcitrance and as a basis for subsequent negotiation. Corporations frequently identified as potentially responsible parties claimed that they were singled out due to their deep pockets and were forced to settle for more than their fair share of the toxic debt. The implication of these critiques is that generator industry corporations held the upper hand in the earlier period while the agency was the dominant player in the later period.

Examination of enforcement outcomes provides insight into the conditions associated with EPA's ability to bring about settlements and whether the agency or responsible parties dominated the settlement process. Between January 1981 and March 1986 EPA initiated 234 cases at 224 National Priorities List sites. Responsible parties reached settlement with the agency in 137 of these cases and signed administrative orders or consent decrees specifying the cleanup activity to be undertaken.[9] In the remaining ninety-seven cases, the agency issued unilateral orders or referred the case to the Justice Department for litigation. The statistical analysis presented in the appendix to this chapter relates private and public sector resources and EPA strategy to the agency's ability to reach a settlement and to settlement terms. As above, the cleanup activity covered by a settlement is measured in terms of phases of the cleanup process and the cost of completing these phases. Reference to more extensive cleanup activity therefore means either that more phases of the cleanup process are involved in a case or that the phases involved are more costly to implement (for example, a remedial action is more costly than a removal).

The differential success of EPA regional offices in achieving settlement is clearly reflected in statistical analysis of enforcement outcomes; a case is more likely to be settled if the site in question is the responsibility of a regional office with a greater overall settlement success rate.[10] For example, settlement is about twenty percentage points more likely when a case is negotiated by Region 5 (with a high settlement score) than when it is negotiated by Region 1 or Region 9 (with low settlement scores). Relative success in achieving settlement reflects some combination of regional facility to bring responsible parties to the negotiating table, to organize and oversee negotiations, to effectively use the options allowed under agency settlement policy, and to acquire and allocate enforcement resources. EPA allocations of enforcement staff and attorneys to the regions is also significant in explaining relative regional accomplishments (see chapter 6).

The analysis demonstrates that when conditions surrounding negotiations are such that the agency is more likely to prevail, it also is more likely to achieve settlement on its preferred terms. A doubling of the likelihood of settlement results in a 20 percent increase in the extent of cleanup activity agreed to by responsible parties. The latter are willing to agree to more extensive settlement terms to avoid the costs associated with confronting the agency when it is likely to win in that confrontation.

The availability of state hazardous waste program resources also affects enforcement outcomes. They impact on the terms of the settlement, although they have no direct effect on whether or not a case is settled. Settlements are for slightly less extensive cleanups where state resources are ample in contrast to situations where state resources are more limited. As argued in chapter 6, the ability of a state to accept lead responsibility for enforcement expands along with state hazardous waste program funding. Since state enforcement usually involves sites with less expensive or less complex cleanup problems, expansion in state enforcement activity raises the average cost and complexity of sites left to be addressed through the federal enforcement program. EPA must then offer greater concessions in terms of work to be performed to bring about settlement. Balanced against this negative is the fact that the total number of settlements resulting from state and federal enforcement is potentially much larger than the number from federal enforcement alone.

On the other side of the negotiating table, the magnitude of responsible party resources influences the probability of settlement. A settlement is three to four percentage points more likely when the site in question is located in a state with substantial generator industry resources than when it is located in a state with more limited generator industry resources. Responsible parties are more willing to settle when they possess more ample resources to satisfy agency cleanup requirements. At the same time, settlement terms bear no relationship to the availability of generator industry resources. The first finding suggests that EPA can exercise a limited dominance over the settlement process. A regional office can apply strategy and allocate enforcement staff to capture responsible party resources at sites where these resources are more substantial. The second finding contradicts the oft-repeated argument that major hazardous waste generators are forced to make greater contributions to cleanup solely on the basis of their corporate wealth.[11]

The second finding lends itself to two interpretations, both of which are relevant to an understanding of settlement outcomes. The absence of a relationship between settlement terms and responsible party resources suggests that EPA does not base its settlement conditions on the corporate wealth of the parties sitting across the negotiating table. It also suggests that more resource-rich corporations can effectively threaten not to settle in response to agency demands for greater cleanup contribution even if EPA does choose to pursue deep pockets. A wealthier corporation can underwrite the cost of an expensive legal conflict with the agency and induce it to settle for less. With limited resources, EPA is constrained in its ability to use the threats of treble damages, fund-financed cleanup with cost recovery, and strict, joint and several liability to achieve dominance over recalcitrant private parties. Settlement progress at other sites would be sacrificed were the agency to allocate a greater share of available enforcement resources to do battle with all deep pockets. Stated simply, EPA's ability to exercise its potential dominance is constrained by its resources.

Change in EPA enforcement strategy following upon the mid-1983 Sewergate scandal had a substantial impact on enforcement outcomes. As reported above, the Ruckelshaus/Thomas administrations concluded three times as many settlements as did the Burford administration. However, a case brought under the Ruckelshaus/Thomas administrations has a sixteen percentage point *lower* chance of being settled relative to a case brought under the Burford administration. The average terms of settlement in Burford administration cases also are more favorable to the agency, although the absolute difference attributable to the change in strategy, per se, is uncertain.[12]

These last findings are striking in light of extensive criticism of the Burford enforcement strategy. They can be explained primarily in terms of the incentives and threats that operated under the two strategies. First, the Burford administration strategy promoted settlement in a number of major cases by offering a broad release from future liability in exchange for a near-term cleanup action. Responsible parties were willing to undertake remedial design and remedial action since they were in turn protected from liability for any future problems at the site, in particular those that related to future ground water contamination. These lenient terms were the subject of considerable criticism in Congress and the press as the Sewergate scandal ran its course. As a result, the settlement policy that emerged under the Ruckelshaus/Thomas administrations set tough conditions for granting release from future liability. As noted in chapter 6, EPA seldom agreed to grant this release in relationship to as yet undetected ground water contamination. The regional offices were effectively denied use of a valuable incentive in cases where it might have been justified as a condition for settlement.

Second, the Burford administration promoted settlements by agreeing to cleanup activity involving minimal and less costly measures. As discussed above, the National Contingency Plan constrained the agency to apply the same standards at enforcement sites as for fund-financed actions. The Burford administration selected limited and inadequate removal actions and impermanent remedial actions when these activities were financed out of the Superfund and apparently imposed similar standards for privately financed cleanup. Responsible parties were willing to conclude settlements with the Burford administration since they required less effective remedies that were also less expensive.[13] Both the adequacy of removals and the permanence of remedial actions improved after 1984. Consequently, the cost to a responsible party undertaking these actions also increased.[14] The Ruckelshaus/Thomas administrations pursued a different strategy for reducing a responsible party's response costs as an inducement to settle. Consistent with its proposed revisions to the National Contingency Plan, EPA agreed to settlements for phased and partial cleanup activity. The responsible party could agree to conduct the remedial investigation/feasibility study only or could agree to conduct a surface cleanup only.[15] This approach was particularly successful in promoting responsible party–financed remedial investigation/feasibility studies. Due in part to its focus on phased agreements, the strategy resulted in proportionally fewer agreements to conduct remedial designs and remedial actions.

Finally, the Ruckelshaus/Thomas administrations utilized threats with greater frequency than did the Burford administration. During the Burford administration the agency was severely criticized by Congress for issuing few unilateral orders with treble damage penalties for noncompliance, for referring few cases to the Justice Department, and for its resistance to financing cleanup via the fund in the face of responsible party recalcitrance. The Ruckelshaus/ Thomas administrations issued seventy unilateral orders (in contrast to six issued by the Burford administration) and referred twenty-five cases to the Justice Department (in contrast to seven referrals under the previous administration). Over a quarter of these actions involved demands that responsible parties conduct remedial designs and remedial actions. The agency also used the fund to conduct remedial studies as a basis for negotiation. It threatened responsible parties with legal action to reimburse agency costs. EPA records indicate that as of March 1986 many responsible parties were in compliance with unilateral orders issued after mid-1983. In these cases, the agency apparently achieved through conflict what it did not achieve through voluntary settlement. However, there were limits to what it could achieve through reliance on threats. Regional offices reported that all too frequently the agency did not follow through on recovery of cleanup costs from responsible parties when these parties did not take action and cleanup was consequently financed through the fund. In addition, EPA initiated few cases involving cost recovery for fund-financed remedial action, in part because these remedial actions were yet to be completed. The responsible parties that should have financed these actions could put off payment for several years. Agency activism was also constrained by reluctance on the part of the Justice Department to pursue litigation, a reluctance related to that department's own resource constraints as well as to its adherence to White House deregulatory tenets.

The differential use of incentives and threats that characterizes these two strategies represents substantial differences in EPA's desire to dominate the negotiation process. Agency dominance was not a goal of the Burford administration since it was inconsistent with the deregulatory ideology that shaped its view of enforcement. The negotiating position of responsible parties was strengthened as the agency emphasized incentives for settlement and shied away from the use of threats against the recalcitrant. In contrast, the aggressiveness of EPA strategy after mid-1983 represents a clear effort to dominate the negotiation process. Efforts to dominate, however, were limited by the need to place more emphasis on threats to counterbalance a reduced emphasis on incentives and by political and economic constraints on effectuating its threats. Within the political arena, corporations responsible for hazardous waste site conditions protested their victimization at the hands of EPA and forced the agency to defend its strategy before some hostile members of Congress (see chapter 8). At the same time, responsible parties recognized that EPA could threaten action but had only limited capacity to absorb the cost of litigation should it follow through on these threats. They could refuse to settle or could negotiate less expensive settlements than otherwise would be possible. Despite efforts at greater aggressiveness after 1983, EPA's enforcement budget was not adequate to its task until 1985. In that year enforcement outlays were almost double those for the preceding four years. With limited resources, EPA could not fully exercise its potential dominance.

Efficiency and Equity

Evaluation of the Burford and Ruckelshaus/Thomas administration strategies suggests that both left room for enhanced efficiency and that both sacrificed efficiency to politics. The Burford strategy, guided by a desire to minimize the cost of regulation, erred in an excessive use of incentives that exposed the program to substantial future costs. In contrast, the Ruckelshaus/Thomas administration strategy, constrained by congressional pressure to offer less attractive incentives and driven by a desire to generate a more respectable settlement record, erred in an excessive reliance on threats. Since it did not have the resources to follow through on these threats, a relatively greater reliance on incentives would have produced more efficient outcomes. As discussed in the next chapter, many critics of the program argued that a more judicious application of incentives and threats than attempted by either the Burford or Ruckelshaus/Thomas administrations would have enhanced enforcement efficiency.

Superfund enforcement is ultimately justified on equity grounds. Since enforcement absorbs both agency and corporate resources, the total cost that society must bear to achieve hazardous waste site cleanup is lower if simply financed through government revenues.[16] The social judgment to make polluters pay indicates a willingness to sacrifice some efficiency in the pursuit of equity. The Burford administration was far less in accord with this social judgment than were the Ruckelshaus/Thomas administrations. The former designed its strategy to be inequitable in its responsiveness to generator industry interests and its rejection of a public desire to make polluters pay. In contrast, the Ruckelshaus/Thomas administrations did attempt to increase corporate contributions to site cleanup. They achieved a substantial increase in settlements (relative to what had come before) and more frequently took aggressive action against parties that refused to accept their responsibilities for contamination problems. The remedies covered in these settlements improved in tandem with those applied in fund-financed actions. Statistical findings do not support responsible party claims that deep pocket corporations were systematically forced to contribute more than their fair share of cleanup costs.

ROOTS OF FAILURE

The story of Superfund implementation through 1985 illustrates the intertwined roots of its failure: the absence of cleanup standards, the preference for containment versus permanent treatment technologies, the strategies applied to promote fund- and responsible party–financed cleanup, and the program's budget constraints. These roots were planted in the conflict over who would pay the toxic debt; they supported inefficient and inequitable program outcomes.

The failure of Congress to mandate the use of cleanup standards left the decision to EPA's discretion. The deregulatory ideology that shaped agency strategy under Administrator Burford mandated both the exclusion of standards from the National Contingency Plan and the associated emphasis on cost minimization and impermanent remedies. The desire to reduce the burden of regulation and guarantee that there would be no Son of Superfund necessitated severe restrictions on the scope of removal and remedial actions. It also required emphasis on incentives rather than threats to induce responsible party contributions to cleanup. The willingness to promote generator industry profits at the expense of increased risk to public health and the environment defines the essential inequity of Superfund implementation.

Sewergate freed EPA strategy from severe ideological constraints but left the agency to contend with the legacy of Burford administration decisions and performance as well as a continuing Office of Management and Budget preference for cost containment. EPA selection of removal and remedial measures for both fund-financed and responsible party–financed actions still needed to conform to the 1982 National Contingency Plan. Enforcement was burdened by agency hesitancy to offer settlement incentives that could expose it to renewed congressional criticism. In this instance, agency self-interest as well as Reagan White House policy guided enforcement decisions.

Critiques of fund and enforcement outcomes after 1983 fed a congressional desire to more narrowly circumscribe EPA decision making and to insulate agency decisions from Reagan administration constraint. Anticipating some of the changes that would be included in a reauthorized Superfund, EPA revised the National Contingency Plan to recognize federal and state cleanup standards and to place greater emphasis on permanent treatment technologies. By 1985 both removal and remedial actions were influenced by these changes in EPA strategy.

Throughout the period under review, the promotion of efficient and equitable program outcomes remained subject to staff and cleanup resource constraints. The inadequacy of EPA staff resources limited oversight of cleanup contractors as well as of responsible party submittals and compliance. Inefficient remedies were accepted in part because they were less expensive in terms of staff time. Staff limitations restricted the ability of the Ruckelshaus/Thomas administrations to follow through on enforcement threats and to induce responsible party settlement and compliance. The inadequacy of the Superfund to clean up a growing universe of hazardous waste sites contributed to the need to minimize costs. Funds were insufficient to clean up priority sites where responsible parties were not identified. This insufficiency was magnified by the need to clean up sites where responsible party recalcitrance required fund-financed cleanup and subsequent cost recovery actions. The inadequacy of state cleanup resources imposed an additional restriction on an aggressive application of the fund and on the potential to match expenditures to needs. In general, staff and fund resources were inadequate to achieve a significant reduction in the risk that hazardous waste sites posed to public health and the environment.

Congressional oversight committees were as sensitive to EPA's resource constraint as to the strategies that determined the use of agency resources to satisfy the Superfund mandate. As discussed in the next chapter, the reauthorization debate was dominated by conflict over the size of a workable Superfund program and the burden that funding and enforcement would place on hazardous waste generator industries.

APPENDIX: DETERMINANTS OF PROGRESS

This appendix examines the determinants of cleanup progress at National Priorities List sites addressed under EPA's fund and enforcement programs through early 1986.

Fund-Financed Cleanup

The extent of progress at sites where cleanup is financed solely through expenditures out of the Superfund depends on regional, state, and site-specific characteristics. Progress is examined at 239 sites where EPA conducted a removal and/or a remedial action as well as at 199 sites where the agency initiated a remedial investigation/feasibility study as prelude to remedial cleanup. The relationship of cleanup progress to fund obligations also is examined at these 199 sites.

The regional office with responsibility for a site is an important determinant of progress in initiating phases of the cleanup process. The variable REGFND measures the weighted percentage of necessary cleanup phases completed at fund-lead priority sites within each region. This is the fund progress score discussed in chapter 6. Unless otherwise noted, the variables and data sources used in the following analysis are the same as those utilized in the appendix to chapter 6.

Three state-level characteristics are considered. State hazardous waste program resources per National Priorities List site (the variable STFDNPL) determines capacity to share in the cost of cleanup. Site ownership determines the percentage of cleanup costs borne by a state. The qualitative variable STOWN identifies state-owned sites. Each state can designate one site as its top priority for cleanup and expect the region to give priority to this site. The qualitative variable TPS identifies state top priority sites.

Site conditions are characterized using EPA hazardous ranking system scores. The total score (the variable TOTAL) summarizes the risks posed via air, surface water, and ground water contamination routes. The risk posed via a ground water route is indicated by the variable GW.

Since cleanup is a time-intensive process, the extent of removal and remedial action at each site depends on when the site was added to the National Priorities List. The variable UPDATE specifies the revision to the NPL when each site was proposed for listing. A higher number indicates a more recent addition. For those sites where remedial action has begun, the extent of cleanup depends in part on when the remedial investigation/feasibility study was initiated. The variable FQRIFS identifies the fiscal quarter in which funds were obligated for study of site conditions.

Progress at each site is measured by the weighted percentage of cleanup phases initiated (the variable FUNDSCR). The weights and phases are the same as used to calculate regional scores.[17] FUNDSCR is the dependent variable in the estimates of fund-financed progress. The dependent variable OBLIGATION measures dollar obligations from the fund to finance removal and remedial actions at each site.[18]

Ordinary least squares regression estimates of factors accounting for the extent of progress at priority sites are presented in the first two columns of table 7.1. The first column shows estimates for 239 sites where a removal and/or a remedial action was initiated. The second-column estimates are for 199 sites where a remedial investigation/feasibility study was initiated and where additional remedial measures may also have been undertaken. All nonqualitative variables are expressed as natural logs. The corresponding coefficients represent the elasticity or responsiveness of change in the dependent variable to change in an independent variable. The adjusted R^2 for both estimates are reasonably high for a cross-section study. The F ratios are significant at the 1 percent level, indicating that the independent variables as a set are determinants of the dependent variable.

The variable REGFND is positive and significant in both equations, demonstrating the impact of regional office progress on the level of site-specific cleanup. The extent of cleanup is considerably more responsive to overall regional progress when sites with removals as well as sites with remedial investigation/feasibility studies are included in the sample. A doubling of the regional score brings about a 175 percent increase in average site progress for this sample in contrast to a 24 percent increase for the smaller sample.

The variables STFDNPL and STOWN are included only in the estimate of

Table 7.1. Determinants of Fund-Financed Cleanup

	FUNDSCR[a]	FUNDSCR[b]	OBLIGATION[b]
Intercept	2.7	74.6 ***	147.25 ***
	[1.29]	[4.02]	[4.60]
FUNDSCR			0.92 ***
			[7.32]
REGFND	1.75 ***	0.24 **	
	[4.28]	[2.07]	
STFDNPL	0.077 ***		
	[3.63]		
TPS	0.88	0.5 ***	
	[1.21]	[2.79]	
STOWN	−0.74 **		
	[2.32]		
TOTAL	−0.32	0.29 **	0.63 ***
	[0.66]	[2.43]	[3.19]
GW	−0.06	−0.03 **	0.11 ***
	[1.17]	[2.43]	[4.41]
UPDATE	−0.88 ***		
	[3.42]		
FQRIFS		−11.4 ***	−21.1 ***
		[4.17]	[4.43]
Adj. R^2	0.21	0.24	0.046
F	10.16	13.27	42.36
No. Obs.	239	199	199

*Significant at .10   **Significant at .05   ***Significant at .01
[a]Sample includes sites with removal and/or remedial action.
[b]Sample includes sites with remedial investigation/feasibility study initiated.

progress at sites with removal and/or remedial actions. The availability of state resources affects whether a site becomes a priority for remedial action but does not affect the initiation of subsequent phases once a remedial study is initiated. Similarly, cost-sharing requirements affect the decision to initiate remedial studies but do not affect initiation of subsequent actions. STFDNPL is positive and significant at the 1 percent level, suggesting that a site located in a state with greater hazardous waste program resources is more likely to experience an initiation of remedial action. STOWN is negative and significant at the 5 percent level. The negative sign indicates that action at state-owned sites tends to be limited to removal actions. The coefficient indicates that as many as three out of four state-owned sites do not proceed beyond this phase. The final state-level variable, TPS, is not significant in the removal and/or remedial action equation but is positive and significant at the 1 percent level in the second equation. The latter finding suggests that the regions respond to a state's designation of a site as its top priority by accelerating progress through the remedial action phases.

The site characteristic variable, TOTAL, is positive and significant at the 5 percent level in the second equation but is not significant in the first. The coefficient in the second equation implies that the severity of the overall contamination risk posed by a site affects the speed at which remedial action phases are initiated. The coefficient of the ground water score variable, GW, is negative (though low in absolute value) and significant at the 5 percent level in the second equation. This statistically significant coefficient little different from zero indicates that ground water conditions have virtually no impact on the sequence of remedial action phases initiated. This is consistent with oversight study findings that surface problems are the primary focus of remedial cleanup action. It also suggests that the presence of ground water contamination problems do not affect whether a site is selected for surface cleanup. If the agency consistently selected sites for surface cleanup as a precondition for addressing ground water problems, the coefficient on GW presumably would be substantially and significantly positive.

Finally, the positive coefficients on UPDATE and FQRIFS demonstrate that the extent of progress for both samples depends on when the site was available for regional consideration.

The estimates of OBLIGATION appear in the third column of table 7.1. The primary reason for estimating this equation is to determine whether obligations for phases of the remedial action process are affected by the nature of site conditions. The four variables included in the estimate are FUNDSCR, TOTAL, GW, and FQRIFS. The adjusted R^2 is relatively low, but the high F ratio indicates that the independent variables as a set are determinants of agency obligations. The coefficient of FUNDSCR is positive and significant at the 1 percent level. Its value is close to one, suggesting that obligations increase in rough proportion to the percentage of total cleanup phases initiated. The coefficients of TOTAL and GW are both positive and significant at the 1 percent level. The coefficient of TOTAL indicates a significant increase in dollar obligations when a site poses a greater overall risk to public health. In contrast, the very low coefficient of GW indicates a minimal increase in dollar obligations when ground water contamination poses a greater risk to public health. This implies that agency obligation of funds for remedial investigation/feasibility studies is no greater when ground water problems need to be addressed and that the agency's commitment of funds for design and construction of a remedy is no greater when ground water problems are present. Consistent with the other estimates, dollar obligations are smaller for sites with a more recent initiation of a remedial investigation/feasibility study.

Privately Financed Cleanup

EPA settlements with responsible parties are a product of negotiations conducted at the regional level. The regional office attempts to maximize the financial burden placed on responsible parties in a manner consistent with cleanup requirements and agency guidance. The basic goal of responsible parties in negotiation is to minimize their financial burden. A corporation with liability for hazardous waste site conditions will evaluate the strength of EPA's case, the cost of settlement, and the potential cost of recalcitrance. Settlement limits responsible party costs to those associated with cleanup. In contrast, confrontation imposes substantial litigation costs on top of potential cleanup costs. Consequently, the stronger is the agency's case, the more likely is a responsible party to settle. Further, when the agency has a strong case, a responsible party will agree to settle for a more expensive cleanup to avoid the additional cost of litigation.

This characterization of the negotiation process requires estimation of two sequential outcomes: the likelihood (i.e., probability) of settlement and the terms of settlement. The likelihood of settlement depends on regional, state, and responsible party characteristics, on site conditions, and on agency strategy. The terms of settlement depend on these factors as well as on the likelihood of settlement. A greater likelihood of settlement indicates a higher probability that the agency can win on its preferred terms and therefore a greater cost to recalcitrance.

Regional progress in settlements is measured by the regional settlement score discussed in chapter 6. It is the weighted percentage of necessary cleanup phases voluntarily agreed to in settlements for all priority enforcement sites in the region (the variable REGSETL). The availability of state hazardous waste program resources per priority site (STFDNPL) and the designation of a site as a state's top priority for cleanup (TPS) are measured as above.

The availability of responsible party resources (the variable PRP) is indicated by the percentage of generator industries firms with profits sufficient to finance cleanup at a representative site (see the appendix to chapter 5). The squared value of PRP is also included as a variable (PRP2) since initial estimation indicated a nonlinear relationship between PRP and the probability of settlement. As discussed above in the text, the relationship between responsible party resources and settlement outcomes is ambiguous, a priori. The variable PRP is calculated at a state level of aggregation. A multiplicative variable (STFDNPL*PRP) is included to examine the interrelationship of state hazardous waste program resources and responsible party resources.

Site conditions include hazard ranking system scores (the variables TOTAL and GW) and an estimate of cleanup costs by generic site type (the variable COST). Finally, the qualitative variable STRATEGY distinguishes between cases settled under the Burford administration (January 1981 through March 1983) and cases settled under the Ruckelshaus/Thomas administrations (April 1983 through March 1986). STRATEGY equals zero for cases settled in the earlier period and equals one for cases settled after March 1983.

EPA settled 137 out of the 234 cases initiated between January 1981 and March 1986.[19] The remaining 97 cases involved additional conflict between the agency and responsible parties. The dependent variable LIKELIHOOD has a value of one if the case was settled and a value of zero if not settled. A logit estimation is used to identify conditions that distinguish between cases with settlement and cases in conflict. As discussed in the appendix to chapter 6, a logit estimation is appropriate when the dependent variable is dichotomous and bears a nonlinear relationship to the explanatory variables.

The extent of cleanup in a settled case is measured by the weighted percentage of cleanup phases covered by the settlement (the variable EXTENT). The weights and phases are the same as used to calculate the regional variable and the extent of progress at sites included in the fund program. The estimation of EXTENT is derived through an ordinary least squares regression and uses a sample that includes the 137 cases with settlements. The predicted probability of settlement derived from the estimate of LIKELIHOOD (the variable PSETL) is included as an argument. The variable REGSETL is not included in the estimate of EXTENT. It was not significant in initial estimations and biased other coefficients given its close relationship to PSETL. Exclusion of REGSETL substantially raises the significance level of several coefficients and generally improves the significance of the overall equation.

The estimation of LIKELIHOOD is presented in the first column of table 7.2. The chi-square is significant at the 1 percent level, indicating that the independent variables as a set are determinants of the dependent variable. Regional progress in achieving settlements has the most substantial impact on

Table 7.2. Determinants of Enforcement

	LIKELIHOOD	EXTENT
Intercept	1.64 [1.11]	0.3 [1.24]
PSETL		0.094 * [1.57]
REGSETL	7.27 *** [2.86]	
STFDNPL	0.000207 [0.17]	0.00046 ** [1.97]
STFDNPL*PRP	–0.0016 [0.15]	–0.0048 ** [2.37]
PRP	–41.08 * [1.68]	–0.72 [0.21]
PRP2	190.03 * [1.69]	7.9 [0.51]
TPS	–0.74 [1.44]	0.16 [1.48]
TOTAL	0.011 [0.69]	0.0021 [0.76]
GW	–0.0083 [1.16]	–0.00038 [0.30]
COST	0.015 [0.84]	–0.0012 [0.46]
STRATEGY	–0.7 * [1.76]	0.107 [1.43]
	$\chi^2 = 23.15$ d.f. = 10 Sig. level = .01	Adj. $R^2 = 0.15$ F = 3.51

*Significant at .10   **Significant at .05   ***Significant at .01
Note: One-tail test on PSETL. Two-tail test on remaining variables.

the probability of settlement. The coefficient of this variable is positive and significant at the 1 percent level. The probability of settlement also increases with the availability of responsible party resources. The coefficients of PRP and PRP2 are both significant at the 10 percent level. The derivative of LIKELIHOOD with respect to PRP is generally positive, indicating agency potential to dominate the negotiation process and induce responsible party settlement on the agency's preferred terms.[20] The coefficient of STRATEGY is negative and significant at the 10 percent level. The coefficients of the state resource variable (STFDNPL) and of the site condition variables (TOTAL, GW, COST) are not statistically significant. While the coefficient of the top priority site variable (TPS) is not significant at the 10 percent level, a relatively high t-statistic suggests that the relationship between this designation and the likelihood of settlement is negative. An interpretation of this last finding appears below.

The probability of settlement was calculated for alternative values of REGSETL and PRP under the Burford and Ruckelshaus/Thomas strategies.[21] The probability of settlement is 73 percent for cases initiated by the Burford administration and 57 percent for those initiated by the Ruckelshaus/Thomas administrations. A case managed by a regional office with a high settlement score has an 82 percent chance of settlement under the Burford strategy and a 70 percent chance of settlement under the Ruckelshaus/Thomas strategy. A case managed by a regional office with a low settlement score has a 63 percent and 46 percent of chance of settlement, respectively, under the two strategies. Variation in responsible party resources yields a minimal three to four percentage point change in the probability of settlement. The probability of settlement is higher under the Burford strategy for any level of responsible party resources.

The estimate of EXTENT is presented in the second column of table 7.2. The adjusted R^2 is reasonably high for a cross-section estimation. The predicted likelihood of settlement (PSETL) affects the extent of cleanup agreed to by responsible parties. The coefficient of this variable is positive and significant at the 10 percent level.[22]

The coefficients of the state resource variable (STFDNPL) and the multiplicative state variable (STFDNPL*PRP) are positive and negative, respectively, and are both significant at the 5 percent level. The derivative of EXTENT with respect to state resources is generally negative, suggesting that the extent of cleanup agreed to by responsible parties is smaller when a site is located in a state with more abundant waste program resources. As discussed in chapter 6 as well as in the current chapter, enhanced state enforcement capacity reduces the number of cases while raising the average cleanup cost and complexity of cases left to be addressed in the federal enforcement program. This in turn forces the regional office to accept settlement for fewer phases of the cleanup process. The negative sign of the STFDNPL*PRP variable indicates that the importance of state resources is greater when responsible party resources also are greater. (Recall that the variable PRP is measured at a state level of aggregation.) Greater responsible party resources facilitate state-level enforcement and thus further magnify the complexity and cost of cleanup for cases that are left to be addressed by the regional office. The top priority site variable (TPS) is not significant at the 10 percent level. However, the t-statistic is high enough to justify faith in the positive sign of the relationship. The negative relationship between TPS and LIKELIHOOD in combination with the positive relationship between TPS and EXTENT implies that the likelihood of settlement on a region's preferred terms is reduced as the region attempts to satisfy state expectations by demanding more extensive cleanups.

Finally, the coefficient on STRATEGY is positive but not significant at the 10 percent level. As with the variable TPS, the t-statistic is high enough to justify faith in the positive sign of the relationship, though not in its magnitude. A chi-square test shows that the variable STRATEGY belongs in the equation and generally improves the statistical power of the estimate. The interpretation of the impact of strategy on enforcement outcomes is discussed above in the text.

The experience of the first half of the 1980s shattered congressional expectations that Superfund as initially conceived would substantially alleviate the threats posed by uncontrolled hazardous waste sites. Congressional investigation into the cause of failure merged into a debate over solutions and the design of an effective Superfund program. Early congressional hearings highlighted the Environmental Protection Agency's faltering development of the rules and guidelines necessary for implementation. By 1982 oversight hearings were dominated by congressional investigation into the efforts of the Reagan administration to derail the program and guarantee that there would be no Son of Superfund. By mid-1983 examination of agency implementation shared the center stage with congressional debate on redesign of the program. From 1984 to 1986 the debate over redesign progressed against the background of EPA efforts to revitalize the Superfund and continued in a joint congressional conference committee until passage of the Superfund Amendments and Reauthorization Act (SARA) in October 1986.

The desire by many in Congress to redesign Superfund was motivated in large part by the failures associated with agency promulgation and implementation. The sense of urgency was fed by greatly expanded estimates of the number of traditional Superfund sites. The intrusion of deregulatory politics into EPA decision making suggested the need to limit agency discretion and to supplement congressional oversight with expanded avenues for public pressure. Congress debated the wisdom of holding EPA to mandatory cleanup schedules, requiring that cleanup satisfy uniform national standards, requiring a preference for permanent cleanup technologies, and allowing citizen suits to force agency action. Controversies surrounding EPA's enforcement program suggested the need to rationalize the settlement process. Congress was divided on liability issues and on how to avoid the expense and delay associated with litigation.

Reauthorization hearings addressed issues left unresolved by CERCLA as well as newly emerging issues. Provisions for victim compensation and a federal cause of action were again considered and hotly debated. Newly emerging issues included cleanup of hazardous waste sites on federal property as well as contamination problems posed by leaking underground storage tanks, pesticides in ground water, and mining sites. The tragic consequences of a chemical release in Bhopal, India, catapulted a right-to-know title to a position of prominence on the redesign agenda.

An expanded Superfund mandate and a rapidly growing list of priority sites would require a substantial increase in EPA responsibilities and in the size of the response fund. Whether EPA could carry out a far greater program without squandering resources became central to defining a feasible program. With resolution of this issue and agreement on the size of the fund, focus shifted to the source of funding. Conflict over who would pay engendered the most protracted debate. By late 1985 an absence of agreement on this issue threatened to shut down the Superfund program.

This chapter traces the course of the reauthorization debate and examines the factors accounting for the redesigned program that emerged. A summary of leading bills fashioned in the House and Senate highlights the major issues addressed and the solutions proposed. Against this background, I examine those reauthorization issues that are most closely linked to the threats posed by hazardous waste sites: the pace and extent of cleanup, settlement policy, citizen suits, victim compensation, and the source of funding. Finally, I discuss the changes in Superfund mandated under SARA and the political economic forces that produced a vastly expanded cleanup program.

THE REAUTHORIZATION DEBATE

The House began debating Superfund reauthorization in 1984.[1] At least ten bills were introduced during the Ninety-eighth Congress, with four reported out of committee. The bill that passed the House on August 10, 1984, was introduced by James Florio (D-N.J.), a severe critic of the Reagan administration's handling of the Superfund program. H.R. 5640 created a five-year, $10.1 billion program.[2] Revenues would be raised through a $2.76 billion tax on crude oil (a tenfold increase over the $200 million tax imposed by CERCLA), a $5 billion tax on an expanded list of chemical feedstocks (a threefold increase over the CERCLA tax), and $2.3 billion in general revenues. Placing the major burden on crude oil and chemical feedstocks retained the polluter-pays concept of the 1980 law. At the same time, the increased share coming from general revenues was appropriate because "responsibility for abandoned waste sites *partially* falls outside of the industries which pay the petroleum and feedstock taxes" (emphasis added) (U.S. Congress, House, 1984c: pt. 2, 22).

H.R. 5640 limited EPA's discretion while expanding the agency's responsibilities and powers. The bill imposed mandatory cleanup schedules and required that agency cleanup remedies satisfy uniform national cleanup standards. It mandated public participation in remedial decision making and allowed for citizen suits to force EPA action. It limited agency ability to shift cleanup costs onto states by requiring that the 90 percent federal/10 percent state matching share formula of CERCLA also be applied to long-term operation and maintenance costs. The agency's enforcement program would be strengthened through affirmation that liability was strict, joint and several; through increased civil and criminal penalties for noncompliance with EPA orders; and through a provision that an order would not be subject to judicial review until the agency acted to enforce that order or recover cleanup costs. The latter was to address EPA's claim that preenforcement review was a major source of delay in carrying out fund-financed cleanup at sites with recalcitrant responsible parties. EPA was directed to develop a program for addressing the risks posed by leaking underground storage tanks.

Florio's bill also included provisions to reduce several barriers to compensation for individuals injured through exposure to toxic chemicals. A victim compensation title had been dropped from CERCLA to fashion compromise legislation in 1980. Subsequent study by a Superfund Task Force reinforced earlier conclusions that toxic tort suits brought in state courts faced substantial barriers to compensation. The House bill created a federal cause of action allowing suits to be brought in federal court; made the liability of responsible parties strict, joint and several; and established a three-year statute of limitation. To alleviate the informational burden placed on those bringing suit, it directed the Agency for Toxic Substances and Disease Registry (ATSDR) to prepare toxicological profiles of the 100 chemicals most frequently found at Superfund sites. ATSDR, housed within Health and Human Services, had been created under CERCLA but was left underfunded and ineffective by EPA. Earlier House bills introduced by Representative Florio went further in allowing the fund to compensate victims for injury and damages.

Dissenting voices within the House committee characterized H.R. 5640 as an "ill-conceived, 'slap-dash,' purely political bill that not only offers EPA no constructive help, but could severely hinder the agency in its effort to do its job" (U.S. Congress, House, 1984c: pt. 2, 64). Standards, schedules, citizen suits, and the federal cause of action were subject to the most pointed criticism. The increased tax burden placed on the petrochemical industry was deemed unfair and likely to severely or even fatally damage this struggling industry. Echoing the position taken by the Reagan administration, these representatives noted that Superfund taxing authority would not expire until September 1985 and asked why it was necessary to deliberate in such haste.

In contrast to the extensive redesign passed by the House, the Senate Environment and Public Works Committee reported a bare-bones five-year, $7.5 billion measure (S. 2892).[3] General revenues would provide about $1 billion with the remaining $6.5 billion to come from special taxes. The committee, deferring to the jurisdiction of the Senate Finance Committee, did not propose a specific funding mechanism. The report on S. 2892 laid out a number of previously discussed alternative funding mechanisms and also included an alternative advocated by the petrochemical industry: a corporate net receipts tax. It noted that this option would spread the tax over broad segments of the economy and would require quite low rates. Further, it would "bring the tax base closer to the principle of the 1980 law, namely that those who most directly caused the problem should pay for its solution" (U.S. Congress, Senate, 1984b: 44). The responsiveness of Senate committees to the pleas of the petrochemical industry for tax relief and their acceptance of the guiding principle that society as a whole has contributed to the release of toxic chemicals placed them in direct conflict with an expressed House committee preference for taxing the petrochemical industry to make polluters pay the toxic debt. This rift was a primary cause of the greatly protracted reauthorization debate.

The Senate, in contrast to the House, was not concerned with narrowly circumscribing EPA's options. The proposed law would direct EPA to consider long-term as well as short-term costs in evaluating alternative remedies and to prefer actions leading to permanent remedies over containment. Acknowledging that "[n]o rigidly uniform remedy would likely be the best" at all sites, the Senate proposed that "all remedial actions must attain a degree of cleanup and control of further release which, at a minimum, assures protection of human health and the environment. . . . [T]he specific remedy at each site should be relevant and appropriate to the circumstances at the site" (U.S. Congress, Senate, 1984b: 6). This was the approach that EPA would subsequently follow in its 1985 revision to the National Contingency Plan. Rather than strengthening agency enforcement powers, the Senate bill directed EPA to consider complementing its aggressive enforcement policy with a greater emphasis on negotiated settlements.

The Senate did share with the House a desire to reduce the financial burden placed on the states and proposed that the fund cover 90 percent of the operation and maintenance costs associated with ground water and surface water treatment for a five-year period. The current one-year limit imposed an added strain on state budgets and was an incentive to EPA selection of pump and treatment remedies. At the same time, state responsibilities would expand under a provision that a state could not receive Superfund money for remedial action unless it provided assurance of adequate capacity and access to facilities for the treatment or disposal of all that state's hazardous wastes for the next twenty years. This provision was to encourage the states to be more aggressive in their efforts to site new hazardous waste facilities.

The Senate did not follow the House lead in writing a broad victim compensation title but instead proposed a $30 million a year Victim Assistance Demonstration Program to be funded by the federal government and implemented by five selected states. Like the House, the Senate recognized the need to close the enormous data gap associated with industrial chemicals so as to rationalize the cleanup process and address some of the legal barriers faced by those seeking compensation. It proposed a more active role for the Agency for Toxic Substances and Disease Registry.

The proposal emerging from the Senate Environment and Public Works Committee was criticized by some of its members for going too far and by others for not going far enough. Senator Symms (R-Idaho), the sole vote against reporting S. 2892 to the Senate, pointed out that an EPA Superfund Task Force found that no major deficiencies required legislative change and argued that the bill posed a very harsh economic threat to the nation's economy and its trade stability. Reauthorization was premature. Symms, along with Alan Simpson (R-Wyo.), saw the victim assistance proposal as a demonstration program in name only. The specifics of the proposal suggested a program of enormous and unprecedented size. In contrast, Senator Lautenberg (D-N.J.) felt that the bill should enhance the pace of Superfund implementation and that a fuller consideration of how clean is clean was necessary. The Ninety-eighth Congress ended with the bill in the Finance Committee.

The Senate acted first in the Ninety-ninth Congress, passing a $7.5 billion reauthorization (S. 51) on September 26, 1985, with $5.4 billion to be raised through a broad-based Superfund excise tax. The CERCLA tax on crude oil and chemical feedstocks was left unchanged. The bill did contain a provision for citizen lawsuits against EPA for failure to implement the program.

Action in the House took longer because five committees had jurisdiction, and a sixth reported a research and development bill. The broad-based tax was a major point of contention; the House rejected it in a close vote in favor of a combination of a feedstock tax, a waste-end tax, and general revenues. In the aftermath of Bhopal, the House passed a right-to-know amendment requiring industries to make public an annual report on their emissions of substances that were linked to cancer, birth defects, and other chronic health problems. But the House rejected a provision for a citizen's right to sue dumpers in federal court for injuries from hazardous substances (the federal cause of action). The revised bill passed the House on December 10, 1985, and a conference with the Senate was requested.

House refusal to agree to the Senate's broad-based tax stalled further action until mid-1986. House and Senate conferees agreed on programmatic issues in July 1986 and finally resolved the tax issue in October. In the interim, emergency appropriations of $198 million were required to keep Superfund afloat after expiration of its taxing authority in September 1985. President Reagan signed the bill on October 17, 1986, in spite of his strong opposition to a new tax on corporate receipts.

REAUTHORIZATION ISSUES

Disagreement between and within the House and Senate reflected the strong and often diametrically opposed positions staked out by participants in the reauthorization debate. A broad coalition of labor and environmental groups demanded legislation at least as expansive as that initially proposed by the House and also emphasized the correspondence between feedstock taxation and a polluter-pays principle. The petrochemical industry was equally strong in its insistence that the program focus solely on traditional Superfund sites and be funded through some combination of general revenues, a broad-based tax on corporate receipts, and a waste-end tax on hazardous waste disposal. It emphasized the counterproductive nature of EPA's enforcement program and asked for legislation that would produce a more equitable assignment of liability. In particular, it desired an increase in the share of cleanup costs borne by the fund and a corresponding reduction in the share imposed on generator industries through enforcement. Other manufacturing industries joined with the insurance industry in asserting the need to end EPA's inequitable system for imposing cleanup liability. They were greatly divided, however, on a source of funding; alternative funding mechanisms would impose differential burdens across manufacturing and nonmanufacturing industries. The states wanted the federal government to bear a greater share of the public cost of cleanup but were not unified on funding issues. Individual states, like individual indus-tries, recognized the disproportionate burdens associated with the various funding alternatives. Finally, EPA articulated the Reagan administration preference for a no-frills, $5 billion program financed one-third through a feed-stock tax and two-thirds through a waste-end tax. The administration argued that the financial and siting responsibilities of the states should be expanded and that EPA's enforcement authority should be strengthened. The administration proposal would codify existing EPA guidance and its proposed revisions to the National Contingency Plan. It would not clarify the principle of strict, joint and several liability, a cornerstone of agency enforcement policy.

Schedules, Standards, and Size

The expansiveness of a redesigned Superfund would determine the magnitude of funding needs and liability exposure. How large a program was necessary depended on the number of sites and contamination problems requiring cleanup, the standards to be achieved, the technologies to be applied, and the speed of cleanup. How large a program was feasible depended on EPA's administrative and technical capabilities.

The 1980 act mandated a number of studies by EPA on the pace, scope, and impact of the program as well as on future funding needs and the economic impacts of funding alternatives. Many who counseled against a rush to legislation in 1984 argued that conclusions on program needs were premature prior to publication of these EPA studies. When released in December 1984, the studies contained EPA's projection that 1,500 to 2,500 priority sites would require cleanup actions at a cost of $6 to $12 million per site. The higher cost estimate applied to sites with ground water problems (25 to 50 percent of sites) and sites where cleanup needed to comply with Resource Conservation and Recovery Act regulations and other environmental and health standards. Allowing for cleanup undertaken or financed by responsible parties, the agency estimated future Superfund needs at $7.6 to $22.7 billion. Its baseline estimate was $11.7 billion (U.S. Environmental Protection Agency, 1984d: 4–10).[4] A subsequent estimate by the General Accounting Office using EPA data projected as many as 4,170 priority sites with federal cleanup costs ranging from $6.3 to $39.1 billion. The Office of Technology Assessment suggested that the problem extended well beyond the traditional Superfund sites considered by EPA and that the federal cost of cleanup could reach $100 billion if remedial action was guided by more demanding environmental standards and placed greater reliance on permanent treatment technologies.

The projected cost of cleanup depended substantially on the standards and technologies applied. As discussed in earlier chapters, the 1980 law left resolution of how clean is clean to the agency. The case-by-case approach contained in the 1982 National Contingency Plan and critical evaluations of cleanup remedies selected by the agency fueled demands for imposition of specific standards. The strict approach contained in the 1984 House bill reflected that advocated by the labor–environmental group coalition. "The legislation," read the House report, "would accomplish this crucial goal [of establishing uniform national cleanup guidelines] by applying appropriate standards and criteria developed under the other major environmental laws to Superfund remedial actions. These provisions will ensure that once cleanup at a Superfund site is completed, the environment will not be contaminated at levels in excess of these permitted under . . . other federal laws" (U.S. Congress, House, 1984c: pt. 1, 28). The chemical waste management industry as well as major generator industry groups acknowledged the importance of standards but then emphasized that a blanket application of standards without case-by-case judgment might not provide the most cost-effective protection. EPA, anticipating that its flexibility would be severely constrained if it did not place greater emphasis on standards, revised the National Contingency Plan in 1985. The new NCP recognized applicable or relevant and appropriate federal requirements as guides to cleanup. The bills passed by the Senate in 1985 would essentially codify this more flexible approach.

Debate over appropriate cleanup technologies followed a path similar to that over standards. The 1984 House bill expressed the preference for permanent remedies over containment that was advocated by the states, labor and environmental groups, the Office of Technology Assessment, and the General Accounting Office. A "bias toward a permanent cleanup solution" was incorporated in the Reagan administration legislative proposal and acknowledged in Senate bills.

The application of specific standards and a preference for permanent treatment technologies would raise the cost of cleanup above that projected by EPA. The cost would be even higher if Congress mandated an expansion of the program beyond cleanup at traditional Superfund sites. Prominent candidates for inclusion in a broader program were the 1.4 million underground tanks in which gasoline and other hazardous substances were stored. Petroleum industry experts estimated that as many as 75,000 to 100,000 of these tanks were leaking and that 350,000 could develop leaks within five years. State experience indicated that leaking tanks were the source of a substantial number of ground water contamination cases. Many states facing this threat to underground drinking water sources sought greater federal regulation and funding to help solve the problem (U.S. Congress, House, 1984c: pt. 1, 31). Other candidates for an expanded program included ground water supplies contaminated by agricultural pesticides, mining sites, buildings containing asbestos, and homes exposed to radon gas.

Finally, the cost of the program over the next five years would depend on the pace of site cleanup. By 1985 EPA had completed cleanup at six sites (a number frequently quoted, to the agency's dismay) and projected that it could clean up 170 priority sites at most under the 1980 law. To those drafting reauthorization legislation in the House, the history of the program demonstrated unequivocally that the agency needed firm timetables to organize its cleanup efforts. The 1984 House bill would direct EPA to place no fewer than 1,600 sites on the National Priorities List by January 1988 and to begin on-site work at a minimum of 150 sites annually. These timetables would serve as insurance against a repetition of the mismanagement and lax enforcement that plagued the program over its first few years (U.S. Congress, House, 1984c: pt. 1, 28).

Critics of the federal government's cleanup efforts argued that these proposed limitations on discretionary action should apply to federal facilities as well as to those eligible for cleanup under Superfund. An estimated 1,100 to 1,400 individual sites were located on federal property in 275 congressional districts. Although cleanup could not be financed by Superfund, agreements with other federal agencies gave EPA some oversight authority over cleanup plans. In a characteristic critique, Blakeman Early of the Sierra Club testified that "[t]he federal facilities program has been proceeding at a snail's pace. Since the funding of all cleanup activities comes out of each agency's budget, there is a tremendous incentive not to take expeditious action. And this has been reinforced by a Department of Defense estimate that cleanup costs have risen from $1.5 billion to between $5 and $10 billion" (U.S. Congress, House, 1985b: 165). Representative Moody (D-Wis.) emphasized that "[t]he Justice Department would not sue another federal agency. They refused to get involved and every agency was on their own based on their likes and dislikes as to how fast they wanted to move. Many of them were not moving at all. This was hardly fair to let a federal agency pollute in a way we would not find acceptable from the private sector" (U.S. Congress, House, 1985b: 587). To solve this problem, these critics argued, federal sites should be subjected to the same enforceable schedules proposed for private sites.

EPA strongly opposed limits on its discretion as well as proposed expansions in Superfund's scope. Administrator Thomas asked Congress to restrict the program, by statute, to its original intent; he did not want Superfund to become a broad-based public works program for the improvement of a vast array of projects at the local level. He cautioned against attempts to force the cleanup program into arbitrary schedules (U.S. Congress, House, 1985b: 540–46). His predecessor, William Ruckelshaus, warned Congress that setting deadlines by law that were impossible to comply with would lead to erosion of public trust in the agency.

Thomas was equally adamant in arguing that a $1 billion a year program was the maximum feasible size. Many reports had highlighted staffing problems as a very significant constraint on effective implementation. High turnover rates and a related drain of staff to private sector contractors limited creation of a cadre of experienced project managers. Thomas, pointing to Office of Technology Assessment and Congressional Research Service (CRS) estimates of technical staff availability, emphasized that staffing needs would impose a major constraint on effective program expansion. A study by the House Appropriations Committee also supported a maximum $5 billion program. "We've tripled the budget and we've doubled the staff in about 18 months. . . . It just gets to the point that it is getting beyond [our] management ability and management staff to . . . manage 600 to 800 complex site operations around the country" (U.S. Congress, House, 1985b: 565–66). Thomas warned that there was potential for considerable waste and abuse were the program to go beyond the $5 billion level and advocated no expansion in scope to conserve resources.

As compelling as the agency's case against a threefold increase in program size was, advocates of an even larger program referred to the same studies in support of their position. Florio introduced the Congressional Research Service report into the record and emphasized its conclusion that "with few exceptions, available facilities and personnel could support a substantial expansion of the Superfund program over the next five years" (U.S. Congress, House, 1985a: 402–7). The CRS did acknowledge that the adequacy of waste treatment and disposal capacity could constrain the growth of Superfund spending. Most damaging to EPA's position was the conclusion that the adequacy of state funds to satisfy federal cost-sharing requirements was likely to be the main barrier to accelerating the rate of Superfund cleanup. The Reagan administration desired legislation that would increase this burden on the states. Since the CRS study was based on EPA estimates of resources and capacity to support a $5 billion program, it was unclear whether its conclusions would hold as well for a $7.5 to $10 billion program.

Representatives of chemical, oil, and manufacturing corporations and their industry associations endorsed the EPA position on limiting the size and scope of the program. They affirmed their support for reauthorization and, recognizing that they would pay for a large percentage of the program, had an interest in efficient implementation. Referring to proposals to spend three times as much per year as EPA deemed feasible, Louis Fernandez, chairman of the board of directors of Monsanto and representing the Chemical Manufacturers Association, told Congress that "[i]f these numbers can be justified on the basis of rational projected annual spending needs, such a justification ought be made public" (U.S. Congress, House, 1984a: 659). The National Association of Manufacturers reiterated the constraints on expansion identified by the agency and stressed that EPA's current level of activity was already taxing the limits of its professionalism (U.S. Congress, House, 1985b: 1065). The American Petroleum Institute cautioned that expanding the coverage of Superfund to matters tangential to the cleanup of abandoned hazardous waste sites would merely lengthen the time needed to accomplish the cleanup task (U.S. Congress, House, 1985b: 1039). These industries anticipated bearing some of the resentment if future implementation was as problematic as earlier experience. Limiting the size and pace of the program would cap their potential tax burden and exposure to future liability.

Settlement Policy

EPA's increased aggressiveness after 1983 magnified industry's dissatisfaction with the Superfund enforcement program and its goals. Although EPA had revised its settlement policy, it wanted Congress to affirm its new emphasis on incentives. Industry shared this view. The central issues producing agency/industry conflict were the mechanism for distributing liability among responsible parties and the use of the fund as a tool for encouraging settlement. Reagan administration EPA proposals emphasized the need to speed up the enforcement process by putting off court consideration of responsible party challenges and by minimizing government involvement in determining an ultimate distribution of liability. EPA preferred that the burden of apportioning liability be shifted substantially onto potentially responsible parties. In contrast, industry emphasized the desirability of increasing the fund's share of cleanup costs (at the expense of enforcement), restricting the applicability of strict, joint and several liability, and developing a more effective process for negotiated settlement.

The agency and the Department of Justice defended EPA's recently promulgated settlement policy as a basis for a redesigned enforcement program and asserted that the current policy was fair.[5] The administration proposal would codify this policy and would also institute barriers to responsible party practices that delayed negotiation and fund-financed cleanup. In particular, delay was attributed to the fact that parties sued by the government were bringing contribution suits against other potentially responsible parties in the same judicial action. In several cases, EPA argued, this strategy resulted in massive and potentially unmanageable litigation. Enforcement delays would be minimized if apportionment of liability (contribution) occurred only after conclusion of the government's case. "It has been our experience that a clear determination of the remedy and its costs leads to more expeditious settlement than when the remedy and costs remain indeterminate" (U.S. Congress, House, 1985b: 663).

The administration proposal would postpone the hearing of defendant contribution claims while affirming their right to such hearing. Parties found liable under Superfund would have a legislated right of contribution to sue other parties. This would encourage settlement by creating a guaranteed mechanism for parties that settle for more than their fair share to be compensated by those that refuse to settle. The proposal also would preclude preenforcement judicial review of government decisions on the appropriate extent of remedy and the liability of responsible parties until after the government acted to enforce the order or collect penalties for noncompliance. EPA argued that preenforcement review allowed responsible parties to delay initiation of fund-financed cleanup actions. Compliance would be encouraged by allowing responsible parties to seek reimbursement from the fund if they could show that they were not liable or that the response action was not in accordance with the law. Penalties for noncompliance would also be increased.

In essence, this proposal would allow EPA and the Justice Department to establish aggregate liability, use incentives and threats to promote settlement, and then shift the burden of conflict over apportionment to responsible parties. Regardless of whether the litigation cost of apportionment would be reduced, the agency would avoid bearing many of these costs and, most important, would reduce the attendant delay in cleanup.

Industry representatives as well as some members of key congressional committees were highly critical of EPA settlement policy and the changes the agency proposed. "I must emphasize," said William Rusnack of Atlantic Richfield Company, "that the most significant detriment to expediting site cleanup is that the EPA and the Justice Department approach settlement from an enforcement, rather than a cleanup philosophy" (U.S. Congress, House, 1985b: 266). Testimony on behalf of a broad array of potentially responsible parties supported this critique with reference to a recent detailed analysis of agency policy by environmental law professor Frederick R. Anderson for the Administrative Conference of the United States (Anderson, 1985). Anderson argued that EPA erred in applying a settlement policy designed for litigation to a negotiation process intended to achieve voluntary compliance. The development of a negotiation alternative, favored by a growing body of opinion inside and outside of EPA, would encourage settlement, lower litigation costs, and expedite cleanup. Anderson believed that the private sector had a strong financial incentive to explore the negotiation option: it faced higher costs when negotiation failed. The Senate bill acknowledged Anderson's analysis in stating that EPA should complement its aggressive enforcement program with openness to the negotiation option.

Atlantic Richfield (ARCO), the Chemical Manufacturers Association, the American Petroleum Institute, and the insurance industry all proposed settlement strategies designed to increase the portion of cleanup financed by the fund, place greater emphasis on negotiation, and provide greater incentives to voluntary settlement. ARCO, for example, proposed that Congress distinguish between problems created before final Resource Conservation and Recovery Act hazardous waste regulations were adopted in 1981 and those occurring afterward.[6] Strict liability would apply for the post-RCRA problems while for pre-1981 activities only those who were negligent should be punished. Given that a substantial percentage of National Priorities List site problems were created before 1981, this proposal would shift a large percentage of the cleanup burden onto the fund. Further, since pre-1981 disposal practices often conformed to a relatively lax legal/regulatory framework, showings of negligence might be the exception rather than the rule. ARCO and other generators did not emphasize these facts. However, they did stress that since most funding proposals would increase their financial burden, a corresponding reduction in their retroactive liability was reasonable and equitable. Speaking for the administration, Assistant Attorney General Henry Habicht II disputed the claim that this proposal would enhance equity: "An effective and fair liability scheme, one which has been tested in the courts, is a more accurate way of allocating the cost of the . . . cleanup program than is a massive tax, which necessarily seems to be a more arbitrary way of imposing the cost of cleaning up hazardous waste sites" (U.S. Congress, House, 1985b: 546).[7]

ARCO further advocated abandonment of joint and several liability as a basis for negotiation. "Our experience has shown that joint and several liability discourages settlements and voluntary cleanups. A responsible party who wants to settle must convince all other parties to settle or else pay a disproportionate share of the cleanup costs himself. He has no way of recovering those costs short of more costly litigation" (U.S. Congress, House, 1985b: 267). Litigation under joint and several liability transferred responsibility for apportionment to the courts. ARCO claimed that the courts would generally apportion liability among responsible parties using the same evidence that EPA used to make its case. Were EPA to perform this apportionment prior to negotiation and also agree to fund the remainder, or orphan share, attributable to insolvent or unidentified parties, the agency would gain from lower transaction costs and from earlier settlement.

Representatives of major generator industries claimed that the so-called delaying tactics highlighted by EPA were in fact reasonable measures to protect private parties against the imposition of an unfair cleanup burden. The American Petroleum Institute, for example, argued that without preenforcement review, a private party had no recourse short of willful disobedience (with subsequent exposure to treble damages and penalties) for raising claims of administrative abuse in a neutral forum (U.S. Congress, House, 1985b: 828). EPA's proposal that hearings on contribution be put off until after the settlement of the agency's case also elicited a strong response. The Chemical Manufacturers Association, for example, argued that this restriction on the right of contribution would impose excessive burdens on settling parties and would thus inhibit settlement. It would not encourage all parties to come to the negotiating table at an early date since those not likely to be named by the agency in its suit could gain from the delay. This provision also allowed abuse of agency discretion.

EPA refuted these arguments in general with reference to their impact on the timing of cleanup actions and the availability of a judicial avenue for fair apportionment. The agency took particularly strong exception to the proposition that it should apportion liability. Administrator Thomas argued that a determination of fair share can be a complex, difficult, and time-consuming process. "In many cases, there is no non-arbitrary way of determining shares of liability, such as when a particular site involves both high toxicity, low-volume wastes and low-toxicity, high volume wastes. . . . In our experience, even when waste volume is a reasonable criterion for apportionment, information on the specific volumes sent to the site by particular parties is frequently unavailable or highly speculative and not independently verifiable" (U.S. Congress, House, 1985b: 665). The government could not obtain the necessary information simply by examining the site; multiple parties send similar wastes, and the waste is unlabeled, untraceable, and mixed together in a toxic soup.[8] "Given these intractable realities of the enforcement process, requiring any sort of apportionment before the government could obtain private party action would effectively remove such action from the Superfund program" (U.S. Congress, House, 1985b: 665).

The insurance industry was also highly critical of EPA settlement policy. William Bailey, president of Aetna and past chairman of the American Insurance Association (AIA) told Congress that "[t]he insurance industry's ability to provide a market for current and future environmental liability insurance has been crippled by legislative and judicial decisions that dramatically affect the liability of insurance companies under policies which, in many cases, expired a large number of years ago" (U.S. Congress, House, 1985b: 1243). The root cause of this insurance crisis was EPA's imposition of strict, joint, several, and retroactive liability; responsible party efforts to shift the cost onto insurers; and recent court decisions that expanded the scope of coverage of liability insurance policies.

Like other potentially responsible parties, the insurance industry objected to the transaction costs it had to absorb in suits over apportionment and contribution. Beyond the costs stemming from disputes with responsible parties over insurance coverage, insurers also could be required to pay the cost of agency/responsible party litigation if policies were in force or if the courts decided they were in force. The issue of transaction costs thus loomed doubly large for the insurers. The AIA commissioned a study by Putnam, Hayes, and Bartlett to investigate the magnitude of litigation costs associated with cleaning up 1,800 priority sites.[9] Based on unreleased insurance industry data, the study estimated that litigation costs could exceed $8 billion compared to $14.6 billion in direct cleanup costs. Private party litigation costs accounted for 79 percent of this total, while government costs and coverage litigation costs accounted for 15 percent and 6 percent, respectively. If two-thirds to three-quarters of a $5 billion best estimate of Superfund transaction costs could be eliminated, 400 to 450 additional sites could be cleaned up at no additional cost to society. The study attributed high transaction costs to the complexity of litigation and extensive data gathering, the factual uncertainty of technical data, government action and policy, and secondary litigation.

The settlement policy debate confronted Congress with a set of difficult choices with uncertain outcomes. The least uncertain was that associated with ARCO's proposal to draw a distinction between cleanup problems created before and after 1981. Acceptance of this proposal would significantly increase the burden on the fund and correspondingly decrease transaction costs. Neither the House nor Senate expressed an inclination to exclude any National Priorities List sites from the enforcement program.

Since EPA's proposal built on its current settlement policy, its outcome in practice was reasonably predictable. The major uncertainties therefore were those associated with the industry proposals, in particular the potential for EPA to craft a mutually acceptable apportionment formula, the size of the orphan share implied by this formula, and the agency's exercise of skill and discretion in using the orphan share to induce settlement. If, as claimed by the agency, the complexities of apportionment suggested that responsibility was in practice indivisible, responsible party proposals would lead either to a substantial orphan share or to an increased reliance on EPA discretion in the conduct of negotiations. The possibility of a greater orphan share left Congress with the choice of either creating a larger fund to absorb the orphan share or accepting less ambitious cleanup goals. The possibility of increased EPA discretion required Congress (in particular the House) to abandon its preference for reducing agency discretion and shielding it from the temptation to achieve settlement through sweetheart deals. In its place, Congress would rely on agency ability to use the orphan share to induce responsible parties to contribute some of their transaction cost savings to the achievement of cleanup goals. If, as claimed by responsible parties, an apportionment formula always would emerge eventually (i.e., contribution is in practice divisible), the major unknown was the size of the orphan share. However, since responsible party objections to current agency policy were based on the stated or implied assumption that they were forced to accept far more than their fair share, it was reasonable to expect a large orphan share. Congress therefore was left essentially with the same set of choices: either expand the fund or affirm EPA enforcement discretion. It eventually did both. However, the expanded fund was to allow a larger program rather than a reduction in responsible party cleanup burden.

Citizen Suits

The debate over settlement policy focused on the legal relationship between the government and responsible parties. In contrast, the debates over citizen suits and victim compensation focused on legal remedies available to aggrieved private citizens vis-à-vis responsible parties and the government.

Efforts by the Reagan White House to limit EPA actions suggested the desirability of allowing citizens to play a role in the enforcement process. Citizen suit provisions were a standard feature of major environmental laws passed since the early 1970s. The 1985 Senate bill (S. 51) provided a citizen right to sue in federal court "to enforce standards, regulations, conditions, requirement and orders under the Act and to seek performance of nondiscretionary duties by the President or delegees of the President" (U.S. Congress, Senate, 1985d: 61). No action could be brought if a state or the federal government was "diligently prosecuting" an enforcement action. Various other safeguards were included. For example, a court could award litigation costs to any substantially prevailing party, thereby encouraging private enforcement and discouraging frivolous suits.

The Reagan administration and generator industries opposed a Superfund citizen suit provision while environmental, labor, and citizens' groups voiced strong support. Opponents argued that citizen suits would interfere with the enforcement priorities of EPA and the Department of Justice and would increase the federal caseload generated by Superfund. The provision would allow any person to be a private attorney general. "Beyond the disruption of priorities, waste of private and judicial resources on transaction costs and delay of the overall cleanup program," speculated attorney Edmund B. Frost on behalf of the Chemical Manufacturers Association, "citizens suits would also drain very substantial amounts of extra resources from the federal courts and the Department of Justice" (U.S. Congress, Senate, 1985c: 525). The Department of Justice doubted that the public benefits flowing from citizen suits would justify the increase in litigation.

Citing a recent study by the Environmental Law Institute for EPA, representatives of CMA and the American Petroleum Institute (API) pointed to a surge of citizen suits under federal environmental statutes. "The majority of these suits," argued the president of API, "are brought by well-financed, national environmental groups which are bent upon using the federal courts to establish programs and policies which they may have unsuccessfully advocated before congress and EPA. Few of these groups have any real nexus to waste sites. Citizens living around sites are not without significant remedies at common law. . . . The right of citizens to disrupt negotiations, attack voluntary cleanups and bring ancillary claims into enforcement action should not be allowed. . . . Congress should serve as guardian, rather than assigning the role to private groups to carry out through litigation" (U.S. Congress, House, 1985b: 827).

Janet Hathaway, staff attorney for Public Citizen's Congress Watch, disputed the position that there was an explosion of excessive and unjustified citizen suit litigation.[10] She emphasized that the Environmental Law Institute (ELI) study found a total of 349 actions between 1978 and 1984, two-thirds of which were under the Clean Water Act. This concentration reflected the fact that the act's self-reporting provisions allowed citizens to identify statutory violations. The up-front cost of bringing a suit and the difficulty of documenting statutory violations were, in general, a deterrent to citizen suits. ELI found that "[m]ost citizen suit cases . . . were acknowledged [by government enforcement personnel] to be either 1) cases which EPA would have initiated in the normal course, or 2) cases which were 'enforcement worthy' but were not high on EPA's priority list" (quoted in U.S. Congress, Senate, 1985c: 320). Further, the study found that nearly half the cases were dropped because negotiations were initiated, about 20 percent were dropped for other reasons, and around a quarter were settled before a judicial decision was made.

The desire of both the government and industry to limit participation in negotiations and cleanup decisions was understandable. Nevertheless, Hathaway believed that "[a] citizen suit provision is crucial to ensure that violations of the Act or of regulations, which the Justice Department overlooks or is unable to devote enforcement resource to, are not continuing unabated" (U.S. Congress, Senate, 1985c: 317). Rather than unnecessarily absorbing enforcement resources, citizen suits complement government actions.

Congressional concern that EPA might not sustain the aggressive enforcement program it initiated after 1984 and a degree of skepticism regarding responsible party motives in opposing citizen suits mitigated pressures to delete the provision from a reauthorized Superfund act.

Victim Compensation

The degree of uncertainty and the potential costs associated with alternative settlement policies were small in comparison to those associated with proposals for a victim compensation title. The debate over victim compensation pitted environmental advocacy groups, labor unions, and representatives of communities with hazardous waste sites against generator industries, the insurance industry, and the Reagan administration. The former argued for changes in law to alter a situation in which individuals were victimized by the state court system as well as by exposure to hazardous substances. The latter cautioned against change and were united in their predictions of excessive costs and adverse consequences for private production and a rational public health policy. The concerns of proponents were made palpable by documentation of unexplained, excessive incidence of death, birth defects, and disease. The reservations expressed by opponents were given force by a popular perception of a litigation explosion and an associated crisis in insurability.

Congress, in rejecting a CERCLA victim compensation title, had mandated a Superfund Task Force to examine the need for reform of the state judicial-tort system and to make recommendations for change. The report of the study group in September 1982 formed the basis for much of the ensuing debate.[11] The report highlighted several substantial barriers to victim compensation within the state judicial system: overly restrictive statutes of limitations, extremely demanding burdens of proof, and limited opportunities for class action suits (see chapter 3).

A two-tier system was recommended to reduce barriers to recovery. Tier 1 would provide an administrative remedy for recovery of full medical costs, some lost wages, and some death benefits. Claims would be paid out of a fund initially financed by taxes on industry. Three major findings would be required to establish a "presumption of causation" and trigger payment to a claimant: (1) that there was a release of a hazardous substance(s) and that the claimant was exposed; (2) that the duration and level of exposure were reasonably likely to cause or contribute to the claimant's injury; (3) that it was reasonably likely that such exposure caused or significantly contributed to the type of injury alleged. Tier 2 would allow the plaintiff to resort to the state judicial system for recovery of additional damages, including damages for pain and suffering, and punitive damages. The presumption of causation necessary for a tier 1 claim would guarantee the plaintiff a hearing of his or her case. The plaintiff would not be relieved of the burden of proving the case by the traditional test of a preponderance of evidence.

Environmental groups with support from labor unions argued that the study group's recommendations were a good starting point, but that they did not go far enough.[12] Even with the proposed easing of the victim's burden of proof, the tier 1 administrative system was not likely to be used with success very often.[13] A major problem with tier 2 was that it relied on the state court system and left in place a patchwork quilt of state court remedies. To address this variability in the admissibility of evidence and to help alleviate confusion, a federal cause of action was needed to establish minimum federal rules governing compensation systems. It should stipulate a statutory limitation period beginning when a plaintiff knew or should have known that he or she has been injured and had a cause of action. As of 1983, only thirteen jurisdictions had a period of this duration. It should be available to victims pursuing recovery in either state courts or federal courts. Further, there should be no limits on the amount or type of recovery. The legislation should make clear that the plaintiff's burden of going forward would be met by showing the three elements required for the tier 1 presumption of causation. This would allow the plaintiff to introduce more types of evidence (such as epidemiological studies, animal studies, etc.) without challenges to relevancy and would relieve the plaintiff of the "burden of tracing a molecule of the pollutant from the source into the body to produce injury. . . . [T]his is still a very considerable, expensive burden of proof. . . . [It] does not mean that the plaintiff will always prevail; it does mean giving plaintiff the opportunity to present his case in the only way relevant to modern injuries to the jury" (U.S. Congress, House, 1983c: 1040).

The substantial difficulties involved in linking hazardous waste sites to injury were central to the argument for reform. They were also central to the argument against change. If evidence supported a waste site to injury link, then the small number of cases passing through the state court system indicated the strength of the barriers highlighted by the study group. Alternatively, if evidence could not support this link, reform could loosen a floodgate of spurious claims.

The major problem facing advocates of change was the same as that facing hazardous waste site victims: to make the case that reliance on statistical evidence from laboratory experiments and epidemiological studies was essential for demonstrating the health impact of waste site exposure.[14] Academics with social science, biostatistics, and public health backgrounds pointed out that scientific evidence can establish correlation between a cause and an effect but cannot prove causation; it is easier to disprove than to prove causation.[15] In addition, they argued, those with scientific training tended to underestimate causation unless it was proven beyond a doubt that findings fell within a 95 percent confidence interval. This standard was far in excess of normal legal standards or the social policy standard incorporated in the spirit of the bills put forth in the House. Finally, scientific evidence could be cited selectively to demonstrate that problems were not severe. For example, Nicholas Ashford, director of the Center for Policy Alternatives at MIT, noted that in the worker exposure area, Doll and Peto found that no more than 2 or 3 percent of all cancer is occupationally related. "A close examination of the facts simply do not bear that kind of low figure. We do not know how large it is, but there is a selective quotation of scientific literature to make a point which is not justified in my view" (U.S. Congress, House, 1983c: 280).

The basic conclusion to be drawn from the testimony of these experts was that studies of an exposed population at a specific site cannot be relied on as the only indicator of causation if actual victims are to be compensated. Such studies often cannot prove conclusively (i.e., in a statistical sense) that a particular individual's disease or injury was most likely due to a hazardous waste site release as opposed to a life-style cause (such as smoking), inherent susceptibilities, or other exposure to toxic substances (in an occupational setting, for example). Laboratory and epidemiological findings also must be considered. The burden of proof in testimony before congressional committees was on those who believed on the basis of these collateral studies that a waste site to injury link existed. Discussion of dioxin contamination at Times Beach, Missouri, illustrates that this was a considerable burden.

The recognition of a widespread Missouri dioxin problem began in May 1971 when a child was hospitalized after playing in a horse arena where numerous horses and other animals had become ill and died.[16] It was discovered that the stables had been sprayed with oily waste containing dioxin as a dust control measure. Additional contamination sites were identified. Concern over long-term effects was reduced somewhat in 1975 when a Centers for Disease Control (CDC) report said dioxin's expected half-life was one year. The pace of new site discovery and investigation of health effects then picked up dramatically in the summer of 1982 when EPA reported that the dioxin molecule was far more persistent in the environment than originally thought. Dioxin contamination was subsequently confirmed at thirty-one sites, four of which were placed on the National Priorities List. After a major flood in December 1982, EPA announced a $33 million Superfund allocation to purchase Times Beach property and relocate residents. With attention focused on Times Beach, dioxin came to be popularly referred to as "the most toxic substance known to man."

Marilyn Leistner, mayor of Times Beach, testified that when the dioxin flood disasters hit, Times Beach was nearing completion of a metamorphosis from a rundown, poor river town to a lower-middle-class community. She saw her community transformed from a small and growing town on a scenic Ozark river to a national symbol of something unclean and uninhabitable. Everyone's life was brutally and irrevocably changed. All residents now lived with the fear of long-range health effects, while the less fortunate experienced severe health problems that defied diagnosis as to their cause despite efforts from all parts of the medical community. Mayor Leistner's testimony suggested that if official concern over health effects justified evacuation, a program to allow compensation was equally justified. Yet there was no clear mechanism to compensate those with injury and disease. There was no compensation for the anguish, stress, and resultant mental health problems suffered by the people of Times Beach. The economic injury suffered was neither recognized nor compensated (U.S. Congress, House, 1983a: 7–16).

"The question I am interested in," stated Elliot Levitas (D-Ga.) with reference to the evacuation, is "was this simply a political response to quiet down some hysterical housewives in the area, or was it justified in terms of scientific information?" (U.S. Congress, House, 1983a: 377). Bertram Carnow, a physician and president of an occupational-environmental health consulting firm, had examined over 300 people exposed to dioxin. He assured Levitas and the committee that "it has caused a wide variety of diseases, and I have 30 years of medical and scientific activity which says that those are related to and caused by the exposure to dioxin. . . . From the huge collection of data which has been assembled since 1953 we know that dioxin can affect virtually every major organ system in the body" (U.S. Congress, House, 1983a: 328).

In contrast, expert testimony presented to Congress in the *Interim Report of the Missouri Dioxin Task Force*[17] suggested that the health effects of dioxin might in fact be exaggerated. A University of Missouri dermatologist pointed out that chloracne was considered the hallmark objective health effect associated with exposure to dioxin. It was the only objective finding in populations with low-level exposure in Seveso, Italy. In examples of industrial accidents where there was a high-level exposure, 80 to 90 percent of workers who had some of the more serious effects of dioxin also had chloracne. While all exposed persons would not be expected to exhibit chloracne, it is unlikely that every person would be an exception to this rule. Yet the preliminary report of the Centers for Disease Control examination of 186 residents of Times Beach found no cases of chloracne. A representative of the Veterans Administration reported that their investigation of Agent Orange (a dioxin-contaminated defoliant) concluded that scientific data on the long-term health effects of exposure to dioxin were *at present* insufficient to form a consensus (emphasis in original). [18] A representative of the Chemical Industry Institute of Toxicology stated that numerous "scientific" opinions for the existence or absence of toxic effects as a result of exposure of experimental animals or humans to dioxin were not *consistent* with the existing scientific data (emphasis added). A representative of Syntex (the source of the toxic wastes and a developer of a process to detoxify dioxin) stated that in humans, no *conclusive* evidence existed that dioxin had caused cancer, reproductive effects, or birth defects (emphasis added). [19]

Other experts testifying before Congress cast further doubt on the risks posed by dioxin. Dr. John Beljan reported on the findings of an American Medical Association study of Agent Orange. The study found conclusive evidence of a cause and effect relationship only with respect to chloracne. There was *insufficient data* to establish a definite relationship between human exposure and other claimed adverse health effects (emphasis added). Dr. Beljan could offer no explanation of why there was an apparent lack of severe problems in human populations exposed to dioxin if it was known to be toxic to laboratory animals. "There is a large body of evidence that would tend to indicate that there have been large populations who have been exposed to dioxin and it would appear as if the human being is one those creatures who may be particularly resistant to it" (U.S. Congress, House, 1983a: 1133). He went on to say that he did not personally want to ingest it.

Medical representatives speaking for responsible party interests disputed the existence of any waste site to injury link. Dr. Bruce Karrh, general director of medical, safety, and fire protection for DuPont and representing the Chemical Manufacturers Association, testified that a CMA study of the relationship of health problems to waste sites "[f]ound that claims of such relationship run counter to the experience of CMA member companies. Moreover, independent epidemiological surveys have failed to detect significant health problems. . . . [O]ccupational exposure and health data should provide an indication of the health effects that might be expected if similar exposure patterns were encountered by the public. Since we saw no significant increased incidence of chronic disease among employees in the chemical industry, we concluded that widespread increased incidence of chronic disease among the public is also unlikely" (U.S. Congress, House, 1983a: 359).

Courtney Riordan, representing EPA, reinforced this testimony with discussion of findings at Love Canal and Woburn, Massachusetts. He noted that the only study of Love Canal which so far seemed to have demonstrated a statistically significant difference between exposed and comparison groups related to birth weight. He went on to say that it was difficult to interpret what this finding meant in terms of potential health effects. At Woburn, Massachusetts, a cluster of adverse health outcomes were cited in support of legislation for toxic victim compensation. "Although there was an increase in leukemias around the Woburn area, case-control questionnaire data failed to identify any lifestyle differences among the cases and controls. For the one compound known to have heavily contaminated the area, arsenic, previous human epidemiological studies have shown increased rates of lung and skin cancer following arsenic exposure, but not leukemia. In other words, investigators were unable to discern whether any of the potential chemical exposures could account for the clustering of leukemia cases" (U.S. Congress, House, 1983a: 370–74).

Riordan's observations are particularly striking when contrasted to the conclusions drawn by Marvin Zelen, director of the Woburn health study. Dr. Zelen noted that in 1979 two municipal wells serving as the water supply of east Woburn were shut down after samples from them were found to have excessive concentrations of chlorinated organic solvents. Little was known about the history of these wells prior to 1979, what toxins they may have contained, or their concentrations. An abandoned lagoon was also discovered with heavy contamination of lead, arsenic, and metals. Ground water was discovered to be heavily concentrated with organic pollutants and metals. A study by the Massachusetts Department of Public Health could not find any relationship between a high relative incidence of leukemia and contaminated water supply. In contrast, the subsequent Woburn questionnaire health study found that (1) children with leukemia had twice the access to water from the contaminated wells compared to children not having leukemia; (2) perinatal mortality was higher for pregnant women who had at least 50 percent of their water coming from these wells; (3) pregnant women having access to water from these wells had children with a higher incidence of birth defects; and (4) higher levels of lung/respiratory childhood disorders and kidney/urinary disorders were observed for children having access to water from the contaminated wells. "The aggregate of evidence," continued Dr. Zelen, "is overwhelming that the well water is positively associated with some adverse health effects. . . . It is not possible for such [an observational study] to prove cause and effect relationships" (U.S. Congress, House, 1984a: 182–83).

Parties with potential liability for victim compensation highlighted the uncertain and inconclusive nature of the scientific evidence in their attack on reform proposals. A representative of a large group of property-casualty insurers expressed the insurance industry's concern with predictability and affordability and stated that virtually all victim compensation proposals before Congress were uninsurable. "[They] would so weaken the evidential and burden of proof requirements in the common law as to cast upon defendants and their insurers what we view as the impossible task of identifying which of the millions of Americans with long latency disease and other health problems did not contract them through exposure to hazardous substance and therefore are ineligible for compensation" (U.S. Congress, House, 1983a: 1050). The underlying premise was that a presumption of causation would come to substitute for the traditional test of a preponderance of the evidence and would shift the burden of proof from the plaintiff to the defendant. If the current system was flawed in its denial of compensation to some of the perhaps 2 or 3 *percent* of claimants with valid claims, the proposed system was flawed in that it would ease the burden on this minority while also allowing compensation to the 97 to 98 percent of claimants that did not have valid claims (emphasis added). The reader will note that this is the 2 or 3 percent in the Doll and Peto study referred to above as an example of selective quotation.

Building on this premise, the American Insurance Association took the position that the study group proposal combined staggering costs, unlimited and unpredictable liability, and abandonment of the traditional requirements of fault and causation. It would be uninsurable, unaffordable, unjust, and unwise. With strict, joint and several liability, insurers would bear a substantial percentage of the compensation costs passed through by deep pocket generators they had insured. Like other opponents, they pointed to the experience of the black lung victim compensation program. That program was initially expected to cost $40 million a year and was currently costing about $2 billion a year. It represented what happens when a presumption of causation is allowed. AIA suggested that the study group's tier 1 might have an annual bill of $28 billion; tier 2 would allow added massive costs (U.S. Congress, House, 1983a: 1065).

Sheila Birnbaum, an academic and lawyer representing the insurance industry, emphasized that the proposed reforms built on the erroneous assumption that compensation was not possible under state tort law. She presented Congress with a compilation of recent verdicts or settlements involving exposure to toxic substances and interpreted the cases as indicating "that there is a tort system presently in place, which is responding and which will continue to respond to claims" (U.S. Congress, House, 1983a: 1060). The cases, however, generally involved toxic substances with established potential for injury (e.g., lead, benzene, DDT, formaldehyde) and/or situations with little uncertainty regarding source and exposure (e.g., chemical explosions, children living in proximity to a lead smelter).

Like the insurance industry, representatives of the National Association of Manufacturers argued against change that they believed would yield an inherently unfair imposition of large liability judgments. Union Carbide expressed its commitment to compensation but believed that revisions in common law should be left to the states. Testimony on behalf of ARCO warned that devising legislation in an emotionally charged atmosphere and without adequate factual underpinnings was fraught with difficulty and peril. Regarding specific proposals, ARCO suggested that if a federal cause of action was adopted, it should have consistent and equitable standards and preempt state law. These standards should be based on actual causation and not upon unproved assumptions. Further, while suits brought by the government would preserve a victim compensation fund and penalize undesirable conduct, they would also continue litigation and elevate the transaction costs that any compensation system should be designed to eliminate (U.S. Congress, House, 1983a: 1291).

The Reagan administration also argued against proposals for a victim compensation title. A 1983 Office of Management and Budget review characterized the Superfund study group recommendations as "adopting *the worst of both worlds: an administrative compensation system* with liberal evidential standards and generous benefits, as well as *continued availability of traditional tort law*. . . . Although its advocates now price Superfund compensation proposals at '*only*' *a few billion dollars*, the amounts at stake are *literally open-ended and potentially enormous*" (emphasis in original) (U.S. Congress, House, 1983a: 1826). EPA's general counsel opposed what he characterized as drastic reductions in the burden of proof. "All victim compensation proposals assume some ability through science to establish a cause and effect relationship between particular substances, exposure levels, and diseases. This may not be the case" (U.S. Congress, House, 1983a: 368). Testimony on behalf of the Department of Justice offered an extensive list of reasons for not adopting a federal cause of action that included the burden on federal courts, federal government exposure to liability for personal injury and a flood of litigation that would dramatically increase the federal deficit, the implications for occupational exposure and workers compensation, and the erosion in the willingness of insurers to underwrite facility risks (U.S. Congress, House, 1985b: 738–40).

As discussed above, James Florio had introduced several bills containing provisions that addressed the problems identified by the Superfund Task Force on victim compensation. However, the bill that passed the House in August 1984 (H.R. 5640) did not allow for compensation of injury out of Superfund. It did mandate studies by the Agency for Toxic Substances and Disease Registry that could be useful in establishing the link between hazardous substances and injury and also allowed members of exposed populations to petition EPA for health effect studies. It further created a federal cause of action. When the House passed a subsequent bill in December 1985, provision for the federal cause of action was rejected. The bill passed by the Senate three months earlier (S. 51) mandated studies by ATSDR and established a victim assistance demonstration project.

By late 1985 supporters of a victim compensation title were fighting to retain the little that remained in major Superfund bills before Congress. Industry and the Reagan administration were adamantly opposed to the limited victim assistance program passed by the Senate. Like the black lung program, they argued, it could serve as a precedent for a more expansive victim compensation program. It had budgetary, policy, and legal implications well beyond the Superfund program that made its consideration inappropriate in the limited context of Superfund reauthorization (U.S. Congress, House, 1985b: 737).[20] In contrast, both the administration and major hazardous waste generators supported studies to clarify the health effects of hazardous substances. The Chemical Manufacturers Association had joined a lawsuit brought by the Environmental Defense Fund to force EPA to establish and fund the Agency for Toxic Substances and Disease Registry. CERCLA had mandated ATSDR as a vehicle for scientific study of waste site/disease relationships. Having based their opposition to a victim compensation title on the insufficiency of cause and effect evidence, industry and government both advocated further study but little else.

Funding Cleanup

Conflict over a source of revenue for an expanded Superfund led to the most protracted of the reauthorization debates and threatened to shut down the existing cleanup program. The House proposed a substantial increase in taxes on crude oil and chemical feedstocks to underwrite a $10 billion fund.[21] The Senate's proposed $7.5 billion fund would be financed primarily through a broad-based corporate tax and an unchanged tax on oil and chemical feedstocks. The Reagan administration's proposed $5 billion fund also would leave the feedstock taxes at current levels and would raise about $3 billion through a waste-end tax.[22] In addition, an increased share of cleanup costs would be financed by the states: a state would pay 20 percent of remedial costs if the site was privately owned (up from 10 percent under CERCLA) and 75 percent if the site was state owned (up from 50 percent under CERCLA). In contrast, House and Senate bills would maintain the original percentages and decrease the states' share of long-term operation and maintenance costs.

Congress's 1980 decision to finance Superfund through feedstock taxation was based primarily on considerations of predictability, ease of administration, and the expectation that most of the tax would be passed through to other producers and to consumers. During the reauthorization debate, the industries paying the Superfund tax emphasized the inequities of the current tax burden and the economic problems each industry faced. Increasing their tax burden would threaten industrial recovery from the 1981–82 recession. EPA, other government agencies, and private sector consultants also expressed serious reservations regarding feedstock taxation. The Reagan administration and EPA preferred to address these reservations through heavy reliance on a waste-end tax. The petrochemical industry preferred reliance on a waste-end tax and general revenues or on a broad-based corporate tax.

In a study of alternative funding mechanisms released in December 1984, EPA had identified several areas of strength and weakness in the current feedstock tax (U.S. Environmental Protection Agency, 1984d). On the plus side, the tax would generally raise chemical prices in proportion to the tax rate and would have small impacts on production.[23] The tax was easy to administer and its revenues were reasonably predictable.[24] On the minus side, the tax did not create incentives for environmental protection. Further, it was unfair in that it overtaxed organic chemicals and undertaxed inorganic chemicals relative to their contributions to cleanup needs.

Several problems associated with a feedstock tax could be addressed by combining it with a waste-end tax. On the plus side, the waste-end tax had a negligible impact on prices and profits at an industry level, created a better match between taxpayers and industrial contributors to Superfund problems, and had desirable incentive effects. A significant percentage of waste stored on land could be expected to shift to waste treatment in response to tax incentives.

On the minus side, a waste-end tax might not generate predictable revenues or be easy to administer. Since a waste-end tax encouraged a movement away from higher-taxed disposal options, the tax base would erode as generators responded to these incentives. In addition, potential taxpayers could avoid the tax through illegal dumping. Despite some findings to the contrary, EPA was convinced that with increased rates to compensate for changes in the tax base and provision of adequate enforcement staff and resources, a waste-end tax would raise substantial revenues at moderate rates while creating relatively strong incentives for a shift to treatment. EPA believed that administration would be manageable if the tax were based on existing reporting and regulatory structures.

Reliance on a waste-end tax had broad appeal. In a 1983 hazardous waste management study, the Office of Technology Assessment emphasized waste-end taxation as a means for discouraging land disposal and for firming the generally disregarded links between Superfund and the Resource Conservation and Recovery Act (see discussion in chapter 5). Joel Hirschhorn, OTA project director for Superfund, told Congress that much more than the $600 million per year proposed by the administration could be generated from a waste-end tax (U.S. Congress, House, 1985b: 36, 45). The Association of State and

Territorial Solid Waste Management Officials and many environmental groups also supported waste-end taxation. The petrochemical and oil industries believed it was a preferable alternative to an expanded feedstock tax.

In contrast to this optimism, other participants in the debate raised serious reservations regarding the heavy reliance the Reagan administration proposal placed on a waste-end tax to finance cleanup. The Congressional Joint Committee on Taxation and the House Ways and Means Committee among others noted that there was substantial uncertainty regarding the revenues that could be generated. EPA had built a case for predictability with reference to state experience. However, it acknowledged that it was unclear how relevant state experience was to a $1 billion waste-end tax. The same could be said of a $600 million waste-end tax. A representative of the environmental/labor coalition expressed concern that, in favoring deep well injection, the proposed tax schedules might create a whole new generation of underground Superfund sites. Concern was also expressed that the tax might be difficult to administer since, among other problems, rates would change with any alteration in Resource Conservation and Recovery Act disposal rules and hazardous waste listings.

Strong objections were also voiced by the producers of inorganic chemicals who anticipated an increased financial burden under a waste-end tax. Kennecott, the nation's leading producer of copper, argued that the copper industry could not absorb the burden of a waste-end tax (U.S. Congress, House, 1985b: 1066–68). Similarly, other producers claimed that a waste-end tax would undercut their international competitiveness since a similar increase in cost would not be borne by their foreign competition. Domestic producers would need to either absorb the added cost or reduce or terminate production and withdraw from contested markets. Further, a waste-end tax was unlikely to reduce waste generation in mining industries since these industries faced no real alternative to current land disposal practices (U.S. Congress, Senate, 1984a: 372). Inorganic wastes cannot be destroyed and will not disappear. Industries producing these wastes, such as automotive, machinery, primary metals, and electroplaters, were currently facing severe economic conditions. A waste-end tax system would exacerbate their economic problems (U.S. Congress, House, 1985b: 90).

Within the context of the Reagan administration proposal for a $5 billion program, creation of a waste-end tax would avoid increased reliance on feedstock taxation. However, reservations regarding the predictability and revenue-raising potential of a waste-end tax and the fact that the House and Senate were seeking $10 billion and $7.5 billion, respectively, in Superfund tax revenues suggested the strategic need for an additional alternative. In the absence of such an alternative, increased feedstock taxation seemed inevitable. Clearly perceiving this possibility, Atlantic Richfield Company sponsored a major study of funding alternatives by economics professor William Nordhaus in conjunction with the Management Analysis Center, Inc. The study highlighted problems with feedstock taxation and advocated the alternative of a broad-based tax on net corporate receipts.

ARCO introduced the broad-based tax concept to the House in early 1984. In this and subsequent testimony ARCO representatives discussed the economic problems facing the chemical industry and relied on the Nordhaus study to emphasize the negative international trade and equity implications of feedstock taxation. The chemical industry was facing severe economic problems: "Over the past several years, this industry has suffered from both overcapacity, and significantly increased costs for the petroleum fractions and natural gas streams used in production. Annual growth in the industry has dramatically slowed from levels in excess of 10 percent down to about 3–4 percent per year. Profit margins on many products were reduced or eliminated during the recent downturn" (June 13, 1984, testimony, reprinted in U.S. Congress, House, 1985b: 489). ARCO pointed out that in an industry with excess production capacity, it was not possible to pass on the feedstock tax to their downstream customers. Free market pressures, including foreign competition, mitigated against pass-through and forced domestic producers to absorb the tax. The recent recovery only allowed ARCO to raise the percentage of the tax collected from customers from 39 percent in 1981 to 53 percent in 1983 (U.S. Congress, Senate, 1984a: 521).[25] Further, the current Superfund tax primarily burdened a small number of petrochemical companies; only twelve companies paid 70 percent of the feedstock tax. For these companies, petrochemical manufacturing operations represented 5 to 20 percent of their capital assets. "[I]t is unrealistic to expect the management and stockholders of these companies to continue to manufacture petrochemicals when these operations can only be expected to generate continuing losses, and are not essential to the companies' overall viability" (June 13, 1984, testimony, reprinted in U.S. Congress, House, 1985b: 492).

The Nordhaus study highlighted the consequences of expanded feedstock taxation for the international competitiveness of the petrochemical industry and its continued domestic operations (Nordhaus et al., 1985). It concluded, first, that the burden of the tax fell on nonhazardous as well as hazardous feedstock derivatives. Second, the lost revenues due to reduced domestic and export sales were double the increased feedstock tax to be collected under the proposed House bill (H.R. 5640). Third, imports of key petrochemical derivatives would increase by as much as 400 percent and exports of petrochemical derivatives would fall by 4 to 18 percent. Fourth, the estimated loss to U.S. industry was $190 million annually for just two chemicals analyzed; this would come at a time when the positive petrochemical trade balance enjoyed by the United States was already eroding. Faced with the prospect of continuing unprofitable operations, many domestic producers could find plant shutdowns to be the most attractive economic option.

Other expert testimony supported these projections of a negative trade impact. A representative of the International Trade Administration (Department of Commerce) emphasized the need to maintain competitive industries. Asked what would be the impact of a fivefold increase in the feedstock tax applied to chemicals, he responded that "I believe for the organic chemical business this could be a downright disaster" (U.S. Congress, House, 1985a: 854). Due to overcapacity and international competition, it was also unlikely that producers of inorganic chemicals could pass an increased tax downstream. These projections did little to allay the concerns of members of Congress from Louisiana and Texas and AFL-CIO representatives from these states regarding the impact of an increased feedstock tax on their industries.

A less pessimistic assessment was offered by the Congressional Research Service. A 1984 CRS study concluded that "[i]t is highly unlikely that the Superfund taxes played a major role in the weakening of U.S. primary petrochemical use in 1981 and 1982" (U.S. Congress, House, 1985a: 848). The study estimated that taxes explain *no more than* 10 percent and 5.5 percent of the industry's decline in output in 1981 and 1982, respectively (emphasis in original). National economic recession and dollar appreciation account for most of the decline in output. A 1985 CRS study estimated that virtually all of the first-year increase in feedstock taxation would be passed forward to users in the form of higher prices. Profit margins would be little affected. Since imported primary petrochemicals would be subject to the Superfund tax increase under a House proposal, the competitiveness of domestic producers vis-à-vis imports would not be affected (U.S. Congress, House, 1985a: 851–52). When the staff of the Congressional Joint Committee on Taxation examined the Congressional Research Service evidence, it concluded that "[w]hile the feedstock tax could, in theory, harm U.S. trade, it is unlikely that the actual damage to the U.S. chemical industry is large" (U.S. Congress, Senate, 1985b: 59).

Beyond its findings on international competitiveness, the Nordhaus study also offered support for petrochemical industry claims that feedstock taxation was not equitable. The chemical and oil refining industries were currently paying 84 percent and 16 percent, respectively, of the feedstock tax. In contrast, these industries accounted for only 44 percent of identifiable National

Priorities List site disposers. Further, 18 percent of the sites were owned by chemical or oil companies while 55 percent were owned by other untaxed industries and the owners of 37 percent of the sites were unknown. Finally, the organic chemical industry produced 54 percent of chemicals identified at Superfund sites and paid 66 percent of the tax, the inorganic chemical and nonferrous metal smelting and refining industries produced 30 percent of these chemicals and paid 18 percent, and the petroleum refining industry produced 6 percent of these chemicals and paid 16 percent of the tax.

It should be noted that these estimates as well as similar estimates produced by EPA[26] suffered from substantial data limitations. It is possible to determine how frequently a chemical appears at a Superfund site and how frequently the name of a disposer appears on site records. However, there is no particular reason to expect a tight relationship between these frequencies and the volume or toxicity of the wastes disposed of at the site. Although the data used by Nordhaus and EPA were the best available, they did not necessarily provide an accurate picture of relative contribution to Superfund problems. Consequently, they can suggest the inequity of feedstock taxation, but cannot establish its extent. These data limitations are similar to those involved in apportioning liability in negotiation and settlement.

The development of a truly equitable tax was perhaps impossible, observed the ARCO study authors. "The past benefits of the products that have caused hazardous waste problems, and of today's cleanup, are widely dispersed. To properly apportion cost to all groups, everyone who has ever used a styrofoam cup, bought pantyhose, taken aspirin, or wrapped a sandwich in plastic wrap would have to be taxed. . . . No tax could be levied that would remotely succeed in approximating the benefits of past actions or present cleanup" (U.S. Congress, House, 1985b: 297, 300). A broad-based tax on corporate net receipts, however, could more fully acknowledge the societal nature of the problem and distribute the burden accordingly across industry. The proposed tax would be paid by manufacturing (54.5 percent); mining (4.7 percent); transportation and utilities (16.8 percent); wholesale and retail trade (12.5 percent); and finance, insurance, and real estate (8 percent) (U.S. Congress, House, 1985b: 403). Although the Nordhaus study did not break out the percentage burden falling on the chemical and oil industries, it is possible that these industries would pay about 30 percent of the tax imposed on manufacturing, that is, about 16.2 percent of the total.[27] The other advantages of a broad-based tax were that its revenues were virtually guaranteed, administration was simple, and economic dislocation was minimal.

The broad-based tax received strong support from the Chemical Manufacturers Association and from other industries likely to suffer a greater tax burden under alternative proposals. The American Petroleum Institute gave qualified support to the ARCO proposal. The petroleum industry would experience a tenfold tax increase under the House bill. API argued that the petroleum refining industry could not pay more without a serious negative impact on its future. The industry was suffering from substantial idle capacity (despite the U.S. economic recovery), plants had shut down, and those still in operation were only marginally profitable. Over the past few years, petroleum refiners had experienced lower demand, heightened competition from imports, high costs of upgrading refining facilities, and substantial additional environmental control costs. "Singling out the U.S. refining industry for increased CERCLA taxes, when they already are paying more than their fair share, would make even worse an economic environment that has already seen a loss of 11,000 jobs" (U.S. Congress, House, 1985b: 1046). API advocated no change in the feedstock tax, institution of a $300 million per year waste-end tax, and raising any additional funds through general revenues. As a last alternative, it would support a broad-based tax.

In contrast to the chemical industry, the oil industry could not claim that an increased tax on oil would have adverse trade impacts. The tax was imposed on imported as well as domestic oil. The Nordhaus study had evaluated a hydro-carbons tax (i.e., a tax on crude oil, coal, and gas), and although this option was not discussed in any detail, it did note that only modest economic distortions were likely if tax rates were modest. The House-proposed increase from 0.79 cents per barrel to 4.5 cents per barrel would result in a 0.002 percent increase in the price of a $20 barrel of oil, an increase that could be passed on in full to consumers.

Senate committees with jurisdiction over Superfund legislation (the Environment and Public Works Committee and the Finance Committee) were sympathetic to positions taken by the chemical and petroleum refining industries. Senator Lloyd Bentsen (D-Tex.), a member of both committees, told his colleagues that "we all know that the fund must be and will be expanded, but as more revenues are required, they must be raised with a full recognition that a more equitable revenue base is necessary. . . . [T]he narrowly drawn feedstock tax places an unfair economic burden on certain chemicals and areas of our national economy. For example, there are estimates that 50 percent of the petrochemical feedstock portion of the tax is raised from plants in Texas. . . . It is not to the benefit of any area of our Nation for us to encourage the production of these chemicals outside of the United States. . . . I am disappointed that the [administration] proposal fails to include a broader based revenue source that is both necessary and fair" (U.S. Congress, Senate, 1985a: 3). The Environment and Public Works Committee had advocated a broader tax base in its deliberations during the Ninety-eighth Congress. Several members of the Finance Committee introduced legislation establishing a broad-based tax in the Ninety-ninth Congress.

The broad-based tax concept drew criticism from groups that questioned its underlying assumption of severe economic dislocation and its presumption of equity. Blakeman Early of the Sierra Club told Congress: "We believe that the oil and chemical feedstock tax should continue to be the principle source of funding for Superfund. The passage of H.R. 5640 by the Ways and Means Committee and subsequently by the House, with triple the rates of the current tax . . . indicates that [they] also believe that an increase can occur without a major adverse impact on the chemical and oil industries. . . . The chemical industry is the fourth lowest taxed industrial sector among 18 industries studied by the Joint Tax Committee" (U.S. Congress, House, 1985b: 163). He went on to say that a broad-based tax gets away from the polluters-pay principle in that it taxes some industries that have nothing to do with handling hazardous substances and hazardous waste. A representative of the Steelworkers Union expressed an oft-repeated view that industry frequently holds out the threat of plant closings, employment loss, and diminished international competitiveness in its opposition to environmental legislation: "[T]here is a lesson to be learned when we're dealing with industries in any environmental issue . . . another form of the old saw 'if you don't do something for us, then we're either closing down or going overseas'. . . . [T]his has not been the case. . . . [The] environmental issue is a smoke screen issue" (U.S. Congress, House, 1985b: 195).

Strong objections to a broad-based tax also came from EPA and the Reagan administration. EPA argued that it would not target the tax to the industry segments that use or produce hazardous substances and hazardous wastes. A large percentage of such taxes would be paid by firms not directly responsible for Superfund expenditures (U.S. Congress, House, 1985b: 658). Beyond any concern with equity, the Reagan administration was opposed to tax increases, expanded social programs, and, in particular, to the creation of a new method of taxing corporate activity that could then easily expand into other areas of government finance. Senator Bob Dole (R-Kans.) expressed this view in his critique of the Senate Finance Committee bill: "I do not think it is a coincidence that the Committee found it easy to vote for a $7.5 billion program when that program is largely funded by a very small tax on a large number of manufacturers. I fear that coupling this broad new tax with a popular program both removes considerations of fiscal restraint from our deliberations and guarantees that this tax bill expend [sic] by leaps and bounds in the not too distant future" (U.S. Congress, Senate, 1985e: 32).

SUPERFUND HIATUS

A congressional deadlock emerged in December 1985 when the House approved legislation to create a waste-end tax and to impose an increased share of Superfund taxes on the chemical and petroleum industries and the Senate approved a broad-based tax. The following six months witnessed complex and often heated negotiations between conferees appointed to draw up a compromise. By July 1986 final agreement was reached on all issues except how to raise the money (Bureau of National Affairs, August 8, 1986: 523). The compromise would create an $8.5 billion hazardous waste site cleanup program and a $500 million program for leaking underground storage tanks. The Reagan administration threatened to veto the bill if more than $5.3 billion was sought and, in particular, if funding was via a broad-based tax or substantial increases in chemical feedstock or petroleum taxes. An aide to Administrator Thomas discounted the threat, noting that the bill gave so many new responsibilities to EPA that the agency could not effectively carry them out with $5.3 billion. EPA warned of the dire consequences of not passing a bill in 1986 and asked for special appropriations to avert a collapse of the cleanup program (Bureau of National Affairs, September 19, 1986: 731).

By late September 1986, conferees were under pressure to have a bill on President Reagan's desk to avoid a pocket veto. They agreed to accept the Senate concept of a broad-based tax imposed on corporations subject to the alternative minimum tax as computed under the pending Tax Reform Act of 1986.[28] Speaking for House conferees, Representative Downey (D-N.Y.) argued that the Senate tax on petroleum was too low and not serious and that the broad-based tax was too high.[29] The House was committed to a polluter-pays concept. Further, the elimination of a waste-end tax from the proposal would pose enormous difficulties politically. Speaking for Senate conferees, Senator Bentsen reiterated the plight of the petroleum industry and oil producing states. (Crude oil prices had plummeted from $24 to around $13 a barrel between 1985 and 1986.) He argued that waste-end tax revenues had never lived up to expectations and that their collection would strain the capabilities of the IRS. Texas Representative J. J. Pickle told conferees that the oil industry already would be taking an $8 to $10 billion hit under pending tax reform legislation and that CERCLA would tax the industry repeatedly with its chemical ingredient tax, petroleum tax, and a tax to finance an underground storage tank cleanup fund.

Finally, on October 2, a compromise was reached between conferees. The legislation authorized $8.5 billion for hazardous waste site cleanup to be financed primarily through a petroleum tax ($2.76 billion), a chemical feedstock tax ($1.37 billion), a corporate environment tax ($2.5 billion), and general revenues ($1.25 billion). A higher tax was levied on imported oil than on domestic oil due to efforts by Senator Bentsen to protect jobs in the domestic oil industry. A tax on imported chemical derivatives ($57 million) was imposed to address the international competitiveness concerns of the organic chemicals industry. The compromise legislation was passed by the Senate, 88 to 8, on October 3 and by the House, 386 to 27, on October 8 (Bureau of National Affairs, October 10, 1986: 853).

Treasury Secretary Baker, Energy Secretary Herrington, and Office of Management and Budget Director Miller all recommended a veto (Bureau of National Affairs, October 17, 1986: 907). Representative Lent (R-N.Y.) said a veto would have a bad effect on Republican House and Senate members involved in close reelection races. President Reagan remained undecided. Public information campaigns were waged by interest groups in support and in opposition. In favor of the legislation were several environmental engineering firms and laboratories with Superfund contracts, the Hazardous Waste Treatment Council, environmental groups, chemical companies, and mining firms. In opposition were oil companies and a coalition against the broad-based tax spearheaded by the Grocery Manufacturers of America. Mobil Oil ran an ad in the *Washington Post* stating that "One industry—ours—has been singled out to shoulder 30 percent of the $9 billion program. No other industry would pay anything close to this amount." The new tax "will doubtlessly hurt the oil industry's ability to find new energy sources for America, and its ability to compete against foreign companies overseas" (Bureau of National Affairs, October 17, 1986: 907). The conservative Heritage Foundation asserted that the legislation would abandon the polluter-pays concept and "tax corporations as though all were guilty" to create a "lucrative source of public works projects." "Only a very small number of toxic waste dumps," the foundation said, "pose an urgent and expensive problem. Yet the proponents of the legislation give the impression that the whole country is awash with dangerous chemicals, dumped by unknown polluters" (Bureau of National Affairs, October 17, 1986: 907).

President Reagan signed the Superfund Amendments and Reauthorization Act of 1986 on October 17. In a statement, the president said that he did so because his "overriding concern has been the continuation of our progress to clean up hazardous waste sites" (Bureau of National Affairs, October 24, 1986: 955).[30]

SUPERFUND AMENDMENTS AND REAUTHORIZATION ACT (SARA)

The redesigned Superfund Act was more extensive and complex than the 1980 act. It limited EPA discretion while expanding its responsibilities, powers, and funding.[31]

SARA set cleanup schedules and standards and stipulated that a permanent remedy must be chosen when possible. States were given the opportunity for a more active role in the cleanup process. Federal facilities were subjected to cleanup timetables and EPA was given an oversight/management role analogous to its relationship with other responsible parties.

To encourage state siting of new treatment and disposal facilities, each state was required to provide assurance by November 1989 that it had capacity for all hazardous wastes expected to be generated within the state for the next twenty years or to forgo access to fund-financed cleanup. To ease the financial burden of cleanup on the states, they would no longer have to pay 100 percent of operation and maintenance costs after the first year for ground water and surface water treatment. The Reagan administration position that the states should bear a larger percentage of cleanup costs was rejected.

To encourage settlement with responsible parties, SARA essentially formalized EPA's existing settlement policy with some additions to encourage negotiation. Among other provisions, the agency could prepare a nonbinding allocation of cleanup costs among responsible parties when it would aid settlement. Establishment of these procedures reflected House, Senate, and industry concerns that EPA settlement policy left little room for negotiation and provided little guidance to responsible parties in their deliberations over apportionment. Further, mixed funding was authorized where responsible parties would conduct cleanup with financial assistance from the Superfund—essentially fund coverage of a portion of the orphan share to induce settlement. To limit responsible party use of the courts to delay cleanup, judicial review was limited to the administrative record established by the agency as a basis for selecting a remedy (i.e., the record of decision). Challenges to removal or remedial decisions could not be reviewed by federal courts prior to EPA enforcement actions.

The discretion granted EPA was circumscribed by a citizen suit provision advocated by both the House and Senate. Citizens could commence a civil action against any party (including the United States) for violation of any standard, regulation, condition, requirement, or order under Superfund (including federal facilities) and could commence a civil action against the government for failure to perform a nondiscretionary duty under Superfund.

Most proposals to address barriers to victim compensation were excluded from the House and Senate bills passed in December 1985. The House rejected a federal cause of action. The Senate Finance Committee killed the victim assistance demonstration program. As in 1980, the potential burden of these proposals on hazardous waste generators, insurers, and the government was given greater weight than their potential for easing the financial and emotional burden of victims. SARA did alter state statutes of limitations by setting as a minimum limitation period the date the victim knew that damages were caused by hazardous substances. SARA also required the Agency for Toxic Substances and Disease Registry to prepare a list of at least 275 of the hazardous substances most commonly found at Superfund sites and to prepare toxicological profiles of these substances. ATSDR was also directed to perform a health assessment at each Superfund site to assist in determining whether to take additional steps to reduce human exposure and to collect additional information. Citizens could petition ATSDR for health assessment. To preclude EPA or the president from again short-circuiting these provisions through depriving ATSDR of resources, minimum employment and funding levels were mandated.

A remedial cleanup program for leaking underground petroleum storage tanks was established and the states were required to inventory underground storage tanks containing hazardous substances. A cleanup trust fund would be financed by taxes on various fuels. A new Title III contained the Emergency Planning and Community Right-to-Know Act, providing for safety information, emergency planning, and notification programs to strengthen public protection from industrial use of hazardous chemicals. Making this information readily available to the public would put pressure on producers to reduce their hazardous waste generation and to emphasize source reduction. The deaths of thousands in the December 1984 Bhopal chemical disaster guaranteed passage despite a desperate lobbying campaign by manufacturers, White House opposition, and denouncement by powerful legislators who thought the bill would overly burden industry.[32] A new Title IV contained the Radon Gas and Indoor Air Quality Research Act, requiring EPA to establish a radon gas and indoor air quality research and development program, including health effects research and demonstration of methods for mitigation or elimination of radon gas and other pollutants.

POLITICAL ECONOMY OF SARA

The design of SARA, like that of the 1980 Superfund law, was a product of environmental threats, economic concerns, and conflicting political pressures. In contrast to the earlier debate, the one over SARA proceeded against a background of accumulated information on the extent of public health and environmental threats posed by Superfund sites. In 1980 generator industries could easily challenge EPA estimates of the number of potential cleanup sites. They also could challenge cost estimates since no cleanups of the Superfund type had yet been executed. By the mid-1980s EPA estimates of the number of potential National Priorities List sites were accepted by many observers as conservative. Further, it was generally accepted by EPA, cleanup contractors, and congressional oversight offices that remedy selection must incorporate standards and promote permanent solutions. The agency's December 1984 estimate of cleanup costs assumed neither specific standards nor permanent cleanups. Its $6 billion minimum-size program assumed cleanup costs in the $8 million range. With application of specific standards and permanent cleanup technologies, cleanup costs would be a multiple of this amount. The accumulation of information placed generator industries in the position of having to acknowledge the substantial scope of the problem and having to fight against expansion beyond the $5 billion program advocated by EPA. Their potential to effectively exercise political pressure was constrained.

In designing the 1980 act, Congress recognized that EPA implementation of other hazardous waste legislation did not always live up to expectations. Implementation failure, however, was not attributed primarily to White House opposition. In contrast, SARA was designed specifically to preclude Reagan administration inaction on environmental protection. Until the 1980s the congressional paradigm for coping with regulatory problems remained largely unchanged: the legislature formulated broad policy objectives and the agencies devised the means to achieve them (Florio, 1986: 375–78). The appropriations process provided the greatest opportunity for congressional influence over agencies. Lawsuits by regulated parties and the beneficiaries of regulation helped to ensure that agencies implemented statutes as written. In the early 1980s, Reagan administration efforts to eviscerate regulatory agencies as a deregulatory strategy demonstrated that the traditional paradigm was insufficient to promote environmental protection. Confronted with a "wide discrepancy between the public's desire for vigorous environmental protection and the Reagan administration's ideological preferences for regulatory relief" Congress was forced, in the words of James Florio, to become a "reluctant regulator" (Florio, 1986: 376). Public demands for action (as indicated by public opinion polls) and pressure from environmental and labor groups and the states buttressed a congressional desire to preclude a replay of the early 1980s cleanup experience.

SARA's stipulation of work schedules and cleanup standards is the clearest manifestation of this change in the relationship between Congress and the Environmental Protection Agency. Schedules and standards are a concrete statement of congressional intentions regarding cleanup program goals. They give form to the Superfund directive to minimize threats to public health and the environment. They expand the realm of nondiscretionary action and in so doing attempt to insulate the agency from a White House preference for inaction. SARA's citizen suit provisions further reinforce congressional intent by sharing oversight responsibilities with individuals and organizations.

The schedules contained in SARA, however, do have inherent limitations. First, they direct EPA to start physical cleanups but do not set related goals for completions. The omission of completion goals in part reflects the fact that specific answers to how-clean-is-clean questions remained elusive. Also, since few cleanups had been completed, there was little basis for setting a completion target date. Second, they force the agency to give priority to satisfaction of nondiscretionary over discretionary goals. As discussed in the next chapter, the need to meet schedules resulted in a clear agency preference for fund-financed over privately financed cleanups and a sacrifice of environmental to nonenvironmental performance goals.

In setting schedules and standards, Congress substantially raised the expected five-year cost of the program. The $8.5 billion fund would cover the federal government's share of cleanup costs. States would have to pay around $1 billion. Responsible parties would need to contribute some $5.7 to $12.8 billion via settlements with EPA. Bringing finances in line with program goals required a reduction in the financial burden placed on states as well as an effective enforcement program. State cleanup cost matching requirements were eased so that the program would not as readily fall victim to state budgetary constraints. Settlement provisions reduced responsible party potential to adopt delaying tactics. The codification of the existing settlement policy expressed congressional intent that EPA should use the incentives already contained in its settlement policy, such as release from liability and mixed funding, to encourage private party–financed cleanups. At the same time, the addition of special negotiation procedures and nonbinding preliminary allocations of liability addressed criticisms by industry that EPA downplayed incentives and avoided meaningful negotiations. EPA could now emphasize negotiations when they were likely to bring about satisfactory settlements and emphasize aggressive enforcement when negotiation threatened to retard cleanup progress. Citizen suits would complement EPA enforcement efforts and also would help to keep the agency honest.

Advocates of an expanded Superfund saw SARA as "the most significant piece of environmental legislation this decade."[33] In contrast, industry representatives felt they were shut out of reauthorization negotiations and that environmental groups, the Environmental Protection Agency, and the states were the only real players.[34] Industries liable for Superfund problems did not achieve three of their primary goals: elimination of the "draconian imposition" of strict, joint and several liability; a related increase in the orphan share of cleanup costs to be borne by the fund; and mandatory EPA apportionment of the remaining cleanup costs as a basis for fair share settlement offers. Their potential liability was reduced, however, with elimination of most proposed changes in victim compensation procedures. Further, they could be expected to benefit from the toxic substances and health assessment studies to be conducted by the Agency for Toxic Substances and Disease Registry if, as some industry representatives claimed, threats to public health did not justify many site cleanup plans. The failure of Congress to include a victim compensation title suggests that the political pressure exerted by advocates of change was offset by that of industry, by information on the potential though uncertain cost of the title, and by agency and White House opposition.

The resolution of the funding debate produced both winners and losers among industries. The chemical industry was a winner. Its burden under the feedstock tax remained unchanged while a tax on imported chemical derivatives modified the adverse trade effects attributed to a feedstock tax and facilitated its pass-through to consumers. The industry would bear some 4.3 percent of the corporate environmental tax.[35] Overall, the chemical industry would pay directly about $1.29 billion or 16.3 percent of all Superfund taxes and, given ARCO estimates discussed above, would be able to pass at least half this amount on to customers. The chemical industry learned from its experience during the first Superfund debate. It was more unified and did not rely on claims of adverse impacts that were unsupported by data (see chapter 4).

If the chemical industry was a winner, industries not subject to the original Superfund tax were losers. Manufacturers other than the chemical and petroleum industries would pay about $1 billion of the corporate environmental tax (12.6 percent of all Superfund taxes). Nonmanufacturing industries would pay about $1.28 billion (16.2 percent of all Superfund taxes). Congressional hearings provided little indication of the percentage of this direct burden that could be passed on to consumers.

The petroleum refining industry defined itself as the biggest loser. Mobil claimed that petroleum refiners would pay 30 percent of fund-financed cleanup, a percentage substantially above estimates of their contribution to the problem. The total tax imposed on oil can be roughly estimated at $3 billion (39 percent of total Superfund taxes), although only half this amount would be raised from domestic production. The size of the tax increase placed on oil can be attributed to several factors: First, there was resistance to a further increase in general revenues due to concern over the mounting federal budget deficit. Second, the chemical industry could make a stronger case for economic dislocation if the chemical feedstock tax was increased. Third, less than half the increase would fall on domestic refiners. Finally, it was expected that refiners could pass SARA's minuscule percentage increase in oil prices on to consumers in full. If the last two of these assumptions are correct, the domestic refining industry would end up suffering a tax increase well below their contribution to Superfund cleanup problems.

Having argued that society as a whole was the primary beneficiary of the chemical revolution and thus should bear a major portion of the toxic debt, generator industries would deem any increase in their burden to be inequitable. SARA's reaffirmation of the precedent of using industry as a conduit for environmental taxation was therefore troubling on several counts. First, there was no guarantee that the Superfund tax could be passed on in full. Second, industry could be used as a conduit for funding other environmental programs. As their direct tax burden increased, the percentage to be passed on could decrease. Finally, even with substantial pass-through, generator industries retained the stigma of bearing a primary responsibility for creation of Superfund cleanup problems.

As in the 1980 debate, the ability of opposing interests to exert political pressure was limited by broader structural constraints on congressional choice. The advocacy of environmental groups was made compelling by extensive information on the extent of the environmental threats posed by Superfund sites, while the opposition of industry was made compelling by a slow recovery from the 1981–82 recession and a deteriorating trade balance. Congress had to weigh the need to expand the program to address these threats against the need to minimize adverse economic impacts. Stigmatizing generator industries as the cause of the problem could legitimize Congress by establishing it as a champion of public over private interests. Spreading the direct burden of the Superfund tax over a wide range of industries and concentrating the greatest burden on an industry most likely to pass on the tax in full reduced the economic impact. Legitimacy also required a stronger enforcement program and a guarantee that congressional intentions would not succumb to White House intransigence. Even with limits on agency discretion, SARA granted increased autonomy to EPA to accomplish Superfund site cleanups. The need to sustain legitimacy and promote capital accumulation circumscribed the ability of affected parties to fully shape SARA's final form to their self-interests.

CHAPTER 9

The Superfund Amendments and Reauthorization Act enhanced EPA powers and circumscribed its discretion. It set the stage for a substantial increase in fund- and responsible party–financed cleanup activity, for environmentally effective and permanent cleanups, and for increased state and community involvement in cleanup decisions.

A redesign of EPA's implementation strategy was needed to meet these expectations. The goals of SARA would define the ends to be achieved while an incorporation of new powers would become the means. EPA did not pursue this course of action. Rather, the agency made modifications to its existing strategy and set fund conservation and the fulfillment of nonenvironmental performance goals as its primary ends. It soon became apparent that within the confines of its strategy, resources, and leadership, EPA could not align these ends with the environmental expectations of SARA or the broader expectations of an efficient and equitable program.

Superfund implementation continued to be constrained by Reagan administration hostility to environmental protection expenditures and by an EPA leadership resistant to change. The election of George Bush and the appointment of conservationist William Reilly to head EPA promised to resolve mounting conflicts between Congress and the agency. Acknowledging the need for a mid-course correction, Reilly soon produced a management review containing an insightful and straightforward evaluation of program failings. The review was followed by announcement of a new strategy built on the dual principles of enforcement first and worst sites first.

By late 1990 quantitative measures of Superfund activity suggested that the program was finally on the right track. EPA still faced the challenge of resolving other program-related conflicts initiated under the Reagan administration. The National Contingency Plan, a blueprint for Superfund implementation, and a related document to guide corrective action cleanups at operating hazardous waste facilities both bore the imprint of the Reagan EPA and the Reagan Office of Management and Budget. Although Reilly withdrew a highly controversial section of the National Contingency Plan that would allow EPA to defer cleanup to other programs, he failed to overcome Bush Office of Management and Budget preference for cost reduction over risk reduction.

The prospect of a 1991 reauthorization debate also threatened to kill the agency's new momentum: a replay of the 1985–86 funding hiatus and a successful effort by generators and their insurers to convert Superfund into a public works project were real possibilities. Both threats were quietly eliminated by inclusion of refinancing and reauthorization provisions in the 1991 federal budget.

Through 1991 EPA continued to build on its post–management review accomplishments and also began to place increased emphasis on waste reduction and recycling as the only truly long-term solutions to hazardous waste threats. Publication of data on toxic waste emissions, negotiation with polluting industries, and a widening of the Superfund liability net encouraged major polluting corporations to set significant waste reduction goals. At the same time, controversy mounted over the potential liability faced by lending institutions, successor and parent corporations, and municipalities for Superfund site cleanup. Controversy continued over weak government commitment to clean up contaminated federal facilities, the cost of cleanup, and EPA oversight of cleanup contractors.

This chapter begins with a critical examination of the post-SARA Superfund strategy developed and implemented by EPA through mid-1989. I then focus on the related debate over solutions to Superfund's continuing failure and two events that shaped that debate: the expectation of reauthorization in 1991 and the replacement of Lee Thomas by William Reilly as EPA administrator. Next, changes in EPA strategy and achievements are evaluated from the time of Administrator Reilly's mid-course correction to early 1992. In the final section, I evaluate the conflict over Superfund since 1986 and the implications for a successful hazardous waste site cleanup program.

FAILURE TO IMPLEMENT SARA, 1986–1989

The passage of SARA did not resolve underlying conflict between congressional expectations and the Reagan administration deregulatory ideology. By

1987 the Reagan administration interpreted four years of economic expansion and a fall in the rate of inflation as validation of its economic program. For the administration, the foremost challenge was the high level of federal spending and a mounting budget deficit. The deficit had nearly doubled since 1981 as a "bloated" increase in outlays outpaced increased receipts. The White House intended to solve this problem through continued reliance on private sector initiatives, state and local solutions to social problems, and decreased federal regulation and spending. Federal government programs were still perceived by the administration as a source of unnecessary interference in private economic decisions. They impeded operation of markets, inhibited competition, or imposed costs on firms and raised prices faced by consumers without providing commensurate benefits (U.S. Council of Economic Advisors, 1988: 3–10). Deregulation and the justification of cost by benefits remained cornerstones of administration policy.

As in 1981, EPA had to set a strategy that would resolve contradictions between congressional expectations and administration policy. Both Congress and the White House favored a strategy that would conserve the fund. For Congress, this would allow Superfund resources to address the greatest number of sites. For the Reagan administration, this would reduce federal outlays, contribute to deficit reduction, and forestall reauthorization of an even larger Superfund. Further, Congress expected EPA to use the fund to leverage its position with responsible parties and to supplement this incentive to settle with aggressive enforcement. The anticipated increase in the cost of on-site clean-ups made a strong enforcement program even more crucial. The Reagan administration desired a substitution of private for public cleanup expenditures on budgetary grounds but remained ideologically opposed to aggressive en-forcement programs. It had cut the examination staff of savings and loan regulators and had also virtually eliminated antitrust enforcement. In addi-tion, Congress instructed EPA to involve the states in cleanup decisions and to minimize their financial burden. For the Reagan administration, fiscal re-sponsibility demanded that the states make a maximum contribution. Finally, Congress mandated the application of strict standards, a preference for perma-nent solutions, and a limited role for cost considerations in selecting cleanup remedies. The Reagan administration still questioned the value of public health and environmental benefits to be derived from site cleanup and was firmly committed to cost-benefit analysis as a basis for program decisions.

The immediate challenge facing EPA was to regain the momentum lost during the funding hiatus of 1985–86 so as to meet site evaluation and cleanup deadlines. The reauthorized Superfund required EPA to complete pre-remedial studies (i.e., site inspections and preliminary assessments) at approximately 25,000 hazardous waste sites by January 1, 1989. By 1990 EPA was required to determine which of these sites should be added to the National Priorities List for cleanup under the program. Remedial investigation/feasibility studies at 275 sites were to be completed by 1990 and on-site remedial action at 175 sites was to be initiated by October 1989. Meeting these deadlines would move EPA from a concentration on site studies to a greater emphasis on actual cleanup.

EPA chose two goals as cornerstones of its Superfund strategy: conservation of the fund and satisfaction of mandated work schedules. The former goal was consistent with congressional and White House expectations. The latter was consistent with congressional expectations and the maintenance of agency autonomy. Major components of the strategy included, first, limiting the size of the National Priorities List and deferring responsibility for cleanup to private parties and to other programs. Both would reduce demand for fund expenditures and facilitate compliance with work schedules. The second component required interpreting SARA to allow cost-benefit evaluations to offset the high projected cost of strict standards and permanent remedies. This would promote fund conservation and settlement with private parties. SARA would be interpreted through revision to the National Contingency Plan. The third component required utilization of incentives for responsible party cleanup. In particular, EPA would continue to rely on its fund-first strategy. Responsible parties would be offered the opportunity to conduct site studies as an incentive to settlement. If responsible parties would not settle, site studies would be financed out of the fund and EPA would then negotiate or litigate private party contribution to the selected remedy.

Although EPA's post-SARA Superfund strategy built on its existing guidance to the regions, some revision was necessary. EPA advised the regions to make greater use of enforcement tools that had been used only infrequently in the past: for example, combining fund and responsible party resources to clean up a site, and allowing minor contributors to settle for a fixed cash payment. Its guidance on cleanup reiterated nine criteria contained in SARA for evaluating alternative remedies: compliance with standards under federal laws; reduction of toxicity, mobility, or volume; short-term effectiveness; long-term effectiveness and permanence; implementability; cost; community acceptance; state acceptance; and overall protection of human health and the environment.[1] The guidance advised the regions to consider effectiveness, ease of implementation, and cost in selecting a remedy and to choose the remedy that provided the *best balance* among these factors. EPA included this policy in its proposed revision to the National Contingency Plan. The vagueness of these instructions and their implication that the regions take a cost-benefit approach in selecting remedies would soon cause mounting conflict between EPA and Congress.

EPA was well aware that its initial implementation actions would be carefully scrutinized. However, it did not anticipate that evaluations of its 1987–88 decisions would produce a torrent of critical studies establishing that the Superfund was going in the wrong direction. The panoply of program decisions and oversight responsibilities were criticized in reports by congressional committees and offices and by environmental and industry groups. The reports revealed a general consensus that Superfund's failure was rooted in contradictions between the articulated goals of SARA and those that drove agency decisions. EPA's strategy was consistent with the nonenvironmental performance goals imposed by SARA and with the need to take some action at a large number of sites. It was inconsistent with SARA's mandate to protect public health and the environment and the need to make efficient use of public and private resources. Most reports pointed to the inability or unwillingness of top agency officials to resolve these contradictions in a manner consistent with the law. EPA was not seen as solely responsible for unacceptable program outcomes. Several reports acknowledged sources of failure rooted more broadly in the decisions of other agencies that impacted on the program (e.g., the Department of Justice, the Office of Management and Budget) as well as in the actions of Congress.

At the front end of the program, EPA efforts to limit the size of the National Priorities List had turned the NPL into a policy tool to control the distribution of cleanups among Superfund and other cleanup programs. Rather than asking whether a site may require cleanup, EPA was now asking whether site contamination was bad enough to warrant cleanup. Under this strategy, EPA was willing to accept false negatives (i.e., a problem site is excluded from the National Priorities List) while attempting to avoid false positives (i.e., a non-problem site is added to the priority list). The impact of these decisions was to facilitate EPA compliance with nonenvironmental performance goals while increasing the number of non-NPL sites left to be addressed by the states (U.S. Office of Technology Assessment, 1989b: 85–129).

If a site did qualify for the National Priorities List, EPA proposed a deferral policy that provided the option of shunting that site to another cleanup program. The policy would prevent sites from being placed or maintained on the Superfund cleanup list if they could be addressed by other federal or state programs or by responsible parties. While Superfund was the largest cleanup program, cleanup expenditures under other federal and state programs and by private parties combined were around 50 percent greater than Superfund expenditures (U.S. Office of Technology Assessment, 1989b: 193). A deferral policy had been advocated by the Reagan administration during the reauthorization debate and was included in EPA's proposal for revision to the National Contingency Plan. In a report for the Senate Subcommittee on Superfund, Ocean and Water Protection, Senators Lautenberg (D-N.J.) and Durenberger (R-Minn.) characterized this proposal as a clear circumvention of the unique provisions and requirements contained in Superfund. It was the "exception that threatened to swallow the law." In particular, sites deferred to other programs could be subjected to less stringent cleanup standards and health assessment requirements. This expectation was fueled by White House proposals to weaken corrective action cleanup guidelines for operating hazardous waste facilities. Further, under a deferral policy, community involvement would not be financed through SARA's technical assistance grants and Superfund's liability and enforcement powers might not apply (Lautenberg and Durenberger, 1989: 78–83).

The General Accounting Office questioned the effectiveness of a deferral policy, noting that most states were unable to clean up large hazardous waste sites (U.S. General Accounting Office, 1989a). The Office of Technology Assessment noted that state programs rely extensively on land disposal and containment remedies which ultimately will prove to be impermanent. Superfund may increasingly be required to fix poor cleanups executed under other programs, just as it was originally conceived to address poor waste disposal practices (U.S. Office of Technology Assessment, 1989b: 13, 193–217). EPA subsequently acknowledged that it had done little research into the states' ability to handle cleanups before proposing the deferral policy. It had pushed this policy, nevertheless, as a way to save resources for other cleanups (Bureau of National Affairs, November 17, 1989: 1303).

A controversy over listing a site owned by the city of North Miami, Florida, on the National Priorities List highlighted potential differences between Superfund and municipal cleanup goals and raised questions regarding the wisdom of deferring cleanup decisions to the states.[2] North Miami, arguing that its Munisport landfill site contained no hazardous waste, applied political pressure to avoid its listing on the priority list. City attorneys said the site could be cleaned up better and faster under Florida law at a cost of $11 million. EPA had initially proposed a cleanup plan costing twice as much. In an apparently political decision, the agency then proposed delisting based on its finding that the site posed no threat to human health. Dade County opposed delisting and allowing state oversight of cleanup, noting that as a former owner, the state had a clear conflict of interest. EPA subsequently reversed its position again upon finding that leachate from the site could cause substantial damage to a sensitive, endangered mangrove preserve. Florida questioned the basis for this conclusion. For those opposing a deferral policy, several factors magnified the significance of this federal/state conflict and of any precedent the agency established at Munisport: Some 20 percent of National Priorities List sites are municipal landfills. States are required to provide a 50 percent cost contribution to a fund-financed remedy at these sites. EPA had made some attempts to shield municipalities from cleanup liability. A policy to defer decisions to states and municipalities could provide EPA with another avenue for reducing state and municipal cleanup burdens and could produce cleanups substantially inferior to those demanded by Superfund.[3]

Conservation of the fund was EPA's stated rationale for limiting the size of the program. Conservation could be associated with a range of cleanup scenarios: at one extreme, expenditures could be spread thinly over a large number of sites; at the other extreme, expenditures could be concentrated at the worst sites. The first scenario would more likely satisfy cleanup schedules at the expense of environmental protection. The second would more likely maximize environmental protection at the expense of meeting schedules. Evaluations of cleanup decisions through 1988 suggested that EPA chose the spread-the-fund-thinly scenario. A Hazardous Waste Treatment Council/environmental group report, appropriately titled *Right Train, Wrong Track*, reviewed the seventy-five records of decision (RODs) issued by EPA in 1987. (As noted earlier, a ROD summarizes the findings of site studies and proposes a cleanup remedy.) The report found that despite the clear and explicit directive of the Superfund law to use permanent treatment remedies to the maximum practical extent, 68 percent of the remedies selected in 1987 failed to use any treatment whatsoever on the source of contamination. Another 24 percent used only partial treatment or ineffective treatment options. Only 8 percent used treatment technologies to the maximum practical extent. The report also found that EPA ignored existing environmental standards, set cleanup goals unscientifically, exempted Superfund cleanups from the environmental regulations it imposed on waste management facilities, and generally ignored the impact of Superfund sites on natural resources (Environmental Defense Fund et al., 1988: 1–2). Further, EPA guidance provided justification for ignoring explicit standards. "[C]leanup level decisions for each site are made in a flaccid framework comprised of whatever cleanup levels appear convenient and above all, cheap" (Environmental Defense Fund et al., 1988: 54).

A follow-up study, *Tracking Superfund*, evaluated the 150 RODs issued in 1988 (Environmental Defense Fund et al., 1990). It found that at a majority of sites (54 percent), cleanup standards had not been established for ground water, surface water, and soil. At sites where standards were set, EPA often relied on risk assessments rather than on objective standards and criteria. A risk assessment involves an estimation of the probability of developing cancer or other health effects as a result of direct exposure to toxic chemicals. The risk assessments reviewed often contained suspect and unsubstantiated assumptions. For example, a cleanup level associated with a high cancer risk was chosen under the assumption that people would stay away from the contamination. The follow-up report found a continued preference for impermanent remedies. Forty-four percent of the remedies selected merely minimized exposure to contamination with fencing and capping. Bogus treatment technologies, such as stabilization of high organic content wastes, continued to be selected for some sites despite EPA's own data showing that these technologies were ineffective. The report also found that contamination of ground water was often written off rather than cleaned up. When ground water contamination was addressed, the remedy frequently called for provision of alternative water supplies, plugging wells, imposing institutional controls to prevent further usage, or for relying on natural attenuation to cleanse an aquifer, a euphemism for no action (Environmental Defense Fund et al., 1990: 3–4).

The Lautenberg-Durenberger report and several studies by the Office of Technology Assessment (U.S. Office of Technology Assessment, 1988, 1989b) identified similar failings in the remedy selection process. They concurred in the conclusion that these environmentally unsound decisions were rooted in a failure of agency leadership to promote consistency in remedy selection and a related White House focus on minimizing the cost of cleanup. The Lautenberg-Durenberger report emphasized that the Reagan administration's proposed revision to the National Contingency Plan provided the apparent theory upon which EPA applied cost in remedy selection. The revision directed EPA to compare the cost and effectiveness of alternative remedies to determine which alternative offered results "proportional to their costs such that they represent a reasonable value for the money" (Lautenberg and Durenberger, 1989: 59). This is a formula for a cost-benefit analysis, not for the cost-effectiveness analysis mandated by SARA.

Similarly, the Office of Technology Assessment concluded that EPA had transformed the statutory directive to minimize cost, after cleanup objectives were identified, into a cost-benefit approach which could reduce cleanup objectives to reduce cleanup costs. The remedy selection process contained in SARA was essentially reversed: cost justified objectives rather than objectives justifying cost. This approach allowed any cleanup decision to be rationalized and undermined the environmental goals of Superfund (U.S. Office of Technology Assessment, 1989b: 16–17). Clean Sites, Inc., a nonprofit organization involved in mediating Superfund site settlements since 1984, also faulted EPA for its backwards and illogical approach to cleanup. They contended that an initial setting of cleanup objectives would facilitate open discussion of remedies and would eliminate many unnecessary, costly studies (Clean Sites, Inc., 1990).

EPA, Congress, and the Reagan administration all agreed that an effective enforcement program was an essential component of fund conservation. During the reauthorization debate many, including EPA, also had emphasized the equity of enforcement to make polluters pay. Further, the performance of cleanup studies by responsible parties helped EPA meet its mandated deadlines and provided an added incentive to conduct an active enforcement program. Nevertheless, oversight investigations found that other constraints often dominated these incentives and rendered them insufficient to produce desirable enforcement outcomes. Several basic failings were identified: EPA was negotiating cleanup as an inducement to settlement, EPA was not using the enforcement tools available under Superfund, and EPA was giving the recalcitrant a free ride at the expense of "good citizen" responsible parties.

EPA had long emphasized that it was in the interest of responsible parties to conduct the remedial investigation/feasibility studies that provided the basis for remedy selection. Early involvement at a site afforded greater participation in cleanup decisions. However, responsible party involvement was not intended to provide a means to circumvent an application of strict standards and a preference for permanent remedies. Investigations into the enforcement program found that responsible party involvement did in fact allow such avoidance. A comparison of 1987 and 1988 records of decision revealed an increased application of treatment and permanent technologies when cleanup of on-site contamination was financed by the fund. Similar progress was not noted at sites where a responsible party performed site studies and was expected to finance the remedy. For records of decision issued in 1988 to address a source of contamination, about 84 percent of proposed fund-financed remedies utilized treatment technologies and about 12 percent utilized impermanent containment technologies. In contrast, about 56 percent of remedies selected by responsible parties utilized treatment technologies and about 42 percent utilized containment. In addition, selection of a most permanent treatment technology was about three times as likely when the remedy was to be fund-financed (U.S. Office of Technology Assessment, 1989b: 163–64; Lautenberg and Durenberger, 1989: 148–51). Further, cleanup standards were established somewhat less frequently when responsible parties carried out remedy selection studies (Environmental Defense Fund et al., 1990: 52). EPA data showed that remedies selected by responsible parties were more likely to be at the low range of remedy costs compared to those selected for fund-financed cleanup (U.S. Office of Technology Assessment, 1989b: 164).

These findings led to the disturbing conclusion that responsible party performance of remedy selection studies threatened to compromise environmental protection. To minimize their costs, responsible parties had clear incentives to conduct incomplete remedial investigations that minimized the apparent extent of contamination. It was also in their interest to propose inexpensive and ineffective remedies and to bias risk assessments. The latitude to act on these incentives was provided by the dearth of EPA guidance on how clean is clean. Opposition by community groups to less protective remedies was minimized by agency policy: EPA had failed to initiate a technical assistance grants program and was willing to exclude community groups from discussion of settlements. At the same time, the latitude to act on these incentives was facilitated by EPA's willingness to negotiate the selection of a remedy. In this regard, the Office of Technology Assessment concluded that "[c]leanup standards, the extent of cleanup, the permanency of cleanup, and the selection of cleanup technologies are often compromised in formal and informal negotiations to obtain settlements with responsible parties" (U.S. Office of Technology Assessment, 1989b: 161).

Senior EPA administrators rejected this critique. First, they argued that the data did not support the basic finding that remedies selected by responsible parties were in fact different from those selected for fund financing. The definition of treatment used in drawing this conclusion, however, suggests the possibility that the agency's findings were biased.[4] It is also likely that EPA site project managers viewed the agency's rebuttal with some skepticism; many claimed that responsible parties were producing studies guided by self-interested assumptions and conclusions. EPA did acknowledge that risk assessments were vulnerable to manipulation and subsequently said they would not be performed by responsible parties. Second, these administrators argued that it made no sense to select a remedy if a responsible party was unwilling to provide the money.

This last response is striking in light of the strong enforcement tools available to EPA. It is, however, consistent with oversight findings that EPA placed insufficient reliance on the incentives and threats afforded by these tools. The agency's fund-first strategy was not working because the enforcement program did not guarantee that recalcitrance had a high cost. EPA was failing to identify all potentially responsible parties and was lax in notifying those that had been identified. Staff shortages caused search delays and precluded the early involvement of some responsible parties in remedial studies (U.S. General Accounting Office, 1989b: 21–35). EPA was using unilateral orders sparingly to close lengthy negotiations or to force action when negotiations were unsuccessful (U.S. General Accounting Office, 1989b: 3–4). Further, only about one-quarter of orders issued in 1988 were for the remedial design/remedial action phase of cleanup, the major cost component of the remedial process. Few orders were referred to the Department of Justice for enforcement. While 1989 data indicated an improvement, numbers remained low relative to expectations for responsible party–financed cleanup.[5]

EPA was also giving a low priority to the recovery of costs from responsible parties after a cleanup action was completed. By mid-1989 it had only recovered about 35 percent of the amount it had targeted for 1991 and conceded that this target would not be met. Fund-financed cleanup had pushed recoverable costs, those associated with completed studies and the initiation of actual cleanup, to some $1.5 billion. EPA had recovered only 6.5 percent of these costs (Lautenberg and Durenberger, 1989: 118–34).

Oversight reports were highly critical of EPA's failure to induce responsible party financing of on-site cleanup activity. Good citizen responsible parties, those willing to settle with EPA, were equally critical of agency policy for giving the recalcitrant a free ride. If unilateral orders were not issued, the recalcitrant would pay no more by waiting. The greater the delay in the initiation of a cost recovery action, the greater the gain from recalcitrance. Why, asked the good citizens, should any responsible party agree to settle under these conditions? The initiation of contribution suits by settling parties against the recalcitrant was not seen as a viable option. The cost of litigation might wipe out the potential recovery. The treble damage threats available to EPA were a more effective means to induce compliance and to guarantee equitable settlements.

The failure of the enforcement programs was due in part to the high priority EPA placed on meeting deadlines. Negotiations and enforcement actions took longer than simply using the fund. Failure also was due to EPA willingness to pass responsibility for allocation of cleanup costs to responsible parties and to severe EPA staffing constraints. Enforcement required relatively more staff time and effort, but staffing levels were insufficient to meet all program needs. Since the fund was finite, a weak enforcement program would result in its premature exhaustion. Once depleted, the fund could be used neither to keep sites flowing through the pipeline nor to induce private party settlements.

These shortcomings attributed to strategy, per se, were magnified by EPA dependence on contractors to perform a wide range of program activities. Responsibility for crucial decisions was shifted to the private sector while EPA was left with inadequate staff to manage and oversee contractors. Heavy dependence on outside contractors had emerged from an early 1980s perspective that Superfund was a short-term program. Rapid implementation was to be achieved through drawing on the technical expertise that existed in the private sector. Dependency was also encouraged by Reagan administration policy to privatize the federal government. The creation of an enlarged EPA bureaucracy was neither desirable nor necessary. Rather, private sector firms would do the work with EPA limiting its role to oversight. Over the first eight years of Superfund, contractors received between 80 and 90 percent of annual program expenditures. Between 1988 and 1989, external spending increased by 27 percent to $1.24 billion as EPA pushed to meet its work schedules (U.S. Office of Technology Assessment, 1989a: 3). Contractors were involved in all aspects of fund- and responsible party–financed removal and remedial decisions, from initial site evaluation to actual cleanup. They were integrally involved in developing policies and regulations as well as in management and oversight.

Evaluations of contractor performance challenged the deep-seated belief that reliance on the private sector enhanced efficiency. It did not seem unreasonable to contract out for actual cleanup services. However, this was not where the money was going. By mid-1988, 103 sites were at the remedial action stage whereas 641 were still undergoing site studies. The bulk of contractor services were for the critical analyses that set the direction of cleanup. Dependency on contractors to provide these studies had created "a huge new industry of environmental consultants who put . . . [billions] into their pockets by studying sites, taking literally years to figure out what the site is like and what kind of remedies might be used" (comment by the Hazardous Waste Treatment Council, quoted in U.S. Office of Technology Assessment, 1989a: 28). A 1988 Office of Technology Assessment study of records of decision pointed to the poor quality of contractors' technical work. The report warned that these deficiencies were at odds with the environmental mission of the program as well as with the desire for a cost-effective program (U.S. Office of Technology Assessment, 1988: 6). Studies by the General Accounting Office and EPA's inspector general also linked program failure to the quality of contractor work (U.S. General Accounting Office, 1989c, 1989d; and Bureau of National Affairs, May 1, 1987: 4).

EPA dependence on contractors produced conflicts of interest that contributed to documented and suspected inefficiencies and delays. There was an inherent conflict between a contractor's drive for profits and program goals. This was manifest in an escalation of the cost of site studies and in the time required for their completion. A single pool of engineering and consulting firms contracted their services to the federal government, to state governments, and to responsible parties. Contractors working for responsible parties were more likely to emphasize reduced cost, tolerate more risk, and view certain cleanup technologies and approaches as more permanent than did local communities. They were less likely to serve the best interests of the state or the federal government. Further, a contractor working for EPA could use inside information it might acquire to benefit responsible parties (for example, in negotiating a settlement with the agency). Finally, a contractor with a proprietary interest in a cleanup technology was more likely to choose this technology over a more effective and less costly alternative (U.S. Office of Technology Assessment, 1989a: 35–37).

The inefficiencies of the contracting system were traced back to EPA policy as well as to congressional and White House decisions. A revised remedial action contract award system introduced by EPA in 1988 left prime contractors with substantial responsibilities, including oversight of subcontractors. The Office of Technology Assessment argued that this revision was driven by a desire to enhance timeliness as opposed to cleanup quality. Further, the new system was unlikely to increase competition for awards or to provide incentives for enhanced efficiency (U.S. Office of Technology Assessment, 1989a: 15–20). The complexities of administering contracts contributed to the relatively higher cost of government-financed versus responsible party–financed cleanup activity. While the contracting system did inhibit growth of government bureaucracy, it produced an external bureaucracy suffering from the same inefficiencies long attributed to government. The General Accounting Office also faulted EPA for its willingness to provide contractors with a blanket indemnification from liability (U.S. General Accounting Office, 1989e). During the reauthorization debate, contractors had emphasized that problems of obtaining liability insurance would keep many from entering the industry. EPA's blanket indemnification policy eliminated incentives to acquire private insurance and to exercise due care. It also left the fund liable for poor contractor performance.

Any contracting system EPA devised would be likely to fail so long as the agency lacked adequate staff for management and oversight. The inability of EPA to perform these functions was a direct consequence of congressional actions that reconfirmed a policy to contract out the Superfund program. In particular, EPA administrative expenses were not allowed to grow in line with the associated increase in its management and oversight responsibilities. Between 1982 and 1989, the total Superfund budget grew by 600 percent while administrative expenses grew by only 360 percent. Restrictions on staff growth left EPA's Office of Inspector General with insufficient resources to carry out the level of auditing and investigation it deemed necessary for Superfund (U.S. Office of Technology Assessment, 1989a: 11, 39). The inspector general had warned that a contracting system with minimal oversight was highly susceptible to fraud and abuse. Fraud by Department of Defense contractors following upon the huge defense expenditure increases of the early 1980s provided a clear parallel to what could be anticipated at EPA. Testimony during the reauthorization debate could leave little room to doubt that increased contractor expenditures unmatched by increases in management oversight would produce inefficiency.

Despite these warnings, the mismatch of contractor and agency resources was exacerbated by SARA. In 1986 the program was estimated to be 36 percent understaffed relative to new program needs (U.S. Office of Technology Assessment, 1989a: 31). Enforcement staff subsequently grew but remained insufficient. Private and public sector demand for technical staff increased substantially while EPA's ability to compete for the best staff declined. The higher pay and advancement opportunities offered by contractors produced high turnover rates for EPA. By 1988 turnover in the Superfund program was the highest for all EPA programs and exceeded that for all federal employees by one-third (Lautenberg and Durenberger, 1989: 109–10). Experienced agency staff took jobs with contractors, leaving EPA with the less experienced. And as these inexperienced staff gained hands-on training with the agency, many of them moved on to the private sector. Most of the large increase in contractor staff did not come from EPA, however, and this also created a problem in that new staff lacked agency training. When contractors sent these inexperienced staff into the field, the need for agency oversight of their performance increased.

The absence of a stable and experienced technical staff placed EPA at a severe disadvantage vis-à-vis contractors and responsible parties. Increasingly, site project managers lacked the experience to successfully critique contractor studies and proposals and to effectively oversee contractor performance. Their inexperience placed them in an equally weak position in negotiating with responsible parties and in overseeing state performance of delegated cleanup activities. In sum, EPA's inability to effectively manage and oversee those with substantial responsibility for program performance magnified the failures inherent in its Superfund strategy.

TO REDIRECT OR REDESIGN?

Events converged to make the years 1989–90 a transition period for EPA. First, critical studies of Superfund decisions between 1987 and 1989 were released through early 1990. Private and public sector oversight studies contained proposals for change as input into the next reauthorization debate. SARA's funding authority would expire in October 1991. Second, the 1989 appointment of William Reilly as EPA administrator and his subsequent review of the program set a new direction for Superfund. Third, conflict between Congress and the White House over the National Contingency Plan and a related corrective action plan for operating hazardous waste facilities was finally resolved, although not on terms that would necessarily enhance environmental protection. With a Superfund blueprint and a potentially viable implementation strategy in place, Congress quietly reauthorized Superfund in late 1990. It was necessary to see what the new Superfund program could accomplish before engaging in another lengthy and disruptive reauthorization debate.

Critical studies of Superfund suggested that change was essential. However, the nature of that change was a matter of considerable dispute. Office of Technology Assessment studies and the Lautenberg-Durenberger report emphasized the need for more effective leadership and an increase in program administration funding. Inadequate staffing levels, high staff turnover, and low staff experience were seen as basic determinants of EPA's poor record of cleanup decisions, lax enforcement, and weak contractor oversight. EPA's ability to carry out other recommended changes in its cleanup strategy were not possible in the absence of a realistic level of financial support.

The House Appropriations Committee advocated increased congressional control over EPA actions through manipulation of the agency's budget. The goal was to promote conservation of the fund and a more aggressive enforcement program (U.S. Congress, House, 1988: 9–13). In contrast to this approach, many generator industry corporations and their insurers continued to attack EPA's litigiousness and Superfund's imposition of liability. A group of sixteen major corporations advocated a less adversarial approach to settlement, remedy selection, and allocation of cleanup costs (Bureau of National Affairs, February 24, 1989: 2304). For others who would bear the toxic debt, CERCLA's strict, joint and several liability standard was seen as integral to program failure.

A major insurer, the American International Group, proposed elimination of the current liability system in favor of a public works approach to be financed through a tax on commercial and industrial pollution insurance premiums (Bureau of National Affairs, September 22, 1989: 857). This scheme would significantly reduce the high transaction costs associated with lengthy negotiations and expensive litigation. The cost of cleanup would shift back to the polluting industries. A RAND Corporation report (Acton, 1989) and an American Bar Association panel attributed Superfund failure to the delays and high costs associated with its litigious atmosphere. The latter supported a public works approach (Bureau of National Affairs, August 10, 1990: 759). The Committee on Economic Development proposed replacing the current liability standard with an apportionment of costs in proportion to contribution (Bureau of National Affairs, May 19, 1989: 146). The Coalition on Superfund, comprised of twenty-two major corporations and insurance companies and organized by William Ruckelshaus, proposed that cost considerations be given a greater role in the remedy selection process. Like other industry evaluations, the coalition argued that a related change in the preference for permanent solutions was necessary. With the average cost of cleanup reaching $25 million, quantitative cost-benefit analysis was essential to determine whether the cost of cleanup was commensurate with its benefits (Bureau of National Affairs, September 22, 1989: 857). Advocates of a cost-benefit approach pointed to EPA's own analysis of relative environmental risk to support their claim that hazardous waste site risks were overstated. A 1987 EPA report concluded that inactive hazardous waste sites ranked eighth among environmental cancer risks (Bureau of National Affairs, February 27, 1989: 1822).[6]

Under Administrator Thomas, EPA's response to its pro-environmental critics was generally defensive. Superfund chief Winston Porter attacked the Office of Technology Assessment's 1988 study on remedy selection and the *Right Train, Wrong Track* study for their incomplete, superficial views of the law's requirements (Bureau of National Affairs, July 15, 1988: 358–59). Enforcement chief Lloyd Guerci argued that the lack of state money and the poor financial condition of some responsible parties contributed to the selection of remedies viewed inadequate by agency critics (Bureau of National Affairs, July 29, 1988: 419).

EPA's defensive posture fed the long-standing hostility between the agency and Congress. The perception that EPA was resistant to change and averse to admitting past error was further reinforced when Administrator Thomas proposed in August 1988 to commission a study of reauthorization issues. Thomas felt that the expectations of the Superfund law were at the heart of agency problems. The proposal was immediately faulted for its focus on political issues in lieu of actions to correct serious management problems. Equally suspect was its possible relationship to the Coalition on Superfund study organized by Ruckelshaus. Thomas said that participation by Ruckelshaus would be helpful given his experience as a two-time EPA administrator. Environmentalists saw his involvement as most inappropriate given the coalition's expected efforts to dilute CERCLA's tough cleanup and enforcement standards. Opponents in the House of Representatives stated that it was also inappropriate to launch a costly study in the final days of the Reagan administration. The agency should be directing its efforts to completing the already overdue National Contingency Plan and to initiating a technical assistance grant program for community involvement in site decisions (Bureau of National Affairs, August 26, 1988: 734). Thomas eventually scaled down his proposal. His sympathy for the position taken by responsible parties is indicated by the fact that he was hired to head the Coalition on Superfund a year after leaving EPA (Bureau of National Affairs, January 19, 1990: 1630).

The election of George Bush in November 1988 and his naming of William Reilly as EPA administrator in December 1988 promised to bring needed change. Standing before a polluted Boston Harbor, the Republican candidate had pledged to be the environmental president. His appointment of Reilly was in accord with this promise. William Reilly, former head of the Conservation Foundation and the World Wildlife Fund, was considered a moderate on environmental issues. Soon after joining the Conservation Foundation in 1973, he began a program advocating direct cooperation between business leaders and conservationists in solving divisive resource and environmental policy issues. As head of the Conservation Foundation in 1984, he was instrumental in established Clean Sites as a mediator in Superfund cleanup disputes. Reilly was a negotiator, an advocate of alternative dispute resolution, and a conservationist. Environmental groups generally approved the appointment. The Chemical Manufacturers Association saw the appointment as indicative of the importance president-elect Bush placed on environmental issues. CMA expected Reilly to take a pragmatic, realistic approach (Bureau of National Affairs, December 30, 1988: 1771).

While there was no reason to question Reilly's credentials as an environmentalist, there was good reason to question whether he would be given sufficient latitude by a Bush White House to solve the many problems that plagued EPA's hazardous waste cleanup program. As vice-president, Bush was integral to the design and implementation of the Reagan administration deregulatory agenda. His political history suggested a far greater concern with producing oil than with addressing the safe disposal and cleanup of its petrochemical derivatives or with promoting conservation. President Reagan had appointed William Ruckelshaus in 1983 in the wake of Sewergate. The appointment did not change Reagan White House opposition to the Superfund program. Whether a similar tension would exist between a Reilly EPA and a Bush White House would be revealed as EPA strove to address two general problems: EPA management, staffing, and strategy, and EPA promulgation of a National Contingency Plan and a corrective action plan for operating hazardous waste facilities. These issues are the subject of the following section.

REDIRECTING SUPERFUND

Reilly announced his intention to redirect Superfund at his confirmation hearing. The hearing coincided with release of several of the highly critical reports discussed above. In contrast to his predecessor, Reilly stated that he would make corrections in the program, not reexamine its goals. A management review would be initiated in March and completed in ninety days. It would guide EPA in setting enforcement as a top priority. Reilly told Congress that "if you can create these incentives [to negotiate settlements], if you can make clear that there is nothing in it for a responsible party to stay away from the table, to be recalcitrant, to decline to negotiate, settlement ought to be possible" (Bureau of National Affairs, March 3, 1989: 2337).

A *Management Review of the Superfund Program* was released in June 1989 (Reilly, 1989). The report offered no apologies for past failures. Rather, it highlighted the need to devise a Superfund strategy consistent with a set of fair and realistic expectations. The report emphasized the inherent conflict among basic Superfund goals: The pursuit of health standards at each site often conflicted with prompt and effective action at all sites. The expectation of prompt cleanup also conflicted with the need for full and responsive public participation in the cleanup process. The pursuit of quantitative milestones to meet congressional deadlines conflicted with pursuit of qualitative cleanup progress. EPA recognition of these conflicts was not new. What was new was the basic strategy EPA chose in the context of these conflicting expectations.

The principles of enforcement first and worst sites first were made cornerstones of the new strategy. The report implied that the fund-first strategy pursued since 1984 was flawed. Aggressive enforcement could induce responsible parties to bear more of the cleanup burden, but only if the fund remained sufficiently robust to pose a credible resource for direct federal action. The use of enforcement to multiply Superfund's impact argued against pouring out the fund to attack too many sites simultaneously. In contrast, a worst-first approach would utilize fund resources to achieve necessary cleanup at the most dangerous sites as quickly as possible. An enforcement-first approach would further conserve the fund and maximize responsible party contributions. (Reilly, 1989: 5–6). Aggressive enforcement combined with a regularized negotiation process would encourage settlement. As envisioned by Reilly, "the first requirement of superfund is a clenched fist, but we will also offer an open hand" (Bureau of National Affairs, June 16, 1989: 428).

The announcement of the revised strategy was lauded by environmentalists, industry, and members of Congress for its sharp shift from the approach taken under the Reagan administration. The program mandated by CERCLA and reauthorized under SARA was predicated on strong enforcement. Yet critical evaluations throughout the 1980s had faulted EPA for its unwillingness to construct such a program. Despite both mandate and critique, this was the first time a senior EPA official had expressed a preference for enforcement first.

Senator Lautenberg anticipated that the new strategy would restore a measure of confidence in the program and would reduce hostility with Congress. Congress expressed support for EPA's new direction by authorizing an additional $27.5 million and 460 new staff positions for enforcement in EPA's fiscal 1990 budget (Bureau of National Affairs, July 21, 1989: 557). Richard J. Fortuna, director of the Hazardous Waste Treatment Council, noted that "[f]or the first time in nine years, we now have both an administrator committed to the program, the resources necessary to carry it out, and a fundamental recognition that policy and management changes are necessary in order to make this program a success" (Bureau of National Affairs, June 23, 1989: 462).

EPA soon took a number of significant steps to set its new strategy in motion. New enforcement guidance was issued to the regions instructing them to focus on the use of unilateral orders for actual cleanup. They were to initiate cost recovery and treble damages actions at all sites with nonsettling responsible parties unless manifestly inappropriate (Bureau of National Affairs, March 2, 1990: 1813). EPA also announced that it would tighten enforcement program oversight by requiring state or federal officials to conduct health risk studies. This change was the result of an agency finding that private companies might be understating threats to residents near a site.[7] The agency produced a model consent decree for use by the regions to facilitate consistency with its deadlines and settlement requirements and to reduce enforcement delays (Bureau of National Affairs, July 27, 1990: 533). Major generator industry corporations and associations objected to the last two policy changes, arguing that they would produce resistance and delay settlements.

Actions at a number of enforcement sites provided early evidence that EPA was finally willing and able to build an aggressive enforcement program on a foundation other than the fund-first threat. Following initiatives to impose penalties and bring suits against nonsettlors at the Cannons Engineering Corporation sites, EPA warned all nonsettling parties that "this decision sends an important message. If you reject a settlement offer made by the government, you will face significant risks, including the risks of more costly settlement terms or much greater liability" (Bureau of National Affairs, August 25, 1989: 730). Agreements in December 1989 on nine consent decrees totaling $69.5 million were offered as an indication of the momentum of the new strategy (Bureau of National Affairs, December 29, 1989: 1448).[8]

Administrator Reilly carried through on another major management review initiative in significantly altering technical assistance grant requirements. SARA had created the grant program to allow greater citizen participation in remedy selection but EPA had delayed issuing rules for awarding these grants until March 1988. Critics charged that grant requirements set by Administrator Thomas had effectively thwarted citizens' efforts to obtain federal money to evaluate remedy selection documents. The demanding requirements were motivated by an EPA view that citizen participation was a source of delay in moving sites through the remedial action pipeline. While SARA required applicants to provide a minimum 20 percent match for any federal grant, the Thomas EPA had set the minimum at 35 percent. Commenting on the grant application process, Representative Markey (D-Mass.) noted that "[i]t is so hard to penetrate EPA's bureaucracy that you could line a superfund site with it and it wouldn't leak" (Bureau of National Affairs, March 17, 1989: 2469). Reilly reduced the matching requirement to 20 percent and also removed other financial and bureaucratic impediments (Bureau of National Affairs, December 1, 1989: 1353).

Reilly's ability to redirect EPA demonstrated an evolving White House perception of the Superfund program. The Bush administration, recognizing that the public placed a high priority on environmental cleanup, did not want to be seen, like the Reagan administration, as anti-environment. It was willing to support more aggressive enforcement to reduce the government's cleanup burden. Since reauthorization, EPA enforcement staff had increased by about 60 percent (Bureau of National Affairs, January 13, 1989: 1827). To further movement in this direction, the Bush administration recommended authorization of $1.7 billion for Superfund in its fiscal 1990 and 1991 budget requests.[9] Congress had authorized only $1.5 billion in 1990. In contrast to this support, Reilly's failed attempt to establish stringent cleanup requirements for abandoned and operating hazardous waste facilities demonstrated that the Bush administration still shared its predecessor's preference for cost reduction over risk reduction. The Bush administration would allow the program to go forward but would limit its cost and reach.

Under the reauthorized Superfund, EPA was required to publish a revised National Contingency Plan by April 1988. The revision was to include procedures and standards for remedial actions consistent with the requirements of SARA. Under the 1984 amendments to the Resource Conservation and Recovery Act, EPA also was to publish corrective action cleanup guidelines for operating hazardous waste facilities. Corrective action provisions were to be included in the permits issued to these facilities. Since the National Priorities List contained at least 100 former RCRA sites, EPA was aware of the need to coordinate the two sets of guidelines. If the RCRA standards were less stringent, a facility that took corrective cleanup action and then closed could become a Superfund site. Further, many federal facilities were subject to both the Resource Conservation and Recovery Act and Superfund. The availability of two disparate cleanup standards could propel these facilities toward the less stringent standards.[10] EPA announced its intention to merge Resource Conservation and Recovery Act and Superfund cleanup approaches soon after passage of SARA.

Controversy over revision to the National Contingency Plan had begun in early 1987. SARA required that ground water and surface water cleanups comply with the requirements of the Safe Drinking Water Act. Under that act, EPA established two sets of standards. The stricter standards were based solely on the level of a contaminant that would not cause any adverse health effect. For carcinogens, the level was generally set at zero. The less strict standards were based on contamination levels that could be economically achieved. The cost of attaining a given level of cleanup would determine the acceptable level of risk. EPA proposed that the latter standards be applied to Superfund cleanups. Key members of Congress criticized the choice, arguing that SARA ruled out the use of cost considerations in determining the amount of risk allowable after cleanup had occurred; EPA's policy was therefore illegal. Administrator Thomas defended the choice as both legal and protective. Cleanup would be too expensive if a site had to be left absolutely free of contamination. EPA guidance on this issue would apply until the National Contingency Plan was issued (Bureau of National Affairs, April 17, 1987: 2115).

In late 1988 Representative Dingell (D-Mich.) expressed concern that the White House Office of Management and Budget was delaying release of the National Contingency Plan. He pointed to court rulings and Reagan administration guidelines that prohibited OMB from interfering with EPA compliance with a nondiscretionary statutory deadline. EPA announced that the plan would be issued after the upcoming presidential election. When finally released on November 17, 1988, the plan contained a number of highly controversial elements. It included EPA's deferral policy to allow states and responsible parties to keep sites off of the National Priorities List if they could be cleaned up under other, often weaker, authority. It also included EPA's less strict Safe Drinking Water Act standards and a less stringent risk range for carcinogens. The risk range set the number of allowable cancers to be achieved by a cleanup remedy. For almost six years EPA had set the upper limit at one cancer per 10 million people exposed to the contaminant. The Office of Management and Budget set the upper limit at one cancer per million people exposed. EPA would take comments from the public and issue a revised plan in November 1989.

Over EPA objection, Dingell released documents that revealed the sweeping scope of the Office of Management and Budget review of the plan and its efforts to weaken cleanup standards on economic grounds. The documents contained EPA warnings to the White House office that weakening the standards would create a firestorm of protest. They also indicated that EPA's concern was over the public outcry, not over whether more stringent standards protected public health (Bureau of National Affairs, March 17, 1989: 2462).

In June 1989 Administrator Reilly shelved the deferral policy in the face of extreme opposition from environmental groups and congressional staff. The final National Contingency Plan was issued in early 1990 in settlement of a suit brought by the Natural Resources Defense Council (Bureau of National Affairs, June 9, 1989: 323). It retained the less restrictive provisions demanded by the Reagan Office of Management and Budget. Several states soon filed court challenges to the plan's cost-sharing provisions. The states charged that the revised plan compelled them to bear the burden of running treatment plants (Bureau of National Affairs, June 15, 1990: 340). States also objected to Office of Management and Budget use of cost as a factor in setting cleanup standards (in violation of the Superfund law) and to OMB definition of acceptable cleanup. In particular, the office had induced EPA to allow an incomplete cleanup if the future use of the site was restricted through a fence or a deed restriction. Such actions would be considered a cleanup (Bureau of National Affairs, January 11, 1991: 1644).

In that the National Contingency Plan was drafted by the Thomas EPA and delayed by the Reagan Office of Management and Budget, it is not immediately apparent how it would have fared under the Reilly EPA and the Bush Office of Management and Budget. The extent of Reilly's opposition to the final National Contingency Plan is unclear. His concern over the risk range issue may have been tempered by EPA data showing that its more restrictive upper limit had never determined selection of a cleanup remedy (Bureau of National Affairs, March 17, 1989: 2462). Further, with the agency under court order to issue a final plan by February 1990, there was little time to rewrite the massive document. In contrast to this uncertainty, the parallel conflict over a corrective action plan for operating hazardous waste facilities made clear that Bush administration efforts to minimize costly regulations would be little different from those under the Reagan administration. A pro-environment EPA administrator would have only limited ability to overcome this preference.

The 1984 amendments to the Resource Conservation and Recovery Act required operating treatment, storage, and disposal facilities either to certify compliance with ground water monitoring and financial responsibility requirements by November 1985 or to close. Around 1,000 facilities chose to go out of business rather than to meet RCRA land disposal requirements. A closure plan was required for all of these facilities and a corrective action plan also was required if contaminants had migrated beyond site boundaries. In late 1987 the General Accounting Office reported to Congress that EPA delay in executing closure plans threatened public health and the environment and could create additional Superfund sites. Seventy percent of the sites assessed by EPA were leaking contaminants. Over 2,500 operating sites could require corrective action at a cost as great as $22.7 billion. At least 800 RCRA facilities could be transferred to Superfund (U.S. General Accounting Office, 1987c).

EPA had been issuing permits containing corrective action provisions since 1984. However, it had not published the corrective action standards that would guarantee both consistency among RCRA facility cleanups and consistency with Superfund cleanups. The plan had gone to the Office of Management and Budget in the closing days of the Reagan administration. The Bush OMB delayed its publication for twenty-one months while EPA was forced to agree to a weakening of key provisions. First, the upper end of the risk range for carcinogens was lowered as in the National Contingency Plan. Second, hazardous waste facilities would be considered cleaned up when contamination problems beyond facility borders were addressed. Hazardous waste could still remain within the borders. Third, stringent remedy selection standards would not be required to address a source of contamination. Fourth, several contaminated units within a facility could be treated as a single unit. This would allow untreated hazardous waste to be transferred between these units without being subject to a Resource Conservation and Recovery Act ban on land disposal of untreated waste. All of these concessions would substantially diminish the scope of cleanup and could substantially increase public health and environmental risks. Further, limiting cleanup to the area outside of a facility's borders would allow thousands of sites to escape corrective action rules and would greatly increase the number of Superfund sites (Bureau of National Affairs, May 18, 1990: 187).

The Office of Management and Budget questioned whether the cost of corrective action would produce reciprocal benefits. EPA estimated the cost to the private sector at $7 to $42 billion and the cost to the federal government at $2 to $200 billion. The vast majority of cleanup costs would be borne by the federal government if it was required to eliminate contamination at Department of Defense military bases and the Department of Energy's nuclear weapons complex. The anticipated federal cost was at the heart of Office of Management and Budget opposition. The Departments of Defense and Energy, as well as other affected federal agencies, supported the Office of Management and Budget position (Bureau of National Affairs, May 18, 1990: 187). OMB efforts to thwart pressure for federal facility cleanup was a continuation of its actions during the Reagan administration. The office had successfully vetoed giving EPA and the states enforcement powers to guarantee federal agency compliance with environmental laws.

Administrator Reilly could not have the corrective action rule published without making concessions demanded by the Office of Management and Budget. Although OMB Director Darmen had recently stated that delaying tactics should not be used in disputes over EPA rules and regulations, he reportedly did not want the rule issued at all (Bureau of National Affairs, May 1, 1990: 187). EPA agreed to OMB demands that it perform new cost estimates. Final action would be delayed for at least eighteen months and possibly for several years (Bureau of National Affairs, July 13, 1990: 474). Within months of this agreement, President Bush issued a regulatory impact analysis guidance that touched on such issues as the measurement of risk and the evaluation of benefits. It noted that agency risk assessments are biased to yield worst-case estimates that may distort regulatory outcomes. Like President Reagan's 1981 executive order, it required submission of rules and regulations to the Office of Management and Budget. The rules must be justified on the basis of cost-benefit analysis (Bureau of National Affairs, August 24, 1990: 821).

By late 1990 a new Superfund strategy was in place and gaining momentum and a National Contingency Plan was published. The program now faced a threat from a new quarter: Gramm-Rudman-Hollings. The Bush administration had proposed more money for Superfund in its fiscal 1991 budget. However, the inability of Congress and the White House to agree on a budget package consistent with Gramm-Rudman-Hollings deficit reduction goals would trigger a cut in Superfund appropriations of some $613 million. The Office of Management and Budget noted that this cut would be the most visible in the environmental area and would undermine public confidence in the cleanup effort (Bureau of National Affairs, August 10, 1990: 758). In a surprise last-minute move, Congress reauthorized Superfund for three years and extended its taxing authority for four years.[11] This action reflected agreement that another reauthorization debate was premature until it was established whether a newly altered Superfund program would work. The extension was supported by a broad coalition of environmental and industry groups. It was opposed by those hoping to change Superfund's liability standards. Congressional sources expressed dismay at the lack of vocal support for the extension on the part of the Bush White House (Bureau of National Affairs, November 16, 1990: 1374).

These episodes in the first years of the Bush presidency point to a grudging White House support for Superfund. They also reveal the constraints the administration would impose on the program and EPA's latitude within these constraints. EPA would be given more room to satisfy public demands for cleanup action and for participation in cleanup decisions. Enforcement would also be encouraged, but only with reference to nonfederal hazardous waste sites. It would be preferable to impose cleanup costs on the private sector while protecting the federal budget and the budgets of polluting federal agencies. The weaker Resource Conservation and Recovery Act corrective action requirements, when finally issued, would afford private parties some latitude for avoiding the burden of Superfund liability. Cost would continue to play a major role in cleanup decisions. Cost considerations would limit the extent of cleanup and the liability burden to be borne by the private sector. These constraints to be imposed on Superfund were effectively identical to those advocated by the Reagan administration. In contrast to the Reagan era, a preference for cost reduction over risk reduction would no longer find as clear a voice in senior EPA officials. EPA was now more likely to push up against White House constraints.

SUPERFUND INTO THE 1990s

Reauthorization opened a window of opportunity for EPA to demonstrate what it could accomplish under new leadership and a new Superfund strategy. Statistics issued as of late 1991 support agency claims that a corner has been turned in the enforcement program.[12] By the end of fiscal 1990, 134 unilateral orders were issued, nearly double the number recorded in fiscal 1988. Compliance with these orders rose from 43 percent in fiscal 1989 to nearly 58 percent by late fiscal 1991. By fiscal 1991, unilateral orders had outdistanced the previously more common consent decrees, a strong indication of a new aggressiveness. The ratio of unilateral orders to administrative orders on consent rose from 46 percent in fiscal 1988 to 117 percent by late fiscal 1991. Further, unilateral orders for design and construction of a remedy, the most expensive phase of the cleanup process, increased from thirteen in fiscal 1989 to forty-four in fiscal 1990. The greater reliance on orders to compel cleanup induced responsible parties to enter into voluntary agreements in order to avoid the high cost of litigation. While the value of design and construction activity covered by unilateral orders increased from $65 million in fiscal 1988 to $357 million in fiscal 1990, the sum of this activity covered by consent decrees increased from $263 million to $731 million over the same period.

Regarding its worst-sites-first strategy, EPA reported taking or planning emergency response actions at all newly evaluated sites posing immediate threats to the public or the environment. Further, the agency increasingly used treatment to address a site's principal source of hazardous waste contamination. Seventy-five percent of these source control threats involved treatment in 1990 versus 50 percent in 1989.

EPA has been less successful in implementing other initiatives promised in its program review, in particular improvements in management and oversight of contractors. A late 1990 report charged that cost overruns continued to pervade public cleanups. The cost of fund-financed remedies jumped 75 percent between stipulation of a cleanup plan and the completion of cleanup. In contrast, comparable private party cleanup costs increased by only 15 percent (Bureau of National Affairs, November 30, 1990: 1485). The implication that EPA is still unable to effectively manage its multibillion-dollar program is reinforced by a House panel finding that the agency failed to pursue potential waste and fraud in some $8.6 billion worth of contracts. The panel charged that the agency's Office of Inspector General conducted superficial investigations into allegations against one of the largest cleanup contractors and is generally plagued by serious leadership failures (Washington Post, 1991).

Both critics and supporters of the program also question whether the remedies EPA selects are justified by risk. While a desire to return sites to a preindustrial condition is laudable, they argue that a more narrow focus on saving lives is a far more economical use of limited environmental cleanup resources. Pointing to EPA estimates that some 1,000 cancer cases annually can be linked to hazardous waste exposure in contrast to the 5,000 to 20,000 lung cancer deaths from indoor exposure to radon, they suggest that less ambitious Superfund cleanup goals could free up funds to substantially address problems like radon (Passell, 1991; and Portney, 1988).

The agency's aggressive enforcement program has produced both predictable and unexpected results. A recent *Washington Post* investigative report found that nearly one-third of the $200 million the government has spent since 1988 to clean up sites has gone to administrative expenses of private contractors rather than to actual cleanup activity (Weisskopf, 1991). The percentage has been increasing. Senior EPA officials have attributed this situation to the agency's stepped-up enforcement effort. The ten-year agreements with contractors that the agency entered into in 1988 were based on the assumption that a much higher percentage of cleanup activity would be undertaken by the government. The contracts set fixed payments for program management. As fund-financed cleanups declined, contractor administrative costs have come to absorb a larger percentage of total outlays. While EPA's interpretation is reasonable, critics argue that the problem is broader: the agency has more contractors and equipment than it needs, has not attempted to control costs, and has made bonus awards to contractors whose performance is deemed unsatisfactory. The cost control and oversight problems noted above give force to this more critical evaluation.[13]

Increased enforcement activity, rising cleanup costs, and lax control over contractors have all contributed to an escalating conflict over the imposition of Superfund liability.[14] Major generators claim that EPA has failed in negotiation to accompany its clenched fist with an open hand. EPA attorneys, they charge, treat the agency's model consent decree as carved in stone and exhibit little willingness to alter provisions that are solely to the EPA's advantage. Further, EPA has not made extensive use of its power to simplify negotiation and apportionment through settlements with minor contributors. It also has made scant use of SARA's mixed funding provisions that allow EPA to cover some portion of the orphan share as an inducement to settlement. Major targets of EPA enforcement actions still see themselves as being held liable for far more than their proportionate share of cleanup costs. Under these circumstances, they are increasingly willing to reject consent decrees and to accept unilateral orders (see the data at the beginning of this section). The elimination of preenforcement review precludes their challenging these orders before the work is done. Since noncompliance with a unilateral order can result in treble damage penalties, responsible parties see their only viable option as compliance with the order followed by actions to recover costs from the fund (if they can prove that the cleanup response was not necessary) or through third party contribution suits. From EPA's perspective, the plight of responsible parties indicates the success of the enforcement program. From an industry perspective, EPA accomplishments bring with them a substantial and unnecessary increase in transaction costs. Industry has attempted to highlight the unfairness of agency policy as well as to bring political pressure to bear by targeting municipalities in third party contribution suits.

Municipal landfills comprise about 20 percent of the sites on the National Priorities List; municipalities also have sent their solid waste to privately owned priority sites. Although solid waste contributes to the total cost of cleanup, the agency and environmentalists argue that it is the hazardous waste coming from nonmunicipal generators that creates the need for cleanup action.[15] Beyond this perception of who is to blame, EPA also remains sensitive to the volatile political ramifications of forcing local governments to pay for cleanup. Recently a district court ruled that EPA's policy of not naming generators or transporters of municipal solid waste as potentially responsible parties is a legitimate exercise of discretion and rationally related to efficient use of agency resources. It further noted that private responsible parties could sue municipalities in subsequent contribution actions (Bureau of National Affairs, March 22, 1991: 2090).

Big corporations targeted by EPA are increasingly pursuing this option.[16] DuPont, Rohm and Haas, Texaco, and others have brought suit against fifty municipalities for cleanup costs at a New Jersey landfill. B. F. Goodrich and Uniroyal Chemical Company have targeted twenty-four Connecticut communities while General Electric and Polaroid are among those suing twelve Massachusetts municipalities. At the Operating Industries site in California, Occidental Petroleum, Lockheed, Proctor and Gamble, and sixty-one other companies are demanding that twenty-nine Los Angeles suburbs pay 90 percent of a cleanup expected to cost from $650 to $800 million. In explaining these actions, industrial generators note that municipal solid waste adds to the cost of cleanup. The cost of capping a landfill is related to the volume of waste present, whether hazardous or nonhazardous. Remedies involve burning off methane gas released from garbage. Corporate plaintiffs also emphasize that household waste may normally contain a fraction of a percent of toxic waste; this is sufficient for Superfund liability. In bringing suit against municipalities, major corporations are simply following the same logic of the Superfund law that allows EPA to target them as responsible parties. The underlying message is that if municipalities consider this situation to be highly inequitable, they should join the already beleaguered plaintiffs in pressuring Congress to change the law. [17]

Like major generators, insurers remain highly critical of the retroactive nature of environmental liability standards including those that underlie EPA's Superfund enforcement program. In response to a General Accounting Office survey, insurers reported a sharp increase in the cost of closing pollution coverage claims. Four insurers said that in 1985 they paid an average of $15,600 on 176 closed claims. In 1989 they paid an average of $64,400 on 786 closed claims. Insurers also reported spending about $158 million on lawsuits involving pollution coverage issues. At the close of the 1980s they were engaged in 1,962 lawsuits with insured parties over coverage involving about 6,000 hazardous waste sites. GAO anticipated that these numbers will continue to increase (U.S. General Accounting Office, 1991a). More recently, a RAND Corporation study estimates that the nation's insurers spent $470 million in 1989 on indemnification of policy holders and on transaction costs related to Superfund sites. [18]

Although the protests of industry and their insurers have been loud and persistent, they have yet to receive as sympathetic a hearing as that accorded another group caught in the Superfund liability net: lending institutions. Under the Superfund law, any party with a security interest in a facility (for example, a lender who can claim property as collateral for a loan) is exempt from cleanup liability if it acts to protect that interest but does not participate in the facility's management. However, the security interest exemption may be voided when a lender acquires full title to contaminated property through foreclosure. This became a source of concern in the late 1980s with an increase in business failures and loan defaults on commercial property. Concern mounted in the wake of spreading savings and loan institution failures and due to Supreme Court refusal to review an appellate court ruling on the liability of a secured creditor. The appellate court ruled in the Fleet Factors case that a secured creditor may be liable, without being an operator, if it participated in the management of a facility "to a degree indicating a capacity to influence the corporation's treatment of hazardous wastes" (Bureau of National Affairs, February 22, 1991: 1891). The level of participation associated with this capacity was not defined, although it is clear that some participation is required prior to the lender losing the exemption.

For situations where a lender is considered an owner when property is acquired through foreclosure and the exemption is lost, SARA created an innocent landowner defense. The defense is available for a purchaser who did not know or had no reason to know that property was contaminated. The standard is satisfied if the purchaser made all appropriate inquiry into the previous ownership and uses of the property at the time of acquisition. SARA also provides government entities with a defense to liability if they inadvertently acquire the property. This defense could be available to properties of failed thrifts and banks acquired through actions of the Federal Deposit Insurance Corporation (FDIC) and the Resolution Trust Corporation (RTC). However, if the property was known to be contaminated, the insurer also may be held liable for cleanup.

Private and public sector financial institutions consider these standards too vague relative to the high cost of cleanup if they are found to be liable. Lenders argue that the uncertainty surrounding these liability issues has produced a credit crunch; in particular, small businesses are being denied credit when they cannot provide lenders with adequate assurances due to the high cost of environmental audits. EPA, however, asserts that "[t]he problem is fear on the part of the commercial lending community for future liability that has not yet materialized" (Bureau of National Affairs, April 19, 1992: 2253). Only 8 of 18,392 formal notices of potential liability under Superfund have gone to private lenders.[19] The National Association of Manufacturers found that only 3 percent of over 2,200 manufacturers with less than 500 employees had been denied application for a new or renewed loan based on their bank's perception of environmental liability problems (Chemical Manufacturers Association, 1991: 5).

The FDIC and RTC maintain that existing law poses serious problems for resolving failed thrifts and banks. They report postponing foreclosure on property held by failed lenders. They also claim that assets with a book value of about $338 million have been identified as having potential hazardous substance problems and that estimated cleanup costs amount to more than one and one-half times the market value of the properties. Like private lenders, they are casting Superfund as a major impediment to financial and real estate transactions and as a potential cause of substantial increase in the cost of the savings and loan bailout.

EPA has attempted to defuse this issue through a proposed rule that would reconcile security holders' interests with the agency's duty to clean up sites and recover costs from institutions that do participate in management. The rule identifies a broad range of lender activities that do not void the security interest exemption. It also specifies that acquisition of property by the FDIC and RTC is an involuntary transfer as needed for the innocent landowner defense (Bureau of National Affairs, June 14, 1991: 430–32). Lending institutions see EPA's actions as a move in the right direction but prefer the solution contained in pending legislation that would further broaden their exemption from liability. The rule may protect them from government suits but does not protect them from the same private third party suits that have come to plague municipalities. The FDIC and RTC want full immunity from Superfund liability as well as exemptions for those who purchase the assets they have acquired from failed institutions.

Environmental and industry groups and several states see EPA's actions and proposed legislation as undercutting Superfund's liability standards and removing major incentives to cleanup; the lender liability crisis is a ruse to justify escape from Superfund liability (Phillips, 1991). The Chemical Manufacturers Association argues that if lenders face a problem, it is because Superfund is working as Congress intended. Both lenders and Congress should recognize the full severity of Superfund's liability standards. "What is needed," argues CMA, "is a comprehensive reevaluation of the entire Superfund liability standard and its impact on all potentially responsible parties plus its impact on the cleanup of this nation's hazardous waste sites in a protective, timely, and cost-effective manner" (Chemical Manufacturers Association, 1991: 17). While environmental groups do not share CMA's general objection to Superfund liability, they also are unconvinced that lenders need special protection or that providing such protection will solve the nation's banking and economic ills. Among other problems, EPA's rule would no longer require lending institutions to conduct environmental audits. Further, a broad exemption could create a major loophole allowing liability to be extinguished in the transfer of property through a bank.[20] Laundering schemes could cleanse sites of liability and leave Superfund with the cleanup bill.

Industrial and financial interests have proposed that the escalating conflicts engendered by a broadening of the Superfund liability net be resolved through substitution of some broad-based tax for the current Superfund liability standards. In support of this proposal, academic studies have argued that environmental enforcement is little more than a highly inefficient funding mechanism (Menell, 1991). While this approach might arguably create a more efficient and equitable system for remedying the environmental abuse of the past, it could at the same time weaken incentives to prevent such abuse in the future.

The case for strict, joint and several liability has always rested in part on the belief that future liability will deter present abuse. If generator corporations are held liable for past abuse, they will be more likely to consider future liability in making current production and disposal decisions. A strong enforcement program will encourage voluntary action to clean up sites before they are added to the National Priorities List. It also will encourage investigation of sites prior to real estate transactions. To avoid liability, lending institutions will demand information on contamination problems as well as the elimination of contamination through cleanup. Critics of this theory point out that a deterrence-through-enforcement approach presumes that current producers and disposers perceive imposition of liability as a certain consequence of their actions. A short-sighted hazardous waste generator or one that underestimates the cost of environmentally dangerous actions will not be sufficiently deterred (Menell, 1991). These are some of the same problems that blunt the deterrence impact of toxic damage suits.

Significantly, the potential deterrent impact of Superfund's liability standards has been reinforced by SARA's Emergency Planning and Community Right-to-Know Act. Publication of the first Toxics-Release Inventory in 1989 shocked generators into recognizing the sheer magnitude of the hazardous waste that industry released into the environment.[21] Some of the nation's largest companies later responded with voluntary programs to reduce their pollution. AT&T said it would stop all emissions of listed chemicals into the air by the turn of the century. The 3M Company announced a plan to reduce hazardous releases by 90 percent by the year 2000; a new emphasis on pollution prevention was needed since its earlier 1975 program was not moving fast enough. Further, while studies did not find that the pollutants it emitted were health risks, 3M could not claim that they were not. Public concern and the expectation that industry would reduce pollution made the setting of new corporate targets necessary. A second Toxics-Release Inventory, published in 1990, showed that toxic chemical releases were concentrated in a few states and were emitted by a small percentage of nearly 20,000 industrial plants. DuPont, Monsanto, and American Cyanamid accounted for 15 percent of the total. Following publication, EPA asked more than 600 companies to voluntarily cut in half (by 1995) emissions of the seventeen most dangerous toxic chemicals, including benzene, cyanide, mercury, and chromium. EPA Administrator Reilly negotiated 80 percent reductions in toxic air emission from the nation's forty worst-emitting plants.

The toxics-release inventories allowed the public to easily identify each generator's contribution to the nation's hazardous waste pollution. In so doing, they brought considerable pressure to bear on corporations that traded on an image of social responsibility and that wished to avoid additional government regulation (Holusha, 1991). They also made concrete the potential cost of liability for damage to public health and the environment. In this regard, they reinforced the waste reduction incentives associated with Superfund's tough liability standards.

The recently elevated priority accorded waste reduction has affected the debate over Superfund liability. While industry and their insurers have attacked retroactive Superfund liability, they increasingly acknowledge the need for prospective liability as a component of the nation's waste minimization efforts. For example, the American International Group proposal to substitute a broad-based tax for the current Superfund standard would include a liability cutoff date. Hazardous waste disposed after that date would still be subject to strict, joint and several liability. It is unclear how this proposal will work in practice. It is possible that it will add substantial complexity to the apportionment of liability.[22]

Generator industries have used announced waste reduction targets as indices of their new environmentally responsible behavior and as part of their argument for release from retroactive liability. In this context, retroactive liability provides an additional political incentive to meet these targets and should not be modified until substantial progress has in fact occurred. Further, there is good reason to question whether announced future actions justify forgiveness for past actions. The claim by generators that they did not know the magnitude of their pollution prior to the toxics-release inventories suggests a high degree of environmentally irresponsible behavior. In light of these considerations, it is clearly too soon to test whether retroactive Superfund liability is an expendable component of the nation's waste reduction system. The arguments for the elimination of this strong liability standard face an extremely difficult burden of proof.

BALANCING NATIONAL PRIORITIES

Events since 1986 highlight a continuing conflict over pursuit of environmental versus economic priorities. The real and perceived costs of environmental protection have increased. The preference for permanent treatment remedies contained in SARA combined with a ban on land disposal of hazardous waste have raised the cost of cleanup. A perception of rapidly increasing costs has been fed by the vocal opposition of generators and their insurers to permanent remedies and strong liability standards. They argue that the transaction costs of a program consistent with the 1980 and 1986 Superfund mandates are far out of line with the environmental benefits secured. Lending institutions claim that a broadly cast liability net threatens the stability of the financial system. Efforts to socialize the toxic debt are frustrated by government's diminished capacity to absorb the economic burden of environmental cleanup due to mounting federal deficits, financial crises that place substantial claims on federal revenues, a recessionary economy, and strong antitax sentiments. EPA recently estimated that annual spending on all pollution control, almost $90 billion in 1987, will grow to $160 billion by the year 2000. Federal agencies such as the Departments of Energy and Defense are expected to bear the greatest increase in their share of these expenditures (U.S. General Accounting Office, 1991b: 4).

Conflict among priorities has intensified with critical evaluations of Superfund potential to reduce environmental risks. EPA's finding that the risk posed by hazardous waste sites is overstated relative to other environmental risks has been used to support the claim that program costs do not produce commensurate benefits.[23] Further, EPA, the General Accounting Office, and industry have argued that affected communities often demand remedies justified by fear rather than by objective threat. EPA responsiveness to community fears results in overly protective remedies and reduces the aggregate reduction in risk achievable with a given pool of cleanup resources. Continuing disagreement over the risk posed by hazardous waste sites encourages this public behavior as does the sense that cleanup decisions are based too often on political and economic considerations. EPA delay in initiating the technical assistance grant program did little to promote more realistic community evaluation of waste site threats.

Through 1992 the White House and many in Congress have remained most sensitive to the economic and budgetary consequences of a strengthened environmental commitment. However, Washington's responsiveness to private sector demands for relief is constrained by two factors. First, even if hazardous waste site risk is overstated, it is still real and substantial. In its 1989 report on Superfund, the Office of Technology Assessment asked the rhetorical question: Do uncontrolled toxic waste sites in fact pose a problem that justifies a multibillion-dollar program? OTA answered with an emphatic "yes" (U.S. Office of Technology Assessment, 1989b: 22–26). Public support for environmental protection remains strong. With Superfund as the most visible of federal environmental protection programs, the political costs of attempting once again to eviscerate it are unacceptably large. Second, since cleanup will occur, promotion of a policy to reduce the burden on the private sector will result in a greater burden being placed on the federal budget. White House and congressional resistance to environmental action in the early 1980s was based primarily on private sector burdens. Resistance in the late 1980s increasingly built on anticipated public sector costs.

Given these constraints, Washington's post-SARA efforts to resolve conflicts between economic and environmental priorities have taken several paths. The potential cost and scope of Superfund cleanups were limited by provisions contained in the National Contingency Plan and in proposed corrective action guidelines for operating hazardous waste facilities. The upper end of the risk range was reduced and the justification of cost by benefits was emphasized. The White House denied EPA and the states the power to force federal facility compliance with environmental law. Congress has yet to successfully challenge this denial through legislation.

The initiation of an enforcement-first strategy and the related increase in enforcement funding emerged from the need to place a greater share of the toxic debt on private responsible parties. For the first time, EPA's Superfund strategy is consistent with the basic logic of the enabling legislation. Of equal significance, it offers the potential for consistency with critiques of regulation and demands by industry for a more equitable settlement process. By interpreting the deregulation movement as a mandate to eviscerate EPA, President Reagan missed an opportunity to reform environmental protection. Many advocates of deregulation acknowledged that hazardous waste cleanup was among those instances of market failure that justified government action. For these critics, the means, not the ends, were in need of reform. Other advocates of deregulation focused narrowly on the cost of environmental protection and argued that economic viability demanded substantial relief. President Reagan's environmental policy was shaped by this latter perspective. In contrast, the appointment of William Reilly by President Bush was more in line with the former perspective. Reilly's background suggested a capacity to promote environmental goals through strong enforcement as well as through dialogue with industry. EPA's ability to sustain an enforcement-first strategy in the face of a mounting backlash will depend in part on its ability to extend an open hand while maintaining a clenched fist.

These changes have allowed EPA to more aggressively pursue private cleanup resources while limiting the cleanup costs that can be imposed. At the same time, White House and congressional sensitivity to economic costs have imposed a derivative sensitivity on EPA. The more forceful is the agency in its efforts to meet program goals, the greater is the political protest from those who bear the costs. When political backlash is anticipated, EPA faces a strong incentive to compromise and protect its discretionary powers. EPA's uncharacteristic speed in drafting guidelines for lending institutions provides a clear case in point. Convinced by anecdote in the absence of hard data, Congress considered limiting cleanup liability out of fear that not doing so would seriously destabilize financial markets. In this setting, EPA acted with haste to preclude congressional action that could produce a more general weakening of liability standards. EPA concern over third party suits to impose cleanup liability on municipalities reflects a similar political constraint. Notwithstanding agency views on the equity of municipal cleanup contributions, EPA has a history of actions to increase the cleanup burden imposed on the states.

The methods chosen to resolve conflict over economic and environmental priorities have several clear implications for the efficiency and equity of the Superfund program. Efforts to protect federal agencies from the full force of environmental laws inevitably diminish overall cleanup efficiency and equity. Even though the Superfund cannot be used to finance these cleanups, all cleanup funds ultimately come from the same pool of private and public resources. If these resources cannot be directed at some of the worst sites because they are owned by the federal government, risk reduction per dollar spent falls. Communities exposed to the contamination released at these sites experience a lesser protection than communities exposed at similar nonfederal sites. The incompatibility of Superfund with corrective action guidelines will also reduce program efficiency and equity by allowing less costly and less protective cleanup options. Such deferral promises to increase the number of future Superfund sites and the overall cost of cleanup. The impact of revisions to the National Contingency Plan are less obvious. An emphasis on cost may improve efficiency but will most likely do so at the expense of protectiveness. If cost is overemphasized, equity will suffer. Enforcement first could enhance both efficiency and equity. If recalcitrance continues to be expensive and EPA begins to rely on incentives as well as on threats, good citizen responsible parties will have increased incentive to settle as will those who have previously chosen to avoid their fair share contribution to cleanup. The enforcement program will experience some reduction in transaction costs and will produce a better match between contribution and responsibility.

The solutions forged in the late 1980s have at least temporarily resolved some Superfund-related conflicts. Opposing evaluations of these solutions will figure prominently in the next reauthorization debate. It is too soon to predict how the Clinton administration's environmentalism will be manifest in a legislative solution to the Superfund dilemma.

Other Superfund-related problems remain unresolved. First, the privatization of the Superfund program remains incompatible with government oversight of contractors. EPA's post–management review initiative to improve the stability and experience of its workforce has yet to produce an efficient contracting system. The current system leaves EPA dependent on private sector firms whose goals conflict with program efficiency and equity.[24] The system allows excessive study, cost overruns, and cleanup delays. Second, the impact of weaker liability standards on waste reduction remains unknown. If enforcement first produces a more efficient and equitable system for assigning liability for past abuse, there will be less tension between cleanup and waste reduction goals. If enforcement first fails, considerable public pressure will be needed to sustain a system that diminishes rather than increases incentives for future environmental abuse.

The story of Superfund's evolution demonstrates the linkage between program failure and conflict over who pays the toxic debt. The goal of this chapter is to highlight this linkage within the political economic framework discussed in chapter 3 and, against this background, to consider the feasibility of a negotiated solution to the Superfund dilemma.

POLITICAL ECONOMY OF FAILURE

Superfund has imposed substantial costs on major polluting industries and their insurers, federal and state taxpayers, and a growing cast of third parties while leaving hazardous waste site host communities exposed to health and environmental threats. Although no one has explicitly willed this outcome, conflict among interested parties has nevertheless produced failure.

Industries targeted to pay the toxic debt have made concerted efforts to limit their tax and liability burdens. They have taken their efficiency and equity arguments to the White House and to Congress with some success. They have exerted pressure on EPA to draft less burdensome cleanup and enforcement strategies and have used their political and economic muscle to resist many agency initiatives and actions. When all else fails, they have acted to pass enforcement costs onto third parties.

The perceived economic consequences of substantial cleanup and transaction costs has magnified the political leverage of polluting industries. Influential voices in Congress have advocated limits on Superfund in the interest of domestic growth and international competitiveness. The Reagan administration, with its faith in the benefits of deregulation, had emphasized these economic goals in its attacks on Superfund. Until its pre-1992 election moratorium on regulation, the Bush White House was more passive in this regard. The stance to be adopted by the pro-environment Clinton administration is unclear at the time of this writing.

Despite these political and economic advantages, the petrochemical, manufacturing, and insurance industries have achieved only limited success in their efforts to constrain Superfund and socialize its costs. The real and perceived consequences of environmental inaction were essential factors in the creation of Superfund and have continued to buttress resistance to industrial pressures. Mounting budgetary problems have constrained moves to more fully spread the cost of cleanup through the tax base. Community, labor, and environmental group emphasis on the inherent equity of a make-polluters-pay principle has reduced congressional sympathy for the plight of polluting industries and has raised the political cost of acting on this sympathy.

Proponents of a liberal instrumentalist theory of the state would argue that this is a conflict ripe for compromise (see chapter 3). In situations where no party can dominate, negotiated compromise is a viable means to minimize a collective loss and to produce a program that does not suffer from excessive inequity or inefficiency. Despite these incentives, a compromise solution has yet to emerge. Rather, review of Superfund makes clear that ongoing conflict has produced a program that embodies contradictory elements and consequently yields inefficient and inequitable outcomes. This is the scenario predicted by the more pessimistic structuralist theory of the state. Polluting industries and their political supporters, lacking power to prevail, have been able to impede initiatives that increase industry's economic burden. Advocates of an enhanced cleanup effort and a make-polluters-pay principle have in turn acted to deny industry the full fruits of these victories. Partial and incompatible victories build contradictions into the program, guaranteeing that too much is spent and too little is achieved. The result is a program marked by failure.

This study has highlighted several of these contradictions that are central to Superfund failure. First, it is clear that failure to resolve conflict over how clean is clean has resulted in costly and impermanent remedies. Congress did place emphasis on standards and permanent remedies in its 1986 reauthorization. It failed to explicitly distinguish between cleanup objectives as the starting point of the remedy selection process and cost as a secondary factor. Responsibility for balancing cleanup decision criteria was passed on to EPA. The agency thus became the locus of conflict between White House, state, community, environmental, and industrial interests. Unable to resolve this conflict, EPA often sacrificed cleanup effectiveness to cost considerations and rationalized its actions in terms of questionable risk evaluations.

As emphasized throughout the study, failure to resolve how clean is clean is a manifestation of a more general inability to resolve conflict over economic and environmental values. Conflict over these values is at the root of the structural analysis of environmental regulation and is characteristic of other areas of environmental policy. Peter Yeager argues in his recent work on Clean Water Act implementation that "the outer bounds of social regulation are set by the systemic needs of the political economic system of capitalist democracies, which are represented in legal determinations in the form of mandated consideration of the *costs* of controls, both those that may be borne by the private sector and those accruing to the state" (emphasis in original) (Yeager, 1991: 306). If cleanup standards are not stipulated, conflict over the justification of cost by benefit politicizes cost-benefit analysis and robs it of any claim to scientific objectivity. If cleanup standards are stipulated but guidelines do not state the priority to be accorded standards as primary objectives relative to cost as a secondary consideration, cost-effectiveness evaluations of remedy selection reduce to a cost-benefit evaluation. Yeager notes that in the absence of clear agreement on the cost to be absorbed to achieve a cleaner environment, government decision makers may choose to obscure the methodological underpinnings of procedures such as cost-benefit techniques that yield environmental and economic outcomes (Yeager, 1991: 323–27).

Second, it is equally clear that inability to resolve conflict over an equitable distribution of the toxic debt has severely compromised program efficiency. Confronted with budgetary problems, real and perceived economic dislocation, and pressure to make polluters pay, Congress left major responsibility for distributing cleanup costs to EPA and its enforcement program. EPA in turn could not resolve the basic contradiction between this expectation, on the one hand, and its willingness and ability to demand industrial compliance, on the other. Under Administrator Burford, EPA sacrificed aggressiveness to industrial accommodation and a White House deregulatory agenda. Under Administrators Ruckelshaus and Thomas, EPA sacrificed cleanup goals to mandated schedules and fund conservation. Under the enforcement-first approach, EPA became more aggressive but was left to contend with the political ramifications of increased third party suits and a related increase in transaction costs.

The staggering cost of hazardous waste cleanup requires EPA to induce giant corporations in major industries to help underwrite the cleanup process. These corporations are notable for their concentrated holdings of corporate resources and their resulting ability to contest agency enforcement efforts. Environmental programs within the United States as well as those in similar industrialized countries reveal significant barriers to imposing enforcement costs upon larger and more powerful corporations and an associated tendency to impose these costs disproportionately on smaller polluters.[1] Superfund will fail to achieve its ends to the extent that EPA cannot prevail against the most powerful polluters, expect that the less powerful have the resources to substantially underwrite cleanup, or negotiate an acceptable distribution of cleanup burden over both large and small polluters.

Third, it is apparent that EPA's staff resources are insufficient relative to its mandate. Staff limitations have generally constrained the efficiency of the remedy selection process, the productivity of enforcement activity, and the oversight of contractors. Blunting agency action through budgetary constraint is a hallmark of an inability to resolve regulatory conflict, as made clear in structural analyses of regulation.[2] In such situations, strong legislation satisfies public demands for action while inadequate funding restricts action and diminishes economic burden.

Finally, failure to resolve conflict between federal funding and federal responsibilities has left elements of the cleanup program dependent on entities that cannot or do not meet Superfund expectations. The demands of the New Federalism have imposed a cleanup and enforcement burden on the states that often exceeds state fiscal capacity. The desire to privatize much of the cleanup process has left EPA dependent on for-profit contractors. Contractor decisions are often driven by goals that diverge substantially from those of the agency.[3]

FORGING COMPROMISE

Although conflict is inherent to Superfund goals, failure is not inevitable.[4] Wresting success from failure requires establishment of firm objectives and procedures that reward compromise and punish recalcitrance. The fact that no one clearly gains from Superfund failure can lead to development of a program that affords opportunities to minimize collective loss and opportunities to more equitably share in the corresponding gains.[5] A program with these characteristics is more likely to produce the efficiency and equity outcomes predicted by the liberal instrumental model. In this final section I sketch out a model of negotiated settlement and consider its feasibility.

Proposals offered by Clean Sites, Inc., are of particular interest in this regard. In 1989 Clean Sites began a project to develop a common understanding of the tensions and difficulties involved in selecting remedies (Sarno, 1991; Clean Sites, 1990). Consistent with a belief in the benefits of negotiation, the project built on participation by major public and private sector interests. Clean Sites found that the ambiguous and implicit nature of the current selection process was central to its failure, a conclusion in accord with the findings of this study. By way of solution, they proposed a four-step explicit and interactive process.

The first step is for EPA to more fully and actively involve affected parties in defining the scope of remedial investigations and in selecting site objectives. To achieve this goal, the agency provides detailed information on risk to human health and the environment and on the specific problems requiring remediation.

The second, and most critical, step is the establishment of site-specific cleanup objectives. To develop objectives, consideration is given to such factors as the future use of the site and its environs, the proximity of residents, the level of contamination of surrounding properties, specific environmental issues, and the views of the state, responsible parties, and directly affected citizens. Making this decision at the outset facilitates resolution of conflicts that typically emerge later on in the remedy selection process.

The third step is the full development of alternative remedies only after site objectives and cleanup levels are determined. All of these alternatives must at least meet site objectives. Permanence, treatment, and long-term effectiveness are then explicitly considered in evaluating alternatives. Long-term effectiveness serves as a next-best option to permanence when the latter is not feasible.

Fourth, an alternative is selected that provides the greatest long-term effectiveness at lowest cost. Cost is compared to primary benefits to select the best alternative.

In a related document, Clean Sites proposes an enforcement strategy to reinforce responsible party incentives to participate in the remedy selection process and to accept compromise positions (Clean Sites, 1989). As in EPA's current enforcement-first strategy, the basic goal is to increase the number of site cleanups while conserving the fund. To achieve these goals, EPA initiates a significant number of administrative and judicial enforcement actions to punish the recalcitrant and impel their participation in cleanup. It also undertakes an increased number of cost recovery actions in a timely manner. To demonstrate visibly its will to enforce, EPA vigorously pursues a limited number of good cases and then aggressively pursues nonsettlors. Regional offices are held accountable for meeting realistically high responsible party cleanup goals. Finally, EPA more fully utilizes incentives for cooperation, such as mixed funding and minor party settlements, structured settlements that penalize nonsettlors in subsequent litigation by forcing them to pay more than if they had settled, and targeting nonsettlors first to cover subsequent cleanup activity. As discussed in chapter 9, EPA has already made some progress in building an enforcement program along these lines.

To facilitate consistency in remedy selection and enforcement, Clean Sites also proposes enhancing regional office accountability. To facilitate effective implementation of all these proposals, Clean Sites advocates an upgrading of project manager positions and provision of needed staff training. Finally, to hold EPA accountable for achievement of program goals, Clean Sites proposes that the agency track measures of success that focus on program outcomes rather than on program inputs. Recent EPA initiatives are in accord with these proposals.

The above program affords potential gains to hazardous waste site victims as well as to major polluting corporations. If host communities are allowed to participate on a equal footing with other interests, they gain through their involvement in remedy selection and through reduced delay in remedy implementation. Establishing objectives at the outset of the process reduces the chance that their interests will be sacrificed to fund conservation or to settlement goals. Major polluters benefit from an enforcement program emphasizing fund financing of orphan shares (e.g., mixing funding settlements) and targeting of nonsettlors. Both reduce their cleanup burden and the transaction costs associated with shifting a portion of this burden onto third parties. They also benefit if a rationalized remedy selection process and an enhanced capacity to oversee contractors contains cleanup costs.

These outcomes promote program efficiency and equity and consequently address industry's demand for a greater socialization of the toxic debt. As noted earlier, polluting industry protests against paying the Superfund tax are based on four propositions: First, society has broadly participated in creating the problem and should therefore participate in paying for the solution. Second, payment of the tax fails to reduce enforcement-related cleanup costs to the extent that the fund does not cover the orphan share and to the extent that EPA allows the recalcitrant to take a free ride. Third, efforts to shift the cleanup burden onto third parties imposes a transaction cost on major targets of EPA enforcement that reduces any net gain secured through shifting the cleanup burden onto third parties. Finally, an absence of EPA control over contractors and the cleanup process produces unnecessarily large cleanup costs that squander the fund and raise the burden of complying with settlement terms.

Continued development of Superfund along lines consistent with the Clean Sites proposals and enforcement first addresses directly three out of four industry propositions. There is reason to expect that industry would drop its emphasis on the first (socialization via the tax base) in exchange for progress on the other three. I believe that the ultimate goal of the socialization argument is to reinforce a public impression that polluting industries are contributing more than their fair share to cleanup and, building on this impression, to demand other concessions.[6] Although the Clean Sites proposal does not promote a direct socialization through taxation, it does promote a fuller socialization of cleanup expenditures via enforcement as well as the prospect of a reduction in transaction costs.

It is naive to assume that the resulting distribution of the toxic debt will satisfy all interests. A reduction in transaction costs may come at the expense of an imposition of a larger cleanup burden on smaller polluters and minor contributors. However, it is equally naive to assume that dissatisfied interests can prevail substantially against a coalition of major corporations and those who have historically supported a stronger and more rational cleanup program.

These optimistic conclusions are predicated on a belief that competing interests can resolve conflict over cleanup goals. Throughout this study, I have emphasized the interdependence between risk and cost evaluations, on the one hand, and conflict over the distribution of the toxic debt, on the other. The Clean Sites remedy selection proposal requires resolution of how-clean-is-clean issues as a precondition for toxic debt distribution via settlement. Setting cleanup objectives clearly requires agreement on site risk to human health and the environment. Comparing cost to primary benefits in selecting a best alternative retains an element of cost-benefit analysis. Polluting industries are likely to support objectives that are sensitive to the greater cost of permanence and long-term effectiveness while exposed communities are likely to support objectives that are more sensitive to risk regardless of cost. Given the substantial uncertainties surrounding identification of hazardous waste site risk, provision of information to all interested parties can reduce, but will not eliminate, disagreement on this central issue.

The most recent round of debate over the dangers posed by dioxin underscores the degree to which self-interest has dominated science in evaluating risk. The pulp and paper industries, highly sensitive to dioxin disposal and cleanup costs, have manipulated scientific findings in a public relations campaign intended to convince EPA and the public that the risks of dioxin contamination have been overstated. Examination of new evidence and subsequent reexamination of existing evidence suggest that the dangers associated with dioxin may in fact be understated (Bailey, 1992).

For industry, cost is the driving force behind evaluations of risk and cleanup effectiveness. Any corporation's share of the toxic debt depends on cleanup costs and their distribution. A remedy selection process that is firmly rooted in objective scientific findings will narrow the range of defensible options and promote agreement. At the same time, a settlement procedure that allows a more equitable distribution of the cleanup burden will reduce the strategic gains associated with emphasizing cost and downplaying risk.

More broadly, resolution of conflict over the toxic debt in the context of procedures envisioned by Clean Sites requires simultaneous change in EPA resources and in the expectations of major players. If EPA staff funding expands to allow a substantial increase in the time and effort it allocates to negotiation, it may attain its settlement objectives without falling prey to excessive accommodation or excessive confrontation. If deep pocket generators believe that they will not have to bear the major burden of costly cleanups, they may find it more in their interest to accept more permanent remedies and to satisfy agency demands. If environmentalists expect that any concessions on their preferred set of cleanup goals will be minimal in contrast to the gains from an enhanced pace of cleanup, they too may support the Clean Sites approach. As suggested above, minor players may not be as pleased with a set of outcomes that satisfy major interests. However, they may possess only limited political and economic power to short-circuit this program.

Compromise on how clean is clean and on the toxic debt burden of major polluting industries will reduce the conflict surrounding third party suits. Fund coverage of the orphan share combined with EPA targeting of nonsettlors and EPA settlement with minor contributors will diminish the frequency and size of suits initiated by major targets of EPA enforcement. Further, although EPA can be expected to seek contribution from municipalities, the burden the agency will attempt to impose on them is considerably less than that demanded by major polluters. The potential for third party suits against lenders also is likely to diminish. While the political ramifications of emphasizing lender liability has served the interests of EPA's primary enforcement targets, the agency is likely to shy away from poking this hornets nest.

Compromise will mute some protest over Superfund liability standards if enforcement no longer places primary emphasis on claims against deep pockets. As argued in chapter 9, strong liability standards are essential to address future disposal problems. An enforcement program that raises the certainty that polluters must pay will make liability a stronger deterrent to future environmentally hazardous economic behavior. The petrochemical industry may demand some relief from retroactive liability in exchange for their announced waste reduction goals. However, it seems premature to consider such a trade-off until hazardous waste generation is in fact diminished.

Compromise may also mute, though not eliminate, insurance industry protests over absorption of cleanup costs and related litigation costs. Polluting industries have promoted a mode of socialization in their efforts to pass cleanup costs on to their insurers. High insurance industry transaction costs, reported in a recent study by Acton and Dixon (1992), demonstrates that industry's resistance to these polluting industry efforts. However, the burden faced by insurers will be diminished to the extent that the fund more fully covers orphan shares and thus reduces insurance claims brought by major responsible parties. It also will be diminished to the extent that major polluters have more extensive insurance coverage than do smaller firms.

The above resolution dynamic evokes an image of three groups of stakeholders meeting around the negotiating table to forge an acceptable compromise. Each group has prioritized its objectives and resolved disagreements among its members. EPA represents the interests of the government, major generators represent the interests of the universe of potentially responsible parties, and environmentalists represent exposed communities. Driven by recognition that conflict costs more than compromise, major players are collectively willing and able to eliminate the ambiguities and implicit guidelines that have historically resulted from an inability to resolve how clean is clean, to forge agreement on an acceptable distribution of the toxic debt, and to guarantee an enforcement budget and strategy consistent with self-interested compliance.

This image stands in stark contrast to the historic realities that are central to the structural analysis of failure. There are substantial differences within and among manufacturing and nonmanufacturing industries as regards risk, cost, and an acceptable distribution of the toxic debt. Environmentalists and exposed communities may disagree on the acceptability of deviation from a zero risk goal. Uncertainties with respect to risk and disagreement with respect to an acceptable balancing of risk and cost promote ambiguous guidelines as means to reach compromise and retain flexibility. The federal budget deficit continues as a significant constraint on EPA staff funding. Further, the decision-making process remains decentralized, allowing each group of stakeholders to push for a preferred outcome through constraint on program elements that serve an opposing group.

To date, self-interested stakeholders have chosen to contend with these issues through a multiplicity of program contradictions. In contrast, the negotiation option is predicated on the assumption that the structural constraints that are central to Superfund failure embody the key to its success. The primary basis for such optimism is that the mounting cost of failure associated with structural constraints will reinforce a movement toward compromise. The substantial political leverage of opposing interests allows contradictions to be built into Superfund. If united by the prospect of a compromise solution, this leverage would be sufficient to remove or minimize these structural constraints. For example, EPA's enforcement budget constraint could be loosened by allowing the agency to pass its costs forward to responsible parties. Such self-financing is generally rejected since it eliminates a constraint on aggressive enforcement. However, were major generators and environmentalists to believe strong and rationalized enforcement was key to a fair distribution of the toxic debt, support for self-financing could increase by an order of magnitude.[7]

Ultimately, resolution of cleanup-engendered conflict in a manner that does not perpetuate Superfund failure depends on forging a social consensus of an acceptable trade-off between efficiency and equity. It also depends on building this trade-off into a program that fully rewards cooperation and substantially penalizes recalcitrance. As a society, we must decide whether it is preferable to err on the side of higher than necessary cost and potentially negative economic impacts or on the side of higher risk and potentially negative public health and environmental impacts. We must choose whether to sacrifice a degree of the equity that flows from a make-polluters-pay principle or a degree of the efficiency that results from holding polluters responsible for their socially harmful actions. If we do not, or can not, come to agreement on these issues, we will continue to expose the public to unacceptably large health risks while squandering valuable environmental and economic resources.

CHAPTER 1

1. This legislation is often referred to by the acronym CERCLA and as the Superfund Act.

CHAPTER 2

1. Information on chemical characteristics presented in this section, unless otherwise stated, is drawn from Epstein, Brown, and Pope, 1982; Miller, 1988; and Sherman and Sherman, 1983.

2. Based on data reported in U.S. Environmental Protection Agency, 1989, chap. 4. This figure includes both releases and transfers.

3. The percentage contributions of chemical groups to Superfund site problems is taken from U.S. Environmental Protection Agency, 1984d: 4–12. Contribution is based on the percentage of National Priorities List sites at which the chemical or its feedstock is found. It does not adjust for concentration, toxicity, or quantity.

4. Dioxin provides a good example of the uncertainty and politics surrounding identification of toxic substance threats. The presence of dioxin-contaminated soil at the Times Beach site in Missouri resulted in a highly controversial evacuation of that town in 1982. The decision to evacuate was defended by EPA during the 1985–86 Superfund reauthorization hearings (see chapter 8). At that time, experts could not agree on whether the evidence established by tests on small mammals confirmed a health threat to humans. More recently, the paper and pulp industries have conducted their own reevaluation of the scientific evidence and, based on a highly questionable assessment of this evidence, have waged a public relations campaign to downplay the risks posed by dioxin. They have successfully pressured EPA to review its policy on dioxin despite a new National Institute for Occupational Safety and Health study suggesting that cancer deaths among chemical-plant workers are higher than expected. The NIOSH study also warns that "it is premature to conclude that [dioxin] is not harmful at low levels of exposure" (as reported in Bailey, 1992).

5. EPA's Toxics-Release Inventory data show that 22.5 billion pounds of chemicals were released or transferred by manufacturing facilities in 1987. In contrast to the earlier studies discussed in the text, TRI data are based on mandatory reporting by industrial firms. The TRI is more reliable in that it is not derived from survey data and extrapolation. Unfortunately, it is not comparable to earlier studies in that it records the quantity or volume of each chemical whereas earlier studies report the volume of a waste stream containing one or more chemicals.

6. Information on petroleum and chemical industry corporations is from *Fortune*

magazine's listing of the 500 largest U.S. industrial corporations (*Fortune*, April 24, 1989), Moody's *Industrial Manual* (1989), and Standard and Poor's *Standard NYSE Stock Reports* (1989).

7. Concentration data are from U.S. Department of Commerce, 1986a.

8. It must be noted that identification of a company as a potentially responsible party does not necessarily mean that it is a major contributor to a Superfund cleanup problem. Under Superfund, liability is not limited to proportionate contribution.

9. As reported in *Business Week*, August 3, 1987, p. 73.

10. See Brown, 1981. Love Canal is discussed at greater length in chapter 4.

11. As reported in Epstein, Brown, and Pope, 1982: 26–29.

12. Those who read the Fred C. Hart study would note that EPA regional offices applied divergent and in some cases unstated methodologies to derive estimates which were ultimately based on data provided by the states. Further, the consultant utilized a speculative EPA estimate that 90 percent of wastes were improperly disposed of to derive a projection of the number of significant problem sites. In that "improper" is a matter of degree, there was little basis for equating improper with significant.

13. As reported in Silka and Brasier, 1980.

14. The following information on ground water characteristics and contamination is taken from the testimony of Robert H. Harris, in U.S. Congress, House, 1980b: 5–10.

15. Additional incidents were reported in 1981 (see U.S. Council on Environmental Quality, 1981: 562–66).

16. These problem areas include (1) nearly 600 operating hazardous waste disposal, storage, and treatment facilities expected to close due to tougher financial and control requirements; (2) an unknown percentage of the nearly 54,000 active and inactive municipal landfills in receipt of hazardous waste; (3) an unknown percentage of approximately 75,000 operating industrial landfills containing hazardous waste; (4) some 10,000 to 64,000 active and inactive mining sites; (5) an unknown percentage of up to 187,500 facilities with underground storage tanks leaking hazardous substances; (6) agricultural use of pesticides that contaminated ground water in over twenty states; and (7) radioactive sites licensed by the Nuclear Regulatory Commission or the states.

17. This estimate may involve some double counting in that a given population can be at risk from several sites. EPA's proportionately lower estimate for 546 sites may have made adjustment for this fact.

CHAPTER 3

1. Government regulation is broadly classified as social or economic. Social regulation is intended to protect public health and safety and the environment from production-related harms. Economic regulation is intended to stabilize price, output, and profits and to control competition by limiting firm entry and exit.

2. The Law and Economics literature is substantial. A seminal work is Coase, 1960. For an in-depth discussion of approach, methodology, and conclusions, see Cooter and Ulen, 1988. For a sampling of critiques, see Kelman, 1979, 1983; Liebhafsky, 1976; and Bromley, 1978.

3. The following discussion of the failure of tort law to achieve cleanup and compensation draws heavily on Strand, 1983.

4. A 1982 study of victim compensation law found that seven states had the worst kind of limitation period, beginning at the time of exposure, while only thirteen jurisdictions had the most appropriate limitation period, beginning when a plaintiff knew or should have known both that the injury occurred and that a cause of action was available. For about half of the states, the right to sue might elapse before the victim knew or could have known that a remedy was available. See U.S. Congress, House, 1985b: 133.

5. Advocates of market-based solutions argue that establishment of property rights in natural resources is necessary to achieve efficient outcomes. The empowerment of public trustees is an alternative solution.

6. See, for example, Brown, 1981; and Epstein, Brown, and Pope, 1982.

7. A 1987 report found that income and race are among the most important community characteristics explaining the location of hazardous waste facilities. It also found that communities with the greatest number of commercial hazardous waste facilities have the highest composition of racial minority and ethnic residents (as reported in Wiley, 1991: 1). A 1990 report by Clean Sites, Inc., found that hazardous waste sites in poor communities that are candidates for the National Priorities List are added only half as often as are sites nationally (Bureau of National Affairs, April 13, 1990: 1961).

8. As described in Epstein, Brown, and Pope, 1982: 99–118.

9. As reported in *New York Times*, June 18, 1989, p. 3-1, and Bailey, 1991.

10. As estimated by U.S. Office of Technology Assessment, 1989a: 3. OTA offers illustrations of the state of the contractor industry based on company reports of some of Superfund's long-time major contractors: Ecology and Environment, Inc., experienced a 204 percent increase in net earning from 1984 through 1988; Roy F. Weston, Inc., experienced a 240 percent increase in earning from 1983 through 1987; ICF experienced a 216 percent increase in sales from 1983 to 1987; Environmental Treatment and Technology experienced a 160 percent increase in net income from 1983 to 1987; and CH2M Hill experienced an 82 percent increase in net income from 1985 to 1987 (U.S. Office of Technology Assessment, 1989a: 11). EPA has been subject to substantial criticism for the share of total Superfund expenditures going to cleanup studies by contractors.

11. A generic instrumental model is based on common conceptual characteristics of conservative, liberal, and radical analyses. Characterization of the conservative variant draws on Bardach and Kagan, 1982a, 1982b; MacAvoy, 1979; Niskanen, 1971; Noll and Owen, 1983; Stigler, 1975; Weidenbaum, 1981; Wilson, 1980. Characterization of the liberal variant draws on Downing, 1981; Derthick and Quirk, 1985; and Shapiro, 1984. Characterization of the radical variant draws on Herman, 1981; and Yeager, 1983. For related discussion of these variants, see Bates, 1976; Shover, Clelland, and Lynxwiler, 1983; and Williams and Matheny, 1984.

12. The reader should note that this perspective does leave room for prior commitments to influence legislator decisions. Some argue that individual legislators have a historic commitment to specific issues or groups such as the environment, health and safety, the elderly, or low taxes that cannot be explained simply in terms of self-interest. To think of congressional decision making in terms of self-interest means that legislators without strong prior commitments are guided predominantly by the consequences of their actions for political support. While legislators with strong prior commitments can

act altruistically, a self-interest perspective assumes that they too can be placed in situations where strong political opposition leads to compromise.

13. For an excellent recent discussion of capture that recognizes participation by competing interest groups in the regulatory process, see Ayres and Braithwaite, 1989.

14. The characterization of the structural model draws on Barnett, 1981; Bates, 1976; O'Conner, 1973; and case studies by Calavita, 1983; Donnelly, 1982; Shover, 1980; and Szasz, 1984. See also Yeager, 1991.

15. The mounting budget deficits that resulted from Reagan administration tax reductions and the high interest costs associated with government borrowing have limited expansion of social programs. The growth in government debt has contributed to high long-term interest rates and a resulting increase in the cost of private finance.

16. Versions of this argument appear in Harvard Law Review, 1986; Anderson, 1985; and recently, Menell, 1991.

CHAPTER 4

1. See Yeager, 1991: 167; and Seneca and Taussig, 1984: 196–99.

2. A summary discussion of RCRA appears in Epstein, Brown, and Pope, 1982: 195–96. For a more detailed discussion and critique, see U.S. Office of Technology Assessment, 1983.

3. Epstein, Brown, and Pope argue that OMB had no intention of giving EPA enough money and personnel to issue permits promptly to all disposal facilities. OMB was equally unwilling to shut down the disposal industry for the time required to issue all the permits (Epstein, Brown, and Pope, 1982: 193)

4. See the chronology of events at Love Canal to October 1980 presented by Senator Moynihan of New York during the congressional debate on Superfund (U.S. Congress, Senate, 1983, 1:700–704).

5. The following draws largely on Portney, 1978: 119–28.

6. Hugh Kaufman, then manager of EPA's hazardous waste assessment program, claimed in RCRA oversight hearings that the agency ordered him to halt his search for dumps that were in violation of RCRA's imminent hazard provision (Brown, 1981: 315–18).

7. House and Senate bills along with accompanying reports and debate are contained in the two-volume legislative history of the Comprehensive Environmental Response, Compensation, and Liability Act of 1980 (U.S. Congress, Senate, 1983). The following overview draws primarily on this source.

8. In White House meetings to hammer out this proposal, representatives of the Department of Commerce, the Council of Economic Advisors, the Office of Management and Budget, and the Council on Wage and Price Stability argued for a cleanup fund totally generated from general government revenues. In opposition, representatives from the EPA, HEW, OSHA, and the Council on Environmental Quality argued for a fund paid for by both industry and government. Carter decided to support the latter proposal. See Mahon and Post, 1987: 66.

9. Initially, the fund was related to the concept of government-required insurance, with fees imposed on generators to compensate government and other parties for damages where unrecoverable. Testimony by representatives of the insurance industry

emphasized the difficulty of establishing a fee structure given substantial uncertainty regarding the quantification of damages. See, for example, statement of American Insurance Association, U.S. Congress, Senate, 1979: 672–78.

10. EPA projected the economic impact of a $400 million annual fee placed on petroleum, petrochemicals, and inorganic chemicals (U.S. Congress, Senate, 1979: 77–89). This analysis suggested that a $100 million annual fee placed on petroleum would be passed on to consumers via a 0.09 cent per gallon increase in the price of gasoline. The president of Union Oil did not dispute this projection (U.S. Congress, Senate, 1979: 503). A $200 million annual fee on petrochemicals would be passed through to consumers via a .067 percent increase in final domestic prices. This could reduce the expected 2 to 10 percent rate of growth in domestic sales by 0.25 percentage points. Further, after-tax profits from industry exports would fall by $6.5 million with an additional after-tax loss of $12 million from import displacement. A $100 million annual fee on inorganic chemicals would also be passed through with no significant economic impact. However, manufacturers facing difficult times (e.g., manufacturers of ammonia) would have to absorb the fees and, in the extreme, would be forced to close plants.

11. Testimony of Louis Fernandez on behalf of the Chemical Manufacturers Association, *Congressional Record* 126, pt. 20 (September 19, 1980): 26341–42.

12. Senator Randolph noted that "[u]nless otherwise provided in this act, the standard of liability is intended to be the same as that provided in section 311 of the Federal Water Pollution Control Act. I understand this to be a standard of strict liability. It is intended that issues of liability not resolved by this act, if any, shall be governed by traditional and evolving principles of common law. An example is joint and several liability. Any reference to these terms has been deleted, and the liability of joint tortfeasors will be determined under common or previous statutory law" (U.S. Congress, Senate, 1983, 1:686).

13. The cost to the chemical and petroleum industries of their fund contributions can be estimated by looking at the ratio of payments to profits over a five-year period. The before-tax burden is 3 percent of industry profits for 1976–80. The after-tax burden is 1.5 percent for the same period. (Profit data are from U.S. Council of Economic Advisors, 1982: 329.) If EPA estimates of pass-through are applied, the after-tax burden is less than one-half of 1 percent.

14. Discussion of chemical industry strategy draws largely on Mahon and Post, 1987.

15. While Stockman's position expressed in this quote was consistent with his position as Reagan's head of OMB, his related position on the budget was not. As a representative, he advocated that the Treasury Department, not industry, finance cleanup.

16. See U.S. Council of Economic Advisors, 1982: 27–46.

17. Rumors circulated in 1981 that Joseph Coors and Senator Paul Laxalt (R-Nev.) had been given control over appointments to Interior and EPA. Coors, a Colorado brewer, was a major contributor to the Reagan campaign and an important figure in right-wing Republican politics; Laxalt chaired the president's national campaign organization in 1980 (Andrews, 1984: 145).

18. For discussion of EPA planning in anticipation of CERCLA passage, see Cohen and Tipermas, 1983.

19. An additional 133 sites were proposed in September 1983 and 244 were proposed in October 1984.

20. Discussion of EPA strategy under Administrator Burford is based on U.S. Congress, House, 1982a, 1982b; and U.S. Environmental Protection Agency, 1982a, 1984a.

21. See, for example, the testimony of Representative Whittaker in U.S. Congress, House, 1982b: 16–18.

22. The following is based on Crandall and Portney, 1984; and testimony of Khristine Hall and David Lennett on behalf of the Environmental Defense Fund, U.S. Congress, House, 1982b: 20–25.

23. Andrew Szasz suggests that the name Sewergate derived from the fact that the participants in EPA events saw themselves caught up in a process which was very much akin to Watergate. He notes that the rhythms of the events were shaped in part by the symbolic legacy left by Watergate, a verbal tag with certain vague memory traces and emotional connotations. For a detailed chronology of Sewergate, see Szasz, 1986.

24. Results of a Washington Post/ABC Poll, March 5, 1983, as reported in Szasz, 1986.

25. Quote and preceding from Andrews, 1984: 177–78. See also Shabecoff, 1983d.

26. The following discussion of change in Superfund strategy after May 1983 draws on U.S. Environmental Protection Agency, 1984a. CERCLA mandated a set of EPA evaluations of the Superfund program, known as the 301 Study. When issued in December 1984, it served as a format for an agency mea culpa. The executive summary of the program effectiveness report notes that "[a] number of policy changes resulted from a major analysis and reevaluation of the program undertaken in the spring and summer of 1983. These policy changes resulted in significant shifts in approach and emphasis in the Superfund program." Additional data are from Acton, 1989.

27. The Burford EPA did win several important precedents in court challenges to CERCLA authority and agency interpretation. For a discussion of these rulings, see Frank and Atkeson, 1985.

28. The agency had early indications that this strategy was not productive when only 1 percent of letters notifying private parties of their potential liability at hazardous waste sites elicited a response.

29. At the Seymour site (Seymour, Indiana), EPA settled with twenty-four generators for surface cleanup in return for a federal covenant not to sue for any further cleanup costs. At the General Disposal site (Santa Fe Springs, California), the Inmont Corporation settled for EPA's bottom-line position (reportedly after that position was leaked by an assistant to Administrator Burford) and obtained a release from all federal claims under all statutes. At the Chem-Dyne site (Hamilton, Ohio), EPA settled for responsible party contributions far below the minimums stipulated in its enforcement guidelines, agreed not to sue settlors for costs if greater than estimated, and agreed to compensate settlors out of the fund if they were sued by nonsettling responsible parties who were sued by EPA (Anderson, 1985: 283). Anderson does note that some three dozen other agreements concluded prior to mid-1983 escaped criticism (Anderson, 1985: 284).

30. See, for example, Crandall and Portney, 1984; and Andrews, 1984.

31. The following discussion of Burford's policy agenda draws on Andrews, 1984: 167–73.

32. Whether EPA's Superfund policy would have changed in the absence of Sewergate is of course an open question. Many scholars argue that scandals have an impact on

support for regulatory policies (see Szasz, 1986). I believe that while the timing of change was dependent on the scandal, the direction of EPA policy would have led inevitably to a clash with Congress with the agency as the loser.

CHAPTER 5

1. A conceptual analysis of the dynamic interaction of these factors at the state level is provided by Goetze and Rowland, 1985.

2. Protection of ground water is also dependent on state-level efforts. Although six federal laws address specific aspects of ground water contamination (Clean Water Act, Safe Drinking Water Act, RCRA, CERCLA, Surface Mining Control and Reclamation Act, and Uranium Tailings Radiation Control Act), no federal legislation is directed toward comprehensive ground water protection (U.S. General Accounting Office, 1984c: iii). A 1984 General Accounting Office study of federal and state endeavors in this area found state-level activities to include developing ground water protection strategies, mapping aquifers and land use in the vicinity of aquifers, and developing hydrology data. The study found variation across states in the level of these activities, in the commitment of state resources, and in general concern over ground water quality (U.S. General Accounting Office, 1984c: vi).

3. The analyses of the California and Texas programs, respectively, draw on Morell, 1983, and Kramer, 1983.

4. The 1983 rankings are quoted in the Morell, 1983, and Kramer, 1983, articles. The 1987 ranking is from U.S. Environmental Protection Agency, 1989: 8.

5. The following discussion of RCRA implementation problems in the early 1980s draws primarily on U.S. General Accounting Office, 1983, 1984b, 1988a. For additional discussion of RCRA sites as future Superfund problems, see U.S. Office of Technology Assessment, 1985: 137–59.

6. An interim status facility is one in operation on or before November 19, 1980, that has not been issued a final permit.

7. The following discussion draws on U.S. General Accounting Office, 1988a.

8. This requirement was effective in October 1989, three years after enactment. To satisfy the requirement, a state did not necessarily need sufficient hazardous waste management capacity within the state but did need to show solid agreements with other states to manage wastes. Most states have attempted to meet this requirement through agreement with other states in their EPA region (see Bureau of National Affairs, September 1, 1989: 742).

9. The following is based on Andrews, 1988.

10. Interestingly, a 1985 General Accounting Office report found that removals at nonpriority sites provided more complete cleanups than those at priority sites. The priority site removals were designed as stop-gap measures pending full-scale remediation. In contrast, the nonpriority sites generally received complete surface cleanup since EPA policy for these sites was that no additional actions beyond the initial one could be undertaken unless immediate and significant threats occurred or the site was placed on the priority list (U.S. General Accounting Office, 1985b: 17).

11. These criticisms of the federal program were in response to a 1988 EPA-proposed revision to the National Contingency Plan that would allow states to administer the

cleanup of hazardous waste sites that would otherwise be included on the National Priorities List. This so-called deferral program is discussed at greater length in chapter 9.

12. State use of property liens may be weakened by a recent Supreme Court ruling that similar authority under the 1986 Superfund Act violates the due process clause of the Fifth Amendment (see Moses, 1991).

13. A fourth factor of importance is the percent of sites owned by a state, a county, or a municipality. Cleanup at these sites requires the state to provide 50 percent of the cost of cleanup in contrast to the 10 percent requirement at privately owned sites. By 1986 one-third of the states did not have any state-owned sites on the National Priorities List.

14. After the replacement of Administrator Burford, agency cost projections assumed thicker clay caps for waste contained on-site and more extensive action to address soil and ground water contamination (U.S. Environmental Protection Agency, 1985a: 7–9, 11).

15. These estimates are based on the following computations: A 539-site National Priorities List and an average cleanup cost of $7.2 million yields a total cleanup cost of $3,881 million in 1983. EPA estimated in 1984 that 50 percent of cleanup costs would be covered by responsible parties. The number of settlement outcomes before mid-1983 in comparison to outcomes between mid-1983 and 1986 (reported in chapter 7), in conjunction with the above-noted EPA estimate of responsible party settlements, suggests a 16 percent responsible party share in 1983. With a 10 percent state match requirement, the states' share of the remaining $3,260 million in cleanup costs is $326 million. For the 1986 estimate, an average cleanup cost of $8.1 million and an NPL with 795 nonfederal facilities yield a total cleanup cost of $6,440 million. Taking EPA's estimate that responsible parties will cover half of this cost, the state share of the remaining $3,220 million is $322 million.

16. The 1988 estimate is based on the following computations: An average cleanup cost of $21 to $30 million (U.S. General Accounting Office, 1989a: 12) and an NPL with 1,088 nonfederal sites yield total cleanup costs of $22,848 to $32,640 million. Responsible parties covered about 40 percent of cleanup costs as of 1988 (U.S. General Accounting Office, 1989a: 29). The states' share of the remaining $13,709 to $19,584 million in cleanup costs is $1,370.9 to $1,958.4 million.

17. The author's calculations based on General Accounting Office data for twelve nonpriority sites suggest an average cleanup cost of $3.54 million (U.S. General Accounting Office, 1989a: 29). The total cost for 28,192 nonpriority sites is $99,799.7 million. If responsible parties cover about 61.5 percent of these costs (U.S. General Accounting Office, 1989a: 29), the share falling on the states is $38,422.9 million.

18. The pearson correlation coefficient on the relationship between the number of priority and nonpriority sites across states is .66 and significant at the 1 percent level.

19. New Jersey authorized taxation of oil and chemical products as a means to fund cleanup. In response to a suit brought by the five companies, the New Jersey Supreme Court ruled that Superfund does not preempt the state law if the spill fund is used to compensate hazardous waste cleanup costs that are not covered or not actually paid for under the federal law. The companies then asked the U.S. Supreme Court to review the New Jersey court's decision (Frank and Atkeson, 1985: 72–73). The issue was ultimately laid to rest through elimination of section 114(c) in the 1986 Superfund reauthorization.

20. Telephone interviews with Robert Wages of the Oil, Chemical and Atomic Workers, September 4, 1986, and with Dick Edgington of the Chemical Workers Union, September 5, 1986.

21. Bruce Yandle argues that union support for environmental regulation has additional self-interest dimensions. First, environmental regulation that raises the cost of capital induces firms to substitute labor for capital, thus increasing the labor income share. Second, both labor and capital gain when the costs of environmental regulation are socialized. Third, environmental regulation raises the cost of entry to new firms and reduces competition. Both labor and capital gain from the resulting increase in firm profits. Using state data, Yandle finds union membership to be positively associated with nonagricultural employment and public expenditures on pollution control. He also finds firm investment in pollution control equipment to be positively associated with union membership. See Yandle, 1985.

22. By the end of 1988, the states completed cleanup at 1,736 (7 percent) of 28,192 known nonpriority sites requiring a response, while EPA and the states completed cleanup at 38 (3 percent) of 1,174 priority sites (U.S. General Accounting Office, 1989a: 28). The higher completion rate at the nonpriority sites is attributed to the fact that many of these sites pose less complex cleanup problems as well as to the nature of the remedy, as noted in the text.

23. The general approach taken and the data used to measure some of the independent variables draw on an analysis of hazardous waste regulation across states presented in Williams and Matheny, 1984. Several findings and conclusions do not correspond to those reported by these authors.

24. Actual and anticipated appropriations as of 1983, as reported to ASTSWMO, appear in U.S. Environmental Protection Agency, 1984c: 3-2, Exhibit 3-1.

25. See Association of State and Territorial Solid Waste Management Officials, 1988.

26. A weighted sum of remedial actions taken at nonpriority sites as of 1988 was regressed on state hazardous waste program funding. The actions include initiation of remedial design, the initiation of remedial construction, and the completion of remedial construction. The weights are the relative cost of each of these cleanup phases as reported in U.S. General Accounting Office, 1989a. The adjusted R^2 is .90; the F value and the regression coefficient are significant at the 1 percent level. The sample includes forty-two states.

27. State population data are from U.S. Department of Commerce, Bureau of the Census, *1980 Census of Population, United States Summary* (Washington, D.C.: U.S. Government Printing Office, 1983), pp. 124–25. Population at risk is calculated as the sum of population at risk from contamination via air, surface water, and ground water. These data are from MITRE, 1986. For a discussion of the hazard ranking system scoring model, see U.S. Environmental Protection Agency, 1984e.

28. Private pollution control expenditure data are from U.S. Department of Commerce, 1985: 3–7. Private expenditures are calculated as the average expenditure (1980–83) for capital and gross annual costs. Public pollution control expenditure data are from U.S. Department of Commerce, 1982: 20–21. Public expenditures are calculated as the sum of expenditures for water, land, and air quality control in 1980, the last year for which these data are available.

29. Data on federal facilities are from MITRE, 1986.

30. State revenue data for 1983 are from Council of State Governments, 1986: 228.

31. State employment data are from U.S. Department of Commerce, Bureau of the Census, *Statistical Abstract of the United States: 1985* (Washington, D.C.: U.S. Government Printing Office, 1985), p. 411

32. This definition might appear to oversimplify the problem in that a firm that is liable for only a fraction of cleanup costs is financially viable if profits are sufficient to absorb this fraction. At large multiparty sites, 10 percent of responsible parties may account for 90 percent of the waste with 90 percent of PRPs accounting for the remaining 10 percent. Examination of the *Census of Manufactures* data indicates that only a fraction of 1 percent of all establishments could absorb 100 percent of average cleanup costs. This figure, however, understates the capacity to absorb cleanup costs in that *Census of Manufactures* data are based on establishments, not enterprises (i.e., companies or corporations). An establishment is a single physical location engaged in a specific line of business. Since large corporations operate many separate manufacturing establishments, the financial viability of the latter is ultimately based on that of the former (assuming liability can be passed upstream when the establishment and enterprise bear a subsidiary/parent relationship).

33. To translate size into financial viability, a $8.1 million average cost of cleanup is divided by 4.1 percent, the 1980–85 national ratio of after-tax profits to sales (U.S. Council of Economic Advisors, 1986: 355). This calculation yields the level of sales that will generate profits equal to cleanup costs. The ratios of value added to sales and value added to employees is then used to calculate the establishment size sufficient to absorb these costs. Value added data by industry and state are from U.S. Department of Commerce, 1986b: 1-161–1-169.

34. Value added data by industry and state are from U.S. Department of Commerce, 1986b: 1-45–1-80.

35. Employment data by industry and state are from U.S. Department of Commerce, 1986b: 1-45–1-80.

36. Membership is compiled from data provided by environmental groups and is calculated as the sum of members in the Audubon Society (1983), Environmental Defense Fund (1984), Natural Resources Defense Council (1984), and Sierra Club (1983).

37. This also implies that environmental group membership will be higher in states where public expenditures are low relative to perceived need, a problem to be addressed below.

38. These three variables are not expected to affect the level of environmental group membership in that they represent potential resources to address environmental problems as opposed to actual program funds or perceptions of environmental problems.

39. As mentioned in note 37 above, environmental group membership is not independent of the level of program funding since, for example, low funding can induce greater membership. Specification error results from the incorrect treatment of ENVGRP as an exogenous variable. A solution to this interdependency is to regress ENVGRP on those exogenous variables that might determine both STFUND and ENVGRP and then use the predicted value of ENVGRP in estimation of STFUND. The predicted value of ENVGRP derived from the regression reported in table 5.2 is substituted for the actual value of ENVGRP in generating the funding equation results reported in table 5.3. This procedure is not followed in the enforcement equation.

Since aggregate enforcement decisions (a product of agency action) receive considerably less publicity than aggregate funding decisions (a product of legislature action), they are not expected to affect the level of environmental group membership.

40. In general, the results reported in table 5.3 are robust. The results of an F-test on the joint hypothesis that nonsignificant variables in each equation have zero coefficients indicate a rejection of the hypothesis. It follows that all included variables contribute to an explanation of funding and enforcement levels. However, multicollinearity may be a problem in both equations as indicated by a condition number greater than thirty. The condition number is a regression diagnostic proposed in Belsley, Kuh, and Welsch, 1980. The variables FEDOWN and ECONOMY are excluded from the enforcement equation. They were initially included but were not significant and, at the same time, lowered the significance of other independent variables and increased multicollinearity.

41. ASTSWMO survey data on number of sites with state enforcement actions since 1981 are reported in U.S. Environmental Protection Agency, 1984c: 2–38.

42. The pearson correlation coefficient is .57, significant at the 1 percent level.

43. Priority list site characteristics are drawn from MITRE, 1986. The date of listing on the NPL is based also on U.S. Environmental Protection Agency, 1984f.

CHAPTER 6

1. Region 9 interview, May 1986.

2. As discussed below, these are remedial investigation/feasibility study, remedial design, remedial action, interim remedial measures, or removals.

3. The classification of sites is based on data obtained from EPA. Obligations for fund-lead and enforcement-lead activity are from EPA's Site-Specific Remedial Funding Report dated March 31, 1986, and the agency's Site-Specific Removal Funding Report of the same date. Federal enforcement-lead activity (other than fund obligations) is from EPA's Enforcement Case Management System Report of March 1986. State-lead data is from EPA's State-Lead Enforcement Site Summary of March 1986.

4. The breakdown of sites using EPA categories applies to a 540-site priority list whereas the breakdown in figure 6.1 applies to 813 sites. It is likely that this classification understates the percentage of sites EPA would categorize as enforcement-lead.

5. I did not conduct an analysis of the choice between fund- or enforcement-lead since this division should simply reflect whether or not a responsible party is identified for the site in question.

6. Interview with Emil Knutti, EPA, Washington, D.C., June 6, 1987; and U.S. Environmental Protection Agency, "FY 1986 Budget Output Assumptions" (no date).

7. In visits to several regional offices, I was struck by the number of fresh college graduate project managers whose responsibilities pitted them against older and more experienced industry representatives, some of whom received their training as project managers. Section chiefs (who supervised project managers grouped by state) were project management veterans in their mid-to-late twenties.

8. Regions with greater potential case loads are generally limited in their ability to move cases to the point where a consent order or decree is signed, a unilateral order is issued, or a case is referred to and filed by the Justice Department. The enforcement

personnel constraint helps explain why only 34.3 percent of the sites in figure 6.1 are enforcement sites whereas 60 percent of sites are categorized by EPA as enforcement-lead. Backlogs and delays would reduce the number of sites with reported (signed) orders, decrees, and case filings.

9. Interview with Norman Niedergang, Region 5, June 11, 1987.

10. Additional discussion of HRS media scores and critiques of the HRS appear in subsequent notes.

11. Since many years of activity may be required before a site is considered clean, the number of cleanups completed is too broad and long-term a measure of progress to draw meaningful distinctions. An index of the portion of necessary work completed would be useful, but no such measure has been published. EPA has recently suggested alternative measures of progress, such as the volume of waste removed from a site (see Reilly, 1989).

12. EPA has generally evaluated its progress in terms of initiations rather then completions. Critics note that this presents a misleading index of accomplishments, since initiation may include minor as well as major work. Further, it is far easier for the agency to meet its goals when expressed in terms of an action begun rather than an action completed. The agency acknowledges this problem but has offered no hard index of progress. Where possible, minor actions have been excluded in quantifying regional accomplishments.

13. For more detailed discussion of cleanup phases, see U.S. Environmental Protection Agency, 1982b; and U.S. Office of Technology Assessment, 1983: 305–9.

14. Acton (1989) advocates the use of obligation and expenditure variables to measure Superfund progress.

15. EPA estimates the average cost of a remedial investigation/feasibility study (RIFS) to be $800,000, the average cost of a remedial design (RD) to be $400,000, and the average cost of a remedial action (RA) to be $7,600,000 (U.S. Environmental Protection Agency, 1984b: 4–5). Note that these are pre-1986 reauthorization estimates. The author's calculations using EPA remedial and removal data indicate that the average obligation for an interim remedial action (IRM) is 27.4 percent of that for a remedial action and that the average obligation for a removal is 10.8 percent of that for a remedial action. The corresponding relative weights are RIFS (.127), RD (.07), RA (.603), IRM (.135), and removal (.065). To score each region, the weight is multiplied by the number of sites at which each phase is initiated and these products are summed. The sum of weighted values is then divided by the number of fund or enforcement sites. In computing the denominator, it is assumed that a removal and an IRM are conducted at each site. While this is not a strictly realistic assumption, it is not unreasonable given the emphasis placed on removals as an initial phase of cleanup after 1983 (U.S. Environmental Protection Agency, 1984a).

16. Region 9 interview, May 1986.

17. Quotes in this paragraph are from U.S. Office of Technology Assessment, 1983: 312–13.

18. Unless otherwise noted, information and quotes in this paragraph are from U.S. Office of Technology Assessment, 1985: 105–6.

19. See chapter 4, note 29.

20. The policy was originally drafted in late 1983 (see Habicht, 1985: 3).

21. Unless otherwise noted, the following discussion draws on U.S. Environmental

Protection Agency, 1985c. A lengthy analysis and critique of the settlement policy appears in Anderson, 1985. For additional discussion and critique, see the articles in "Superfund: A Game of Chance," *Natural Resources and Environment* 1, no. 3 (1985).

22. A minor contributor is a low-volume, low-toxicity disposer who would not normally make a significant contribution to the costs of cleanup in any case.

23. Discussion of the Region 2 removal approach is based on Mugdan, 1986; and interviews at Region 2, June 1987.

24. The following is based on an interview with Norman Niedergang, Region 5, June 11, 1987.

25. Discussion of the Region 9 approach is based on Toxics and Waste Management Division, Region 9, "Enforcement at Immediate Removal Sites" (draft, no date); and Region 9 interviews, May 1986.

26. The fund score bears a positive relationship to the ratio of state resources explicitly available for cost share relative to estimated cost-share requirements. The rank order correlation coefficient is 0.56, significant at the 10 percent level.

27. U.S. Environmental Protection Agency, "Interim Settlement Policy" (draft version, December 5, 1984), p. 11.

28. This allocation scenario is consistent with regional experience. For example, Region 5 reports that Minnesota's active enforcement program has generally addressed smaller sites with a limited number of on-site parties. Region 5 interview, June 1986.

29. The total sample of 813 final and proposed sites is not used since values for one or more variables could not be obtained for all sites.

30. The number of attorneys by region as of September 30, 1985, is from U.S. General Accounting Office, 1986a: 13. The number of sites by region is computed by the author from MITRE, 1986.

31. The date of proposed listing on the NPL is from U.S. Environmental Protection Agency, 1984f, and subsequent agency releases.

32. The numerator used to construct the variable STFDNPL is the measure of state program funding (STFUND) discussed in the appendix to chapter 5. The denominator is the variable NPL83, also discussed in that appendix.

33. State top priority site designations are taken from MITRE, 1986.

34. Site ownership is reported in MITRE, 1986.

35. Computation of the variable PRP is discussed in the appendix to chapter 5.

36. The total score is a linear combination of media scores and does not present inherent problems of multicollinearity. EPA published a description and discussion of the HRS in appendix A to the 1982 National Contingency Plan (see U.S. Environmental Protection Agency, 1982b: 31219–43).

37. Hazard ranking system scores (TOTAL and GW) are from MITRE, 1986.

38. The Office of Technology Assessment is highly critical of the hazard ranking system. In a 1983 report, OTA argues that the HRS does not adequately reflect the risk posed by release at a site (U.S. Office of Technology Assessment, 1983: 383–85). In a 1985 report, OTA notes additional factors that bias site scores (U.S. Office of Technology Assessment, 1985: 162). In a recent report, OTA argues that experience with rescoring proposed sites indicates high error rates and the likelihood of false positive and false negative scoring decisions. It notes the findings of EPA studies that suggest that the HRS underestimates risk (U.S. Office of Technology Assessment, 1989b: 115–21).

39. Site-specific cleanup cost estimates are unpublished data obtained from EPA

under the Freedom of Information Act. The agency does not authorize or support use of these data in the current study.

40. The variables ACTION and FEDERAL are based on the same data used above to determine lead responsibility.

41. EPA notes that the "HRS does not quantify the probability of harm from a facility or the magnitude of the harm that could result, although the factors have been selected in order to approximate both those elements of risk" (U.S. Environmental Protection Agency, 1982b: 31182). In an amendment to the National Contingency Plan, the agency expressed its confidence that the HRS is an effective tool for approximating risk and that differences of more than a few points in score generally are meaningful in discriminating between sites. The agency states that funding of response actions will not necessarily take place in order of the sites' HRS ranking on the priorities list, but that the agency does intend in most cases to set priorities for site studies largely on the basis of HRS scores and the states' priorities simply because at this early stage these may be the only sources of information regarding the risk presented by a site. Subsequent action is less likely to occur in order of HRS scores (U.S. Environmental Protection Agency, 1983b: 40659).

42. The Office of Technology Assessment critiques of HRS scores noted above may lead the reader to doubt these conclusions. If scores are poor indices of risk, the results reported here and in chapter 7 do not support the conclusions I have drawn. Further, results may be simply a product of spurious correlation. Acknowledging these problems, I argue that the consistency among results obtained for all applications of HRS scores reported in this study strongly suggests that they contain information utilized by EPA in making some site cleanup decisions and approximate information utilized by EPA in other cleanup decisions. As noted in chapter 7, other studies find HRS scores to be good predictors of EPA Superfund decisions.

43. The discussion of logit estimations and the methodology for calculating probabilities is based on Aldrich and Nelson, 1984: 40–47.

44. To calculate PRP at the regional level, the value of PRP for each state in the region is multiplied by the ratio of state NPL sites to total regional NPL sites and these products are summed.

45. To calculate the availability of state resources at the regional level, the value of STFDNPL for each state is multiplied by the ratio of state NPL sites to total regional NPL sites and these products are summed.

46. These data are contained in EPA's Enforcement Case Management System Report of March 1986.

CHAPTER 7

1. The data presented in this section are from Acton, 1989, unless otherwise noted.

2. See the discussion of regional enforcement strategies for removal actions in chapter 6.

3. The following is based on U.S. Office of Technology Assessment, 1985: 223–42.

4. For a more detailed discussion and critique of available technologies, see U.S. Office of Technology Assessment, 1985, chap. 6. This report also contains detailed discussion of emerging permanent treatment technologies.

5. A continuing general preference for containment over permanent treatment was

also highlighted in a study published by the National Campaign Against Toxic Hazards six months before the General Accounting Office report was released (see National Campaign Against Toxic Hazards, 1986).

6. A recent study of federal expenditures at National Priorities List sites through 1988 reveals similar results with respect to contamination pathways. Using hazard ranking system pathway scores, the author finds site expenditures most responsive to air scores, slightly less responsive to surface water scores, and considerably less responsive to ground water scores. He also finds that HRS air scores are much more important than ground water scores in explaining whether any cleanup activity is initiated. Further, while both air and surface water scores help explain whether a record of decision or a remedial action is initiated, ground water scores have no statistically significant impact on initiations. See Hird, 1990. An unpublished study of the pace and extent of cleanup through 1990 uses disaggregated HRS data to construct indices of population at risk, waste toxicity/quantity, and risk (a composite of population and waste characteristics). Correlations between HRS scores and these indices suggest that scores weigh primarily population factors as opposed to ecological risk. The author finds toxicity/quantity to be positively related to both cleanup obligations and outlays. Neither population at risk nor HRS scores are statistically significant. See Franzini-Bhargava, 1992.

7. EPA subsequently reported additional settlements. By the end of 1985, 195 settlements worth $484 million were negotiated with responsible parties.

8. Fund-financed actions require regional project manager oversight of EPA contractors (as discussed in chapter 6). The enforcement program, in addition, requires project manager oversight of responsible party compliance with the terms of a settlement and oversight of all responsible party submittals to the agency. Submittals include works plans, safety plans, and plans for sampling substances at the site, as well as the analysis and results of the remedial investigation and feasibility study.

9. This is a smaller number of settlements than reported by the agency to the General Accounting Office as of December 1985. Some cases may not have been recorded in EPA's computerized Enforcement Case Management System.

10. As discussed in chapter 6, a region's settlement score is the weighted value of necessary cleanup activity voluntarily agreed to by responsible parties as a percentage of the total value of necessary cleanup activity for all sites in the region's enforcement program.

11. It may still be the case that some corporations bearing responsibility for site conditions are forced to pay more than their proportionate share of cleanup costs. However, the finding suggests that this is not the case for deep pockets as a group.

12. The average value of work agreed to in settlements under the Burford administration is almost twice as great as that under the Ruckelshaus/Thomas administrations. However, the coefficient that indicates the magnitude of this difference attributable to strategy per se is not significant at a 10 percent confidence level. Nevertheless, the t-statistic is sufficiently high to support a conclusion that the Burford administration strategy in and of itself did produce an average extent of cleanup greater than that under the Ruckelshaus/Thomas strategy. The magnitude of this difference cannot be stated with statistical confidence.

13. If the responsible party does not obtain a release from future liability, agreeing to undertake a less effective remedy is very shortsighted. Near-term cost savings may be small compared to future expenditures.

14. In this context, it is interesting to note the cleanup standard assumptions applied in EPA estimates of remedial action costs in late 1983 (soon after the replacement of Administrator Burford) and again in late 1984. The 1984 standards required thicker clay caps when waste was to be contained on-site and required more extensive actions to address soil and ground water contamination problems. Under the 1984 standards, average remedial construction costs were greater by an estimated 30 to 50 percent (U.S. Environmental Protection Agency, 1985a: 7–9, 11). In an accompanying discussion of these cost estimates, EPA notes that it applied its experience and decision rules to date on site-specific problems to "prescribe remedies that are consistent with remedial actions taken at other sites, with EPA policies and guidance, and with good engineering practice applied to site conditions" (1985a: 2). To the extent that these alternative standards reflect actual EPA practice before and after mid-1983, the cost and effectiveness of a given cleanup was considerably less under the Burford administration.

15. Agency settlement policy immediately after Sewergate required a responsible party to accept the agency's choice of a remedy in exchange for allowing the responsible party to conduct the remedial investigation/feasibility study. This condition was subsequently dropped due to protest by generator industry corporations that it imposed a major obstacle to settlement.

16. Responsible parties have a clear incentive to minimize the cost of implementing a cleanup remedy. In contrast, agency employees may be more concerned with minimizing their oversight responsibilities. Consequently, responsible parties may promote a degree of efficiency lacking when cleanup is fund-financed.

17. A phase is assumed to be initiated when the agency obligates funds for its implementation.

18. EPA remedial action obligations at each site are from the agency's Site-Specific Remedial Funding Report dated March 31, 1986. Obligations for removal actions are from the agency's Site-Specific Removal Funding Report of the same date. The former report also provides the date of fund obligations used to construct the variable FORIFS. Acton argues that expenditure data are superior to obligations data as a index of progress (Acton, 1989: 30). As discussed in the text, remedial action expenditures are significantly below obligations. Obligations data are chosen in the current application since they indicate agency intentions. The potential bias created by a difference between expenditures and obligations is minimized in calculating the variable FUNDSCR in that this measure of progress focuses on phases rather than on dollar magnitudes.

19. Enforcement data are from EPA's Enforcement Case Management System Report of March 1986. The report includes the type of order issued (e.g., administrative, unilateral, referral), the phase(s) of cleanup covered by the order, and an estimate of the value of work involved.

20. The derivative of LIKELIHOOD with respect to PRP is positive when evaluated at or above the mean value of PRP. It is negative at low values of PRP, implying that settlement is not likely when the pool of responsible party resources is small.

21. The values for the first two variables are mean values and mean values plus and minus one standard deviation. Population means are used for the remaining variables.

22. The coefficient of this variable is evaluated under a one-tail test of statistical significance since there is no theoretical reason for expecting a negative relationship between the predicted probability of settlement and the extent of cleanup agreed to by responsible parties. A negative sign implies that the greater the probability that these

costs would be imposed, the less a responsible party would pay to avoid the consequences of not settling.

CHAPTER 8

1. The following overview of the reauthorization debate is based on U.S. Library of Congress, 1988; Congressional Information Service, 1986: 365–97; and various congressional committee reports noted below.

2. Discussion of H.R. 5640 is based on U.S. Congress, House, 1984c.

3. The following is based on U.S. Congress, Senate, 1984b.

4. For other estimates, see U.S. Office of Technology Assessment, 1985: 14.

5. Where not specifically cited, discussion of EPA and Department of Justice positions on settlement policy is based on oral and submitted testimony of Lee Thomas (EPA) and Henry Habicht II (assistant attorney general for natural resources, Department of Justice) in U.S. Congress, House, 1985b: 540–740.

6. See testimony of William Rusnack on behalf of ARCO in U.S. Congress, House, 1985b: 266–87.

7. Since EPA estimated that responsible parties would contribute around 50 percent of total cleanup costs, a $5 billion fund therefore implied a $5 billion responsible party contribution. If a pre/post-1981 distinction reduced responsible party contributions by half, the fund would need to increase by $2.5 billion to meet agency cleanup goals.

8. It was also emphasized that these same considerations confounded efforts by responsible party committees to apportion liability as a basis for settlement with the agency. Different apportionment formulas could yield wide variation in the distribution of burden among parties and forestall or preclude agreement.

9. For the Putnam, Hayes, and Bartlett study, see Butler, 1985.

10. For a broader perspective on the litigation explosion, see Galanter, 1986.

11. The report is reproduced as *U.S. Senate Report #12*, 97th Cong., 2d sess. (Washington, D.C.: U.S. Government Printing Office, 1982).

12. See testimony of Khristine Hall on behalf of Environmental Defense Fund (U.S. Congress, House, 1983a: 1036) and statement of Janet Hathaway on behalf of Public Citizen's Congress Watch (U.S. Congress, House, 1985b: 133). The concern of labor unions regarding reform of the victim compensation system went far beyond that associated with exposure to hazardous waste sites. Exposure in occupational settings arguably were a greater source of death, injury, and disease. The study group's recommendations and the proposed federal cause of action could apply to these claims as well. For testimony on behalf of AFL-CIO, International Union of Operating Engineers, United Auto Workers, and United Steelworkers, see U.S. Congress, House, 1985b: 200–212.

13. See, for example, testimony of Sheila Jasanoff (U.S. Congress, House, 1983a: 1267).

14. The following discussion of problems associated with scientific evidence is based on U.S. Congress, House, 1983c: 280–305, and U.S. Congress, House, 1984a: 164–209.

15. Asked to amplify this statement, biostatistician Marvin Zelen responded: "Let me tell you how . . . one could prove cause and effect of childhood leukemia. You would

have to give the carcinogen, if it was a carcinogen, to children, look and observe them—give a placebo to some other children and after a number of years see what happens. Of course that is impossible!" (U.S. Congress, House, 1984a: 205).

16. The following is based on *Interim Report of the Missouri Dioxin Task Force,* June 1, 1983 (reprinted in U.S. Congress, House, 1983a: 109–275).

17. Expert testimony appears in chapter 2 of the report as reproduced in U.S. Congress, House, 1983a: 147–69.

18. An August 1990 report by a House of Representatives committee concluded that political pressure caused government agencies to suppress or minimize findings of ill-health effects among veterans that could be linked to Agent Orange. A scientific task force sponsored by the American Legion and other veterans' groups recently found a significant correlation between the chemical and two rare cancers and a severe skin disease. Under the Agent Orange Act, veterans with these three diseases can collect disability payments from the Veterans Administration. See Marcus, 1991.

19. Industry subsequently redoubled its efforts to disprove any findings of dioxin's adverse health effects. See Bailey, 1992, and discussion in chapter 10.

20. One implication indirectly suggested but not emphasized by agency and insurance industry testimony was the consequence of a victim compensation title for settlement policy. Litigation produced evidence on responsibility for waste site conditions and could establish liability for a release. Court rulings on these issues could in turn be used by parties seeking compensation for personal injury associated with these sites. In contrast, settlement via a consent decree would not require that a private party accept or deny guilt for the release. EPA did emphasize that by settling, defendants could avoid the possibility of creating an undue precedent for subsequent personal injury actions. The agency did not emphasize that reform of the victim compensation system would enhance these incentives.

21. In the debate over reauthorization, the term "feedstock tax" refers at times to the tax on both chemical feedstocks and crude oil and at other times to the tax on chemical feedstocks only.

22. In contrast to a feedstock tax, which is imposed at the beginning of the chemical production process, a waste-end tax, as conceived by EPA, is imposed on the generation of all hazardous substances under the Resource Conservation and Recovery Act and is collected at treatment, storage, and disposal facilities.

23. The agency subsequently argued that there are economic dislocations and economic disincentives that come to bear fairly quickly (U.S. Congress, Senate, 1985a: 16).

24. Feedstock tax revenues in fact fell about 20 percent short of projections by early 1985 due to recession and appreciation of the dollar (see U.S. Congress, Senate, 1985b: 22).

25. Note that the feedstock tax is a deduction in computing corporate income tax. With this income tax offset, and assuming a top corporate tax rate of 33 percent, the percentage ARCO collected from customers and the IRS is roughly 59 percent in 1981 and 69 percent in 1983. The applicable formula for calculating the incidence of the Superfund tax is one minus corporate tax rate times the Superfund tax times one minus the percentage pass-through.

26. See, for example, U.S. Environmental Protection Agency, 1984d.

27. Based on comparison of chemical and oil industry gross profits to total manufac-

turing industry profits in 1985 (see U.S. Council of Economic Advisors, 1990: 397).

28. Under the Tax Reform Act of 1986, alternative minimum taxable income includes preferences that allow some capital-intensive industries to minimize their profit tax liability (see U.S. Congress, House, 1986: 333–35).

29. The following exchange is from Bureau of National Affairs, September 26, 1986: 771.

30. With passage, Superfund was appropriated $1.46 billion for 1987 and EPA was provided $135 million to hire an additional 600 full-time employees to carry out SARA's numerous requirements.

31. The following description draws on U.S. Congress, House, 1986; Bureau of National Affairs, October 24, 1986: 995–1005; and U.S. Library of Congress, 1988.

32. For a discussion of Title III, see Mason, 1986.

33. Senator Lautenberg (D-N.J.) as quoted in Bureau of National Affairs, October 24, 1986: 955.

34. Attorney George Freeman as quoted in Bureau of National Affairs, September 9, 1986: 780.

35. The following estimates of the distribution of the corporate environmental tax over manufacturing and nonmanufacturing industries is based on actual 1987 tax collections as reported in Internal Revenue Service, *Statistics of Income—1987, Corporate Income Tax Returns* (Washington, D.C.: U.S. Government Printing Office, 1990), table 13, p. 69. The distribution of the tax over manufacturing industries is assumed equal to the each industry's share of 1982 shipments as reported in U.S. Department of Commerce, 1986b: table 3, pp. 1–4.

CHAPTER 9

1. As reported by Environmental Defense Fund et al., 1988: 15.

2. The following is based on a series of articles published in Bureau of National Affairs, *BNA Environment Reporter—Current Developments*, during 1989–90.

3. A compromise was eventually worked out in 1990. Any necessary cleanup at the North Miami landfill would be addressed under state law while the ecological threat would be addressed under Superfund.

4. The Lautenberg-Durenberger report required an EPA analysis of enforcement data to confirm or rebut the subcommittee's findings. EPA's response was published in 1990 (see U.S. Environmental Protection Agency, 1990a). The agency's analysis defines a site as receiving treatment if treatment is used to address any site problem. The report does not state whether treatment at a given site is used to address a major or a minor problem.

5. See Lautenberg and Durenberger, 1989: 118–34. EPA was also criticized for its passive approach in application of SARA authority for settlement with minor contributors and for mixed funding settlements.

6. The argument that Superfund risks were overstated was subsequently given greater circulation in a 1989 *Newsweek* cover story on the cleanup program. See Easterbrook, 1989.

7. EPA's analysis of remedy selection (U.S. Environmental Protection Agency,

1990a) supported the previously made claim that responsible parties could bias risk assessments. In contrast to conclusions drawn in the Lautenberg-Durenberger report, EPA did not find that responsible party cleanups were less protective.

8. Improvements in remedy selection were also noted in a critical evaluation that focused primarily on the pre–management review period (Environmental Defense Fund et al., 1990).

9. President Bush had initially recommended cutting EPA's fiscal 1990 budget below the fiscal 1989 level. His recognition of strong public support for environmental protection brought about a reversal of this position (Bureau of National Affairs, May 5, 1989: 8).

10. The lack of congruence between the two laws is discussed in Hayes, 1987.

11. The reauthorization did not establish new cleanup schedules for the program.

12. Environmental Protection Agency data release, "FY87–91 CERCLA Enforcement Data," September 10, 1991.

13. In October 1991 Administrator Reilly released an agency evaluation of issues raised in the *Washington Post* article. The report acknowledged that management costs as opposed to direct cleanup costs were too high. EPA would reduce these costs and eliminate $2 billion in construction capacity. EPA also announced that it would take action to accelerate cleanup (Bureau of National Affairs, October 10, 1991).

14. Cost overruns for fund-financed cleanups can raise the value of liability imposed in subsequent cost recovery actions. The following discussion of industry perspective draws on interviews with Lloyd Guerci (former director of EPA Superfund enforcement division), August 9, 1991, and with Dell Perelman, assistant general counsel, Chemical Manufacturers Association, August 9, 1991.

15. EPA's Interim Municipal Settlement Policy exempts cities from Superfund liability when they only contribute municipal solid waste to landfill sites.

16. See Tomsho, 1991. Additional insights from Lloyd Guerci and Dell Perelman interviews, August 9, 1991.

17. EPA is developing guidelines for allocating costs for municipal solid waste that will probably not be based on volume alone. Under these guidelines, if municipalities enter into settlements with the agency, they will receive contribution protection. Based on an interview with Arthur Weissman, branch chief, Superfund enforcement guidance and evaluation branch, August 8, 1991. See also Bureau of National Affairs, August 2, 1991: 827–29.

18. Some 88 percent of total insurance industry outlays ($410 million) were for transaction costs. In contrast, very large industrial corporations were estimated to face transaction costs equal to about 21 percent of their total settlement costs. See Acton and Dixon, 1992.

19. A Southern Finance Project analysis of EPA data identified only 40 lenders out of 17,095 potentially responsible parties at more than 1,200 Superfund sites (Bureau of National Affairs, March 1, 1991: 1935). There are more than 30,000 banks, savings and loans, and credit unions nationwide.

20. Telephone interview with Linda Greer, senior scientist, Natural Resources Defense Council, August 13, 1991.

21. The following draws on Schneider, 1991; and Bureau of National Affairs, October 12, 1990: 1146, and June 16, 1989: 441.

22. For example, it would create the need to distinguish otherwise identical waste

coming from a given generator in terms of whether disposal was before or after the cutoff date. It would also create the need to distinguish waste at a given site as having been disposed before or after the cutoff date.

23. The findings contained in EPA's 1987 *Unfinished Business* report (U.S. Environmental Protection Agency, 1987) were updated in a September 1990 report (U.S. Environmental Protection Agency, 1990b). The latter report also considers hazardous waste site cleanup as other than a top priority. Its rankings, however, are confusing. While pollutants in drinking water are seen to pose a relatively high risk to human health, pollutants in ground water are classified as a relatively low-risk problem. Further, Linda Greer of the Natural Resources Defense Council notes that the Science Advisory Board subcommittees charged with evaluating risks to human health declined to provide a relative ranking due the absence of sufficient data. Finally, it must be noted that these rankings are a characterization of relative, not absolute, risks. Whether or not EPA's evaluation of relative risk is accurate, the absolute risk posed by hazardous waste sites could still justify current cleanup costs. For a discussion of the 1990 report, see U.S. Environmental Protection Agency, 1991.

24. In contrast to those who have argued that EPA is captured by industry or environmentalists, a strong case could be made that EPA is captured by its contractors.

CHAPTER 10

1. See, for example, Hawkins, 1984; Shover, Clelland, and Lynxwiler, 1983; and Yeager, 1991.

2. See, for example, Herman, 1981, chap. 5; and Calavita, 1983.

3. The overall effectiveness of a national program to address hazardous waste site problems is contingent on resolution of other conflicts that do not impact directly on Superfund implementation. These include mismatch between Superfund cleanups, on the one hand, and Resource Conservation and Recovery Act corrective action and federal facilities cleanup guidelines, on the other, as well as continuing debate with respect to an effective victim compensation program.

4. Some authors are less likely to agree with the statement that failure is not inevitable. For example, Bruce Yandle states that "[t]ales of environmental struggles indicate that the contests themselves sometimes appear to be more important than the end product—an improved environment. The political limits of environmental control suggest final solutions to the problem will not be found, that effective environmental quality regulation is indeed a unicorn." See Yandle, 1989: 153.

5. Lawyers and consultants are an exception to the statement that no one gains from Superfund failure. The magnitude of their financial rewards is dependent on the degree of conflict.

6. Impressions to the contrary, the Superfund tax is already substantially socialized; it is deductible in calculating corporate profit taxes and is to a great extent passed forward through the chain of commerce. Under the highly conservative assumption that 50 percent of the tax is passed forward, its incidence on taxed industries is 33.5 percent. If, perhaps more realistically, 90 percent of the tax is passed forward, the incidence on taxed industries falls to 6.7 percent. Full pass-through results in a tax incidence of zero. Note that assuming a top corporate profit tax rate of 33 percent, incidence is equal to tax

payments minus a 33 percent corporate profit tax deduction minus the portion passed forward plus a 33 percent tax on the portion passed forward. Incidence is therefore equal to .67 times the tax times one minus the percentage pass-through.

7. Interestingly, the Senate passed a bill in 1992 that allows the FDA to charge drug companies for the cost of reviewing the safety of new drugs and to speed up the review process. The *New York Times* reports that "[t]he plan is considered feasible because the companies may make millions of dollars at the same time they pay new fees." EPA is also said to be considering charging companies for the costs of regulation. These user fees set a precedent as a way for federal regulatory agencies to raise money in difficult times. See Hart, 1992.

Acton, Jan Paul. 1989. *Understanding Superfund: A Progress Report*. Santa Monica, Calif.: RAND Corporation.

Acton, Jan Paul, and Lloyd S. Dixon. 1992. *Superfund and Transaction Costs: The Experience of Insurers and Very Large Industrial Firms*. Santa Monica, Calif.: RAND Corporation.

Aldrich, John H., and Forrest D. Nelson. 1984. *Linear Probability, Logit, and Probit Models*. Newbury Park, Calif.: Sage Publications.

Anderson, Frederick. 1985. "Negotiation and Informal Agency Action: The Case of Superfund." *Duke Law Journal* 85 (2): 261–380.

Andrews, Richard N. L. 1984. "Deregulation: The Failure at EPA." In *Environmental Policy in the 1980s: Reagan's New Agenda*, edited by Norman J. Vig and Michael E. Kraft, pp. 161–80. Washington, D.C.: CQ Press.

———. 1988. "Hazardous Waste Facility Siting: State Approaches." In *Dimensions of Hazardous Waste Politics and Policy*, edited by Charles E. Davis and James P. Lester, pp. 117–28. New York: Greenwood Press.

Association of State and Territorial Solid Waste Management Officials. 1987. *State Programs for Hazardous Waste Site Assessments and Remedial Actions*. Washington, D.C.: Association of State and Territorial Solid Waste Management Officials.

———. 1988. *State Funding Mechanisms for Cleanup of Non-NPL and NPL Hazardous Waste Sites*. Washington, D.C.: Association of State and Territorial Solid Waste Management Officials.

Ayres, Ian, and John Braithwaite. 1989. "Tripartism, Empowerment and Game-Theoretic Notions of Regulatory Capture." Paper presented to Law and Society Association, Madison, Wis.

Bailey, Jeff. 1991. "Tough Target: Waste Disposal Giant, Often under Attack, Seems to Gain from It." *Wall Street Journal*, May 1.

———. 1992. "Dueling Studies: How Two Industries Created a Fresh Spin on the Dioxin Debate." *Wall Street Journal*, February 20.

Bardach, Eugene, and Robert A. Kagan. 1982a. *Going by the Book*. Philadelphia: Temple University Press.

———. 1982b. Introduction to *Social Regulation: Strategies for Reform*, edited by Eugene Bardach and Robert A. Kagan, pp. 3–19. San Francisco: Institute for Contemporary Studies.

Barnett, Harold C. 1981. "Corporate Capitalism, Corporate Crime." *Crime and Delinquency* 27 (1): 4–23.

Bates, Timothy. 1976. *Economic Man as Politician: Neoclassical and Marxist Theories of Government Behavior*. Morristown, N.J.: General Learning Press.

Baumol, William J., and Wallace E. Oates. 1979. *Economics, Environmental Policy, and the Quality of Life*. Englewood Cliffs, N.J.: Prentice-Hall.

Belsley, David A., Edwin Kuh, and Roy E. Welsch. 1980. *Regression Diagnostics*. New York: John Wiley and Sons.

Bromley, David W. 1978. "Property Rules, Liability Rules, and Environmental Economics." *Journal of Economic Issues* 12 (1): 43–60.

Brown, Michael. 1981. *Laying Waste: The Poisoning of America by Toxic Chemicals*. New York: Washington Square Press.

Bureau of National Affairs. 1985–92. BNA *Environment Reporter—Current Developments*. Washington, D.C.: Bureau of National Affairs.

Butler, J. C., III. 1985. "Costs of Superfund Litigation." In *Reauthorization of Superfund*, pp. 1300–1321. See U.S. Congress, House, 1985b.

Calavita, Kitty. 1983. "The Demise of the Occupational Safety and Health Administration: A Case Study in Symbolic Action." *Social Problems* 30 (4): 437–47.

Chemical Manufacturers Association. 1991. "Lender Liability under Superfund." Testimony before the U.S. Senate, Committee on Environment and Public Works, Subcommittee on Superfund, Ocean, and Water Protection. 102d Cong., 1st sess., April 10.

Church, Thomas W., Robert T. Nakamura, and Phillip J. Cooper. 1991. *What Works? Alternative Strategies for Superfund Cleanups*. Alexandria, Va.: Clean Sites, Inc.

Claybrook, Joan, and Staff of Public Citizen. 1984. *Retreat from Safety*. New York: Pantheon Books.

Clean Sites, Inc. 1989. *Making Superfund Work: Recommendations to Improve Program Implementation*. Alexandria, Va.: Clean Sites, Inc.

———. 1990. *Improving Remedy Selection: An Explicit and Interactive Process for the Superfund Program*. Alexandria, Va.: Clean Sites, Inc.

Coase, Ronald H. 1960. "The Problem of Social Cost." *The Journal of Law and Economics* 3:1–44.

Cohen, Steven, and Marc Tipermas. 1983. "Superfund: Preimplementation Planning and Bureaucratic Politics." In *The Politics of Hazardous Waste Management*, edited by James P. Lester and Ann O'M. Bowman, pp. 43–59. Durham, N.C.: Duke University Press.

Cole, Henry S., and Amy Roberts. 1984. "Potentially Responsible Parties at Superfund Sites." Washington, D.C.: National Campaign Against Toxic Hazards.

Congressional Information Service. 1986. *CIS/Annual 1986: Legislative Histories of U.S. Public Laws*. Washington, D.C.: Congressional Information Service.

Cooter, Robert, and Thomas Ulen. 1988. *Law and Economics*. Glenview, Ill.: Scott Foresman and Company.

Council of State Governments. 1986. *The Book of the States*. Lexington, Ky.: Council of State Governments.

Crandall, Robert W., and Paul R. Portney. 1984. "Environmental Policy." In *Natural Resources and the Environment: The Reagan Approach*, edited by Paul R. Portney, pp. 47–81. Washington, D.C.: Urban Institute Press.

Davies, Clarence J. 1984. "Environmental Institutions and the Reagan Administration." In *Environmental Policy in the 1980s: Reagan's New Agenda*, edited by Norman J. Vig and Michael E. Kraft, pp. 143–60. Washington, D.C.: CQ Press.

Derthick, Martha, and Paul J. Quirk. 1985. *The Politics of Deregulation*. Washington, D.C.: Brookings Institution.

Donnelly, Patrick. 1982. "The Origins of the Occupational Safety and Health Act of 1970." *Social Problems* 30 (1): 13–25.

Dowd, Richard M. 1988. "Setting Environmental Standards for Hazardous Waste Sites: A Break from the Past or a Continuation." In *Hazardous Waste Site Management: Water Quality Issues*, edited by Water Science and Technology Board, pp. 13–21. Washington, D.C.: National Academy Press.

Downing, Paul B. 1981. "A Political Economy Model of Implementing Pollution Laws." *Journal of Environmental Economics and Management* 8:255–71.

Easterbrook, Gregg. 1989. "Cleaning Up." *Newsweek*, July 24.

Environmental Defense Fund, Hazardous Waste Treatment Council, National Audubon Society, National Wildlife Federation, Natural Resources Defense Council, Sierra Club, U.S. PIRG. 1988. *Right Train, Wrong Track: Failed Leadership in the Superfund Cleanup Program*. Washington, D.C.: Hazardous Waste Treatment Council.

———. 1990. *Tracking Superfund: Where the Program Stands*. Washington, D.C.: Hazardous Waste Treatment Council.

Epstein, Samuel S., Lester Brown, and Carl Pope. 1982. *Hazardous Waste in America*. San Francisco: Sierra Club Books.

Florio, James J. 1986. "Congress as Reluctant Regulator: Hazardous Waste Policy in the 1980s." *Yale Journal of Regulation* (3):351–82.

Frank, William H., and Timothy B. Atkeson. 1985. "Superfund: Litigation and Cleanup." *BNA Environment Reporter—Special Analysis* 16 (9), pt. 2:1–94.

Franzini-Bhargava, Luisa. 1992. "Priorities in Superfund Cleanups." Department of Economics, University of Houston.

Galanter, Marc. 1986. "The Day after the Litigation Explosion." *Maryland Law Review* 46 (1): 3–39.

Goetze, David B., and C. K. Rowland. 1985. "Explaining Hazardous Waste Regulation at the State Level." *Policy Studies Journal* 14 (1): 111–22.

Habicht, Henry F., II. 1985. "Encouraging Settlements under Superfund." *Natural Resources and Environment* 1 (3): 3–6, 45–48.

Harris, Christopher, William L. Want, and Morris A. Ward. 1987. *Hazardous Waste: Confronting the Challenge*. New York: Quorum Books.

Harris, Louis. 1980. "Toxic Chemical Dumps: Corrective Action Desired." *ABC News–Harris Survey*, July 7. New York: Louis Harris Organization.

———. 1981. "Clean Air Act Amendments Are Meeting with Public Resistance." *ABC News–Harris Survey*, October 15. New York: Louis Harris Organization.

———. 1982a. "America Is Not Turning to the Right." *ABC News–Harris Survey*, August 9. New York: Louis Harris Organization.

———. 1982b. "Americans Want Strict Standards on Water Pollution." *ABC News–Harris Survey*, December 16. New York: Louis Harris Organization.

———. 1983. "EPA Investigation Seriously Hurts Reagan Administration." *ABC News–Harris Survey*, March 24. New York: Louis Harris Organization.

———. 1985. "Environmental Pollution Causes Deep Concern." *ABC News–Harris Survey*, April 1. New York: Louis Harris Organization.

Hart, Philip J. 1992. "Senate Passes Bill to Charge Makers for Drug Approval." *New York Times*, October 8.

Harvard Law Review. 1986. "Developments in the Law—Toxic Waste Litigation." *Harvard Law Review* 99:1458–1661.

Hawkins, Keith. 1984. *Environment and Enforcement: Regulation and the Social Definition of Pollution.* New York: Oxford University Press.

Hayes, David J. 1987. "EPA's RCRA, Superfund Programs Are Growing Apart, Not Together." *BNA Environment Reporter—Analysis and Perspective,* January 2, pp. 1504–6.

Herman, Edward S. 1981. *Corporate Control, Corporate Power.* London: Cambridge University Press.

Hird, John A. 1990. "Superfund Expenditures and Cleanup Priorities: Distributive Politics or the Public Interest." *Journal of Policy Analysis and Management* 9 (4): 455–83.

Holusha, John. 1991. "Chemical Makers Identify a New Hazard: Their Image." *New York Times,* August 12.

Kelman, Mark G. 1979. "Consumption Theory, Production Theory, and Ideology in the Coase Theorem." *Southern California Law Review* 52:669–98.

———. 1983. "Misunderstanding Social Life: A Critique of the Core Premises of 'Law and Economics.'" *Journal of Legal Education* 33 (2): 274–84.

Kramer, Kenneth W. 1983. "Institutional Fragmentation and Hazardous Waste Policy: The Case of Texas." In *The Politics of Hazardous Waste Management,* edited by James P. Lester and Ann O'M. Bowman, pp. 112–38. Durham, N.C.: Duke University Press.

Lautenberg, Frank R., and David Durenberger. 1989. *Lautenberg-Durenberger Report on Superfund Implementation: Cleaning Up the Nation's Cleanup Program.* Report to U.S. Senate Subcommittee on Superfund, Ocean and Water Protection. Washington, D.C.: U.S. Government Printing Office.

Liebhafsky, H. H. 1976. "Price Theory as Jurisprudence: Law and Economics, Chicago Style." *Journal of Economic Issues* 10 (1): 23–43.

Lucero, Gene. 1988. "Son of Superfund." *Environmental Forum* (March–April): 5–12.

MacAvoy, Paul W. 1979. *The Regulated Industries and the Economy.* New York: W. W. Norton and Company.

Mahon, John F., and James E. Post. 1987. "The Evolution of Political Strategies during the 1980 Superfund Debate." In *Business Strategy and Public Policy: Perspectives from Industry and Academia,* edited by Alfred A. Marcus, Allen M. Kaufman, and David R. Beam, pp. 61–77. Westport, Conn.: Quorum Books.

Mahoney, Joseph, and Edward H. Bowman. 1985. "An Economic Analysis of the Hazardous Waste Industry." Working paper of the Reginald H. Jones Center, The Wharton School, University of Pennsylvania.

Maitland, Leslie. 1983. "Top EPA Official Is Accused of Intervening in Behalf of Company." *New York Times,* March 24.

Marcus, Alfred. 1980. "Environmental Protection Agency." In *The Politics of Regulation,* edited by James Q. Wilson, pp. 267–303. New York: Basic Books.

Marcus, Amy Dockser. 1991. "Veterans Renew Agent Orange Damage Claims." *Wall Street Journal,* March 6.

Mason, Michael J. 1986. "The Emergency Planning and Community Right-to-Know Act of 1986: Summary and Analysis." In *Superfund: The 1986 Amendments.* New York: Practicing Law Institute.

Menell, Peter S. 1991. "The Limitations of Legal Institutions for Addressing Environmental Risks." *The Journal of Economic Perspectives* 5, no. 3 (Summer): 93–114.

Miller, G. Tyler, Jr. 1988. *Living in the Environment*. Belmont, Calif.: Wadsworth Publishing Company.

Mitchell, Robert Cameron. 1984. "Public Opinion and Environmental Politics in the 1970s and 1980s." In *Environmental Policy in the 1980s: Reagan's New Agenda*, edited by Norman J. Vig and Michael E. Kraft, pp. 51–60. Washington, D.C.: CQ Press.

MITRE. 1986. National Priorities List Technical Data Base (February 1986 version). Washington, D.C.: Environmental Protection Agency.

Morell, David L. 1983. "Technological Policies and Hazardous Waste Politics in California." In *The Politics of Hazardous Waste Management*, edited by James P. Lester and Ann O'M. Bowman, pp. 139–75. Durham, N.C.: Duke University Press.

Moses, Jonathan M. 1991. "Court Sets Back EPA on Enforcement for Superfund." *Wall Street Journal*, November 6.

Mugdan, Walter E. 1986. "An Enforcement Approach for Multiple-party CERCLA Cases." New York: U.S. Environmental Protection Agency, Region 2.

National Campaign Against Toxic Hazards. 1986. "Out-of-Sight, Out-of-Mind." Washington, D.C.: National Campaign Against Toxic Hazards.

New York Times. 1988. "Shell Loses Suit on Cleanup Cost." *New York Times*, December 20.

Niskanen, William A., Jr. 1971. *Bureaucracy and Representative Government*. Chicago: Aldine.

Noll, Roger G., and Bruce M. Owen. 1983. *The Political Economy of Deregulation*. Washington, D.C.: American Enterprise Institute for Public Policy Research.

Nordhaus, William, and Management Analysis Center, Inc. 1985. "Financing Superfund: An Analysis of CERCLA Taxes and Alternative Revenue Approaches." In *Reauthorization of Superfund*, pp. 291–476. See U.S. Congress, House, 1985b.

O'Conner, James. 1973. *The Fiscal Crises of the State*. New York: St. Martin's Press.

Passell, Peter. 1991. "Experts Question Staggering Costs of Toxic Cleanups." *New York Times*, September 1.

Pasztor, Andy. 1983. "Dump-Cleanup Effort Gets Mired in Politics, High Costs, Red Tape." *Wall Street Journal*, March 11.

Phillips, Amy T. 1991. "EPA's Lender Liability Rule: A Sweetheart Deal for Bankers?" BNA *Environment Reporter—Special Analysis*, August 23, pp. 1158–62.

Piasecki, Bruce. 1984. "The Politics of Toxic Waste: Why the OMB Weakens EPA Programs." In *Beyond Dumping: New Strategies for Controlling Toxic Contamination*, edited by Bruce Piasecki, pp. 53–67. Westport, Conn.: Quorum Books.

Portney, Paul R. 1978. "Toxic Substance Policy and the Protection of Human Health." In *Current Issues in U.S. Environmental Policy*, edited by Paul R. Portney, pp. 105–43. Baltimore: John Hopkins University Press.

———. 1988. "Reforming Environmental Regulation: Three Modest Proposals." *Issues in Science and Technology* 4 (Winter): 74–81.

Reilly, William K. 1989. *A Management Review of the Superfund Program*. Washington, D.C.: Environmental Protection Agency.

Riley, Richard. 1983. "Toxic Substances, Hazardous Wastes, and Public Policy: Problems in Implementation." In *The Politics of Hazardous Waste Management*, edited by James P. Lester and Ann O'M. Bowman, pp. 24–42. Durham, N.C.: Duke University Press.

Russell, Dick. 1989. "EPA Scandal Leaks Out in 'Dioxinville,' Ark." *In These Times*, August 29.

Sarno, Douglas J. 1991. "Improving Superfund Remedy Selection." *BNA Environment Reporter—Analysis and Perspective*, May 3, pp. 26–30.

Schneider, Keith. 1991. "For Communities, Knowledge of Polluters Is Power." *New York Times*, March 24.

Seneca, Joseph, and Michael K. Taussig. 1984. *Environmental Economics*. Englewood Cliffs, N.J.: Prentice-Hall.

Shabecoff, Philip. 1983a. "Forecast for the EPA Was Stormy from the Start." *New York Times*, February 20.

———. 1983b. "Environmental Agency: Deep and Persisting Woes." *New York Times*, March 6.

———. 1983c. "Toxic Cleanup Delays Laid to Two Ex-aides." *New York Times*, April 9.

———. 1983d. "Ruckelshaus Says Administration Misread Mandate on Environment." *New York Times*, April 28.

———. 1983e. "Political Use of Toxic Cleanups Charged by Dingell." *New York Times*, May 20.

———. 1989. "E.P.A. Seeks to Learn If Polluter Got Grant to Help Clean Toxic Wastes." *New York Times*, June 6.

Shapiro, Susan P. 1984. *Wayward Capitalists: Target of the Securities and Exchange Commission*. New Haven: Yale University Press.

Sherman, Alan, and Sharon J. Sherman. 1983. *Chemistry and Our Changing World*. Englewood Cliffs, N.J.: Prentice Hall.

Shover, Neal. 1980. "The Criminalization of Corporate Behavior: Federal Surface Coal Mining." In *White-Collar Crime: Theory and Research*, edited by Gilbert Geis and Ezra Stotland, pp. 98–125. Beverly Hills: Sage Publications.

Shover, Neal, Donald A. Clelland, and John Lynxwiler. 1983. *Developing a Regulatory Bureaucracy: The Office of Surface Mining Reclamation and Enforcement*. Washington, D.C.: National Institute of Justice.

Silka, Lyle R., and Françoise M. Brasier. 1980. "The National Assessment of the Ground Water Contamination-Potential of Waste Impoundments." In *Toxic Chemical Contamination of Ground Water: EPA Oversight*, pp. 26–35. See U.S. Congress, House, 1980b.

Stigler, George J. 1975. "The Theory of Economic Regulation." In *The Citizen and the State: Essays on Regulation*, edited by George Stigler, pp. 114–44. Chicago: University of Chicago Press.

Stoll, Richard G., and David B. Graham. 1985. "Need for Changes in EPA's Settlement Policy." *Natural Resources and Environment* 1 (3): 7–9, 44–45.

Strand, Palma J. 1983. "The Inapplicability of Traditional Tort Analysis to Environmental Risks: The Example of Toxic Waste Pollution Victim Compensation." *Stanford Law Review* 35 (3): 575–619.

Szasz, Andrew. 1984. "Industrial Resistance to Occupational Safety and Health Legislation: 1971–1981." *Social Problems* 32 (2): 103–16.

————. 1986. "The Process and Significance of Political Scandals: A Comparison of Watergate and the 'Sewergate' Episode at the Environmental Protection Agency." *Social Problems* 33 (3): 202–17.

Tobin, James. 1982. "The Reagan Economic Plan—Supply-side, Budget and Inflation." In *Viewpoints on Supply Side Economics*, edited by Thomas J. Hailstones, pp. 207–20. Richmond, Va.: Robert F. Dame.

Tomsho, Robert. 1991. "Pollution Ploy: Big Corporations Hit by Superfund Cases Find Way to Share Bill." *Wall Street Journal*, April 2.

Trost, Cathy. 1984. *Elements of Risk: The Chemical Industry and Its Threat to America*. New York: New York Times Books.

U.S. Congress. House of Representatives. 1979a. Committee on Interstate and Foreign Commerce. Subcommittee on Oversight and Investigation. *Hazardous Waste Disposal, Part I*. 96th Cong., 1st sess. Washington, D.C.: U.S. Government Printing Office.

————. 1979b. Committee on Interstate and Foreign Commerce. Subcommittee on Oversight and Investigations. *Waste Disposal Site Survey*. 96th Cong., 1st sess. Washington, D.C.: U.S. Government Printing Office.

————. 1979c. Committee on Interstate and Foreign Commerce. Subcommittee on Transportation and Commerce. *Superfund*. 96th Cong., 1st sess. Washington, D.C.: U.S. Government Printing Office.

————. 1980a. Committee on Interstate and Foreign Commerce. *Report on Hazardous Waste Containment Act of 1980*. 96th Cong., 2d sess. Washington, D.C.: U.S. Government Printing Office.

————. 1980b. Committee on Government Operations. Subcommittee on Environment, Energy, and Natural Resources. *Toxic Chemical Contamination of Ground Water: EPA Oversight*. 96th Cong., 2d sess. Washington, D.C.: U.S. Government Printing Office.

————. 1982a. Committee on Energy and Commerce. Subcommittee on Oversight and Investigations. *Hazardous Waste Enforcement*. 97th Cong., 2d sess. Washington, D.C.: U.S. Government Printing Office.

————. 1982b. Committee on Energy and Commerce. Subcommittee on Oversight and Investigation. *EPA Enforcement and Administration of Superfund*. 97th Cong., 1st and 2d sess. Washington, D.C.: U.S. Government Printing Office.

————. 1983a. Committee on Public Works and Transportation. Subcommittee on Investigation and Oversight. *Hazardous Waste Contamination of Water Resources*. 98th Cong., 1st sess. Washington, D.C.: U.S. Government Printing Office.

————. 1983b. Committee on Energy and Commerce. Subcommittee on Commerce, Transportation, and Tourism. *Hazardous Waste Control and Enforcement Act of 1983*. 98th Cong., 1st sess. Washington, D.C.: U.S. Government Printing Office.

————. 1983c. Committee on Energy and Commerce. Subcommittee on Commerce, Transportation, and Tourism. *Implementation of the Superfund Program*. 98th Cong., 1st and 2d sess. Washington, D.C.: U.S. Government Printing Office.

————. 1984a. Committee on Energy and Commerce. Subcommittee on Commerce, Transportation, and Tourism. *Superfund Reauthorization*. 98th Cong., 2d sess. Washington, D.C.: U.S. Government Printing Office.

————. 1984b. Committee on Public Works and Transportation. Subcommittee on

Water Resources. *Reauthorization of and Possible Amendments to the Comprehensive Environmental Response, Compensation and Liability Act of 1980 (Superfund)*. 98th Cong., 2d sess. Washington, D.C.: U.S. Government Printing Office.

———. 1984c. *Superfund Expansion and Protection Act of 1984 (Part 1 and 2)*. Report of Committee on Energy and Commerce. 98th Cong., 2d sess. Washington, D.C.: U.S. Government Printing Office.

———. 1985a. Committee on Energy and Commerce. Subcommittee on Commerce, Transportation, and Tourism. *Superfund*. 99th Cong., 1st sess. Washington, D.C.: U.S. Government Printing Office.

———. 1985b. Committee on Public Works and Transportation. Subcommittee on Water Resources. *Reauthorization of Superfund*. 99th Cong., 1st sess. Washington, D.C.: U.S. Government Printing Office.

———. 1985c. Committee on Energy and Commerce. Subcommittee on Oversight and Investigations. *Groundwater Monitoring Survey*. 99th Cong., 1st sess. Washington, D.C.: U. S. Government Printing Office.

———. 1986. *Superfund Amendments and Reauthorization Act of 1986*. Conference Report. 99th Cong., 2d sess. Washington, D.C.: U.S. Government Printing Office.

———. 1988. *Environmental Protection Agency's Management of the Superfund Program—An Overview*. Report to the Committee on Appropriations. Washington, D.C.: U.S. Government Printing Office.

U.S. Congress. Senate. 1979. Committee on Environment and Public Works. Subcommittee on Environmental Pollution and Resource Protection. *Hazardous and Toxic Waste Disposal*. 96th Cong., 1st sess. Washington, D.C.: U.S. Government Printing Office.

———. 1980. Committee on Environment and Public Works. *Report on Environmental Emergency Response Act*. 96th Cong., 2d sess. Washington, D.C.: U.S. Government Printing Office.

———. 1983. A *Legislative History of the Comprehensive Environmental Response, Compensation, and Liability Act of 1980 (Superfund), Public Law 96–510*. 2 vols. Washington, D.C.: U.S. Government Printing Office.

———. 1984a. Committee on Environment and Public Works. *Amending and Extending the Comprehensive Environmental Response, Compensation, and Liability Act of 1980 (Superfund)*. 99th Cong., 2d sess. Washington, D.C.: U.S. Government Printing Office.

———. 1984b. *Superfund Amendments of 1984*. Report of Committee on Environment and Public Works. 98th Cong., 2d sess. Washington, D.C.: U.S. Government Printing Office.

———. 1985a. Committee on Environment and Public Works. *Superfund Improvement Act of 1985*. 99th Cong., 1st sess. Washington, D.C.: U.S. Government Printing Office.

———. 1985b. Committee on Finance. *Superfund Reauthorization*. 99th Cong., 1st sess. Washington, D.C.: U.S. Government Printing Office.

———. 1985c. Committee on the Judiciary. *Superfund Improvement Act of 1985*. 99th Cong., 1st sess. Washington, D.C.: U.S. Government Printing Office.

———. 1985d. *Superfund Improvement Act of 1985*. Report of Committee on Environment and Public Works. 99th Cong., 1st sess. Washington, D.C.: U.S. Government Printing Office.

———. 1985e. *Superfund Revenue Act of 1985.* Report of Committee on Finance. 99th Cong., 1st sess. Washington, D.C.: U.S. Government Printing Office.

U.S. Congressional Budget Office. 1985. *Hazardous Waste Management: Recent Changes and Policy Alternatives.* Washington, D.C.: U.S. Government Printing Office.

U.S. Council of Economic Advisors. 1982–90. *Economic Report of the President.* Washington, D.C.: U.S. Government Printing Office.

U.S. Council on Environmental Quality. 1981. "Contamination of Ground Water by Toxic Organic Chemicals." In U.S. Congress, House, Committee on Government Operations, Subcommittee on Environment, Energy and Natural Resources, *Environmental Protection Agency: Private Meetings and Water Protection Programs,* pp. 525–628. 96th Cong., 1st sess. Washington, D.C.: U.S. Government Printing Office.

U.S. Department of Commerce. Bureau of the Census. 1982. *Environmental Quality Control.* Washington, D.C.: U.S. Government Printing Office.

———. 1985. *Pollution Abatement Costs and Expenditures, 1983.* Washington, D.C.: U.S. Government Printing Office.

———. 1986a. *1982 Census of Manufactures: Concentration Ratios in Manufacturing.* Washington, D.C.: U.S. Government Printing Office.

———. 1986b. *1982 Census of Manufactures: General Summary.* Washington, D.C.: U.S. Government Printing Office.

U.S. Environmental Protection Agency. 1979. "Preliminary Assessment of Cleanup Costs for National Hazardous Waste Problems" (draft version). Washington, D.C.: U.S. Environmental Protection Agency.

———. 1980. *Hazardous Waste Generation and Commercial Hazardous Waste Management Capacity: An Assessment.* Washington, D.C.: U.S. Environmental Protection Agency.

———. 1982a. "Guidelines for Using the Imminent Hazard, Enforcement and Emergency Response Authorities of Superfund and Other Statutes." 47 *Federal Register* (May 13): 20664–67.

———. 1982b. "National Oil and Hazardous Substances Contingency Plan." 47 *Federal Register* (July 6): 31180–31243.

———. 1983a. "National Survey of Hazardous Waste Generators and Treatment, Storage, and Disposal Facilities Regulated under RCRA in 1981: Preliminary Highlights of Findings." Washington, D.C.: U.S. Environmental Protection Agency.

———. 1983b. "Amendment to National Oil and Hazardous Substances Contingency Plan; National Priorities List." 48 *Federal Register* (September 8): 40658–82.

———. 1984a. *The Effectiveness of the Superfund Program CERCLA Section 301(a)(1)(A) Study,* Final Report. Washington, D.C.: U.S. Environmental Protection Agency.

———. 1984b. *Extent of the Hazardous Release Problem and Future Funding Needs CERCLA Section 301(a)(1)(C) Study,* Final Report. Washington, D.C.: U.S. Environmental Protection Agency.

———. 1984c. *State Participation in the Superfund Program CERCLA Section 301(a)(1)(E) Study*, Final Report. Washington, D.C.: U.S. Environmental Protection Agency.

———. 1984d. *The Feasibility and Desirability of Alternative Tax Systems for Superfund, 301(a)(1)(G) Study*, Final Report. Washington, D.C.: U.S. Environmental Protection Agency.

———. 1984e. *Uncontrolled Hazardous Waste Site Ranking System: A User's Manual*. Washington, D.C.: U.S. Environmental Protection Agency.

———. 1984f. *National Priorities List: 786 Current and Proposed Sites in Order of Ranking and by State*. Washington, D.C.: U.S. Environmental Protection Agency.

———. 1984g. "EPA/State Relationship Guidance." Washington, D.C.: U.S. Environmental Protection Agency.

———. 1984h. "Participation of PRPs in RIFS." Washington, D.C.: U.S. Environmental Protection Agency.

———. 1984i. "Issuance of Administrative Order for Immediate Removal Actions." Washington, D.C.: U.S. Environmental Protection Agency.

———. 1985a. "Estimation of the Costs of Remedial Actions at Sites on the National Priorities List: Background Document." Washington, D.C.: U.S. Environmental Protection Agency.

———. 1985b. "National Oil and Hazardous Substances Contingency Plan; Final Rule." 50 *Federal Register* (November 20): 47913–79.

———. 1985c. "Interim Settlement Policy." 50 *Federal Register* (February 5): 5034–41.

———. 1987. *Unfinished Business*. Washington, D.C.: U.S. Environmental Protection Agency.

———. 1989. *The Toxics-Release Inventory: A National Perspective*. Washington, D.C.: U.S. Government Printing Office.

———. 1990a. "A Comparative Analysis of Remedies Selected in the Superfund Program during FY 87, FY 88 and FY 89." Washington, D.C.: U.S. Environmental Protection Agency.

———. 1990b. *Reducing Risk: Setting Priorities and Strategies for Environmental Protection*. Washington, D.C.: U.S. Environmental Protection Agency.

———. 1991. "Setting Environmental Priorities: The Debate about Risk." *EPA. Journal*, March–April, 2–51.

U.S. General Accounting Office. 1981. *Hazardous Waste Facilities with Interim Status May Be Endangering Public Health and the Environment*. Washington, D.C.: U.S. Government Printing Office.

———. 1983. *Interim Report on Inspection, Enforcement, and Permitting Activities at Hazardous Waste Facilities*. Washington, D.C.: U.S. Government Printing Office.

———. 1984a. *Cost-Benefit Analysis Can Be Useful in Assessing Environmental Regulations, Despite Limitations*. Washington, D.C.: U.S. Government Printing Office.

———. 1984b. *Inspection, Enforcement, and Permitting Activities At New Jersey and Tennessee Hazardous Waste Facilities*. Washington, D.C.: U.S. Government Printing Office.

————. 1984c. *Federal and State Efforts to Protect Ground Water.* Washington, D.C.: U.S. Government Printing Office.

————. 1984d. *EPA's Efforts to Clean Up Three Hazardous Waste Sites.* Washington, D.C.: U.S. Government Printing Office.

————. 1985a. *Hazardous Waste: Federal Agency Hazardous Waste Disposal at Kettleman Hills, California.* Washington, D.C.: U.S. Government Printing Office.

————. 1985b. *Clearer EPA Superfund Program Policies Should Improve Cleanup Effort.* Washington, D.C.: U.S. Government Printing Office.

————. 1985c. *Cleaning Up Hazardous Wastes: An Overview of Superfund Reauthorization Issues.* Washington, D.C.: U.S. Government Printing Office.

————. 1986a. *Hazardous Waste: Adequacy of EPA Attorney Resource Levels.* Washington, D.C.: U.S. Government Printing Office.

————. 1986b. *Hazardous Waste: Responsible Party Clean Up Efforts Require Improved Oversight.* Washington, D.C.: U.S. Government Printing Office.

————. 1986c. *Hazardous Waste: EPA's Consideration of Permanent Cleanup Remedies.* Washington, D.C.: U.S. Government Printing Office.

————. 1986d. *Hazardous Waste: EPA's Superfund Program Improvements Result in Fewer Stopgap Cleanups.* Washington, D.C.: U.S. Government Printing Office.

————. 1987a. *Hazardous Waste: Uncertainties of Existing Data.* Washington, D.C.: U.S. Government Printing Office.

————. 1987b. *Superfund: Improvements Needed in Work Force Management.* Washington, D.C.: U.S. Government Printing Office.

————. 1987c. *Hazardous Waste: Corrective Action Cleanups Will Take Years to Complete.* Washington, D.C.: U.S. Government Printing Office.

————. 1988a. *Hazardous Waste: New Approach Needed to Manage the Resource Conservation and Recovery Act.* Washington, D.C.: U.S. Government Printing Office.

————. 1988b. *Hazardous Waste: Future Availability of and Need for Treatment Capacity Are Uncertain.* Washington, D.C.: U.S. Government Printing Office.

————. 1989a. *Hazardous Waste Sites: State Cleanup Status and Its Implications for Federal Policy.* Washington, D.C.: U.S. Government Printing Office.

————. 1989b. *Superfund: A More Vigorous and Better Managed Enforcement Program Is Needed.* Washington, D.C.: U.S. Government Printing Office.

————. 1989c. *Superfund Contracts: EPA's Procedures for Preventing Conflicts of Interest Need Strengthening.* Washington, D.C.: U.S. Government Printing Office.

————. 1989d. *Hazardous Waste: Contractors Should Be Accountable for Environmental Protection.* Washington, D.C.: U.S. Government Printing Office.

————. 1989e. *Superfund: Contractors Are Being Too Liberally Indemnified by the Government.* Washington, D.C.: U.S. Government Printing Office.

————. 1991a. *Hazardous Waste: Pollution Claims Experience of Property/Casualty Insurers.* Washington, D.C.: U.S. Government Printing Office.

————. 1991b. *Observations on the Environmental Protection Agency's Budget Request for Fiscal Year 1992.* Washington, D.C.: U.S. Government Printing Office.

U.S. Library of Congress. Congressional Research Service. 1988. "CRS Issue Brief: The Superfund Amendments and Reauthorization Act of 1986." Washington, D.C.: Congressional Research Service.

U.S. Office of Technology Assessment. 1983. *Technologies and Management Strat-*

egies for Hazardous Waste Control. Washington, D.C.: U.S. Government Printing Office.

———. 1985. *Superfund Strategy.* Washington, D.C.: U.S. Government Printing Office.

———. 1988. *Are We Cleaning Up? Ten Superfund Case Studies.* Washington, D.C.: U.S. Government Printing Office.

———. 1989a. *Assessing Contractor Use in Superfund.* Washington, D.C.: U.S. Government Printing Office.

———. 1989b. *Coming Clean: Superfund Problems Can Be Resolved.* Washington, D.C.: U.S. Government Printing Office.

Wald, Matthew L. 1988. "U.S. Waste Dumping Blamed in Wide Pollution at A-Plants." *New York Times,* December 8.

Waldo, Andrew B., and Mark N. Griffiths. 1986. "Superfund Lessons Learned: Behind the House Funding and Right to Know Votes." *Environmental Forum* (April): 17–22.

Washington Post. 1991. "EPA Auditors Faulted by Hill Panel." *Washington Post,* July 7.

Weidenbaum, Murry L. 1981. *Business, Government and the Public.* Englewood Cliffs, N.J.: Prentice-Hall.

Weisskopf, Michael. 1991. "Administrative Costs Drain 'Superfund.'" *Washington Post,* June 19.

Wiley, Ed. 1991. "Why People of Color Should Think Green." *Black Issues in Higher Education,* January 17, p. 1.

Williams, Bruce A., and Albert R. Matheny. 1984. "Testing Theories of Social Regulation: Hazardous Waste Regulation in the American States." *Journal of Politics* 46:428–58.

Wilson, James Q. 1980. "The Politics of Regulation." In *The Politics of Regulation,* edited by James Q. Wilson, pp. 357–94. New York: Basic Books.

Yandle, Bruce. 1985. "Unions and Environmental Regulation." *Journal of Labor Research* 6 (4): 429–36.

———. 1989. *The Political Limits of Environmental Regulation: Tracking the Unicorn.* New York: Quorum Books.

Yeager, Peter C. 1983. "The Politics of Limits, the Limits of Politics: Systematic Constraints in Environmental Protection Law." Paper presented to the American Society of Criminology, Denver, Colo.

———. 1991. *The Limits of Law: The Public Regulation of Private Pollution.* New York: Cambridge University Press.

Early, Blakeman, 203, 227
Earth Day: ecological paradigm of, 52
Eckhart, Robert, 22
Economic dislocation, 7
Economic growth, 52, 273
Efficiency, 2, 8, 298 (n. 16); and enforcement, 3, 8, 84–85, 182–83, 184; and
remedy selection, 3, 36–37; and cleanup contractors, 3, 248–49; in measuring Superfund failure, 5, 49; and
market failure, 31–35; and design of
Superfund program, 35–38; and state
cleanup programs, 37, 103–4, 110–12,
113, 117; and Burford EPA, 83–85;
and allocation of EPA resources, 161;
and fund-financed cleanup, 166, 174;
and enforcement strategy, 182–83;
and conflict over environmental versus economic priorities, 271–72, 274–
76, 278, 282
Emergency Planning and Community
Right-to-Know Act, 231, 267. *See also*
Right-to-know legislation
Employer flight, 40, 227
Enforcement, federal, 6, 7–8, 45; funding of, 2, 64, 80, 128, 256; and settlement policy, 3, 139–43; evaluation of,
7, 38; nonconfrontational voluntary
compliance, 7, 76, 77, 78, 84; fund-
first approach, 7, 83; use of incentives
and threats, 7, 180–82, 183, 233, 245,
246–47, 277; as inefficient funding
mechanism, 8, 267; and distribution
of toxic debt, 37–38; and assignment
of liability, 38; and imminent hazards,
56, 69, 146; and CERCLA debate,
64–66; expectations for, 68, 125, 175,
275; authority of, under CERCLA, 69;
and Burford EPA, 71–72, 73, 76–78,
80, 84–85, 275, 288 (n. 29); enforced
compliance, 72, 82; negotiated compliance, 72, 82; change by Ruckelshaus, 81–83; progress in, 82–83, 164,
175–76; and efficiency/equity, 84–85,
182–83, 184, 271; and regional office
progress, 134–36, 179, 190, 192; and
variation in regional office strategies,

144–47; and state resources, 148–49,
151, 156–57, 179, 192–93; and industry resources, 149–50, 179–80, 192–
93, 276; and settlements, 175–76;
analysis of progress in (1981–85), 175–
82; evaluation of settlements, 176–77;
and bias toward fund-financed cleanup, 177; and regional office guidance,
177, 240; and EPA versus industry
domination, 177–78, 180, 182; cases
initiated, 178; comparison of Burford
and Ruckelshaus/Thomas strategies
and outcomes, 180–82; and federal
resource constraints, 182, 183, 184–
85, 246, 247, 255, 276, 281; and SARA
debate, 205–10; provision for, in
SARA, 230; and Thomas EPA, 240,
245–47, 275; and selection of permanent remedies, 245; and Reilly EPA,
255, 261, 262, 263–67; and reform
of remedy selection, 277. *See also*
Cleanup strategy; Settlement policy
Engineering criteria, 91
Environmental decade, 51–57
Environmental Defense Fund, 75, 220
Environmental degradation: awareness
of, in 1970s, 5, 52, 53, 274
Environmental groups, 2, 7; and state
cleanup programs, 6, 106–9, 115–19;
and industry liability for cleanup, 37;
and political action, 40, 85; in theory
of regulation, 43–46, 48; and 1985
revisions to National Contingency
Plan, 139; and SARA debate, 200,
232; and lender liability, 266
Environmental interests: and conflict
with industrial interests, 5, 69, 280;
and political economy of regulation,
43–46
Environmental Law Institute, 211
Environmental legislation, 5, 33; in
1970s, 51–57. *See also specific acts*
Environmental Protection Agency
(EPA): and interdependence with
state programs, 6, 42, 87, 96–99,
109–12; and relationship to regional
offices, 6, 76, 123; limits on discretion